RIVALS IN THE STORM

RIVALS IN THE STORM

How Lloyd George seized power, won the war and lost his government

DAMIAN COLLINS

BLOOMSBURY CONTINUUM
LONDON · OXFORD · NEW YORK · NEW DELHI · SYDNEY

BLOOMSBURY CONTINUUM
Bloomsbury Publishing Plc
50 Bedford Square, London, WC1B 3DP, UK
29 Earlsfort Terrace, Dublin 2, Ireland

BLOOMSBURY, BLOOMSBURY CONTINUUM and the Diana logo are trademarks of Bloomsbury Publishing Plc

First published in Great Britain 2024

Copyright © Damian Collins, 2024

Damian Collins has asserted his right under the Copyright, Designs and Patents Act, 1988, to be identified as Author of this work

Every effort has been made to trace copyright holders and to obtain their permission for the use of copyright material. The publisher apologizes for any errors or omissions and would be grateful for notification of any corrections that should be incorporated in future reprints or editions of this book.

For legal purposes the Acknowledgements on pp. 334–6 and the Picture Credits on p. 337 constitute an extension of this copyright page

All rights reserved. No part of this publication may be reproduced or transmitted in any form or by any means, electronic or mechanical, including photocopying, recording, or any information storage or retrieval system, without prior permission in writing from the publishers

Bloomsbury Publishing Plc does not have any control over, or responsibility for, any third-party websites referred to or in this book. All internet addresses given in this book were correct at the time of going to press. The author and publisher regret any inconvenience caused if addresses have changed or sites have ceased to exist, but can accept no responsibility for any such changes

A catalogue record for this book is available from the British Library

Library of Congress Cataloguing-in-Publication data has been applied for

ISBN: HB: 978-1-3994-0710-6; eBook: 978-1-3994-0711-3; ePDF: 978-1-3994-0713-7

2 4 6 8 10 9 7 5 3 1

Typeset by Deanta Global Publishing Services, Chennai, India
Printed and bound in Great Britain by CPI Group (UK) Ltd, Croydon CR0 4YY

To find out more about our authors and books visit www.bloomsbury.com and sign up for our newsletters

For my parents, Fearghal and Diane Collins, and their love, encouragement and example.

Contents

Prologue — ix

1. The Brewing Storm — 1
2. Man of Push and Go — 25
3. The Cabal — 43
4. The Powers That Be — 55
5. Submit or Resign — 70
6. Gentlemen and Players — 86
7. The Valley of the Shadow of Death — 102
8. Mud Sticks — 124
9. The Man Who Won the War — 143
10. Prime Minister for Life — 180
11. The Rules of the Road — 205
12. Solver of the Insoluble — 222
13. Things Fall Apart — 242

Notes — 269
Acknowledgements — 334
Picture credits — 337
Index — 338

Prologue

At 3 p.m. on Saturday 19 September 1914, 3,500 people packed into The Queen's Hall[1] in London's Langham Place, with 10,000 more thronging in the streets outside.[2] The First World War had started just seven weeks before, and the man they had come to see, the Chancellor of the Exchequer David Lloyd George, was set to make his first major speech of the military campaign. He was the people's champion, a 'cottage-bred man'[3] brought up in the small community of Llanystumdwy on the Llŷn Peninsula of north-west Wales. Unlike most other statesmen of his age, Lloyd George was in his own words a 'ranker' who'd 'not passed through the Staff College of the old Universities'.[4] As a consequence, he would say, 'I have never judged a man by the college he went to. I judge by what a man can do and has done rather than by his old school tie. I learned that principle long years ago in Wales.'[5] His tutorials back in those days were fireside chats with village elders in the cobbler's workshop of his Uncle Lloyd,[6] and the first lectures he heard were from the chapel pulpit. Driven by an impulse to 'get on',[7] David Lloyd George had made his way as a local solicitor, before being elected in 1890 as a Liberal Member of Parliament for Caernarvon Boroughs. When in 1909 he presented his 'People's Budget' to the House of Commons, which introduced new taxes to pay for social reform, he called it 'a War Budget. It is for raising money to wage implacable warfare against poverty and squalidness.'[8] Now, in September 1914, he would have to address the war for freedom and democracy to which Great Britain was committed.

The Queen's Hall was London's principal concert venue with excellent acoustics, a major consideration in the days before microphones and speakers. Its ornate stone façade, with colonnades and busts of famous composers, made for a suitably imposing Victorian edifice. Yet inside, it had a certain democratic quality, as a place where people of different classes came together. Later in the day for two shillings, visitors could have enjoyed one of Sir Henry Wood's Promenade concerts;[9] a price that E. M. Forster[10] noted in his 1910 novel *Howard's End* was 'cheap, even if you hear it in the . . . dreariest music-room in London'.[11] The Hall had, in Forster's view, an 'oppressive' atmosphere as well as a rather drab interior and cramped seating.

In 1914 the only chance that people had to hear the voice of a leading politician was in person. Lloyd George liked to give big speeches on Saturday afternoons not just so that working people could attend, but also because the text would be reported in the evening newspapers that day, in the Sunday editions, and again by the daily papers on Monday morning, ensuring the largest possible readership. Yet despite his reputation as a great orator, Lloyd George was apprehensive about his upcoming speech, and concerned that the Queen's Hall audience might be 'a stodgy, fashionable crowd that would chill any enthusiasm in my own or anyone else's breast'.[12] Earlier that day he'd lunched at 20 Queen Anne's Gate, the Westminster town house of his great friend George Riddell,[13] who thought that Lloyd George 'was terribly nervous, feeling, he said, as if he were about to be executed'.[14] Riddell had been trying to persuade him for the past month to deliver 'a speech explaining the reasons why we were at war and appealing to the patriotism of the people'. Yet Lloyd George had initially rebuffed him, saying that 'he did not feel like speaking'.[15]

However, political leadership was now especially necessary because the war had come as such a surprise. When the Archduke Franz Ferdinand[16] was assassinated in Sarajevo on 28 June 1914, few had anticipated that this tragedy in the Balkans would create the spark that in turn would ignite the tinderbox of national rivalries and alliances in Europe, involving at first Serbia, Austria-Hungary and Russia. The decision by Germany, allying with Austria-Hungary, to invade Belgium and France, had brought Britain into the conflict in their defence. That fateful evening on 4 August, when war was declared, the Foreign Secretary Sir Edward Grey[17] prophetically remarked, while looking from his window in the Foreign Office out across St James's Park, that 'the lamps are going out all over Europe. We shall not see them lit again in our lifetime.'[18] Lloyd George's late support for the war had been pivotal in securing the agreement of a wavering Cabinet, but he was yet to explain why he had taken that course. Then on Friday 4 September the Prime Minister, Herbert Asquith,[19] gave a major speech about the war at London's Guildhall, the historic meeting place of the City's merchants. The event was chaired by the Lord Mayor, while Asquith shared the platform with the Conservative Party leader, Andrew Bonar Law.[20] Lloyd George could delay no longer and the following Monday it was announced that he would give a rallying address at The Queen's Hall on Saturday 19 September to encourage the London Welsh community to enlist in the armed forces.

Lloyd George was often nervous before giving a speech, but this was the most important of his career so far. His fear was not the social profile of that London audience or dreariness of the hall, but the ghosts from his past that he would have to put to rest if the speech was to be a success. The first ghost was of the Marconi financial scandal, personified by the presence at The Queen's Hall of his friends, Lord Reading[21] and Lord Murray.[22] In 1912, Reading, then the Attorney General, received advice from his brother Godfrey, who was Managing Director of the Marconi[23] company and on the board of its American subsidiary, to buy shares in American Marconi. Lord Reading purchased 10,000 and encouraged Lloyd George and Murray, then the Government Chief Whip, to invest as well. At that time share dealing by government ministers was permitted, but shortly afterwards, the Postmaster-General Herbert Samuel[24] announced that British Marconi had won a lucrative government contract. The newspapers discovered evidence of this ministerial wheeler dealing and questioned whether they had personally profited from inside knowledge. Asquith stood by Reading, Murray and Lloyd George but was required to refer the matter to a parliamentary select committee. This inquiry ultimately cleared the men of corruption, as they had bought shares in the American company which had not received any British government contracts, but it felt like they had got off on a technicality and there was criticism in the House of Commons for their 'want of frankness'.[25] However, by that time Murray had already resigned as Chief Whip and gone to the House of Lords, and later in 1913 Reading left the government to become Lord Chief Justice; the first Jewish man to be appointed to the position. The fierce opposition to this following the Marconi affair was captured by Rudyard Kipling[26] in his 1913 poem 'Gehazi',[27] in particular with the lines:

> Well done; well done, Gehazi!
> Stretch forth thy ready hand,
> Thou barely 'scaped from judgement,
> Take oath to judge the land
> Unswayed by gift of money
> Or privy bribe, more base,
> Of knowledge which is profit
> In any market place.[28]

Lloyd George always claimed that he never made money from buying Marconi shares, but admitted, 'I acted carelessly. I acted mistakenly, but I acted innocently.'[29] However, the whole affair was seen as a major error of judgement on his part, and had made him, even up until the outbreak of the First World War, the constant butt of political jokes.[30] Other statesmen might have suggested that Murray and Reading stay away from a big speech at The Queen's Hall, but their presence was symbolic of both Lloyd George's loyalty to his friends and defiance of his critics. Although Riddell noticed that Murray and Reading had been given seats in the Hall on either side of Lloyd George, so that the Chancellor, in his view, looked 'something like our Lord on the Cross between two thieves'.[31]

The other ghost at The Queen's Hall was of the young Lloyd George who had made his name as a Liberal radical and opponent of the Boer War.[32] Then he'd decried British policy in South Africa as 'damnable' and 'an infamy'.[33] The Welshman felt an instinctive affinity for the independence of the small Boer Republic in its struggle against the might of the British Empire. In one speech he condemned the British use of concentration camps for Boer women and children, stating 'If I were to despair for the future of this country it would not be because of trade competition from either America or Germany, or the ineffectiveness of its army, or anything that might happen to its ships; but rather because it used its great, hulking strength to torture the little children.'[34] In 1901 a speech by Lloyd George at Birmingham Town Hall was disrupted by a mob that broke every window in the building. In the ensuing riot 40 people were injured and two killed, and Lloyd

George himself was forced to escape for his life dressed as a policeman. Before speaking in The Queen's Hall that same year, he'd had to fight his way through baying protesters to reach the auditorium. However, once inside he was greeted with cries of 'Lloyd George for ever' and spoke out against what he called an 'unjust and desolating war'.[35] The Boer War split the nation, as well as the Liberal Party, and Lloyd George was the chief agent of that division. Herbert Asquith, then one of the pro-war Liberal imperialists, even sought to reassure his colleagues that they would not allow their party to 'be captured by Lloyd George and his friends'.[36]

At the beginning of August 1914, Riddell noted in his diary that Lloyd George had been 'bombarded with telegrams from friends like [C. P.] Scott[37] of the *Manchester Guardian* stating that any Liberal who supported war would never be allowed to enter another Liberal Cabinet'.[38] The Attorney General, Sir John Simon,[39] recalled that 'revulsion from the horrible cruelties and inevitable barbarities of war was so strong that, until the last moment of final decision, I was prepared to give up my political career rather than to assent'.[40] But when Germany invaded Belgium, breaking an international treaty guaranteeing its independence, Lloyd George told his wife Margaret,[41] 'all my traditions and even my prejudices will be engaged on the side of war'.[42] The purpose of the Queen's Hall speech was to persuade old opponents that he would invest all his energy in the war effort, and reassure concerned friends that he had done the right thing. If he succeeded, rather than being the divider of the nation, he would become its unifying force.

Lloyd George's 25-year-old private secretary, Frances Stevenson,[43] who was also his mistress, recalled the weight this responsibility placed on him. 'How he worked at that Queen's Hall speech! And how apprehensive he was before it was delivered! With his Boer War record he realised how important it was – a landmark in his career. People would have to be convinced of his sincerity.'[44] Yet as another long-serving aide A. J. Sylvester[45] understood, it was in Lloyd George's nature to go all out in support of whatever decision he made. He 'was a pacifist, so long as pacificism did not involve humiliation or interfere with his plans and schemes. He was never happier than when fighting his opponents, and the harder the fight became, the greater his enjoyment of it.'[46]

Lloyd George composed the Queen's Hall speech at his country home at Walton Heath in Surrey[47] and the day before he returned to London to deliver it, had tea with George Riddell, who noted that Lloyd George 'said he was miserable and inert. His brain would not work. We discussed various suggestions and then he left to consider them during a walk on Walton Heath. He afterwards told me he had walked until it was dark.'[48] Above his bed, Lloyd George kept a framed embroidery with a line of scripture from the Book of Job that read: 'There is a path which no fowl knoweth, and which the vulture's eye hath not seen.'[49] The audience at The Queen's Hall would now discover whether he had found that path on Walton Heath.

The large auditorium of The Queen's Hall was packed with listeners squeezed into every space available. Even at the back of the stage, people were placed in tiered seating behind the places reserved for the speakers. Above them arranged against the great pipes of the hall's organ, hung the flags of Great Britain, the Empire Dominions, and their Allies in the war. At the opening of the meeting, everyone stood to sing a thundering rendition of the Welsh military marching song, 'Men of Harlech', named after the castle that could be seen across Cardigan Bay from Llanystumdwy. As the audience sat, the Chairman, Lord Plymouth,[50] remained standing to address the hall. There had already been heavy fighting in the war, and earlier that month the British and French forces finally stopped the German advance at the Battle of the Marne, just 60 miles east of Paris. That week the first trenches on what would become the Western Front were dug and although it was not directly referenced, all knew that Lord Plymouth's 23-year-old son Archer,[51] a lieutenant in the Coldstream Guards, had been amongst the first casualties – killed by a German shell on 24 August at Landrecies, during the retreat from Mons. With his voice shaking and grief still raw, Lord Plymouth told his audience:

We must learn to say with Mr Rudyard Kipling, and say it with deep conviction:

> 'There is but one task for all;
> One life for each to give.
> What stands if Freedom fall?
> Who dies if England live?'[52,53]

Later Lloyd George would respond with words that visibly brought tears to Lord Plymouth's eyes:

> Some have already given their lives. Some have given more than their lives. Some have given the lives of those who are dear to them. I honour their courage, and may God be their comfort and strength.

The audience responded with a prolonged low murmur of applause.[54]

When Lloyd George was called to deliver his speech, the 51-year-old Chancellor rose, just five feet five inches tall, and wearing a light grey summer suit, which helped him to stand out against the dark backdrop of the hall. He was well groomed, and though his black mane of hair was now greying, his blue-grey eyes were 'flashing fire like a cluster of diamonds in the glare of the footlights'.[55] Before Lloyd George, on a table covered with a dark red cloth, were a few scattered sheets of stiff paper. As usual, he had no full text for his remarks, just notes providing headings for thoughts or the key lines of a peroration. One eyewitness, the journalist Frank Dilnot,[56] recalled, 'I remember how crowded was the hall and how intensely silent was every soul when Lloyd George . . . stepped to the front of the platform. There was none of the old, fierce, gay, fighting glitter about him. His mobile face was touched with gravity, his eyes were thoughtful, not provocative. He stood very erect, but his chin was drawn in a little, and his head canted forward. Responsibility lay on him, and everyone could see it.'[57]

On the stage, after holding the silence of anticipation, Lloyd George started slowly, almost conversationally; 'There is no man who has always regarded the prospect of engaging in a great war with greater reluctance and greater repugnance than I have done through all my political life. There is no man more convinced that we could not have avoided it without national dishonour . . . Why is our honour as a country involved in this war? Because, in the first place we are bound in an honourable obligation to defend the independence, the liberty, the integrity of a small neighbour.'[58] To which the audience responded with cheers and cries of 'quite right!'[59]

Lloyd George used the pretext of Germany's invasion of Belgium, and Britain's treaty obligation to defend her, as a justification for the war.[60] Then drawing an analogy, as he often did, to bring the importance of this idea to life for his audience, he attacked the German Chancellor's[61] dismissal of the treaty as a mere 'scrap of paper':

> 'What is a treaty,' says the German Chancellor. 'A scrap of paper' ... Have you any of those neat little Treasury one-pound notes?[62] If you have burn them; they are only 'scraps of paper' ... I have seen some of them – wretched, crinkled, scrawled over, blotched, frowsy – and yet those little scraps of paper moved great ships, laden with thousands of tons of precious cargo, from one end of the world to the other. What was the motive power behind them? The honour of commercial men. Treaties are the currency of international statesmanship.[63]

Lloyd George then made himself the personification of national honour, connecting his previous support for the Boer Republic, and his belief as a Welshman in the importance of small nations. He told the hall, 'The world owes much to the little nations and to little men ... Germany ... will only allow six-feet-two nations to stand in the ranks.' Then adding, with reference to his own height, 'But all the world owes much to the little five-feet-five nations ... The heroic deeds that thrill humanity through generations were the deeds of little nations fighting for their freedom. Ah yes and the salvation of mankind came through a little nation ... if we had stood by when two little nations[64] were being crushed and broken by the brutal hands of barbarism, our shame would have rung down the everlasting ages.'[65] Sir John Simon, who was in The Queen's Hall for the speech, thought this section was the 'most moving of all'. In his memoirs he recalled Lloyd George's 'Voice, gesture, his devotion to Wales, his short but sturdy figure on the platform, all helped to give the passage ... irresistible power.'[66]

Lloyd George then used another comparison from everyday life to characterize the behaviour of Germany. 'The Prussian Junker is the road-hog of Europe. Small nationalities in his way hurled to the roadside, bleeding and broken; women and children crushed under the wheels of his cruel car. Britain ordered out of his road. All I can say is this: If the old British spirit is alive in British hearts, that bully will be torn from his seat.'[67] There was now a moment of honest reflection, where Lloyd George gave his personal assessment of what it would involve, in stark contrast to the rhetoric of others during the first weeks of the war, who had suggested that it would all be over by Christmas: 'It will not be easy. It will be a long job. It will be a terrible war. But in the end we shall march through terror to triumph.' He then added a new idea, that victory could not just be left to the generals on the battlefield, but would require the active participation of the whole nation, and the full attention and vigour of its leaders: 'We shall need all our qualities, every quality that Britain and its people possess. Prudence in council, daring in action, tenacity in purpose, courage in defeat, moderation in victory, in all things faith, and we shall win.'[68]

As he approached the close of the speech, Lloyd George sought to unite support for the programmes of social reform he had introduced as Chancellor, with the groundswell of public opinion that recognized the need to fight the war:

> I see a new recognition amongst all classes, high and low, shedding themselves of selfishness; a new recognition that the honour of a country does not depend merely on the maintenance of its glory in the stricken field, but in protecting its homes from distress as well. It is a new patriotism; it is bringing a new outlook for all classes . . . and a new Britain is appearing.[69]

This idea also carried clear echoes of a famous speech given four years earlier by his friend and ally in progressive politics, President Theodore Roosevelt,[70] in which he had stated that 'The New Nationalism puts the national need before sectional or personal advantage.'[71]

Then for his peroration, Lloyd George gave what he called his 'appeal'. This was something he described as being 'outside of the main theme of the speech, it is purely emotional'.[72] At such moments he would later recall, 'I pause. I reach out my hand to the people and draw them to me. Like children they seem then. Like little children.'[73] On this occasion he asked his audience to allow him to draw a 'simple parable'. His childhood had been spent attending services in the Welsh Chapel of the Disciples of Christ, and as Thomas Jones,[74] a fellow Welshman and long-serving aide to Lloyd George, noted, 'There are few literary references in the speeches of Lloyd George . . . The Bible is the only exception; much of it he knew by heart and constantly used.'[75] In this case he delivered a story of his own, drawing on the relatable experiences of this childhood, but based on a biblical message.[76] He told the audience of The Queen's Hall:

> I know a valley in north Wales, between the mountains and the sea.[77] It is a beautiful valley, snug, comfortable, and sheltered by the mountains from all the bitter blasts. It is very enervating, and I remember how the boys were in the habit of climbing the hills above the village to have a glimpse of the mountains in the distance, and to be stimulated and freshened by the breezes which came from the hilltops, and by the great spectacle of that great valley. We have been living in a sheltered valley for generations. We have been too comfortable and too indulgent, many, perhaps, too selfish. And the stern hand of fate has scourged us to an elevation where we can see the great everlasting things that matter for a nation, the great peaks of honour we had forgotten – duty and patriotism, clad in glittering white; the great pinnacle of sacrifice pointing like a rugged finger to Heaven. We shall descend into the valleys again, but as long as the men and women of this generation last they will carry in their hearts the image of these great mountain peaks, whose foundations are unshaken though Europe rock and sway in convulsions of a great war.[78]

This passage had a profound effect on those who heard and read it, including 46 years later the future American President, John F. Kennedy,[79] who cited these lines of Lloyd George's 'stirring' speech when seeking to inspire another generation to 'climb to the hilltop'.[80]

When Lloyd George was in full flow as a speaker, the American journalist Isaac Marcosson[81] observed, 'None approaches him in witchery of word or wealth of imagery. His voice is like a silver bell that vibrates with emotion. His almost flawless phraseology is no studied art but a purely spontaneous thing. Words seem to flow from him in a ceaseless stream.'[82] On this occasion Lloyd George received a tremendous ovation, and Riddell too thought that he had spoken 'well and did not give any sign of perturbation, except . . . that his eyes had a peculiar appearance. They looked like two smouldering furnaces.'[83] However, by the end of the speech Lloyd George's shirt was wringing wet, and Frances Stevenson remembered that 'Strangely enough . . . he was intensely depressed. We drove to Walton Heath and on the way down he expressed the opinion that the speech had been a complete failure . . . It was not until the next day . . . when the papers arrived . . . that he was convinced of the success.'[84] This was noted too by Asquith, who wrote to his muse, the beautiful Venetia Stanley,[85] 'I have only glanced at the Sunday papers . . . Ll. George seems to have made a very characteristic speech, with some excellent "purple patches".'[86] John Simon considered that 'Of his oratorical successes, I count it to be his greatest . . . If the oratory of Pericles[87] and Chatham and Pitt[88] rightly holds a high place in the history of liberty, surely this speech . . . deserves to be recalled.'[89]

Over the next two days the newspapers were fulsome in their praise, even those who had previously been critical of Lloyd George. As *The Times* editorial exclaimed on the Monday morning, 'We have often had occasion to criticize his oratorical methods. We have not infrequently found ourselves at variance with his political views. But we have never questioned his great gifts or the purity of his patriotism. Never have those gifts been put to a nobler purpose.'[90] Yet the only critic who mattered was his Uncle Lloyd back home in Criccieth,[91] who had been a father figure to David and in whose honour he'd changed his surname from George to Lloyd George. Uncle Lloyd wrote to tell his 'boy', 'Tremendous! Tremendous!! Success!!! Bravo! *Bravo*!! BRAVO!!! **BRAVO!!!!** All efforts heretofore on war platforms buried in obscurity for good.'[92]

Lloyd George, according to A. J. Sylvester, had always taken a keen interest in 'mob psychology',[93] and Gustave Le Bon,[94] the leading French expert on the behaviour of crowds, who also counted Theodore Roosevelt amongst his followers, recognized the wider significance of the Queen's Hall speech. Le Bon wrote of it that 'public opinion is all-powerful in England, and public opinion has to be won . . . It might well have seemed a difficult task to persuade a nation into taking part in a European war on account of a small and insignificant Balkan State, whose very name was scarcely known to it. In any case, it was an undertaking that required a profound knowledge of the British mind if it were to succeed at all.' Le Bon observed that Lloyd George helped to accomplish this, 'not by speaking to the people of their material interests, but by reminding them of their national dignity and honour – that is to say, of the respect which must be observed by a great nation for the obligations which it has contracted.'[95]

Two and a half million copies of a printed and bound edition of the Queen's Hall speech were purchased, and a record was released by *His Master's Voice* with the text being read by the celebrated actor Arthur Bourchier.[96] More significant, however, than the acclaim he received, was the growing perception of Lloyd George, although not Prime Minister, as a leader of the nation. The London *Evening Standard* exclaimed, 'Thrilling in the extreme was the scene at Queen's Hall on Saturday, when Mr Lloyd George, for the first time since the war began, made himself the mouth-piece of the British people.'[97]

ONE

The Brewing Storm

'Political crises never come out of the blue,' Lloyd George observed in his *War Memoirs*. 'Clouds gather in the sky, sometimes from one quarter, sometimes from many. Suddenly one of those clouds is black with menace, approaches with surprising speed, hangs right overhead, and breaks into angry flashes.'[1] The first wisp from this brewing storm appeared in late September 1914, shortly after Lloyd George completed his speech at The Queen's Hall, yet it was imperceptible to all but the most seasoned observers. However, one such person was Regy Esher,[2] a sleek éminence grise of Edwardian politics, who had counted kings, generals and ministers amongst his intimate circle. In August 1914, Lord Kitchener,[3] the new Secretary of State for War and hero of past Imperial conflicts, asked Esher to go to France to act as his unofficial liaison with the British military commanders, with a view 'to smoothing out those constantly recurring difficulties that were invariably the world of tittle-tattlers and mischief makers'.[4] It was a task made harder by the often difficult relationship between the domineering Kitchener and the more colourful commander of the British Expeditionary Force, Sir John French.[5] Here Esher was required, he recalled, to 'delve down into the psychology of both men . . . and try to find solvents for the acids that lie about their hearts'.[6] As a consequence of his success, by early 1915 Esher would be recognized as the de facto head of British intelligence in France and the chief liaison between Kitchener and the French War Minister, Alexandre Millerand.[7]

Esher's field of campaign was not to be found at General Headquarters or on the front itself, but in the Hôtel de Crillon, at the foot of the Champs-Élysées in Paris, a magnificent hotel, located within an eighteenth-century neoclassical palace. It was there also that Lloyd George stayed, along with his fellow British ministers, officers and officials, when attending Allied conferences in the French capital. During such visits he would often lunch with Esher on the upper terrace overlooking the Place de la Concorde. In that discreet setting the Chancellor too could absorb the latest gossip from a man he believed to be 'general advisor to everybody and liaison officer between everybody and anybody – a most useful kind of person if he possesses tact, discernment, and experience. Lord Esher had these qualities in a superlative degree.'[8]

Esher's method of gathering evidence and information was through human intelligence, utilizing the unique collection of well-placed people he had made it his business to cultivate. Lloyd George too was a man of secrets and wheels within wheels. He worked through networks rather than hierarchies, using his contacts to seek out the truth rather than waiting for it to reach him. This was driven in part by a great intellectual curiosity, as he confided in Frances Stevenson. 'I am always interested in people – wondering who they are – what they are thinking about – what their lives are like.'[9] A. J. Sylvester remembered that 'Lloyd George never liked matters of detail. His strength lay in his ability to conceive, direct and drive.'[10] Rather than ploughing through great volumes of briefing papers, Lloyd George wanted to see the issues for himself and discuss them with people who had practical knowledge and direct experience. As his Cabinet colleague, Charles Hobhouse,[11] observed, 'Lloyd George is in Council as in every other relation wonderfully versatile, adroit and quick, with an unrivalled, indeed miraculous, power of picking other people's brains.'[12]

Lloyd George created a tight-knit private office to further his interests and guard his secrets, protected by his two ever-present personal secretaries, J.T. Davies[13] and Frances Stevenson. J.T., as he was always known, had been born into a Carmarthenshire farming family and then, like Lloyd George's father, trained to be a teacher. They had met in 1911 during the investiture of the Prince of Wales[14] at Caernarvon, and the following year J.T. joined Lloyd George at the Treasury. As well as being highly efficient J.T. could confer in Welsh with Lloyd George during meetings, so that their otherwise public conversations remained private. Years later, J.T. joined the board of the Ford Motor Company and was asked to compare the working styles of Lloyd George and the great motor magnate, Henry Ford.[15] He recalled that 'they both work a great deal from instinct. Ford is a man of genius, and he has no plan, no rigid system. He works by a series of inspirations and has never blundered. L.G. is very much the same. Over and over again during the war, we thought he was doing the wrong thing. But . . . he was always right. L.G. is absolutely tireless. I've never met his equal.'[16]

Frances Stevenson herself was one of Lloyd George's secrets, an attractive, elegant yet demure young woman, who had been a student at Clapham High School in South London at the same time as Lloyd George's daughter Mair,[17] the second eldest of the five children he had with his wife Margaret. Mair's sudden death in 1907, aged just 17, was a devastating blow to the family, which widened the growing separation between the lives of Lloyd George and his wife. Margaret was dignified and dependable, the daughter of a respectable farming family, who had always preferred the calm and quiet of north Wales to the society and smoke of Westminster. For Margaret, home was Brynawelon, the new house they built on the hill above Criccieth with fine views of Cardigan Bay and the Llŷn Peninsula. It was large and bright, but simply furnished in traditional Welsh style, and with space to indulge her love of gardening. Margaret's absences became longer and more frequent following Mair's death and were exploited by Lloyd George to further his already prodigious philandering. In 1912 the family approached Clapham High School for a recommendation for a tutor to their younger children over the summer, and as a result Frances came to stay with them at Criccieth. She was less than two years older than Mair would have been, and at first almost replaced her role within the structure of the family. As a fluent French speaker, Lloyd George asked her to translate some documents and then suggested further work of assistance. By the end of the year, he made the indecent proposal that she take up the interwoven and inseparable roles of mistress and private secretary. Frances recalled in her memoirs that:

> So great was the power and mastery that he had already exercised over me that I did not doubt for one moment that *he* was in command of the situation. He had made me realise that I was necessary to him. I knew instinctively that in the relationship I was contemplating there would be hurts and humiliations, but it seemed to me that nothing I could ever do would be so worthwhile as to help this man with whom I wished to join my life. L.G. himself, with his

knowledge of the world, must have visualised the possible danger to his own career from our relationship, but I, in my inexperience, felt complete confidence in his power to shield us both.[18]

From then on commenced Lloyd George's dual domestic existence, with his wife in Wales, who would always take precedence when she was by his side, but a second secret life of domesticity in London with Frances, who shared both his love and the cares of his office. J.T. Davies was aware of the relationship and would help to protect and facilitate it. To be truly within Lloyd George's inner circle required knowledge of all his secrets and devoted loyalty to the master.

Lloyd George was always the centre point of his network, and the only one who knew everything that had happened, and how much was yet to come. His other key confidants included Lord Reading, a new man whose life journey had so far taken him from a market stall in the East End of London to become Lord Chief Justice of England. He would often accompany Lloyd George on ministerial visits, dispensing legal and political advice. David Davies,[19] the wealthy Montgomeryshire Liberal MP, whose grandfather had founded the Barry Docks in south Wales, was his parliamentary private secretary and kept him in touch with the mood of the backbenchers in the House of Commons. Closest of all at that time, though, was George Riddell, two years younger than Lloyd George. He had been born in Brixton, South London, and was the son of a photographer. Like his Welsh friend, he'd started work as a solicitor's clerk, but then gone on to make a fortune in the law, before investing in newspapers. Frances Stevenson thought him 'at first rather forbidding, with his piercing blue eyes, gaunt figure, and his habit of cross-examining everyone with whom he came into contact'. However, as a newspaper proprietor he had 'all the gossip of the day, and since politics dominated L.G.'s every working hour, he naturally found Riddell a good companion'.[20] They golfed every Saturday at Walton Heath, where Riddell had arranged for Lloyd George to have a house built right next to the course. It was a large but simply arranged Edwardian villa, mainly furnished, Frances Stevenson recalled, 'from left-overs from L.G.'s former houses'. She thought it 'lacking comfort and adequate heating', but nevertheless 'L.G. loved to get away down there . . . to sleep and wake up in the fresh air.'[21]

Lloyd George's willingness to work hard at new problems had impressed his critics during the financial crisis that threatened to engulf the world's financial markets at the start of the war. In late July 1914 foreign banks made large withdrawals from London, then the centre of global finance, and the City's institutions were struggling to recover funds owed to them from overseas clients. Lloyd George 'resolved to consult every person whose ability, knowledge and experience would assist'.[22] He assembled a team of experts, including Lord Reading, old opponents like the financier Lord Rothschild,[23] and the two former Conservative Chancellors of the Exchequer, Austen Chamberlain[24] and Lord St Aldwyn,[25] to work with the Treasury and Bank of England to help navigate the storm. The brilliant young economist John Maynard Keynes[26] was also summoned by the Treasury from King's College Cambridge, arriving in haste on a Sunday afternoon, in a motorcycle sidecar.

The banks wanted to suspend the rules that then required the convertibility of paper money into gold. This had previously been done in wartime and Lloyd George was sympathetic to their request. However, both Lord Rothschild and Keynes advised against this, believing that it would undermine confidence in the banking system. Instead, the Bank of England would underwrite the liabilities of other banks without any repayment due until one year after the war. Gold convertibility would, though, remain.[27] This decision, Lloyd George recalled, 'marked the main difference between our treatment of the situation and that adopted by other countries . . . [and] did greatly help us to recover financial normality, because it tended towards a restoration of confidence which was so vitally necessary'.[28]

Lloyd George noted of this period that 'Financiers in a fright do not make an heroic picture',[29] a sentiment that Keynes shared. He wrote in the *Economic Journal* in August 1914 that 'The leaders of the City were many of them too much overwhelmed by the dangers . . . At this point the Minister and the Civil Servant, with no affairs of their own to divert them from the affairs of the country, alone stood possessed of the qualities which were instantly required.'[30] Of Lloyd George he considered that he had acted with 'rapidity and with courage' combining 'a regard for principle with practical good sense in action'.[31]

Lloyd George never deferred to people in positions of authority when he thought they were wrong. As a young lawyer he had made his name representing the non-conformist Roberts family against Richard Jones, the Church of England vicar of Llanfrothen village in north Wales. Believing they had the right under an 1880 Act of Parliament to bury their father in consecrated ground, Lloyd George advised the family to break into the churchyard at night to do so, despite the objections of Reverend Jones who had locked the gate. The following morning the vicar applied for a court summons against the family, but Lloyd George won the case, ultimately taking his argument all the way to the Royal Courts of Justice. When campaigning in 1909 for his 'People's Budget', Lloyd George had decried the 'shabby rich men'[32] who wanted to block his new taxes to pay for social reform and questioned the right of the House of Lords to vote against his proposals. In a speech at Walworth Town Hall in south London he told his audience, 'How do they ascertain the wishes of the people? Have you seen any dukes about the Walworth Road? Before the budget was thrown out, did any earls leave their visiting-cards upon you?'[33] In Thomas Jones's view, Lloyd George 'was never much impressed by rank or authority, by dukes or field-marshals . . . and he did not enjoy being treated by them as an amateur'.[34]

In the autumn of 1914 the dark storm clouds on the horizon that Regy Esher could observe from his vantage point in Paris related to the changing nature of the war, from movement to entrenchment, which would require a completely new approach to supplying and equipping the army; in particular, the need for machine guns and high-explosive shells, in quantities that would have previously been unimaginable. Regy could see that 'the War Office was not yet awake to the novel picture of the war',[35] but also that Sir John French knew 'his army was badly equipped with modern instruments of fighting'.[36] On 28 September, French sent a message to the War Office warning that 'a shortage of ammunition for Field Artillery might be attended with the gravest results. It might be thought that the nature of the recent operations have been abnormal, but in my opinion future operations in this campaign will to a great extent be of a similar kind . . . the proposed rate of ammunition supply cannot possibly suffice to meet demands.'[37] Despite his repeated warnings, at the end of year Sir John French wrote again to the War Office stating, 'The present supply of artillery ammunition has been found to be so inadequate as to make offensive operations, even on a small scale, quite out of the question.'[38]

At this time French stated his requirements to supply the principal artillery for his forces as follows. For the 18-pounder guns, 50 rounds per gun per day, instead of the 6 rounds he was receiving. For the 4.5-inch howitzers, 40 rounds per gun per day, instead of 4.6 rounds, and for the 4.7-inch howitzers, 25 rounds per gun per day instead of 7.6 rounds. French's estimates were no exaggeration. Sir William Robertson,[39] then the Chief of Staff for the British Expeditionary Force, recalled, 'In October [1914] at the height of the first battle of Ypres . . . the 18-pounder expenditure averaged 80 rounds per gun per day, and in some cases as many as 300 rounds per gun per day.'[40]

Although Lloyd George was then unaware of the communications between Sir John French and the War Office, he too had concerns about munition supplies, and was seeking to understand the problem in more detail. That autumn he had visited Britain's principal works at Woolwich Arsenal in south-east London where he'd 'found stacks of empty shells which were being slowly and tediously filled, one at a time, with ladles by hand from cauldrons of seething fluid'.[41] The issue was not due to lack of funds, but poor organization, and Lloyd George had 'repeatedly made it clear that as far as the Treasury was concerned no obstacle would come from that quarter in providing every supply that could possibly aid us to victory'.[42] Lloyd George led a delegation from London to France where they were briefed on how the military authorities had brought munitions workers back from the front and converted civilian factories for the manufacture of armaments, in particular the Renault[43] motor works. All of this was reported back to Kitchener and the War Office along with an offer of technical assistance from the French, but none of it was followed up.

At that time Lord Kitchener's personal prestige was immense; he was almost the personification of the British Empire. Lloyd George believed the trouble was that he was 'held in such awe at this date that his colleagues did not dare challenge this authority'.[44] Having never held political office before, Kitchener was brought into government by Asquith to inspire public confidence in the war effort, and with his glaring eyes and massive moustache, was an instantly recognizable public figure. Kitchener was also one of the first to understand that it would be a long war, at least three years in his estimation, and that it would require the recruitment of a vast continental army in the millions, rather than the six divisions, a mere 100,000 soldiers, that the British

Expeditionary Force had sent to France. He became the public face of the recruitment campaign with the famous 'Lord Kitchener Needs You' posters,[45] in which his pointing finger and penetrating stare seemed to directly challenge the viewer from whichever angle they observed it. The success of this advert led the waspish Margot Asquith,[46] the wife of the Prime Minister, to quip that Kitchener was 'not a great man, he is a great poster'.[47] Lloyd George had pressed for the creation of a Cabinet committee to look at the question of munitions contracts and supplies, but this was strongly resisted by Lord Kitchener, who saw the request as civilian interference in war work. Lloyd George's growing frustration was that the Cabinet, and Asquith in particular, continued to defer to the old soldier and declined to act.

The combination of Asquith and Lloyd George had dominated British politics for the previous six years, through two general elections, a constitutional crisis over House of Lords reform, and passing great programmes of social reform. However, the maelstrom of the First World War would provide new and unforeseen challenges that would test beyond limits whether the government could respond to events with sufficient speed. That September, George Riddell had dined alone with Arthur Balfour,[48] the languid and cerebral former Conservative Prime Minister, and over the course of the evening they came to discuss the different styles of Lloyd George and Asquith as parliamentary speakers. Balfour was certainly a qualified authority, having been a member of the House of Commons long enough to have seen both Disraeli and William Gladstone[49] in their prime, as well as being an accomplished speaker himself. According to Riddell, Balfour, 'spoke highly of L.G., and said that he was interesting because he had so many styles of oratory – violent, wheedling, and humorous – and in all he was equally as good. He and Asquith made a remarkable combination. Each had what the other lacked. Asquith possessed great judgement, great dexterity and a wide, capricious mind; L.G., vehement fire, power of action, and tact.'[50] The Lloyd George and Asquith speaking styles also reflected their personalities. Lloyd George, raised outside of the establishment, was decisive, impulsive and a seducer; a man who upset orthodoxies. Asquith, ten years Lloyd George's senior, was the son of a west Yorkshire wool manufacturer, who had sought acceptance, working his way into the inner circle. He'd won a scholarship to study Classics at Balliol College, Oxford, where he also went on to become President of the Oxford Union Society,[51] before being called to the Bar. A barrister by profession, and with a formidable intellect, he was more suited to the High Court than twentieth-century politics. As the First Lord of the Admiralty, Winston Churchill[52] observed of him, 'In Cabinet he was markedly silent. Indeed he never spoke a word in Council if he could get his way without it. He sat like the great Judge he was.'[53]

Where Lloyd George sparkled with vitality, Asquith was solid, square cut, orderly and disciplined. In dress, Lloyd George paid a great deal of attention to the style of his personal appearance, whereas Asquith had the slightly shabby appearance of an ageing Oxford academic. Their Cabinet colleague John Simon also observed that Asquith had 'a sturdiness, physical and mental, which compelled admiration', however 'he was not a spell-binder who aroused emotion as Lloyd George and Churchill could'.[54]

By Christmas 1914 it was clear that there was no end to the war in sight. With no imminent breakthrough on the Western Front thought likely, Cabinet ministers started to question why alternative strategies were not being considered, so that, as Winston Churchill put it, soldiers were not just being sent to 'to chew barbed wire in Flanders'.[55] Lloyd George wrote to Asquith on New Year's Day 1915 with what the Prime Minister thought was a 'quite good'[56] letter urging a more active prosecution of the war from Downing Street. This he suggested should include regular meetings of the War Council, the creation of a new committee with executive power to oversee the supply of munitions to the armed forces, and consideration of landing forces at Salonika in Greece, to bring that country into the war and launch a campaign in support of Serbia. Churchill had also advocated an attack on the Gallipoli peninsula in the eastern Aegean Sea to enable the Royal Navy to gain control of the Dardanelles straits and then open the route to Constantinople. The Dardanelles plan was eventually agreed to by Kitchener, but only in Lloyd George's opinion because it was wrongly believed it would require a smaller commitment from the army than the landing at Salonika. However, delays in launching the attack on Gallipoli meant the element of surprise would be lost, and the mission would be doomed from the start.

Yet the growing divide within the Cabinet was not just over questions of military supply and tactics. It was increasingly about whether the members believed the task before them was so great that it would require completely rethinking every principle of wartime government that had gone before. Or if not, could this all be left to the generals, who would deliver the victory efficiently and with the minimum required effort. On this question Lloyd George and Churchill were natural allies, just as they had been on social reform before the war, when in Winston's words he'd acted as the Welshman's, 'lieutenant . . . and shared in a minor way in the work'.[57] They were also friends, rather than merely good colleagues, and had been since Churchill left the Conservatives to join the Liberal Party in 1904. Four years later, Lloyd George was the only senior member of the Cabinet to attend Winston's wedding to his wife Clementine,[58] as well as being one of the three witnesses to the marriage.[59] It was in many ways an unlikely partnership between the cottage-bred Lloyd George and Churchill, grandson of the Duke of Marlborough,[60] who had been born at Blenheim Palace. They were of similar stature, being just five and a half feet tall, but compensating through towering personalities, to which they were both attracted. Churchill was one of Lloyd George's few aristocratic friends.

Winston's politician father, Lord Randolph Churchill,[61] had been an advocate of *Tory Democracy*, a variation of the progressive *One Nation* Conservatism of Benjamin Disraeli.[62] But if Winston Churchill was now a Liberal, he was from the start a Lloyd George liberal. They both enjoyed, as Churchill would later reflect, 'to talk politics and let their fancy play over the swiftly-moving scene . . . [throwing] themselves with zest into the discussion of current events'.[63] Just before the outbreak of war, Lloyd George also reminded Churchill that 'For ten years there has been hardly a day when we haven't had half an hour's talk together.'[64] Together they could be an energetic force as ministers who believed government intervention could, when well directed, be both necessary and positive. In this regard they were both willing to challenge the conventional wisdom of the experts, an approach that in wartime seemed in increasingly stark contrast to the more wait-and-see attitude of the Prime Minister, Herbert Asquith.

On 22 February 1915, Lloyd George decided that the time had come for the Cabinet to assert its authority on the war effort. In a memorandum circulated to its members he gave his analysis of the issues that needed to be addressed. 'The first and greatest difficulty is equipment,' he stated. 'The number of men we could put in the field is seriously limited by the output of guns and rifles . . . I do not believe Great Britain has ever yet done anything like what she could do in the matter of increasing her war equipment . . . I sincerely believe that we could double our effective energies if we organised our factories thoroughly.'[65] In response to this challenge he called for 'full powers' to be taken 'to mobilise the whole of our manufacturing strength for the purpose of turning out, at the earliest possible moment, war material'.[66]

As a consequence of this memo, in March the government granted itself the power to take control of civilian factories and direct them to war work. Lloyd George presented the measures to the House of Commons and in so doing found an ally in the Conservative leader Andrew Bonar Law, who argued, 'if there is that shortage [of munitions], I do not think the industrial resources of the country have been used to the greatest advantage. I cannot understand why, if this Bill is necessary today, the necessity of it could not have been foreseen in August or September, and why it should not have been introduced then.' In response Lloyd George stated that the government was looking for businessmen of 'push and go' to help deliver what was required, a phrase that captured the public attention of those who in his words 'awaited the advent of the "man of push and go"'.[67]

Lloyd George and Bonar Law had, according to the Chancellor, for years enjoyed 'terms of greater cordiality . . . than is usual between political adversaries who are taking a strenuous part in party conflicts'.[68] They were certainly unlikely political allies. Lloyd George was a champion of free trade and Home Rule for Ireland, whereas Bonar Law was a strong Unionist and a great advocate for trade tariffs on goods from outside of the Empire. Bonar Law was a tall, spare man with a Scottish accent, a consequence of his Glasgow upbringing, rather than his early childhood in New Brunswick, Canada. His speech was lucid, and in debate he made his points methodically, like the hammer of a Clydeside shipbuilder striking a rivet. Unlike Lloyd George, his recreations and vices were limited to chess and rice pudding, although both men enjoyed smoking cigars. As the son of a Minister in the Free Church of Scotland, Bonar Law nevertheless felt a certain affinity with the chapel-bred Welshman, and did not believe he was an entirely lost soul. They were both political outsiders, as Bonar Law had made his way in business, and like Lloyd George, hadn't taken a university degree. He was also the first leader of the Conservative Party from outside of the aristocracy since Disraeli.

In the spring of 1915, Lloyd George also contacted Arthur Balfour, who was then the only Opposition politician included on the War Council and the Committee for Imperial Defence. Lloyd George recalled in his memoirs that 'From time to time I had poured into his ears my misgivings as to the whole position . . . I had an implicit belief in his patriotism and a great admiration for his high intellectual gifts. Moreover, he had some war experience. He knew his Generals well. He had not forgotten the incompetent complacencies of the Boer War. He had suffered from them at that time. Their blunders had helped to discredit his administration.'[69] In letters Lloyd George impressed upon Balfour his wish that he should be more involved in government discussions on the war effort so that his 'Influence and position' might help effect a change in outcome.[70] Balfour also reciprocated that interest, writing to Lloyd George that he could see no improvement in the problems of supplying war materials, 'unless you will take in hand the organization of the engineering resources of the country'.[71]

One of Lloyd George's gifts as a politician was his ability to view the whole chessboard, and not just the pieces directly in play. Although Asquith had completed over seven years as Prime Minister, the longest period of continuous service in that office for nearly a century, his position was precarious. The Liberals lacked an overall majority and at the last general election in December 1910 had only recorded one more seat in the House of Commons than the Conservative Party. They had only governed thanks to the informal support of the 74 MPs in John Redmond's[72] Irish Parliamentary Party, and the relatively new Labour Party, which at that time had only 42 MPs. Lloyd George could see that it was unlikely the war would conclude before the end of 1915, when the next general election was due, so at some point the Conservatives would have to be brought into the government. Therefore, an alliance of like-minded men, regardless of their pre-war party differences, could be essential to shaping future policy, and in reaching out to Balfour and Bonar Law, Lloyd George was already preparing the ground for such an eventuality. Overall, he doubted that the Prime Minister had the personality to 'get a grip of the situation'.[73] On 7 March he confided to George Riddell; 'Give Asquith his brief; and he will give a splendid opinion. The best opinion I know on stated and agreed facts, but he lacks initiative and takes no steps to control or hold together the public departments, each of which goes its own way without criticism. This is all very well in time of peace, but during a great war the Prime Minister should direct and overlook the machine.'[74]

At 7.30 a.m. on 10 March 1915 the urgent debate within the government about the paucity of munitions supply was articulated most dramatically. The British First Army under the command of General Sir Douglas Haig,[75] including the Indian Corps, launched their most devastating concentrated artillery barrage of the war, on the German lines at the village of Neuve Chapelle.[76] Lieutenant Malcolm Kennedy,[77] who witnessed the spectacle, wrote in his diary, 'There was a deafening roar . . . Heralded by a deep-toned vibrating sound overhead, as though hundreds of express trains were rushing through the air. Hell then seemed to break loose as shell after shell, from guns of all calibres, burst with ear-splitting explosions on the German positions opposite . . . But from time to time great masses of earth could be seen hurtling through the air as shells struck the ground to our front and tore it to bits.'[78] For 35 minutes the British guns pounded away at the German front line, and then for a further 30 minutes at the village itself. In just over an hour more shells were expended than had been fired by the British army during the entire Boer War.

The operation caught the Germans completely by surprise and by nightfall Neuve Chapelle had been captured, but the British were not able to make the progress needed to capture Aubers Ridge beyond. A German counter-offensive was successfully repelled, but the effort exhausted the British artillery supplies. On 13 March a further British offensive was postponed and two days later cancelled altogether. The casualties on both sides after three days of fighting were nearly 24,000 killed, wounded or missing, and no decisive advantage was obtained.

Sir John French complained to Lord Kitchener that the offensive had failed due to 'want of ammunition',[79] and two weeks later, in comments to *The Times*, French stated 'emphatically' the importance of 'the need for munitions'.[80] This was a problem that Kitchener appeared to acknowledge in a statement to the House of Lords on 15 March, where he stated, 'we have unfortunately found that the output [of munitions and equipment] is not only not equal to our necessities but does not fulfil our expectations'.[81] However, in private he demonstrated a continued lack of appreciation of the realities of war on the Western Front.

The Conservative MP Arthur Lee[82] had, like Regy Esher, been sent to France by Kitchener as his personal Commissioner, in this case to the Army Medical Service. Lee was a former soldier and while attached to the British Embassy in Washington had served as a military attaché to the American army forces during the 1898 Spanish-American war. It was at that time he befriended the then Colonel Theodore Roosevelt, who made him an honorary member of his 'Rough Riders', the 1st US Volunteer Cavalry. Lee was quick to report back on the Battle of Neuve Chapelle, recalling in his memoirs, 'I took upon myself to dash home to the War Office and to try and impress upon Kitchener the tragic consequences of hurling men's bodies against uncut wire entanglements and batteries of machine guns. He received this very ill and, almost before I could complete my story burst out into a tirade against what he called the "preposterous waste of ammunition . . . Do you mean to tell me that it has come to this; that the British soldier cannot be relied upon to advance and attack with his bayonet unless the enemy has first been battered into a state of insensibility?"'[83] Herbert Asquith met with Kitchener on 18 March, noting, 'He is really distressed and preoccupied by the reckless way in which ammunition, particularly shells, was expended last week.'[84] That day more bad news arrived from Gallipoli, where an offensive by the navies of Great Britain and France had failed to take control of the Dardanelles straits, so opening the prospect that men and materiel from the army would also need to be diverted to this new theatre of war.

Asquith considered giving way to Lloyd George so he could create a special munitions committee with control over war supply, noting, 'it is quite on the cards that I may create a new office for Lloyd George – Director of War Contracts, or something of the kind – and relieve him of his present duties'.[85] Yet ten days later no progress had been made, and the Prime Minister recalled on 28 March, 'There is a truly royal row on the stocks between Kitchener and Lloyd George in regard to the proposed Committee on Munitions. Neither is disposed to give way. K. threatens to give up his office and L.G. to wash his hands of the whole business, leaving on record all sorts of solemn protests and warnings.'[86] The spotlight now, though, was about to fall on Asquith himself.

'The Intrigue against the Prime Minister' is being organized by people who 'thought it worthwhile to put about by innuendo and suggestion the pretence that he is not fit for the task.' On 29 March the Liberal-supporting *Daily Chronicle* further highlighted how in recent days the Conservative press had seemed 'inclined to exalt [Mr Lloyd George] as a luminary eclipsing his chief'.[87] Indeed, that same day the *Morning Post* criticized Asquith's lack of vigour in his leadership of the war effort, asking, 'During the long winter months has it never occurred to the Prime Minister to ascertain the ability of our armament establishments to supply the munitions of war adequate to the increased and increasing necessities of our forces by land and sea? Apparently, it has not. The powers which as Prime Minister, he should have sought have at length been taken over by the Chancellor of the Exchequer [who has] stepped into the place of this leader.'

The article in the *Daily Chronicle* might in normal times have been dismissed as a minor piece of Westminster gossip, but it marked a break in the political truce that had lasted since the start of the war. Even though there was no agreement between the parties, the Conservatives had so far neither opposed the government's direction of the war, nor publicly criticized it. After reading the article, Lloyd George telephoned George Riddell, 'in a state of great anger and excitement', describing it as 'most injurious and indiscreet',[88] but not wrong. The article had been written by the editor, Robert Donald,[89] who was a friend and neighbour to both Lloyd George and Riddell in Walton Heath. He regularly joined them in golf on Saturday mornings, and occasionally they all attended the theatre together. The credence given by a leading Liberal journalist to this 'intrigue' against Asquith would create suspicion that it was a view sanctioned by Lloyd George as well.

Asquith asked to meet with his Chancellor that day to discuss 'the sinister and . . . absurd interpretations which were being given to the articles in *The Times, Observer,* and *Morning Post*'. The Prime Minister later wrote to Venetia Stanley recording Lloyd George's reaction to the suggestion that there might be a plot against him:

> . . . he declared that he owed everything to me, that I had stuck to him and protected him and defended him when every man's hand was against him, and he would rather (1) break stones, (2) dig potatoes, (3) be hung and quartered (these were metaphors used at different stages of his broken but impassioned harangue) than do any act or say a word or harbour a thought that was disloyal to me, and he said

that every one of his colleagues felt the same. His eyes were wet with tears, and I am sure that, with all his Celtic capacity for impulse and momentary fervour, he was quite sincere.'[90]

Although as one of Lloyd George's Conservative critics once observed, 'Lloyd George was a superb actor and he could produce on the spur of the moment crocodile tears which were indistinguishable from the real thing.'[91] Lloyd George gave Riddell his own recollection of the meeting, stating, 'The old boy was in tears . . . I have never intrigued for place or office. I have intrigued to carry through my schemes but that is a different matter. The Prime Minister has been so good to me that I would never be disloyal to him in the smallest detail. I may criticize him amongst ourselves, as I have no doubt he criticizes me, but we are absolutely loyal to each other.'[92]

The following day, Asquith called a meeting with Lloyd George and the Home Secretary Reginald McKenna,[93] who was also a friend of Robert Donald, to discuss the *Daily Chronicle* article. McKenna had been a Cambridge University rowing blue and barrister before entering Parliament, and was close to Asquith. He saw himself as a leading voice for Liberalism in the Cabinet but lacked Lloyd George's instinct for popular opinion. Margot Asquith considered that the rather prim McKenna was 'a man of affairs but not a man of the world'.[94] At this meeting, however, the Prime Minister recalled that his two Cabinet colleagues were 'fighting like fishwives'.[95] Lloyd George, as he always did on such occasions, used attack as the best means of defence, and began, Asquith thought, 'on a very stormy note, accusing McKenna of having inspired Donald to write the article in the *Chronicle* . . . McKenna hotly denied that he had ever said or suggested to Donald that L.G. was in the plot, while admitting that he had had a talk with him on the subject.'[96] For all to see, that was a carefully worded non-denial, denial. Yet while Asquith, ever the conciliator, noted, 'There was a lot of hitting and counter-hitting between them', he felt that he had 'lowered the temperature' and 'got them into first an accommodating and in the end an almost friendly mood'.[97] Although that was most probably because they both thought they had got away with it. Lloyd George told Riddell though, 'I still believe that McKenna is responsible. He is obsessed by the fear of a coalition government in which there would, of course, be no place for him.'[98]

Overall, the outcome of this episode was that the 'volatile and versatile'[99] Lloyd George, as Asquith described his Chancellor, had succeeded in forcing the Prime Minister into making a decision. On 6 April, Lloyd George wrote to Frances Stevenson to inform her that the 'PM has overruled K. peremptorily & put me in command of Munitions of War! God help me', adding that at Cabinet that day there had been a 'Great row between Winston and K . . . The temper of the Great War Lords is getting worse & worse as their shortcomings are getting more manifest. K. has made a mess of Munitions & Winston a muddle of the Dardanelles & their temper is consequently vile.'[100] On 8 April, Asquith made the official announcement of 'a Munitions Committee with the fullest possible powers',[101] and with Lloyd George in the Chair.

Yet, this did nothing to improve the situation, and Lloyd George was frustrated that even with the committee, it was very difficult to get accurate information from the War Office about the orders they had placed. Eight days later Asquith noted another stormy Cabinet where, according to the Prime Minister, Kitchener, 'who is evidently a good deal perturbed, has been attacking L.G. for having disclosed to the Munitions Committee the figures which he, K., had confidentially communicated to the Cabinet. He declares that he can no longer be responsible for the War Office under such conditions.'[102] The cause of the disagreement was that Lloyd George had told the Committee the number of British servicemen in France was 509,000, a decision he defended on the basis that it was difficult for the Munitions Committee to accurately calculate the supply requirements of the army, if they didn't know how many men they were supposed to be equipping. Charles Hobhouse recalled that at one point during their argument Kitchener announced he had clearly lost the confidence of his colleagues, then 'picked up his spectacles, pushed back his chair, and took 3 slow, very slow steps to the door'. Some members of the Cabinet, including McKenna and Lord Crewe,[103] called out 'no, no', but Hobhouse observed that 'Grey and P.M. said nothing. Lloyd George, Churchill and I also said nothing, they because they were angry, I because I was certain the whole thing was pure farce.'[104] Ever the pacifier, Asquith, managed to calm the situation. He wrote that 'By dint of appeals and warnings and gives and takes and all sorts of devices and expedients I have succeeded in getting us back into more or less smooth water. Still, it leaves a disagreeable taste in one's mouth, particularly as L.G. let slip in the course of the altercation some injurious and wounding innuendoes which K. will be more than human to forget.'[105]

On 20 April, George Riddell met with Lord Northcliffe,[106] the most powerful of all the Fleet Street press barons, to sound him out on the conduct of the war thus far. Northcliffe had founded the *Daily Mail* and *Daily Mirror*, and was the owner of *The Times*. Each morning half of the newspapers read in London were printed on his presses and he believed he had a unique power to feel the pulse of the nation. Northcliffe had a boyish, boisterous personality that could result in acts both of great genius and gross irresponsibility. When others in his opinion blundered, the reaction could be volcanic. The Conservative MP and Canadian-British businessman Max Aitken,[107] who also controlled the *Daily Express*, believed that Northcliffe was 'the greatest figure who ever strode down Fleet Street'[108] and that 'His power was so considerable that it was of the utmost importance in all matters of public interest to secure his assistance or at any rate his neutrality.'[109] Northcliffe had for years warned of a likely conflict with Germany and used his newspapers to vigorously support the war effort. He had also visited the front earlier that month where he'd been given a lengthy personal briefing by Sir John French. For some time, Northcliffe had been concerned that the prosecution of the war was not as effective as it should be. In mid-January he'd confided to Samuel Storey,[110] a fellow newspaper proprietor, that his papers were 'dealing very gently with the government now, because the public, who know nothing about the war, will not tolerate criticism of our public men; but, believe me, we will not be patient much longer.'[111] Riddell noted in his diary following their meeting that Northcliffe's patience was now nearly exhausted, as he 'spoke in violent and contemptuous terms of Asquith and Kitchener. He says that the former is indolent, weak and apathetic. He exercises no control over the various departments. He will never finish the war. L.G. may be the man. He is the best of the lot. Kitchener's brain is paralysed. He is . . . most inefficient. He is also tricky and unreliable'.[112] That evening Asquith gave a speech to armaments workers in Newcastle in which he exclaimed, 'I saw a statement the other day that the operations of our army were being crippled by our failure to provide the necessary ammunition. There is not a word of truth in that statement.'[113] The following day *The Times* dismissed Asquith's argument as 'misleading' and 'not the speech of a statesman rising to the height of a great occasion. It was short of courage and candour.'[114] George Riddell recorded in his diary on 24 April, 'L.G. says we are very short of ammunition. We have plenty of explosives but not enough shells. Our organisation has been deplorable, while the French have made the most of their facilities, which are considerably less than ours. The result is they are turning out four times as many shells as we are doing.'[115] The following day there was yet more bad news from Gallipoli where the British and ANZAC[116] forces had landed on the beaches of that peninsula, sustaining heavy casualties and unable to take their objectives. Further to that, on 7 May a German U-boat sank the Cunard passenger liner, the RMS *Lusitania*, just 12 miles off the coast of Kinsale in Ireland, with the loss of 1,195 lives.

On 9 May 1915 a new British offensive near Lille on the Western Front at Aubers Ridge gave another demonstration of the limitations of the British armaments. Sir John French watched the early hours of the operation from the tower of a ruined church and recalled in his memoir, 1914, 'I clearly saw the great inequality of the artillery duels, and, as attack after attack failed, I could see that the absence of sufficient artillery support was doubling and trebling our losses in men.'[117] When he returned to General Headquarters at St Omer later that afternoon he was handed a telegram from Kitchener directing that 20 per cent of the British Expeditionary Force's armament supplies were to be shipped for use in the Dardanelles. In anger, French 'immediately gave instructions that evidence should be furnished to Colonel Repington, military correspondent of *The Times* . . . that the vital need for high-explosive shells had been a fatal bar to our Army success on that day'.[118] French also directed his private secretary Colonel Brinsley Fitzgerald[119] and his aide-de-camp (ADC) Captain Freddie Guest[120] to return to London to brief Lloyd George on the situation, because he had 'already shown me, by his special interest in this subject, that he grasped the deadly nature of our necessities'.[121] The same information was also presented to Arthur Balfour and Andrew Bonar Law. The Aubers Ridge attack, which was stopped the following day, cost 11,000 British casualties for no material advantage gained. The truth exploded in *The Times* on Friday 14 May, where in addition to Repington's report the editorial column stated coldly and clearly, 'British soldiers died in vain on the Aubers Ridge on Sunday

[9 May] because more shells were needed. The Government, who have so seriously failed to organise adequately our national resources, must bear their share of the grave responsibility.' These words had a particular personal resonance for Lord Northcliffe, whose 20-year-old nephew Lucas King[122] had been killed in action at Ypres six days before. On receiving the news, Northcliffe was said to have exclaimed, 'Kitchener murdered him!'[123]

When Lloyd George received his 'unexpected' visit from Colonel Fitzgerald and Captain Guest he noted that this was the 'first communication on the shell question that I had received from the Commander in Chief'.[124] It was also clear to him from the documents he was shown that 'vital telegrams from the front on the subject of the shell shortage had been withheld from me, even when I was Chairman of the Committee appointed by the Prime Minister to consider the munition question'.[125] As a consequence, Lloyd George wrote Asquith a letter that was not sent until 19 May, setting out the information he'd received and concluding that 'the proceedings of a Munitions Committee from which vital information of this character is withheld must be a farce. I cannot, therefore, continue to preside over it under such conditions.'[126] Lloyd George knew that if he resigned and spoke out, it would bring the government down. He was also aware that the Conservative leadership were insistent now on either full participation in the government, or outright opposition to the management of the war effort. On Saturday 15 May the situation was made worse by the resignation of Lord Fisher[127] as First Sea Lord, because of disagreements with Winston Churchill over the commitment of naval resources for the Dardanelles campaign.

On the Monday morning, 17 May, Andrew Bonar Law went to the Treasury to meet Lloyd George in his rooms. It is telling that Bonar Law should have approached Lloyd George first, and not Asquith, to discuss the crisis. However, what had brought them together was, as Lloyd George put it, 'a genuine conviction on the part of many who had no desire to provoke a Ministerial crisis that if an improvement were not soon effected, we should lose the war'.[128] In addition to this, 'Underlying the various specific grounds for anxiety in different directions was a sense of revolt against the attitude of the Government and what was regarded as its leisurely and take-for-granted attitude in dealing with vitally serious matters, matters of life and death.'[129] There was also pressure on Bonar Law to act from within the Conservative Party. Earlier in the year Lord Curzon[130] had complained to Bonar Law that the Liberals had 'all the advantages [of a coalition] while we have all the drawbacks . . . They tell us nothing or next to nothing of their plans, and yet they pretend our leaders share both their knowledge and their responsibility.'[131] Curzon was a former Viceroy of India who wanted to secure a high-ranking place in the Cabinet for himself now he was back in England. He was just the sort of grandee on manoeuvres that Bonar Law had to be careful with as well. Never lacking in self-confidence, Curzon had been lampooned as a student at Balliol College, Oxford, with a doggerel verse that stayed with him all his life:

My name is George Nathaniel Curzon,
I am a most superior person.
My cheeks are pink, my hair is sleek,
I dine at Blenheim twice a week.[132]

According to Austen Chamberlain, who was Bonar Law's closest associate at this time, the Conservative leader told Lloyd George on the morning of 17 May that he couldn't allow Parliament to go into the Whitsun recess, due on 20 May, unless there had been a statement on the resignation of Lord Fisher from the Admiralty, which would result in 'a severe attack on the government'. Then, 'Lloyd George burst out passionately, saying that he entirely agreed with Bonar Law – that it was impossible that things should go on as they were, and inveighing against much in the conduct of the war. In particular he said that Kitchener had "put lies in his mouth" as to the supply of munitions and that the situation was altogether intolerable.'[133] According to Max Aitken, who was also in close contact with Bonar Law at this time, when Lloyd George confirmed to him that Fisher had resigned, the Conservative leader had replied, 'Then the situation is impossible.' To which the Chancellor responded, 'Of course we must have a Coalition, for the alternative is impossible.'[134]

Later that morning both Lloyd George and Bonar Law would together visit Asquith at 10 Downing Street, and they effectively presented him with a *fait accompli*. Lloyd George later recalled, in 'an incredibly short time'[135] the agreement for a coalition was made, and with it the death sentence given to the last entirely Liberal government in British history.

According to Austen Chamberlain, Bonar Law and Lloyd George 'stated that it was absolutely necessary to get rid of Kitchener . . . Asquith's suggestion was that Lloyd George should be made Secretary of State for War and Bonar Law Chancellor of the Exchequer'.[136] The same day, the Prime Minister wrote to his Liberal ministers to inform them, 'The resignation of Lord Fisher . . . and the more than plausible parliamentary case in regard to the alleged deficiency of high explosive shells, would, if duly exploited (as they would have been) in the House of Commons at this moment, have had the most disastrous effect on the general political and strategic situation . . . Upon a full review of all the circumstances, I have come to the conclusion that, in the best interests of the country, the reconstruction of the Government can no longer be deferred.'[137] That evening Margot Asquith sent a note to Lloyd George from 10 Downing Street:

> How tragic! Our great Cabinet that has stormed crisis after crisis . . . all crumpled up like a scrap of paper! . . . Everyone devoted to you and you quite passionately loyal to me and Henry.[138] The break-up of colleagues is to me very tragic. It's true you'll most of you be there but it can never be the same again. I don't care for the other side. I don't admire their brains or their behaviour. BL is a mixture of slimness and simplicity. Lansdowne[139] has a Conservative maidenly mind. Austen is more of a shopkeeper than a merchant – he has no greatness and is a bore . . . Curzon a peacock. You can take the whole lot! I see no use for them . . . Do come and tell me what you think. I'm in my bedroom but very visible and rather lonely. It's all pillows. That vile *Morning Post* and *Times* how they will rejoice.[140]

Regy Esher recalled that London 'was full of rumours. It was said that Lord Northcliffe was working for Mr. Lloyd George to form a new government . . . to substitute Mr. Lloyd George for Lord Kitchener at the War Office.'[141] How much contact the men had at that time is not clear, but Riddell noted that Northcliffe had what he called a 'very useful'[142] hour with Lloyd George on 17 May, the day that the decision in principle to form a coalition government was made. Northcliffe was not the only newspaper man keen to consult Lloyd George about the crisis. The Chancellor's old friend C. P. Scott of the *Manchester Guardian* wrote to him on 18 May that 'It seems to me we have reached something like a turning-point, and that if this country is going to do its duty and the war is not to be indefinitely prolonged, quite a new spirit and quite a new impulse are needed from the centre of authority. At present I see no sign of these things.'[143]

Over at Northcliffe's offices at Carmelite House just off Fleet Street, Tom Clarke,[144] news editor of the *Daily Mail*, recalled that after Asquith had announced in the House of Commons on 19 May his intention to form a new government, it was also confirmed 'that Kitchener was not resigning. Next morning, by order of Northcliffe, the *Daily Mail* opened its thunderous attack on Kitchener – an attack that stunned the whole country.'[145] On Friday 21 May the *Daily Mail* headline proclaimed, 'The Tragedy of the Shells: Lord Kitchener's Grave Error'. It then went on to state that 'Lord Kitchener has starved the army in France of high explosive shells.' The reaction was violent and immediate. Copies of the newspaper were burnt at the London Stock Exchange, police protection was required outside the *Daily Mail* offices. Nevertheless, that evening Northcliffe calmly strode into the newsroom, 'wearing a blue suit, a green slouch hat, and chewing the end of a big cigar', and announced, 'I have thrown off another string of pearls for you today . . . What's the news?'[146] When told of the newspaper burnings at the Stock Exchange and the attacks on him in the evening papers, he just replied, 'That shows they don't know the truth.'[147]

For Northcliffe, the unforeseen consequence of his attack on Kitchener, and the outpouring of support it generated for the Secretary of State for War, made it very difficult for him to be removed from the War Office. Instead, Northcliffe's focus now fell on whether Lloyd George should lead a new department with full responsibility for war supply. On Sunday 23 May, Northcliffe visited Lloyd George at home in Walton Heath. Frances Stevenson recalled that Northcliffe was 'all for C. [Lloyd George] taking over Munitions, & not allowing the Tories to get it. He told C. that they had begun intriguing already against the Liberals, and that he was afraid the national Government would not last long . . . Dirty work when the country is in peril!'[148] When Riddell heard of this meeting a few days later he noted, 'I have a shrewd suspicion that LG has been a party to the attacks on Kitchener . . . LG is very deep and subtle in his proceedings. He rarely tells me *all* the story.'[149]

On 25 May the positions in the new Cabinet were confirmed, with Kitchener staying at the War Office. Lloyd George would lead a new

Ministry of Munitions, but retain the traditional accommodation of the Chancellor of the Exchequer at 11 Downing Street. Bonar Law did not become Chancellor, which went to the Liberal Reginald McKenna, but instead was appointed Secretary of State for the Colonies. Austen Chamberlain was made Secretary of State for India, Curzon Lord Privy Seal, and the new Attorney General was Edward Carson,[150] the leading voice of Ulster unionism and the first person to sign the Ulster Covenant pledging an oath of resistance to Irish Home Rule.[151]

Arthur Balfour succeeded Winston Churchill as First Lord of the Admiralty. Churchill's removal to the then minor Cabinet post of Chancellor of the Duchy of Lancaster was seen as inevitable by Lloyd George from the moment Jacky Fisher had resigned. Firstly, it was revenge from the Conservatives for Churchill's decision to leave their party and join the Liberals. Secondly, as Lloyd George explained to Frances Stevenson, Churchill had found his 'Nemesis . . . When the war came he saw in it the chance of glory for himself & has accordingly entered on a risky campaign without caring a straw for the misery and hardship it would bring to thousands in the hope he would prove to be the outstanding man in this war.'[152] Years later, Lloyd George criticized the decision to demote Churchill as a 'cruel and unjust degradation. The Dardanelles failure was due not so much to Mr Churchill's precipitancy as to Lord Kitchener's and Mr Asquith's procrastination . . . I reckoned it would have been impossible to keep him at the Admiralty in view of the dispute which had precipitated the crisis . . . But it was quite unnecessary . . . to fling him from the masthead, whence he had been directing the fire, down to the lower deck to polish the brass.'[153] Yet Lloyd George, observing the political realities of the situation, did not fight for Churchill, in contrast to the steadfast loyalty that Winston had shown him during the Marconi affair. Then, Churchill had defended what he publicly called Lloyd George's 'unstained and stainless honour'.[154] Now that the reality of the re-organization of the government was clear, in pain and anger Churchill confronted Lloyd George, stating, 'You don't care what becomes of me. You don't care whether I'm trampled underfoot by my enemies. You don't care for my personal reputation.' To which Lloyd George replied, 'No, I don't care for my own at the present moment. The only thing I care about now is that we win this war.'[155]

TWO

Man of Push and Go

At noon on 27 May 1915 the members of the Coalition Cabinet gathered for their first meeting at 10 Downing Street. Arranged around a long table in the large rectangular Cabinet Room were men who had spent their entire careers as rivals and opponents. Despite the generous proportions of that well-appointed but simply furnished chamber, it felt intimate, with ministers sitting at each other's elbows and face to face with colleagues across the Cabinet table. At the centre of it all sat Asquith in the Prime Minister's chair, with his back to the marble fireplace and the portrait of Sir Robert Walpole[1] staring down behind him. Every word and gesture could be scrutinized and there was certainly no place to hide.

The day before, Andrew Bonar Law had addressed a meeting of Conservative parliamentarians held in the smoking room and library of the Carlton Club in Pall Mall.[2] In that cavernous book-lined and wood-panelled room, populated with comfortable leather armchairs and sofas, the members of the Commons and Lords assembled. The club was not just a social gathering place for Conservatives to plot and gossip when Parliament was sitting, rather it served as the organizing centre of the party machine itself. This was where they gathered when important decisions needed to be made, and the members wanted reassurance from their leader over how this novel form of government, the first coalition for 63 years, would work in practice. Bonar Law, speaking in his typically candid and direct fashion, told them:

> Those of us who are now entering the Government are entering it as colleagues of men to whom, only a few months ago, we were bitterly

opposed, and to men from whom even now, we are divided as far as men can be divided, on almost every question of domestic policy. It is very difficult, but the only chance of the success of this Coalition, is that every member of it should go into it with a fixed determination to act as the loyal colleague of every member of the Cabinet . . . putting aside absolutely everything until the war is finished, and by regarding the war as the only thing we have to deal with.[3]

This statement was greeted with approval, by the stamping of feet and banging of tables, but for many Conservatives, the idea that they would one day be in government with Lloyd George would have been unthinkable. On the big pre-war political issues, like reform of the House of Lords, Home Rule for Ireland, free trade, votes for women and Lloyd George's new taxes to pay for social reform, his positions and those of many leading Conservatives were fundamentally different. As Bonar Law's private secretary J. C. C. Davidson[4] recalled, 'Lloyd George had been anathema to the Tory Party, and it was only with the greatest difficulty that they could be persuaded that it was safe to support him in any of his enterprises, because they always saw him as their main enemy.'[5]

There were also elements of personal dislike and distrust between them. Austen Chamberlain recalled of Lloyd George's attacks on 'the honour' of his father[6] during the Boer War, that they were 'an offence which I had neither forgotten nor forgiven'. He further noted how he 'intensely disliked' Lloyd George's methods, and 'felt a great distaste for his ways and little confidence in his judgement'.[7] Edward Carson had previously dismissed Lloyd George as an 'unscrupulous demagogue',[8] and of the new arrangements he thought, 'We are a strange lot of bedfellows in the Cabinet, but I hope we think only of the country.'[9] Arthur Balfour, despite his private flattery, was also sceptical as to whether Lloyd George would succeed at the Ministry of Munitions. On 11 June 1915, Balfour met with Lord Riddell and told him, 'It's a big task. I wonder whether he will be successful. I am not sure that he has all of the necessary qualities. He has some of them, but not others.'[10]

Lloyd George had pressed for the creation of the Ministry of Munitions and now it was his responsibility to deliver it. Yet, despite its central importance to the war effort, there were men sitting around the Cabinet table who would be happy to see him fail, including some of his Liberal colleagues. Lloyd George reflected in his *War Memoirs* that:

> The personal attitude of my old political friends towards me changed and chilled after I became Minister of Munitions. It found petulant expression in speeches and articles, and I felt myself shunned and even spurned by men who once had greeted me with cordiality and enthusiasm. I was treated as one tainted with the new leprosy of war. I had a sense of political isolation more complete than I had ever experienced during the whole of my lifetime. My old friends were turning their backs on me. The Conservatives had not yet forgotten the part I had played in the bitter controversies of the last few years, and the Liberals were resentful and sulky.[11]

The enormity of Lloyd George's task was manifest from day one, when on 24 May 1915 he arrived at his new office at 6 Whitehall Gardens,[12] a Regency-period residence recently vacated by the Bond Street art dealer, William Lockett Agnew.[13] Accompanied by J. T. Davies and Frances Stevenson, he started the work of the Ministry of Munitions in the drawing room of that elegant house, which was then furnished with just one table and a couple of chairs. The following evening they also received a deadly reminder of the urgency of their work, when Lloyd George had to break to Frances the news that her only brother Paul[14] had been killed by a shell on the Western Front at Festubert.

Given the challenge of creating a new Ministry from scratch, Lloyd George brought in men of talent and experience who shared his energy and commitment to action. Chief amongst these was his former colleague at the Board of Trade, Sir Hubert Llewellyn Smith,[15] who Lloyd George believed was 'the most resourceful and suggestive mind in the whole of our Civil Service'.[16] Llewellyn Smith also attracted some of the brightest and best of the younger officials to join them, including the 36-year-old William Beveridge.[17] Beveridge believed that Llewellyn Smith's work at the Ministry of Munitions demonstrated all of 'his superhuman industry, his speed and his resourcefulness in tackling new problems'. Also, that he made 'the art of Civil Service administration . . . an art of getting things done, and getting the right things done, by consultation and conciliation, by anticipating and answering objections, by never leaving ends loose'.[18]

For his junior minister at the new department Lloyd George chose Christopher Addison,[19] who he believed had 'a high order of intellectual capacity, full of ideas, resourcefulness and courage'.[20] Addison was the son of a Lincolnshire farmer and had gone on to study medicine at St Bartholomew's Hospital in London; just the kind of new man of practical intelligence who always appealed to Lloyd George. In Parliament, Addison had been an advocate for social reform and came to Lloyd George's attention through his assistance in the negotiations with the British Medical Association over the introduction of the 1911 National Insurance Act.[21] Addison would become one of Lloyd George's most trusted lieutenants, someone he kept close by and whose advice he sought. In the autumn they would also be joined by the Conservative MP Arthur Lee, who had been amongst the first to notify the War Office of the danger of the shortage of shells and had fallen out of favour there as a consequence. He too would become a loyal champion of Lloyd George's work and interests.

While Kitchener and the War Office offered their full co-operation with the new Ministry, it was soon clear that there was no real plan to share. No proper assessment had been made of the equipment needs for a large continental army of 70 divisions fighting in the unique and challenging conditions of the Western Front. Lloyd George wanted to know what the requirements were for rifles, high-explosive shells and machine guns, how to create the capacity to manufacture them in the volumes required, and how they were to be supplied to the men at the front. The American journalist Isaac Marcosson observed of Lloyd George at work that summer, that he was like 'an animated human sponge' who was a 'genius of assimilation'.[22] When visiting him at the Ministry of Munitions, Marcosson noted:

> Every day literally hundreds of people tried to see him. One out of every hundred succeeded. He made many engagements, but somehow or other they were almost invariably broken before the appointed hour . . . Lloyd George, I might say, is no respecter of programme. I have seen him wipe out a whole day's slate of appointments that included the notables of half a dozen Allied countries as easily as you would break the most informal engagement for luncheon. He always does the thing that presses the hardest. Likewise, he knows how to concentrate. Whenever he does a thing it becomes the most

important thing in the world while he is engaged on it. It is one of the secrets of his success.[23]

To assist him in his task, Lloyd George also sought out similar men of 'push and go' from business to help direct the work of the Ministry of Munitions. It was, Lloyd George recalled, 'from first to last a businessman organisation',[24] but he wanted businessmen of a certain type. In particular, those who possessed 'the essential gift of translating their knowledge into effective action', including the gifts of 'intuition, rapid decision making, and force which enable an improviser to create and hustle along a gigantic new enterprise'.[25]

Chief amongst these businessmen would be Eric Geddes,[26] a senior executive at the North Eastern Railway company. Lloyd George recalled of their first meeting on 28 May 1915 that 'he had the make of one of their powerful locomotives . . . He struck me immediately as a man of exceptional force and capability.'[27] Arthur Lee thought Geddes was 'a prize-fighter type of man . . . like an unruly school-boy, with an almost childish craving for praise and tangible recognition', but noting that he was 'harried by L.G.'.[28] On one occasion when Geddes returned to the Ministry from the War Office, with confirmation from Kitchener for an order for machine guns, Lloyd George told him to 'Take Kitchener's figure. Square it. Multiply by two. Then double again for good luck.'[29] Lloyd George's eldest son Richard[30] also remembered at that time his father stating with incredulity about Kitchener, 'Can you imagine it? A general saying he could not use more equipment? Like a soldier refusing a free xxxx in a *maison tolérée*.'[31]

Lloyd George's focus on securing the 'leading hustlers'[32] of the day placed an emphasis on getting things done over merely knowing a lot about the subject. As he told the American ambassador Walter Page,[33] 'The Government has experts, experts, experts, everywhere. In any department where things are not going well, I have found . . . boards of experts. But in our department at least I've found a substitute for them. I let twenty experts go and I put in one Man, and things begin to move at once.'[34] Colonel House,[35] the advisor to the American President, Woodrow Wilson,[36] and in Lloyd George's opinion also his 'alter ego',[37] visited the Ministry of Munitions and noted of Lloyd George, 'He reminds me more of the virile, aggressive type of American politician than any member of the Cabinet . . . He has something dynamic within him which his colleagues have not and which is badly needed in this great hour.'[38]

Lloyd George's efforts had also earned the appreciation of Theodore Roosevelt who wrote to tell him that 'the prime business at present for you to do is to save your country; and I admire the single-hearted manner with which you have devoted yourself to this great duty',[39] The two men had first met in London in 1910, at a dinner organized at Brooks's Club[40] by the Liberal Cabinet minister, Lord Haldane.[41] Roosevelt 'took a real fancy to'[42] Lloyd George, adding in a letter to a friend, that he considered him to be 'the most powerful statesman I met in England, in fact the man of power'.[43] Lloyd George also thought Roosevelt was able to 'impress those who for the first time came into close personal contact with him', and believed his political convictions were based on a 'stern and dauntless Radicalism [that] always appealed to me'.[44] Isaac Marcosson, who had interviewed both men, considered that Lloyd George was 'the British Roosevelt'. In particular he thought, 'He is fifty per cent Roosevelt in the virility and forcefulness of his character; fifty percent [William Jennings] Bryan[45] in the purely demagogic phase of his make-up, while the rest is canny Celt opportunism.'[46]

Despite Lloyd George's great energy and determination, it would take time for the new Ministry to expand the production capacity for armaments and recruit people to do the work in the factories. One solution was to bring more women into war production, as was already happening in France, and in this endeavour he found an unlikely ally in the suffragette Christabel Pankhurst.[47] Although Lloyd George was in favour of votes for women, Christabel believed that he was 'always betraying us'.[48] In 1913 her mother Emmeline[49] had openly declared her role in a successful bomb plot against building works for Lloyd George's house at Walton Heath, in order as she put it, 'to wake his conscience'.[50] However, with the aid of a £2,000 grant from the Ministry of Munitions, Christabel Pankhurst organized the *Women's War Pageant*, a great parade through Whitehall and the West End of London on Saturday 17 July 1915, to 'hear women's demand for the right to make munitions'.[51] Despite the rain that day tens of thousands joined the march, which culminated in a delegation being sent to call on Lloyd George at Whitehall Gardens. After their meeting Lloyd George shared a platform with Christabel in front of cheering crowds on the Victoria Embankment, close to the Ministry of Munitions. He told them, 'I believe that men and women alike are prepared to do their best to help the old country through to victory.' Lloyd George had agreed as well to the demand made by the Pankhursts that women in munitions factories should receive the same pay as men for piece work. At one point during his speech he was heckled by a woman in the crowd who shouted, 'What about the vote?' Lloyd George replied, 'We will get her into the shell factory first',[52] a comment that drew laughter, but its meaning was clear. Lloyd George knew that following the great contribution of the women of Britain to the war effort, the vote would be assured when peace came. By that time, over 1.5 million women would be engaged directly or indirectly in work to supply government contracts.

The labour shortages had been made worse, though, by the failure to stop munitions workers from volunteering to fight at the front. Lloyd George believed in the summer of 1915 that there were 120,000 skilled workers serving whose return would solve his immediate need for labour. However, to achieve this they would need to be replaced by new recruits, which in Lloyd George's view would require the introduction of some form of conscription. While volunteer recruitment had worked well since the start of the war, the army was now running short of men. On 3 June in his first major speech as Minister of Munitions, Lloyd George addressed workers and industry representatives at Houldsworth Hall[53] in Manchester. There he told them:

> It is a war of munitions. We are fighting against the best organised community in the world . . . and we have been employing too much the haphazard, leisurely, go-as-you-please methods . . . We want to mobilise in such a way as to produce in the shortest space of time the greatest quantity of the best and most efficient war material . . . When the house is on fire, questions of procedure and precedence, of etiquette and time and division of labour must disappear.

Then on the question of compulsion to serve he added, 'If the necessity arose, I am certain no man of any party would protest. But pray do not talk about it as if it were anti-democratic . . . It has been the greatest weapon in the hands of democracy many a time for the winning and preservation of freedom.'[54] Conscription was already in place in France and had been used by Lloyd George's hero Abraham Lincoln[55] in the

American Civil War. The Lloyd George family had also responded to the call to serve. David and Margaret's sons, Richard and Gwilym,[56] had both joined the army in September 1914, and their daughter Olwen[57] was a Red Cross volunteer working in France.

The Conservatives favoured conscription as well, yet wider Liberal opinion was largely against it, and Asquith noted on 26 August that the Government Chief Whip John Gulland[58] 'tells me that he gets letters from Liberal [constituency] chairmen, etc., all over the country denouncing Lloyd George as a lost soul, and some of them predicting that conscription would bring us to the verge, or over the verge, of revolution'.[59] Lord Northcliffe came out for conscription in his newspapers in September, with the *Daily Mail* declaring, 'The country . . . does not understand sneaking and haphazard compulsion under the guise of "moral pressure" excited by irresponsible canvassers on behalf of the government.'[60] This was in particular a reference to the national registration scheme where people were asked whether they were willing to make themselves available for war service. On 14 September, Lloyd George dined with Churchill and Curzon to discuss conscription, and Frances Stevenson recorded from his recollection of the evening that:

> Curzon says the Tories are going to approach the P.M. & say that they cannot proceed any longer under the present state of things. They will demand conscription and the removal of K. from the W.O. [War Office], as being incompetent and having failed to grasp the military situation. D. & Churchill will throw in their lot with Curzon & his followers, for D. says he cannot possibly be a party any longer to the shameful mismanagement and slackness. He says things are simply being allowed to slide, and that it is time someone spoke out. As I said before, however, he hates going against his party, & he fears the Liberals will hate him violently if he goes against them now. He fears Churchill, too. He is not sure whether Churchill will come too, or whether he will remain & get the P.M. to put him into D's shoes in the Munitions Office. D. says that Churchill is the only man in the Cabinet who has the power to do him harm, and he does not trust him when it comes to a matter of personal interest.[61]

The following day Lloyd George also had lunch with Churchill, along with Carson, Bonar Law and F. E. Smith,[62] and noted that they had 'a most useful & important discussion about the war'.[63] Geoffrey Dawson,[64] the editor of The Times, saw Carson the day after this lunch and observed, 'he was drawing closer to Lloyd George . . . Evidently a strong nucleus was forming inside the Cabinet for more strenuous measures . . . Carson said he believed absolutely in L.G.'s disinterestedness and genuine zeal for the war.'[65]

As well as being the leader of Ulster Unionism, Carson was one of the most brilliant lawyers in the country, famous for leading high-profile cases like his successful defence in 1895 of the Marquess of Queensbury[66] in the libel action brought against him by Oscar Wilde.[67] However, it was Carson's efforts in 1910 to clear the name of a 15-year-old Royal Navy cadet, George Archer-Shee,[68] that became a cause célèbre. Archer-Shee had been falsely accused of stealing from another cadet and was expelled from the Royal Naval College at Osborne, on the Isle of Wight. The case was heard at the Court of Appeal, and when on the fourth day of the trial, the Admiralty, represented by the then Solicitor General Rufus Isaacs (later Lord Reading), withdrew its case, Carson admitted to his friend Lady Londonderry,[69] 'It has been a great victory and I feel quite tearful over it. I was always convinced of the boy's innocence, and I know it all arose from the blundering suggestion of the officers-in-charge.'[70] After the trial, Carson told Archer-Shee's mother Helen, 'Will you please tell him I hope he will always look upon me as a friend . . . He will I am sure, do well at whatever profession he adopts.'[71] The case became the inspiration for Terence Rattigan's 1946 play, The Winslow Boy.[72] However, George Archer-Shee would not enjoy the bright future that Carson had restored to him. He fell victim again to the military authorities when he was killed in action during the First Battle of Ypres, on 31 October 1914, three days after the death of Carson's nephew Francis Robinson,[73] who was the same age and a member of the same regiment. The body of neither man was ever found, and both are commemorated on the same memorial panel at the Menin Gate at Ypres. Carson's great legal mind, in addition to his own personal loss, made him a motivated and powerful ally for Lloyd George.

On 17 September the Liberal Daily News sought to expose what it saw as a conscriptionist plot in an article that proclaimed 'Some of the more powerful Conscriptionist Ministers have determined to force the issue of compulsory service in the Cabinet, if they can, next week. Failing to get agreement on their policy – and failure is to be assumed, since the majority are against them – they intend to precipitate a Cabinet crisis by the resignation of their offices. This they mean to do in order to force a general election on the issue of compulsory service.' The 'Conscriptionist Ministers' were listed as Lloyd George and Churchill, along with the Conservatives, Bonar Law, Lansdowne, Curzon, Walter Long,[74] Austen Chamberlain, Lord Selborne,[75] and Carson. The *Daily News* also informed readers, with what seems like a direct reference to Lloyd George's dinner with Curzon, that 'Behind the scenes the strangest of comradeships were being cemented, comradeships which we should only need to name to fill the British public with scorn and amazement. A certain number of more or less well-intentioned Liberal members were drawn into the intrigue and a dinner party campaign was organised to give an air of responsible backing to the conspiracy.' In response, Frances Stevenson noted in her journal that 'The Liberal papers have lost their head. They are gnashing their teeth over Conscription, & can conceal their rage no longer at finding that D is among the Conscriptionists. Evidently someone has been supplying the *Daily News* with information, and that someone is no doubt McKenna . . . but to this he had added his old scare – "a plot against the Prime Minister" suggesting in a most sinister way . . . that the split in the Cabinet over conscription is only designed with a view to getting rid of the Prime Minister.'[76]

On 30 September, Lloyd George found himself breaking bread at another strange table, when he joined the Conservative peer Lord Milner[77] for lunch at his Westminster home, 17 Great College Street. This meeting had been organized by Geoffrey Dawson, at the behest of both men, and was an occasion that during the height of the Second Boer War would have been unimaginable. Milner had been one of the driving forces behind British policy in South Africa and had administrative responsibility for what Lloyd George then condemned as the 'deplorable' concentration camps that had been built to accommodate Boer refugees.[78] As Governor of the Transvaal, Lloyd George had criticized him for making, 'blunder after blunder and miscalculation after miscalculation, writing violent political articles attacking his opponents and insulting half the population he was governing'.[79] When Milner retired as High Commissioner for South Africa in 1905, the *Daily News* declared that this had been 'inevitable' as 'He stands for everything this country abhors.'[80]

Back in August 1915, Milner had become Chairman of the National Service League to campaign for compulsory military service for the duration of the war. So he and Lloyd George were now brought together in their wish to see a more aggressive prosecution of the conflict. The rumbling thunder of the Battle of Loos,[81] which had started on 25 September, so five days before they met, provided a distant backdrop to their encounter. At the time this was the greatest offensive ever by the British army and for the first time featured the new recruits who had volunteered in response to Kitchener's call to arms. However, it was clear from the start that Loos was going to be – as the young combatant army officer Robert Graves[82] described it in his memoir *Goodbye to All That* – 'a bloody balls up'.[83]

At the lunch Lloyd George stated his belief that Loos had 'made the need for men more urgent', and that he was 'emphatic that conscription was the only way [and] that we couldn't win the war without it'. Overall, Lloyd George described the situation using a golfing analogy, that the Germans were 'four up and five to play'.[84] However, as at Neuve Chapelle and Aubers Ridge, Loos would once again see a shortage of high-explosive shells prevent the British from forcing back the German defensive lines and the offensive was called off on 8 October, with the loss of 59,000 casualties and no material gains achieved. Among the loss of life was Rudyard Kipling's 18-year-old son Jack,[85] who had only been in France for three weeks. He was missing in action during the battle, and his body wasn't found during his father's lifetime. In anticipation of grief, Kipling wrote the poem 'My Boy Jack', the first lines capturing his emotions and those of so many other parents waiting anxiously each day for the news that they dreaded:

'Have you news of my boy Jack?'
Not this tide.
'When d'you think that he'll come back?'
Not with this wind blowing, and this tide.[86]

Lloyd George, anxious to turn this tide, wrote of Loos, 'The infatuation of a breakthrough which haunted the western generals like a disease of the mind still prompted them to organise another, and as they thought, overwhelming attack on the German entrenchments.'[87] He also knew that his ties to the radical element of the Liberal Party, who had been his strongest supporters when he entered government in 1905, were now broken. Yet this was now of little importance to him, telling Riddell on 2 October that:

> There are no real friendships at the top . . . This is a cynical but true observation . . . Some of my friends thought that because the Radical Party were disgruntled with me I was in a dangerous situation. But I know the House of Commons. It is a most unreliable barometer of public feeling. Lobby prophecies can never be relied upon . . . The Radical Party do not control public opinion; the people form their own view. If they are of opinion that in a crisis like this I am useful . . . no threats by the Radical Party and no intrigues against me in Cabinet can injure me.[88]

The failure of the Battle of Loos marked the beginning of the end for Sir John French, who would be replaced by Douglas Haig in December of the British Expeditionary Force. However, the situation on the Eastern Front was even worse. In August the landing of 90,000 men at Suvla Bay on the Gallipoli peninsula failed to achieve the hoped-for breakthrough, and a series of diversionary battles timed to coincide with the landings were all failures. On 23 September the 29-year-old Australian journalist Keith Murdoch[89] wrote from London to the Australian Prime Minister Andrew Fisher[90] a detailed 8,000-word letter, setting out the truth of the situation at Gallipoli based on his own experience there, stating, 'The last great effort, that of August 6-21, was a costly and bloody fiasco.'[91] Murdoch warned of the dangerous condition of the men and the exposed nature of the positions they were holding, all of which would be made worse by the onset of winter.

Armed with a letter of introduction from Fisher, Murdoch also visited Lloyd George at Whitehall Gardens on 24 September to brief him personally on the situation. The impression he made was so great Lloyd George wrote to Bonar Law and Carson, informing them:

> I saw Murdoch the Australian yesterday. He struck me as being exceptionally intelligent and sane. That makes the account he gave me of his visit to the Dardanelles much more disquieting. He left on my mind an impression of impending disaster . . . I agree that Murdoch's report does not differ in essentials from that furnished

to us by Colonel Hankey[92] . . . Under these circumstances I am afraid what Murdoch told me is too true, that unless the Dardanelles Committee[93] immediately reconsider the position in the Gallipoli Peninsula, either with a view to action or evacuation we shall be held responsible personally for the disaster.[94]

Lloyd George also urged Asquith to circulate a copy of Murdoch's report to the Cabinet, which he agreed to, even before receiving a response from the military authorities. The impact was almost immediate. On 15 October, Sir Ian Hamilton[95] was relieved of his command at Gallipoli and recalled to London. The following month the decision was made to withdraw from the peninsula, causing Churchill to resign from the Cabinet on 11 November, and decide to join his old yeomanry regiment, the Queen's Own Oxfordshire Hussars, in France. After eight futile months of fighting, the Allies had sustained 250,000 casualties at Gallipoli, including 46,000 men killed.

At the beginning of 1915, Lloyd George had advocated an alternative operation in the eastern Mediterranean, to land troops at Salonika in Greece to support Serbia and encourage Bulgaria to enter the war on the side of Great Britain and her allies. However, that opportunity had also been missed, with the Serbian position crumbling and Bulgaria agreeing to support an invasion of the country by Germany and the Austro-Hungarian Empire. When on 25 September, Bulgaria declared war on Serbia, Sir Edward Grey promised in the House of Commons that Great Britain would offer 'all the support in our power, in the manner that would be most welcome to them, in concert with our Allies, without reserve and without qualification'.[96] Yet at a Cabinet meeting on 9 October, it had transpired that Kitchener was unaware that Germany had already invaded Serbia, and when pressed by Lloyd George as to what the situation was there, a telegram was produced from the War Office showing that it had received this information 20 hours before. Edward Carson passed Lloyd George a note, which read 'K does not read the telegrams – and we don't see them – it is intolerable.'[97] Carson then proceeded to cross-examine Kitchener like a hostile witness in court. Lady Londonderry recorded in her diary, after receiving a report of the meeting, 'I hear [it] was the most marvellous thing that ever was as to places, times, ships and everything else.'[98] The consequence of this failure in Serbia was not just the loss of one of the small nations that Lloyd George had so eloquently defended in his speech at The Queen's Hall, but that it now gave Germany effective control of the Balkans and a land route to supply the Ottoman Empire and reach the Middle East.

Carson resigned from the Cabinet on 19 October, 'disgusted', Lloyd George wrote in his *War Memoirs*, 'with what he conceived to be the deception practised upon Serbia . . . Mr Bonar Law and I shared his opinion about the whole transaction, but on the whole decided that we could not withdraw from the Ministry at this critical juncture. I am not sure that we were right.'[99] Around this time, though, intelligence reached Regy Esher in France of 'rumours of a secret canvas of the House of Commons, taken by two Privy Councillors, which had revealed so large a measure of support for Mr Asquith and against Mr Lloyd George, that the Prime Minister's position appeared to be more assured.'[100] This also tallied with Asquith's own assessment, telling Arthur Balfour in a letter marked 'most secret' that due to their support for conscription it was 'no exaggeration to say that, at this moment, the two most unpopular and distrusted men in the [Liberal] Party are Lloyd George and Winston Churchill'.[101]

Lloyd George was now on the brink of quitting, whether or not others joined him. On Saturday 23 October he lunched and played golf with George Riddell at Walton Heath, where he admitted, 'I do not want to be in the Cabinet just now. There is going to be a disaster; I have done my best to prevent it. My advice has not been taken. I don't wish to feel that I am responsible for what I cannot avoid.'[102] At the end of the month Lloyd George wrote a long letter to Asquith setting out his concerns about the conduct of the war, the failures of Kitchener and the War Office, and the need for a small War Council of between three and five members. It was the kind of letter that forewarned the Prime Minister of the damning public statement Lloyd George might make if he resigned. However, it also contained a sentence that for the first time reads as a threat to the Prime Minister's own position. He wrote that 'The steadfast loyalty of our own party to your leadership has so far saved the Government, but you will forgive me for saying that I doubt whether that would save us if a catastrophe befell Serbia or our force in the Dardanelles and all the facts on the conduct of the War were dragged out as they would be.' In the letter Lloyd George concluded that he had 'reluctantly come to the conclusion that I can no longer be responsible for the present war direction, and at the Cabinet tomorrow I propose with your permission to raise the real issue'.[103] On 1 November, Bonar Law also wrote to Lloyd George asking, 'Have you any objection to my telling the PM that you said to me that you were satisfied that nothing but disaster lay ahead for us as long as Lord K was War Secretary & that you were going to write to the P.M. that you could not continue to share the responsibility for the continuance of the present arrangement at the W.O. & that I had replied that if that issue were definitely raised I must take the same course.'[104] Yet Asquith brought both men back from the brink, with promises of diminishing Kitchener's influence at the War Office, and the creation of a new six-member War Committee.[105]

The Prime Minister could also gamble that as long as the Liberal Party remained united behind him, no alternative government could be formed. However, Lloyd George was right to consider what might have been if he along with Bonar Law and Carson, and with the support of the Northcliffe press, had brought down the Coalition and forced the general election that would normally have been due by the end of the year. Lloyd George's mood was best summed up by his speech to the House of Commons on 20 December, in which he warned that the war effort so far had been:

> Too late in moving here. Too late in arriving there. Too late in coming to this decision. Too late in starting with enterprises. Too late in preparing. In this War the footsteps of the Allied forces have been dogged by the mocking spectre of 'Too Late'; and unless we quicken our movements damnation will fall on the sacred cause for which so much gallant blood has flowed.[106]

The unresolved issue of conscription, though, would provide the Cabinet with an opportunity to pick up the pace before the end of the year, if it was prepared to take it. As far back as 8 October, Kitchener had informed them that 'The voluntary system, as at present administered, fails to produce the number of recruits required to maintain the armies in the field.'[107] In November and December a final attempt had been made to enlist more men for active service by voluntary means. The Derby Scheme, organized by Lord Derby,[108] who had agreed to take on the role of Director of Recruiting, canvassed able-bodied men to ask them if they would attest to serve, on the understanding that married men would not be called up until all available single men had enlisted. When the results of the scheme were reported back to the Cabinet on 15 December, it was found that out of 2,179,231 single men of military age not enlisted before 23 October 1915, 1,150,000 had either enlisted, attested that they were ready to serve, or been medically rejected by the military authorities. However, of this number, by the time they had excluded those who were unfit for service and men who worked in reserved occupations who couldn't be called up, the actual number of recruits from the Derby Scheme was just 346,386 out of the over 2 million single men of military age not yet serving.[109]

In light of these figures, Lloyd George threated to resign unless a commitment was made at once that all unmarried men would be conscripted, writing to tell his family in Wales on 27 December, 'I have made up my mind. My path is clear in front of me & as you know under these conditions, I am always happy, whatever happens. By 5pm I may be plain Lloyd George.'[110] However, the following day he could report back, 'Cabinet satisfactory. P.M. dropped on the right side. Compulsion for unmarried men. There may be resignations. Not certain. Simon, Runciman & McKenna threaten – but [I] doubt it.'[111] Asquith though, found it a bruising encounter, telling McKenna's wife Pamela, who had also become his new muse, 'In the fullest sense of the word a *Hellish* week. One of the worst even in my storm-tossed annals.'[112] In the end only Sir John Simon would resign, and on 12 January 1916 the Military Service Bill passed its second reading in the House of Commons with only 39 MPs voting against it.

Observing events from across the Atlantic, Theodore Roosevelt wrote again to Arthur Lee in early 1916 asking him to 'Give my heartiest regards to Lloyd George. Do tell him I admire him immensely . . . It is often true that the only way to render great service is by willingness on the part of the statesman to lose his future, or, at any rate, his present position in political life, just exactly as the soldier may have to pay with his physical life in order to render service in battle.'[113] The immense pressure that Lloyd George felt was also evident in his work at the Ministry of Munitions. Lee recalled:

> There were times as the winter of 1915 grew grimmer in all its aspects, when the nerves of all of us were strained beyond endurance

and the atmosphere of the Ministry became sulphurous and unhappy. For this L.G. himself was not a little to blame, because with all his supreme qualities of inspiration, uncanny insight, and exalted courage, he could discourage and break the hearts of men by capricious strokes of injustice and even cruelty. They were not deliberate, and merely reflected the intolerable strain and anxiety to which he, more than any of us, was daily and nightly subjected, but his moods brought many black moments. At times he would break out uncontrollably and insist upon the instant dismissal of men of the highest standing, who had given up their businesses to come and work as unpaid volunteers but who, in his opinion, had failed to make good. On occasions I remonstrated with him, but when he became implacable, I said, 'Well, if you insist upon So-and-So going, you must at least tell him so yourself.' He did not like this and replied, 'No. You must do it. I hate *killing sheep*.'[114]

By this time, Lee recalled that the Ministry had become packed with transferred civil servants and businessmen 'hiving like bees' around Whitehall Gardens.[115] In late January they took over the 600-room Hotel Metropole[116] on the corner of Whitehall Place and Northumberland Avenue, directly opposite the home of the radicals at the National Liberal Club. The *Illustrated London News* commented of the requisitioning of this modern and luxurious hotel that 'The stern business of war has never been officially directed from such palatial offices.'[117] The physical growth of the Ministry was also reflected in the impact it was already having by the end of 1915. Some 73 new 'national factories' had been created for the manufacture of munitions, which by the end of the war had increased to 218. In 1915 the total national shell production was 200,400, and mostly of lighter shells. In 1916 this would increase to 6.7 million, more than half of which were medium to heavy shells. By the end of the war the national factories alone were producing 40 million shells a year. When the Ministry of Munitions was created in July 1915, the British army had only received 1,000 machine guns from an order for 1,700 it had placed at the start of the war. By the end of 1915, machine-gun production had increased to 6,102 in that year, rising to 33,507 in 1916, and 120,804 a year by the end of the war.

Sir Edward Grey observed in his memoirs that Lloyd George's 'fertility and resource [as Minister for Munitions] were wonderful; his energy was never depressed by difficulties or daunted by adversity; his spirit was always high. His activity sought any point of importance, where he thought something was not being done that needed to be, or where he saw his way to set right what was wrong or to give a new impulse . . . but for Lloyd George the country would not have been organized as soon as it was for the work of making munitions.'[118]

Yet this progress only underlined the scandal of the waste of time and resources that had occurred before the creation of the Ministry of Munitions. Lloyd George's achievement had materialized because the decision-making power had been taken away from committees, and ultimately placed into the hands of one man, with full executive authority. As Arthur Lee had recognized on his first day at the Ministry, 'it really consisted of one man . . . quite dauntless and emitting sparks of the highest voltage which boded ill for the War Office, the armament manufacturers, or anyone who got in his way'.[119] The question now was whether the whole national war effort should be organized in a similar way.

THREE

The Cabal

In late January 1916, while billeted in the hamlet of La Crèche de Bailleul, and waiting to go up to the front line at Ploegsteert,[1] Winston Churchill, now commanding officer of the 6th Battalion of the Royal Scots Fusiliers, wrote to Lloyd George. 'How do you come out of all of this? I cannot tell, but from this distance it seems to me that you are even more isolated . . . The coalition which you made brings to the fore intractable forces and personalities who do not view the world as you do. The Tory dream and intention is a Tory Government. You get the unpopularity of conscription with such elements as oppose it. Others get the credit.'[2] Churchill, the energetic First Lord of the Admiralty, was the scapegoat for Gallipoli; Sir John French, who had blown the whistle on the shells scandal, had been blamed for the failure to break through on the Western Front; and Carson, a champion of conscription and Serbia, was languishing on the Opposition benches like a barrister without a brief. Yet Kitchener was still there, Asquith seemed as secure as ever, and Lloyd George was a prophet without honour amongst the radical Liberals. However, unseen by Churchill, back in Westminster, a coalition of the willing was beginning to organize for change. In January, Lord Milner and the Conservative MP Leo Amery[3] began organizing a series of secret meetings that became known as the 'Monday Night Cabal'. Milner believed that the war had created a 'new spirit' in the country, which required organization that cut across the traditional party-political system, 'aiming at nothing more than energy and forethought in the conduct of the war, forethought also for the quite immediate thereafter, so that the end of the war may not land us in complete chaos.'[4]

Gathering mostly at Milner's house, 17 Great College Street, which overlooked the Palace of Westminster, they met at 7 p.m. every Monday when Parliament was sitting, for an hour's discussion, followed by dinner. Such dining clubs, then as now, brought together parliamentarians for discreet yet open conversation, on the perhaps surprisingly well-observed principle that their deliberations are never disclosed. The objective of this 'Cabal', though, was more consequential than mere debates on policy. It was, in Amery's words, 'somehow or other to secure a change of government',[5] away from what he thought was a Cabinet of 'twenty-two gabblers round a table with an old procrastinator in the Chair'.[6] The attendees of the first meeting on 17 January were Milner, Amery, Carson, Geoffrey Dawson, and the influential political writer F. S. Oliver.[7] These core members of the Cabal, with the exception of Carson, were drawn from those young men who had been part of the influential group known in South Africa as 'Milner's Kindergarten'.[8] Dawson, who had worked there for Milner, thought he was 'about the biggest man in England'.[9] Even Lloyd George considered that Milner's Kindergarten, or Round Table as it was also known, was 'a very powerful combination – in its own way perhaps the most powerful in the country'.[10]

The Cabal was also joined by General Sir Henry Wilson[11] when he was back in London from his command on the Western Front, and later by the Conservative MP and newspaper owner, Waldorf Astor.[12] Milner wanted the group to go at it 'wholeheartedly' and be 'prepared to make any sacrifice of time and energy necessary to make it a success'.[13] While Carson would be their champion in Parliament, as the de facto leader of the Opposition, the alternative Prime Minister they sought was Lloyd George. As early as September 1915, Amery had written to Lloyd George, 'urging him to break away from the existing make-believe conduct of the war and claim the leadership for himself'.[14] From the spring of 1916, Lloyd George would also start to make guest appearances at the gathering of the Cabal.

These stirrings may have been reflected in the conversation that he had with Churchill when visiting the front at the beginning of February 1916. That evening, in tones very different to his previous letters, Churchill wrote to his wife Clementine, informing her that Lloyd George 'wants the W.O. [War Office]: & I hope he will get it. Really they need a civilian's drive & the leadership of a gifted man. The group I want to work with & form into an effective Governing instrument is LG: FE: Carson: & Curzon. Keep that steadily in mind. It is the alternative Government, when "wait & see" is over.'[15] That sentiment was certainly alive in Leo Amery's notes for a meeting of the Cabal on 19 February, where he recorded that their purpose was 'in season and out of season' to 'insist . . . that the Asquith-Bonar Law influence . . . is paralytic, and that it is absurd to say that there is no alternative government or alternative spirit'.[16]

On 10 March another wartime leader, the new Australian Prime Minister Billy Hughes,[17] came within the orbit of Lloyd George and members of the Monday Night Cabal. That morning Lloyd George hosted a breakfast at 11 Downing Street so that Hughes could meet some of the leading London newspaper editors and proprietors, including Riddell, Robert Donald, and H. A. Gwynne[18] of the *Morning Post*. The Australian had much in common with Lloyd George, as he had been born to Welsh parents and spent much of his childhood in Llandudno[19] in north Wales. The two men were just a few months apart in age, of similar height, and enjoyed reputations as powerful public speakers and progressive politicians. The previous day Hughes had sat in on the meeting of the British Cabinet at 10 Downing Street, and Lloyd George now took the opportunity to ask him, in front of his breakfast guests, what his impression had been. He replied, 'As I sat there, I looked round the table and I thought the members all looked very clever men. That is your trouble. You have got too many clever men.' To which Lloyd George responded, 'Quite true. Twenty-three clever men could not run anything.'[20] Drawing on his experience as a union organizer before entering national politics, Hughes reflected that 'There is only one way to run a strike: it must be run by one man. You must club the strikers and their committee into subjection. Let them talk as much as they like, provided they talk in private, but one man must decide on the plan and be responsible for its execution. Of course, he must get the best advice he can, but the ultimate decision must rest with him and he must furnish the driving force. I do not profess to know much about naval or military affairs, but so far as I can see, a war must be run on the same lines as a strike.'[21] Gwynne responded that he'd 'been saying that ever since the war started'.[22] Riddell also thought, 'Hughes struck me as an able man. He is . . . remarkably acute and direct in what he says; the ablest Colonial politician I have met.'[23] The Australian Prime Minister became something of a political celebrity during his extended visit to Britain, speaking in favour of greater co-ordination between the nations of the Empire to support the war effort, something with which Lloyd George also agreed. While the Labour leaders in Britain had largely been against conscription, Hughes campaigned for it, and a book of the speeches made during his visit became a bestseller.[24]

One week later, Christopher Addison recalled a long and frank conversation with Lloyd George about the political situation. Addison noted that his chief recognized:

> ... the serious dissatisfaction with the Government that exists, and there is a good deal of it among the Tory section in the Cabinet over the P.M.'s complacent attitude. L.G. has been ... with Hughes, the Australian Premier, who had given him his impression of our statesmen. His summary was that, with the exception of L.G. and Bonar Law, most of the Cabinet Ministers he had met were men who dealt largely with words and were not prepared to put that push and energy into things which the situation demanded. There appears to be a movement amongst the Conservatives to try and get L.G. to take a strong line and they are prepared even to go to the length of recognising him as P.M.[25]

On 31 March, Lloyd George dined with Edward Carson. Riddell noted afterwards that he was 'much dissatisfied and thinks he must leave the Cabinet. He feels he is taking part in a fraud which is sacrificing and will sacrifice hundreds of thousands of lives. Mr A has no plan, no initiative, no grip, no driving force.'[26] These first months of 1916 marked a crucial period in Lloyd George's political life. His focus was still on doing whatever it took to win the war, but the battles over munitions supplies and conscription had demonstrated to him that many of his colleagues, particularly in the Liberal Party, were against him. The decision he would now wrestle with was not just whether he should resign, but if through doing so he could force the creation of a new government built on his ideas on how the war should be won. The consequence of that would almost certainly mean the removal of Asquith and the breaking up of the old Liberal Party – a personally momentous act that would require him to throw over his old colleagues, in order to work more effectively through his old enemies. This was the dilemma he would wrestle with throughout 1916, recognizing that it was perhaps a small sacrifice in order to win the war.

The next Cabinet crisis was again about army recruitment, when it became evident that both the number of volunteers and those single men being conscripted under the 1916 Military Service Act would fall short of the requirements needed to maintain the strength of the British forces on the Western Front. Lloyd George favoured universal conscription, and Addison recalled that there had been 'overtures made to L.G. on behalf of the Tories as to whether he would break on the subject. More or less informal offers were made to him that they would follow him. He says he told them frankly that he could only identify himself with the movement if he was going to have the support at the same time of a solid and sufficient body of Liberals.'[27] Addison also warned Lloyd George over lunch on 5 April against leaving the government, 'purely with the backing of the [Northcliffe] Press and the wild men amongst the Tories and with only a small following amongst the Liberals'.[28] To improve Lloyd George's position, Addison would now work closely with Liberal MPs, like David Davies, Frederick Kellaway[29] and William Glyn-Jones,[30] to confirm those of their colleagues in Parliament who were 'friendly to Lloyd George'.[31] Davies in particular was, according to Addison, 'a very stalwart Liberal [and] out-and-out champion of drastic action', who had wanted Lloyd George to resign if the government failed to deliver conscription.[32]

Lloyd George stayed close to the 'wild men' of the Cabal over the coming days. He met with Northcliffe on 5 April and Addison noted the following day that they received 'a document from Amery, who had been going into the [recruitment] figures at the War Office. The burden of it was that it was impossible to get the men required without general compulsion.'[33] Lloyd George also sought the official recruitment numbers from Sir William Robertson, now Chief of the Imperial General Staff, which confirmed the same. On 7 April, Lloyd George lunched with Carson at Arthur Lee's secluded house in Westminster, at 2 Abbey Gardens. It was the perfect setting, close to Parliament, but tucked away behind the imposing wall of Westminster Abbey's College Garden. Such meetings soon became so frequent that Lee started to refer to his home as his 'secret restaurant for plotting statesmen'.[34] On 16 April the King's private secretary, Lord Stamfordham,[35] visited Lloyd George to try and persuade him not to resign from the government, for fear of the political instability it could unleash. However, Lloyd George told him that he had 'taken an oath which prevents me from doing what you ask. I have sworn to serve my King faithfully.'[36]

The same day C. P. Scott also wrote to Winston Churchill that he was 'certain that Ll. G has made up his mind to go . . . At once, with him &

Carson outside the Government there will be the beginnings of a real Opposition.'[37] On 17 April, Frances Stevenson noted in her diary that:

> Things have come to a head over general compulsion . . . D was the first to take the stand . . . & it was naturally thought that he would be backed by the [Conservatives] in the Cabinet. They have, however, ratted almost to a man (F. E. Smith being the exception) being afraid of losing office apparently. When this happened, D. was torn between inclination & expediency. Fortunately, the Army Council took the same view as D., & they are making a firm stand. If Asquith will not accept compulsion wholeheartedly, then they will resign. D. came up to town last night and dined with Bonar Law & says he has never seen anyone in such a state of abject funk. He (B.L.) does not know which way to turn or what to do. If D. goes out, it's almost impossible for B.L. to stay in without becoming an object of contempt; yet he is very loth to resign.[38]

The Monday Night Cabal had also been unimpressed at Bonar Law's wobbling, with Milner telling Arthur Lee, 'We must try to bear it if he comes with us.'[39]

On 20 April the Cabinet agreed a compromise with some technical exemptions to universal conscription. Asquith put these proposals forward for debate in a secret session of the House of Commons on 25 and 26 April, where the true nature of the recruitment crisis could be discussed. The inevitable drift towards conscription for men of fighting age now drew howls of derision from some elements of the radical liberal press, in particular A. G. Gardiner,[40] a known admirer of Asquith, and the editor of the *Daily News*. On 22 April, Gardiner, after a 'long interview'[41] the day before with McKenna, published a diatribe entitled, 'A Letter to Mr Lloyd George'. In it Gardiner wrote:

> Your friends have been silent too long . . . They have refused to see your figure flitting about behind the scenes, touching the strings, prompting the actors, directing the game, and have agreed to talk of Lord Northcliffe, Sir Henry Dalziel,[42] and the Reverend Dr Sir William Robertson Nicoll[43] when the name that has been in their minds has been the name of Mr. David Lloyd George . . . They have done it because they remembered old associations, because they

allowed much for the strain of this evil time upon an emotional mind like yours . . . But the time for these concealments has passed . . . In the heated and overwrought atmosphere of your mind you do honestly believe that you are the Man of Destiny . . . Your brilliant success, your fascinating personality, your various, though wayward and superficial powers encourage the belief.

Gardiner then followed through with a piece of pure intellectual snobbery, stating, 'Still more do your deficiencies encourage it – your untutored empiricism, your casual and uninstructed habit of mind, your light hold of political principles or, as you call them, "dogmas" . . . You had no faith. You had only emotions, and when the storm came the adventurer that was always latent within you made short work of the democrat.' Then later came the question as to where Lloyd George's loyalties really lay, when Gardiner challenged him by stating, 'In short shall I be wrong in assuming that throughout the life of this Government you have been in close intimacy with some of its chief assailants?' Whatever Lloyd George's motives, that charge was certainly correct, and Gardiner followed up with a statement of fact that even Northcliffe would have agreed with, noting that this was not 'a question of prying into private affairs. It is a question of what are the terms upon which a Government can exist.'[44] Yet that poisonous article provided another demonstration to Lloyd George, that his new enemies were mostly to be found amongst his old friends.

The day before conscription was to be debated in the House of Commons, the sense of crisis came closer to home. On Easter Monday morning, 24 April 1916, some 1,200 members of the Irish Volunteers and Irish Citizen Army launched an insurrection in central Dublin, seizing control of the General Post Office in O'Connell Street, where Patrick Pearse[45] then read the 'Proclamation of the Irish Republic'. It would take six days of fighting before the British forces managed to regain control of central Dublin, during which time nearly 500 people were killed.

As the violence in Dublin escalated, German Zeppelin dropped bombs over London on both of the evenings when the House of Commons debated and then rejected Asquith's proposals on conscription. Carson and Milner led the opposition, and it was a sign of the extraordinary weakness of the government that a Coalition with a majority of over 400 MPs could be so easily defeated. The compromise

Bill was withdrawn on 27 April, a decision Lloyd George considered 'a complete justification of the line I took & the Cabinet feel it'.[46] The following day Northcliffe declared at the *Daily Mail* editorial conference, 'There's Ireland in revolt, Kut[47] on the eve of falling, no "big push" ready on the Western Front, the Army calling for more men, and amid all this Asquith holds on to office and says "Wait and See".'[48]

Lloyd George dined with the Cabal on 1 May, and that morning Waldorf Astor had visited Addison where he'd urged him to persuade his chief to 'clear out'.[49] However, that evening Lloyd George pointed out that it would be impossible for him to resign now that they had won the argument on conscription.[50] He personally introduced the new government Bill to the House of Commons on 4 May and a motion to reject it was defeated by 328 to 36. Sir William Robertson wrote to congratulate him, stating that this 'should more than compensate you for the rubbishy Press attacks of the last week or two. The great thing is to get the Bill, and for that the Empire's thanks are due to you – alone.'[51] On 5 May, *The Times* editorial column entitled 'The Right Spirit' praised parliamentary speeches by Lloyd George, Carson and Milner on conscription, 'which will fill the Empire and its friends with new confidence and ring ominously in the ears of our enemies . . . Flinging aside as paltry and unworthy all lesser considerations, they bid us fix our eyes upon the one thing necessary – the winning of the war. The [conscription] measure will hearten the people as a sign that there are men among them who can fight, and fight successfully, for greater vigour and greater foresight. These are the indispensable qualities we require both to win the war and to make a real and an abiding peace. They have not been conspicuous in the Coalition.'[52] This was also the first time that *The Times* had brought together these three men as a single force. In his diary Riddell observed on 21 May that 'There is no doubt that L.G. and Northcliffe are acting in close concert.'[53] He then added in a line that was not included in the version of the diaries published in 1933: 'Lloyd George is growing to believe more and more that he is the only man to win the War. His attitude to the PM is changing rapidly. He is becoming more and more critical and antagonistic. It looks as if Lloyd George and Northcliffe are working to dethrone Mr Asquith.'[54] There were also more sinister rumours in London society about Lloyd George's relationship with Northcliffe. Three days later, Sir Ian Hamilton's wife Jean[55] recalled seeing Mary Spender, who was married to J. A. Spender,[56] a devoted supporter of Asquith's and the editor of the liberal *Westminster Gazette*. She was 'amazing on the subject of Lloyd George, whom she says is intriguing still against the P.M., and that he is entirely in Northcliffe's power as Northcliffe holds Marconi telegrams of his, also several very disloyal letters of his about his colleagues – letters too about his private life – so can blackmail him at any moment, and he [Northcliffe] intends to be S. of S. for War when Lloyd George is Prime Minister.'[57]

The crisis in Ireland, however, would prove to be an important distraction. Following the Easter Rising, Asquith asked Lloyd George to talk to the leading Unionist and Nationalist politicians to see if an agreement could be reached on the government of Ireland. The Prime Minister told him, 'I hope you may see your way to take up Ireland; at any rate for a short time. It is a unique opportunity and there is no one else who could do so much to bring about a permanent solution.'[58] This was also a politically astute move by Asquith. If there was any issue likely to drive a wedge between Lloyd George and the Conservatives, in particular Carson and Bonar Law, it was Irish Home Rule.

Lloyd George recalled that:

> The request came at an awkward moment. For some time, I had been urging on our leaders a measure of closer co-ordination with our Russian Ally and had at last got them to agree to a practical step in this direction. Lord Kitchener was to proceed to Russia via Archangel to consult with the military authorities there about closer co-operation in the field, and it had been arranged that I should go with him to find out for myself the truth about the appalling shortage of equipment . . . and see in what way the Ministry of Munitions could best help to remedy it.[59]

So rather than depart for Russia with Kitchener on 5 June, Lloyd George would stay in London to try and resolve the situation in Ireland.

In meetings held at the Ministry of Munitions in early June, he met separately with Carson and the leading Unionists, and then John Redmond and the Irish nationalists. Rather than holding an open conference where new solutions might be considered, Lloyd George's starting point was where the Home Rule debate had stopped at the outbreak of the war. This was that there should be Home Rule for Ireland within the Empire, with its own parliament in Dublin, but with the initial exclusion of Ulster. The outstanding questions were for how long Ulster would remain within the United Kingdom, and where the border would be drawn on the island of Ireland.[60] At Lloyd George's suggestion, in return for peace and Home Rule in 1916, the Nationalist leaders were prepared to accept the exclusion of six of the counties of Ulster, as well as Carson's condition that they could not be included unless expressly authorized by a new Act of Parliament after the war. In the meantime, the Irish representation in the Westminster Parliament would also remain unaltered. Bonar Law urged his party members to accept Lloyd George's proposal, believing that 'we are bound to do what we think is right in the national interest without regard even to the interests of our Party . . . I am bound to tell you what my conviction is, and it is this, that if we go back on these negotiations now as a Party we shall make a terrible mistake.'[61] To have reached that level of consensus was to achieve, in the opinion of the political writer and Cabal member F. S. Oliver, the 'impossible'.[62]

However, the opposition of Conservatives in the Cabinet, notably Lord Lansdowne, Walter Long, and Lord Selborne, who resigned over the issue, meant that the initiative came to nothing. As Lloyd George lamented in his memoirs, 'The plan which held out such promise for a settlement of the ancient grievance of Ireland, and which was accepted by both parties in Ireland itself, was thereafter deliberately smashed by extremists on both sides.'[63] Yet the negotiations were not entirely unfruitful, as Bonar Law's friend Max Aitken noted. 'For the first time Bonar Law, Lloyd George and Carson had worked together as a team.'[64] F. S. Oliver also thought that while the Cabinet had no doubt hoped that for Lloyd George, Ireland would 'cook his goose', there was now 'a prospect of [him] becoming the most important man in the Government'.[65]

Yet it was still unclear how and when this could happen. The Cabal met for dinner on 5 June and afterwards Henry Wilson, who despaired that the Cabinet was 'a miserable pack of Hesitations and Hiccoughs',[66] noted in his diary that 'Milner sees no chance of getting rid of Asquith and thinks, like me, that his continuance as Prime Minister is a great danger. He looks on Lloyd George as the only chance, but a broken reed as he cannot make up his mind to resign.'[67] Little did the members of the Cabal know that on the same evening, at almost the exact moment they sat down for dinner, tragedy would strike.

On the morning of 6 June, Lloyd George walked from the Ministry of Munitions along Whitehall Place towards 10 Downing Street, to attend the War Council. On his way into the meeting he was pulled to one side by Maurice Bonham-Carter,[68] Asquith's principal private secretary, and told that the previous evening HMS *Hampshire*, the armoured cruiser that was taking Kitchener to Russia, had struck a mine off Marwick Head west of the Orkney Islands. She sank beneath the waves just before 8 p.m., with the loss of 737 crew members and passengers, including Kitchener and all of the personnel supporting his mission to Russia. Lloyd George recalled that when he entered the Cabinet Room, 'I found the Prime Minister, Sir Edward Grey, Mr Balfour and Sir Maurice Hankey sitting at the table all looking stunned by the tragedy. One realised how deep was the impression made by the personality of this extraordinary man on all who came in contact with him. Sir Maurice Hankey and I quite forgot for the moment that had it not been for the Irish negotiations we would also have shared the same fate.'[69]

On Saturday 10 June, at this crucial moment for the government, Lloyd George met with Bonar Law at Cherkley Court, Max Aitken's estate in Surrey. Amidst its gilded-age opulence, Bonar Law agreed to support Lloyd George to become the new Secretary of State for War. The following day, Aitken drove Bonar Law to see Asquith at his country home, The Wharf, at Sutton Courtenay in Oxfordshire, where he found the Prime Minister 'engaged in a rubber of bridge with three ladies'.[70] Asquith offered Bonar Law the War Office, which he declined, and they agreed it should go to Lloyd George. Yet it would be nearly a month before this was settled, and Lloyd George, in anticipation of the appointment, was not sure he wanted to accept.

On 11 June, Reginald McKenna also wrote to Runciman about the vacancy at the War Office, unaware of the negotiations already underway:

> The gloom of Kitchener's death is still hanging over me. Needless to say, that the news was not 24 hours old before claims to the succession were put in by a prominent person. Austen Chamberlain is regarded as the most probable man. Reading and Montagu[71] are sturdy beggars for Ll-G, but so far the P.M. has stood out . . . If past experience is followed, Ll-G will threaten him into acquiescence, but I know he recognises how unsuited Ll-G. is for the office.[72]

Yet Montagu's support for Lloyd George was not as generous as he wished it to have seemed. Writing to Asquith, in anticipation of the long-planned British attack on the Western Front due to commence on 1 July, he advised that it would 'be clearly advantageous to have L.G. at the War Office during the announcement of heavy casualties and a possible unfruitful offensive'.[73]

In his *War Memoirs*, Lloyd George published a letter he drafted to Asquith on 17 June but did not send. In it he sets out not just his wish to resign, but that in so doing he would take his case to the country, with the object of bringing down the government. It was written five days after the confirmation of the death of Captain Hugh Powell Williams,[74] a young man he had watched grow up in Criccieth. He was the son of G. P. Williams[75] the ironmonger, a lifelong friend who'd been Lloyd George's Sunday school teacher, and as a local Liberal Party official, had also helped to secure his nomination to stand for election to Parliament. Lloyd George wrote in his draft letter to Asquith:

> I propose now to take a course which I had determined upon long ago. I have been profoundly dissatisfied for a long time with the progress and conduct of the War. I have expressed my dissatisfaction in writing and orally to you . . . Had it not been for the fact that I had undertaken a task the carrying out of which was vital to the success of our Army, I should long ago have joined Carson, with whom I have been in the main in complete sympathy in his criticisms of the conduct of the War . . . I feel that my position in the Ministry is an anomalous one, as I am completely out of sympathy with the spirit and method of the War direction. I feel we cannot win on these lines. We are undoubtedly losing the War, and nothing can save us but the nation itself. The people do not realise how grave the situation is. I feel they ought to be told.[76]

However, on 6 July, Lloyd George's appointment as Secretary of State for War was confirmed, with Edwin Montagu taking his place as Minister of Munitions. Arthur Lee would also move with Lloyd George to the War Office. Margot Asquith was quick to understand the significance of Lloyd George's appointment, writing in her diary, 'We are out: it can only be a question of time now when we shall have to leave Downing Street.'[77] Since the autumn of 1914, Lloyd George's constant complaint had been against the conduct of the wartime government, and ultimately the leadership of the Prime Minister himself. He would not be content until the war effort had come under his sole direction, with or without Asquith's consent.

FOUR

The Powers That Be

The War Office[1] in Whitehall had been built at the height of British imperial power, to provide a suitably imposing home to the military commanders of the Empire. This large, Edwardian baroque building had been constructed from 26,000 tons of white Portland stone, providing a place of work for 2,500 people in 1,000 offices. They were connected by two and a half miles of corridors, some wide enough to allow messengers on bicycles to pass each other in safety. Once through its grand portal you were greeted by an immense staircase of Italian marble whose red carpet swept you to the first floor where the Secretary of State's rooms could be found. Lloyd George's chamber was vast and oak-panelled, with floor-to-ceiling windows overlooking Downing Street and Horse Guards Parade. This was a setting designed to impress upon visitors that the decisions of the Ministers who resided there, touched the whole world, yet the juxtaposition of power and impotence could hardly have been greater.

On 1 July 1916, five days before Lloyd George's appointment, the Battle of the Somme had commenced. This was Sir Douglas Haig's long-planned great offensive that he believed would achieve a decisive breakthrough on the Western Front, as well as relieving the pressure on the French defence of Verdun. Determined to learn the lessons from the shortage of shells and munitions at Neuve Chappelle and Loos, Arthur Lee recalled that Haig had asked the Ministry of Munitions, 'for a guaranteed steady supply of not less than one million shells a week from 1 July'. Lee noted in his memoirs that he 'was able to inform the Minister and the Commander-in-Chief on 7 June that the goal had already been reached and that production would rise steadily until it attained the two million a week mark, probably by November'.[2] As a prelude to the start of the battle, Haig ordered a seven-day bombardment of the German front lines during which one and a half million shells were fired. This was supposed to break the enemy's defensive positions and provide a walk-over for the advancing British soldiers. Instead, they strode into what one eyewitness, the war poet Siegfried Sassoon,[3] described as 'a sunlit picture of hell'.[4] That day Haig's forces suffered over 57,000 casualties, the equivalent number for the whole of the Battle of Loos, and by the end of the campaign on 18 November there would be over one million casualties on all sides. In just over four months of fighting, the Allies would gain approximately six miles of territory across the front, and none of their major objectives were taken. In his *War Memoirs*, Lloyd George wrote of these terrible losses that 'The Battle of the Somme was fought by the volunteer armies raised in 1914 and 1915. These contained the choicest and best of our young manhood. The officers were drawn mainly from our public schools and universities. Over 400,000 of our men fell in this bull-headed fight and the slaughter amongst our young officers was appalling.'[5] Lloyd George had arrived at the War Office too late to challenge Haig's plans, and without the authority to change his tactics. As far as the military commanders were concerned, it was the task of the Secretary of State to provide them with the men and materials they required, and he should then leave the fighting to them.

On 2 August, Lloyd George went with Frances Stevenson to a private preview screening of the cinema film *The Battle of the Somme*,[6] which showed footage of the first weeks of fighting at the front. While some of the action had been staged for the camera, the film also depicted graphic scenes of devastated villages, barbed-wire entrenchments, and dead soldiers being buried at the front. Frances wrote in her diary that 'To say that one enjoyed [the film] would be untrue; but I am glad I went. I am glad I have seen the sort of thing our men have to go through . . . There were pictures too of the battlefield after the fight & of our gallant men lying all crumpled up & helpless. There were pictures of men mortally wounded being carried out of the communication trenches, with the look of agony on their faces. Then, thinking of her brother, Frances wrote, 'It reminded me of what Paul's last hours were: I have often tried to imagine to myself what he went through, but now I know: and I shall never forget.'[7] After the general release of *The Battle of the Somme* to cinemas on 21 August, it was watched by 20 million people in the first six weeks.

Lloyd George thought the film was 'an epic of self-sacrifice and gallantry',[8] and it focused on an area of the front line that was of particular interest to him. The Fricourt-Mametz section was where the Welsh division had been in the thick of the fighting. The War Secretary would also ask his friend, the war artist Christopher Williams, to paint a picture dedicated to the sacrifices of the Welsh at Mametz Wood.[9] The Welsh poet David Jones,[10] who took part in the battle, also recorded the scene in his poem In *Parenthesis*; 'And here and there and huddled over, death-halsed to these, a Picton-five-feet-four paragon of the Line, from Newcastle Emlyn or Talgarth in Brycheiniog, lying disordered like discarded garments or crumpled chin to shin-bone like a Lambourne find.'[11]

Two weeks before the screening, Lloyd George received news that his friend G. P. Williams had lost another son, Hywel,[12] killed in action at Mametz Wood. This young man had been a childhood friend of Lloyd George's son Gwilym, and when he was asked to unveil a memorial plaque to the Williams boys, he told his own brother William George, 'I had to decline the invitation. I knew I would have broken down in the ceremony. They were handsome, tall and fair headed, as fine and upstanding as any young men you could meet.'[13]

Lloyd George's eldest son Richard had also been working with the Royal Engineers on the Somme, creating roads for artillery and ammunition to supply the front-line troops. When he heard news that the boy was safe, Lloyd George wrote to tell Uncle Lloyd, 'You will be glad to hear that Dick is out of the fight now and without a scratch and he said this morning, "Thanks to Providence."'[14] The War Secretary may not have lost a son on the Western Front, but he knew the agony of having a child taken from you, before they'd had the chance to fulfil their youthful promise. After the death of Lloyd George's daughter Mair in 1907, his friend D. R. Daniel[15] believed that the grief he was suffering was 'tortuous, bordering on madness'.[16] Frances Stevenson also remembered that Lloyd George always had 'an ever-open wound which bleeds again and hurts terribly whenever he is reminded of little Mair'.[17]

At the Ministry of Munitions, Lloyd George had brought in outside experts to advise on the best methods to increase production and improve the supply of armaments to the Western Front. At the War Office it was clear that Sir William Robertson as Chief of the Imperial

General Staff was in lockstep with Douglas Haig, and if Lloyd George wanted to question their strategy he would have to find alternative experts who were prepared to provide that criticism.

Winston Churchill, based on his experiences of the front line that year, had prepared a paper expressing grave concerns about heavy losses during the Battle of the Somme and questioning the strategic objectives of Haig's offensive. He wrote:

> The open country towards which we are struggling by inches is capable of entrenchment defence at every step and is utterly devoid of military significance. There is no question of breaking the line, 'of letting loose the cavalry in the open country behind', or of inducing a general withdrawal of the German armies in the West. No local strategic advantages of any kind have been reaped or can be expected . . . In personnel the results of the operation have been disastrous; in terrain they have been absolutely barren . . . Thus the pent-up energies of the army are being dissipated.[18]

On 1 August it was circulated to the Cabinet by F. E. Smith, and that evening at a dinner Lloyd George was harassed by an excited Lord Rothermere,[19] the brother of Lord Northcliffe, who exclaimed that the officials at the War Office, 'are trying to mislead you. They . . . are feeding you with lies.'[20] Sir William Robertson also warned Haig that 'the Powers that be'[21] were starting to get uneasy about the situation on the Somme. Regy Esher noted as well in his diary a warning from Robertson that 'London critics, especially some members of the Government, talk of [Haig] as the "butcher" because of our losses.'

In Lloyd George's unsent letter to Asquith written on 17 June he had noted that 'The soldiers in this war have not been a conspicuous success. Up to the present there has not been a plan conceived and carried out by them which has not ended in bloody failure.'[22] He was instinctively suspicious of the army high command; an institution he believed to be an 'exclusive . . . profession' where 'social prestige and accomplishment count for so much'.[23] William Robertson was the exception to this rule, one of the few men to have risen from the lowest rank to the highest, but his advancement had been based on his skills as an administrator, rather than as a commander in the field. Robertson, Lloyd George noted, was 'cautious and discreet', whose 'qualities of circumspection in judgement and speech lead even shrewd and experienced observers of all sorts and conditions of men to infer that there was a vast mental hinterland unexplored and unrevealed'.[24] The French called him 'General Non-non', and the French Prime Minister Aristide Briand[25] told Lloyd George that 'Rob-berrt-son says "Non" before he has heard what your proposal is about.'[26]

Sir Douglas Haig on the other hand radiated self-confidence. Everything in his life so far had been a preparation for the role of military hero that he believed he was now destined to play. He was independently wealthy, as an heir of the *Haig* Scottish Whisky distillery business founded by his father. At the Royal Military Academy at Sandhurst he was awarded the Anson Memorial Sword, the prize traditionally given to the cadet who passes out first on the list at the final examination, and he would combine his duties as a cavalry officer with playing polo for England. Haig was also close to King George V and they had been on friendly terms since they'd first met at a Sandringham[27] shooting weekend in 1898.

In early August the King visited Haig at his Advanced Headquarters for the Battle of the Somme, Château Val Vion at Beauquesne, near Amiens. General Headquarters (GHQ) at Montreuil-sur-Mer, about 25 miles south of Boulogne, was considered too far from the front line to be an efficient base for the commander-in-chief during the offensive. Haig understood how important this relationship with the monarch was to guard against political intrigues at home that could jeopardize his position. His wealthy, sleek and well-connected private secretary, Sir Philip Sassoon,[28] also made sure that Haig was kept abreast of important news and gossip, in particular through messages received from Lord Northcliffe and Regy Esher. Northcliffe even sent Sassoon regular bulletins entitled 'News from the Home Front'. In one of them that summer he warned, 'The Secretary of State for War, who is really excellent when he keeps away from what he does not understand, is understood to declare that he has no intention of interfering. His immediate surroundings, however, are not such as to inspire confidence, and his good nature places him at the mercy of ungummed generals and baffled careerists, such as would be Brigadier-General Churchill.'[29] Northcliffe had also visited Haig that summer, recording in his journal, '[The General] showed me his plans. Each time I see him I am convinced of his qualities. We talked of the wobble of the politicians.'[30]

On 11 August, Lloyd George made his first trip to Paris as War Secretary and met with Aristide Briand. Regy Esher had previously noted in his diary; 'Briand thinks Lloyd George possesses a longer view than any of our leaders . . . Lloyd George said to him that being both of them Celts, they perhaps possessed more imagination. Briand found that upon the general direction of the war they were in close sympathy and agreement.'[31] Of their August meeting Esher observed that it was 'curious' to see them together as they were 'alike in so many ways. Of Breton or Celtic blood, physically they resemble each other. Both are eloquent; but Briand has infinitely more knowledge and he plays with Lloyd George.'[32] It was a similarity that Rudyard Kipling had also observed, noting after interviewing the French Prime Minister the year before that he had 'the same L.G.-like shrug and lean forward of the shoulders at critical points – a sort of political bedside manner. A windbag, yes, but of the most unscrupulous.'[33]

The following day Lloyd George joined Haig at Beauquesne, where as expected he assured him that he had 'no intention of meddling'[34] in military strategy, and simply proposed that Eric Geddes should join Haig's staff in order to resolve the logistical logjam, which was slowing the delivering of munitions and supplies to the front. Geddes was appointed Director of Military Railways at the War Office, and by June 1917 had overseen the completion of 1,000 miles of light railways to convey supplies from the ports and railyards to the front line. The working village created to support this effort at Monthouis, three miles from Montreuil, became known as Geddesburg.

Lloyd George thought Haig possessed 'indomitable will and courage',[35] but nevertheless believed he was 'intellectually and temperamentally unequal to the command of an Army of millions fighting battles on fields which were invisible to any Commander . . . He did not possess that eye within an eye which is imagination.'[36] Or, as Lloyd George more simply put it to his son Richard, Haig was 'Brilliant to the top of his army boots.'[37] Haig on the other hand regarded Lloyd George as 'astute and cunning, with much energy and push but I should think shifty and unreliable'.[38] The trouble was that Haig was a man who had never been told 'no', while Lloyd George was someone who wouldn't take 'no' for an answer. This was not a working relationship ever destined to be a success.

Lloyd George's visit to France was kept short so that on 17 August he could return home to Wales to speak at the Welsh National Eisteddfod. For many years this had been an annual visit for Lloyd George and his family, and in 1916 the festival was held in a huge marquee on the Vicarage Field sports ground in Aberystwyth. On arrival, he was accompanied by Margaret and their 14-year-old daughter and youngest child Megan,[39] while cheering and applause followed them all along their route to the speaker's platform. Some 3,000 people were seated in the marquee with a further 2,000 standing in the wings, and when Lloyd George rose to speak, it took a further five minutes for the noise to die down.

Earlier in the year he had written to the organizers recommending the singing of traditional Welsh songs at the Eisteddfod, but this had attracted some criticism in the press as being inappropriate in wartime. In response he told his countrymen:

> Why should we not sing during war? Why, especially, should we not sing at this stage of the War? The blinds of Britain are not down yet, nor are they likely to be. The honour of Britain is not dead, her might is not broken, her destiny not fulfilled, her ideals are not shattered by her enemies. She is more alive; she is more potent; she is greater than ever she was. Her dominions are wider, her influence is deeper, her purpose is more exalted than ever. Why should her children not sing? . . . It is true that there are many thousands of gallant men falling in the fight – let us sing for their heroism . . . I am glad that I came down from the cares and labour of the War Office of the British Empire to listen and to join with you in singing the old songs which our brave countrymen on the battlefield are singing as a defiance to the enemies of human right.[40]

The Times reported that his speech was received with 'tumultuous applause'[41] and then 'the audience formed itself into a choir thousands strong . . . The effect . . . was extraordinary, and the music echoed through the hills and rolled beyond the confines of the town. There were 10 hours of continuous singing.'[42] They sang hymns set to old Welsh folk tunes and some 'songs without words'. Lloyd George told the gathering that 'they could express in song feelings which they could not voice in words. There were emotions surging in the soul of a nation which could not be put into words.'[43] Overall, the experience created a sense of 'hwyl', a Welsh word with no direct translation into English, but representing a heightened, almost spiritual, sense of emotional fervour, generated by music, poetry and the spoken word.[44] The scenes were reminiscent of the great Welsh revivalist movement led just over a decade before by the evangelical minister Evan Roberts.[45] In 1905, Roberts had travelled to Carnarvon to hear Lloyd George speak, and when the two men met the politician had prophetically told the revivalist, 'I wield the sword, you build the temple.'[46]

The attention given to Lloyd George's Eisteddfod speech may have also influenced the writing in 1917 of the war poem 'Anthem for Doomed Youth' by Wilfred Owen.[47] Born in Oswestry on the Welsh borders, Owen and his family took a keen interest in Lloyd George. The poem describes the 'demented choirs of wailing shells' and in particular the last line (of its concluding couplet) reads as a direct reference to Lloyd George's speech ('The blinds of Britain are not down yet, nor are they likely to be'): 'Their flowers the tenderness of patient minds, / And each slow dusk a drawing-down of blinds.'[48] Similarly, Siegfried Sassoon's poem 'Everyone Sang' told how 'My heart was shaken with tears; and horror drifted away . . . O, but Everyone was a bird and the song was wordless; the singing will never be done.'[49] Another soldier poet Robert Graves also recalled seeing Lloyd George speak three months before, at a dinner of the Honourable Society of Cymmrodorion,[50] where he was:

> . . . up in the air on one of his 'glory of the Welsh hills' speeches. The power of his rhetoric was uncanny. I knew that the substance of what he was saying was commonplace, idle and false, but I had to fight hard against abandoning myself with the rest of the audience. The power I knew was not his; he sucked it from his hearers and threw it back at them. Afterwards I was introduced to him, and when I looked closely at his eyes they were like those of a sleep-walker.[51]

Yet Lloyd George's eyes were also open to the lack of progress being made by the British forces fighting on the Somme. On 11 September he returned to France to meet with Ferdinand Foch,[52] the commanding officer of the French northern army group, which had supported the British forces fighting on the Somme. Foch saw Sir Henry Wilson the following day and reported back the questions Lloyd George had raised about the British army. In his diary Wilson noted that 'Lloyd George asked innumerable questions about why we took so few prisoners, why we took so little ground, why we had such heavy losses, all these in comparison with the French. Foch played up well as regards Haig and would not give him away. He simply said he did not know, but that our divisions were green soldiers and his were veterans.'[53]

On 17 September, Foch visited Haig at Beauquesne and after their formal meeting he gestured that they should go for a private talk in the garden. Haig recalled that:

> ... he then told me of Lloyd George's recent visit to his HQ. Lunch was at 12 noon, and LG said he would bring 2 or 3 with him. He actually arrived at 1.45 and brought 8 persons! After lunch, LG using Lord Reading as interpreter, had a private talk with Foch. He began by saying he was a British Minister, and, that he had a right to be told the truth! He wished to know why the British who gained no more [ground] than the French, if as much, had suffered such heavy casualties ... LG also asked his opinion as to the ability of the British generals. Foch said LG was sufficiently patriotic not to criticise the British Commander-in-Chief but he did not speak with confidence of the other British generals as a whole! Foch's reply was that he had had no means of forming an opinion. Unless I had been told of this conversation personally by General Foch, I would not have believed it possible that a British Minister could have been so ungentlemanly as to go to a foreigner and put such questions regarding his own subordinates. Foch thought Reading was a cunning individual.[54]

While Lloyd George was in France, a major British offensive on the Somme front was launched on 15 September, including the first deployment of tanks by any side.[55] This was successful at first, but then once again the initiative was lost. During the battle Lloyd George recalled being driven with Haig from GHQ to the headquarters of General Cavan[56] at Méaulte near Albert, where they were also to meet with the French commander, General Joffre.[57] On the way they observed a long column of soldiers from the Guards regiment marching towards the front line in preparation for an attack. Lloyd George would later learn that amongst their number was Raymond Asquith,[58] the Prime

Minister's eldest son, who was killed in battle near Ginchy. After receiving the news the devastated Asquith wrote, 'Whatever pride I had in the past and whatever hope I had for the future – by much the largest part was invested in him. Now all that is gone.'[59]

Lord Northcliffe wrote to Sir Philip Sassoon to warn him, 'My present move is to combat the statements that the offensives of 1 July and 15 September are practically a repetition of Neuve Chapelle – heavy losses and comparatively few results . . . One of the reasons why this task is a little difficult is that the public were so fooled about the Dardanelles, Loos, Neuve Chapelle and other Allied successes that they are sceptical.'[60] Northcliffe also encouraged Sassoon to stay close to Geoffrey Dawson with updates on senior politicians visiting the front, and the two men corresponded practically every day that autumn. The press baron advised Sassoon that 'It is our system that he should know them and I should not, which we find an excellent plan. They are a pack of gullible optimists who swallow any foolish tale. There are exceptions among them, and they are splendid ones, but the generality of them have the slipperiness of eels, with the combined vanity of a professional beauty.'[61]

Northcliffe retained his high regard for Lloyd George and told Sassoon that he was 'an excellent man – keen to win the war, but he has a habit of rushing in where angels fear to tread'.[62] Yet Northcliffe also had a blind spot when it came to his deference to the generals on matters of military strategy. As Winston Churchill complained in the third volume of his history of the war, *The World Crisis*:

> . . . the foolish doctrine was preached to the public through the innumerable agencies that Generals and Admirals must be right on war matters and civilians of all kinds must be wrong. These erroneous conceptions were inculcated billion-fold by the newspapers under the crudest forms. The feeble or presumptuous politician is portrayed cowering in his office, intent in the crash of the world on Party intrigues or personal glorification, fearful of responsibility, incapable of aught save shallow phrase making. To him enters the calm, noble resolute figure of the great Commander by land or sea, resplendent in uniform, glittering with decorations, irradiated with the lustre of the hero, shod with the science and armed with the panoply of war. This stately figure, devoid of the slightest thought of

self, offers his clear far-sighted guidance and counsel for vehement action, or artifice, or wise delay. But this advice is rejected; his sound plans put aside; his courageous initiative baffled by political chatterboxes and incompetents.[63]

In October, after receiving complaints from Robertson about the War Secretary, Northcliffe reported in a letter to Philip Sassoon that he had descended on his office in Whitehall and told Lloyd George's secretary J. T. Davies that 'if further interference took place with Sir William Robertson I was going to the House of Lords to lay matters before the world, and hammer them daily in my newspapers'.[64] It is not clear whether this was a reference to the rumoured incriminating personal papers of Lloyd George's that were supposedly in Northcliffe's possession. But, if we are to take him at his word, then presenting evidence to the House of Lords under parliamentary privilege, where he would have immunity from legal action, rather than just publishing the information, would imply that the matters he wished to lay before the world were of a sensitive nature. Philip Sassoon certainly believed the rumours and a few months later told a close friend that Northcliffe was in possession of 'compromising Marconi letters that he bought some years ago'.[65]

Despite Lloyd George's difficult relationship with the generals, Regy Esher could appreciate the qualities that Lloyd George brought to the war effort. Writing to the War Secretary's friend and ally Lord Murray, he acknowledged, 'His gifts as an administrator are not of the ordinary peace kind. He does not attempt to exercise minute supervision over detail . . . He has adopted with marked success the plan of cutting away red-tape and of placing reliance upon personal responsibility by bestowing extended powers upon individuals selected for their capacity, vigour and courage. This is the only method in wartime that is conducive to success.'[66] Yet, as the autumn campaign of 1916 drew to a close, the prospects of Britain and her allies remained bleak, with no likelihood of an early and victorious end to the war. Russia was close to collapse, the Balkans dominated by the Central Powers, and the Ottoman Empire reviving thanks to improved supplies from Germany. France was exhausted from its efforts in heroically resisting the brutal German attack at Verdun that lasted from February to December, and the great British offensive on the Somme had failed to achieve the hoped-for breakthrough. At the Battle of Jutland[67] in June 1916 the Royal Navy had held back an attempt by the German fleet to break the blockade of their ports, but U-boat attacks were now sinking increasing numbers of British merchant ships, threatening supplies of food and vital war materials. Yet despite these pressures, and his own concerns about the conduct of the war, Lloyd George was determined to maintain a positive public position. At the end of September, Northcliffe arranged for him to be interviewed by the American journalist Roy Howard[68] at his 'barn of a room'[69] at the War Office. Howard's article would be syndicated at home and across the United States and was intended to show that Britain was not interested in a compromise peace, but would fight through to victory. Lloyd George told Howard that 'Britain has only begun to fight. The British Empire had invested thousands of its best lives to purchase future immunity for civilisation. The investment is too great to be thrown away.' Dismissing talk of a truce, Lloyd George stated that 'the fight must be to a finish, to a knock-out'.[70]

Yet how and where was this knock-out blow to be landed? Lloyd George told George Riddell over breakfast on 1 November, as recorded by Harry Burnham,[71] owner of the *Daily Telegraph*, that 'he could never get out of the General Staff' an answer as to 'how they expect to win the war. The day before yesterday he asked General Robertson again. He always gets the same answer – "Wearing them down."' Lloyd George was concerned that the public were fatigued by the war as well, telling Riddell and Burnham that after his interview with Roy Howard, 'he expected to have support, in the shape of letters of all classes backing him up. Instead of that letters came, mainly from men and women who had lost their sons, and who wanted to avenge their deaths at all costs . . . the losses are heavily felt now, and people are asking whether we have only had a paper victory.'[72]

Later that day, Lloyd George lunched alone with Maurice Hankey in the seclusion of Arthur Lee's house in Abbey Gardens. Again, he chose to have more open and intimate discussions on strategy away from Downing Street and the War Office. Walton Heath and Riddell's house in Queen Anne's Gate provided similar safe havens; so did a flat in St James's Court[73] that David Davies had 'found him' that month, and as Lloyd George told C. P. Scott over breakfast there one morning, 'between ourselves he has paid for and furnished it'.[74] Over this lunch in Abbey Gardens, however, Hankey, whose younger brother Donald[75] had been killed in action a few weeks before, recorded that 'Ll. G. considered that the Somme offensive had been a bloody and disastrous failure; he was not willing to remain in office if it was to be repeated next year . . . I warned him that he was not dealing now with munitions workers . . . but with armies led by the most conservative class in the world, forming the most powerful trades union in the world.'[76]

Yet it would be from the Conservative classes that the pressure for change would now come. A House of Commons debate on a motion relating to the confiscation of enemy property in Nigeria wasn't an obvious cause of concern for the government whips. However, on 8 November it became the focal point for a rebellion against the Coalition that would herald its demise within a month. Earlier that day, Lloyd George met with Carson and Milner at Arthur Lee's house, to discuss the amendment tabled to the government motion by the Conservative MP Leslie Scott,[77] a former legal colleague, and close political associate of Carson. Bonar Law, as Colonial Secretary, would lead that evening for the government in proposing that any neutral or British person or business should be able to purchase German assets, whereas Scott's amendment would restrict such a transaction to the British only.

The debate led to a direct confrontation in the House of Commons between Bonar Law and Carson, with Carson accusing the Conservative leader of speaking 'nonsense' and making statements that were 'absolutely untrue'.[78] The government defeated the amendment by 231 votes to 117, but amongst the Conservatives 65 voted with Carson and Scott, and only 73 with Bonar Law, out of a parliamentary party of 286. Looking back on the vote, Bonar Law recalled, 'My friends and Liberals told me that I had scored a great parliamentary triumph; but I knew better. There were sixty-five of my party against me. They were men who had formerly been my staunchest supporters. The Nigerian debate was simply a symptom of discontent with the Coalition, rather than hostility to myself.'[79]

Carson was also supported by leading Liberals in the voting lobby, including Winston Churchill, and three of Lloyd George's acolytes, Henry Dalziel, Alfred Mond[80] and Hamar Greenwood.[81] The War Secretary himself missed the vote, despite his presence being required by the government whips. When they noticed that Lloyd George was not in the House, a call was put in to 11 Downing Street to find out where he was. Speaking to his wife Margaret, a whip was told, according to the King's private secretary Lord Stamfordham, that Lloyd George must be in Parliament as 'he said he was dining with Sir E. Carson'.[82] The fact that Stamfordham went to the trouble to find out whether Lloyd George had permission to be absent that evening, or had instead decided not to support the government, shows the wider significance that was attached to this division. According to Max Aitken, Lloyd George had been 'dining that night with Lee at his house in Abbey Gardens where several meetings had already taken place between Lloyd George, Carson and Milner. All three had met that evening to discuss the possibilities of co-operation.'[83] Lee's house was less than a ten-minute walk from the voting lobby.

Three days after the vote, Austen Chamberlain wrote to his sister Hilda, 'I dare say we shall be out of office soon. Carson will get us out if he can, & when the LlG, Carson, Churchill ministry is formed I shall feel justified in going on long leave.'[84] On 13 November, Frances Stevenson also noted in her diary that Lloyd George believed there was 'likely to be a break'[85] in the Conservative Party. That day Lloyd George had told Max Aitken, knowing it would get back to Bonar Law, that he was working with Carson to try and secure a new smaller War Council with ultimate control over strategy. At the end of 1915, Aitken had been appointed as the military representative of the Canadian government in London, which position came with a room at the War Office, not far from that of the Secretary of State. This facilitated frequent informal contact with Lloyd George, and through this Aitken could see that the combination of Carson and the War Secretary meant that his old friend 'Bonar Law's position was indeed one of great weakness'. Aitken observed that 'He was little more than the titular leader of the Conservatives in the Cabinet. He had failed over and over again . . . to carry his Conservative colleagues with him.'[86] If Bonar Law failed to act now, he faced revolt from within his own party, something about which, according to Chamberlain, he was 'seriously perturbed'.[87] Aitken was determined that Bonar Law should instead now join forces with Lloyd George and Carson, and press for a reorganization of the government.

The War Secretary now had to leave London to join Asquith at the Inter-Allied war conference in Paris on 16 November, but he encouraged Aitken to stay in touch. This meeting with the leaders of France and Italy would prove to be the last straw for Lloyd George, where he would see for himself, as Hankey had warned, the collective power of the military authorities. In proceedings that he described as 'little better than a complete farce'[88] the generals dismissed his support for greater resources to be dedicated to Salonika and the Eastern Front, and left Lloyd George 'feeling that after all nothing more would be done except to repeat the old fatuous tactics of hammering away with human flesh and sinews at the strongest fortresses of the enemy'.[89] After returning to the Hôtel de Crillon, where the British delegation was staying, Lloyd George walked with Hankey before dinner, and they discussed the fact that 'nothing in the way of a change in the conduct of the War had been accomplished and that in the absence of some dramatic *coup* things would go on as before until we slid into inevitable catastrophe'.[90] As twilight fell on the streets of Paris, they turned into the Place Vendôme. Lloyd George recalled that when they passed the famous column in the centre of the square bearing the statue of Napoleon,[91] Hankey told him, 'You ought to insist on a small War Committee being set up for the day-to-day conduct of the War, with full powers. It must be independent of the Cabinet . . . The Chairman must be a man of unimpaired energy and great driving power.'[92] That night Lloyd George wired Bonar Law and Max Aitken, asking to meet when he returned to London. The coup was at hand.

FIVE

Submit or Resign

At 8 p.m. on Monday 20 November the conspirators gathered for dinner at Max Aitken's grand suite on the fourth floor of the Hyde Park Hotel.[1] It was a most elegant setting for a plot against the Prime Minister to take shape. Aitken believed the moment had now come, but it required getting Lloyd George, Bonar Law and Carson together in a room to agree what needed to be done. In May 1915 it had been the joint action of Lloyd George and Bonar Law that had created the Coalition, and the same force could remake the government again. The Conservative leader was also in a tight spot, as if he wavered he risked losing control of his own party.

Bonar Law was still not sure about Lloyd George and thought that Asquith, despite his failings, was more trustworthy. However, Carson reassured him that in his view the Welshman was a 'plain man of the people, and, though you mayn't trust him, his crookednesses are all plain to see. But the other is clever and polished and knows how to conceal his crookednesses.'[2] Now at the Hyde Park Hotel, in an atmosphere that, according to Aitken, 'seemed unfavourable, not to say strained',[3] Lloyd George set out his plan for a three-man War Council with full executive powers. Asquith would not be included, effectively leaving him as a Prime Minister in name only. The group met again on Saturday 25 November at Bonar Law's home, Pembroke Lodge, at Edwardes Square in Kensington, to agree a modified version of Lloyd George's proposal; this time Asquith would have an external role as President of the new committee but would not be an active member of it. They also agreed that Bonar Law should put it to the Prime Minister that evening in the form of a written memorandum, which had been drafted by Aitken. The tone of Bonar Law's meeting with the Prime Minister when they discussed the proposal, was that of a friendly warning. Unless Asquith initiated their proposed reforms to the War Council, in Bonar Law's opinion, 'criticism might lead to an agitation, and he would be forced to act and thus find himself in a humiliating position. It was quite evident that Mr Asquith did not realize the seriousness of the position.'[4] Later, Asquith wrote back to Bonar Law rejecting the proposal and trying to make him doubt Lloyd George's motives. 'You know as well as I do both his qualities and his defects. He has many qualities that would fit him for the first place, but he lacks the one thing needful – he does not inspire trust . . . Here, again, there is one construction, and one only, that could be put on the new arrangement – that it has been engineered by him with the purpose, not perhaps at the moment, but as soon as a fitting pretext could be found, of his displacing me.'[5]

The members of the Monday Night Cabal were doing all they could to encourage Lloyd George to press on. On Sunday 26 November, General Sir Henry Wilson, back from the Western Front, lunched with Lloyd George at Walton Heath, and during a long talk in the afternoon told him that he:

> . . . had not met a single man in high position since I had been home this time who thought we were going to beat the Boches,[6] and that he [Lloyd George] alone could save us from defeat which must follow on such a train of thought. I told him that the present Government stank in the nostrils of the whole army, and that if he was to break away and raise the standard of victory he would have a unanimous army behind him. He agreed – I think – and thought the margin of safety between victory and indecisive peace was daily becoming narrower.[7]

The Cabal dined together at F. S. Oliver's house at 8, Hereford Gardens in Mayfair the following evening where Carson asked the group, 'Should Lloyd George come out of the Government, which he was convinced was going the best way to lose the war? And was it, or was it not, desirable that Bonar Law should come with him?'[8] Geoffrey Dawson noted that it was 'unanimous' for Lloyd George 'to come out at once', and 'unanimous' that Bonar Law should 'be induced to support him'. Carson then added that he was 'quite convinced himself and gave us to understand that he would at once urge Lloyd George to take action'.[9]

The following morning Dawson 'had a talk' with Arthur Lee, who told him it 'was a pity that L.G. and Northcliffe had not for some time been on speaking terms'.[10] They both decided that a meeting should be arranged when Northcliffe was back in London later in the week.

Most of the Conservative members of the Cabinet were still in the dark about these behind-the-scenes negotiations with Asquith and Lloyd George when Bonar Law briefed them on the situation on 30 November. Unsurprisingly, feeling bounced into reforms they had not previously been told about, Austen Chamberlain recalled that the ministers 'were unanimously of the opinion' that these proposals were 'open to grave objection'.[11] Max Aitken wrote that they believed it was 'simply a scheme for the further aggrandisement of Lloyd George as dictator'.[12] What's more, 'Lloyd George, it was said, was simply using Carson as a tool to stir up dissension and discontent among Tory back-benchers and so frighten the Conservative members of the Ministry into giving way to his inordinate ambitions.'[13] The Conservative grandee Lord Lansdowne told Bonar Law that the meeting had 'left a nasty taste in my mouth. I did not like your plan.'[14] Chamberlain noted, though, that despite these concerns it was 'evident' that Bonar Law had already 'committed himself too deeply to Carson and Lloyd George'.[15]

The following day, 1 December, Lloyd George breakfasted with George Riddell and Harry Burnham, where he told them that the prospects for the war were 'gloomy', and that 'We have only just a chance to win the war. We cannot win unless things are changed. If they are not changed I shall leave [the Cabinet].'[16] Burnham noted after their meeting, 'Lloyd George is not going to stay where he is much longer. He is sick of the soldiers and sick of the Government and sees disaster ahead . . . but there is no doubt he is anxious to be Prime Minister and to have a try. I gathered that, generally speaking, matters are coming to a crisis.'[17]

Later that morning Lloyd George, as arranged by Dawson and Lee, had his first meeting with Lord Northcliffe for several weeks. Before breakfast Northcliffe had telephoned Arthur Lee, 'in one of his ugliest moods', as his wife Ruth Lee recalled, and fuming '"I have wasted I don't know how many hours of my time on L.G. already and he isn't worth it. He will never really do anything and has not the courage to resign."'[18] Yet their meeting was a success and they agreed to meet again that day, after Lloyd George had seen the Prime Minister.

Lloyd George proposed to Asquith a modified version of the plan that Bonar Law had previously discussed with him. The War Committee would still not include Asquith, but as Prime Minister he would have the right to exercise a veto over its decisions, and refer questions to it, subject to the agreement of the Cabinet. Later, Lloyd George reassured Northcliffe that this was at last the moment of make or break. Asquith would either give in to his demands, or Lloyd George would resign. The following morning *The Times* leader column duly reported to its readers that the 'turning-point of war' had come and backed Lloyd George's plan for a 'drastic reconstruction [of the government] based wholly and solely on the qualities required in waging war'.[19]

Asquith wrote back to Lloyd George that while he agreed there needed to be a 'reconstruction and revision' of the government, he believed 'whatever changes are made in the composition or functions of the War Committee, the Prime Minister must be its Chairman', and 'The Cabinet would in all cases have ultimate authority.'[20] For Lloyd George this response was 'entirely unsatisfactory' and 'would effect no improvement and hardly any change'.

Later that evening Aitken, concerned that Bonar Law might be losing his nerve, decided that he should meet with Lloyd George again. Knowing that the War Secretary was dining at the Berkeley Hotel[21] with Lord Reading, Edwin and Venetia Montagu, and the Governor of the Bank of England, Walter Cunliffe,[22] Aitken and Bonar Law set out in a taxi to meet him. After extracting Lloyd George from the dining room, they went on to Aitken's suite at the Hyde Park Hotel and according to Lloyd George, he and Bonar Law 'decided that we should go forward with our plan of reorganisation whatever the consequences'.[23] The following morning, Lloyd George sent Bonar Law a copy of the letter he had received from Asquith the previous day and adding his own note which read, 'The life of the country depends on resolute action by you now.'[24]

Frances Stevenson wrote in her diary on 2 December that Lloyd George declined to meet Asquith at 11 o'clock in the morning and instead drafted his letter of resignation. He saw Northcliffe at the War Office, and clearly left the press baron with the belief that he was about to resign, as Northcliffe then directed his *Evening News* title to start placarding London with the message, 'Lloyd George Packing Up'.[25] Lloyd George then met with Reading and Edwin Montagu, who were now acting as unofficial intermediaries between the War Secretary and Prime Minister. According to Montagu, Lloyd George gave him his resignation letter to pass on to Asquith, who had by then left Downing Street to go to Walmer Castle[26] for the weekend.[27] At Lord Reading's request Lloyd George agreed to wait until the following day before actually resigning, in case a compromise agreement could be reached. Reading then visited Hankey in Downing Street, and both agreed that, as Sir Maurice recorded in his diary, 'The obvious compromise is for the Prime Minister to retain the Presidency of the War Committee with Lloyd George as Chairman, and to give Lloyd George a fairly free run for his money.'[28]

That afternoon Montagu despatched Maurice Bonham-Carter to Kent by car with Lloyd George's letter and one of this own, which warned; 'The situation is probably irretrievably serious. I have just come from L.G., with whom I have spent an hour of hard fighting, but it seems to be of no avail, and I fear he has committed himself.'[29] Montagu also requested that the Prime Minister return to Downing Street immediately.

On Sunday morning, 3 December, as Conservative ministers gathered at Bonar Law's home of Pembroke Lodge, *Reynolds's News*, the newspaper owned by Lloyd George's friend Henry Dalziel, ran the front-page headline, 'Lloyd George to Resign'. While they disliked being put in this position, facing realities they agreed on a statement to be presented to Asquith, which read: 'We share the view expressed to you by Mr. Bonar Law some time ago that the Government cannot continue as it is. It is evident that a change must be made, and, in our opinion, the publicity given to the intention of Mr Lloyd George makes reconstruction from within no longer possible. We therefore urge the Prime Minister to tender the resignation of the Government. If he feels unable to take that step, we authorize Mr Bonar Law to tender our resignations.'[30] Following the meeting, Curzon wrote to Lord Lansdowne, who had remained that Sunday at his Wiltshire estate, Bowood, stating that 'Had one felt that reconstruction by and under the present Prime Minister was possible, we should have all preferred to try it. But we know that with him as Chairman, either of the Cabinet or War Committee, it is absolutely impossible to win the War.'[31]

Asquith left Walmer Castle for London on Sunday morning, arriving at 2.30 p.m. at Downing Street where he had a late lunch with

Montagu, and they were joined by the Liberal grandee Lord Crewe. The Prime Minister then met with Bonar Law, who came directly from Pembroke Lodge armed with the letter of resignation on behalf of the Conservative members of the Cabinet. Asquith, at Bonar Law's suggestion, also sent for Lloyd George, who was at Walton Heath. Lloyd George drove back to London that afternoon with C. P. Scott, editor of the *Manchester Guardian*, who had been his guest for lunch. On the journey Lloyd George explained to Scott that 'he had decided not to go on, on the present footing which was hopeless . . . What was needed was a very small Committee, of say, three, with very large powers . . . He had pressed this view on the P.M. and at the same time offered his resignation.'[32]

Over three hours of negotiations that afternoon and evening, Asquith met with Lloyd George and Bonar Law both separately and together, and according to Bonar Law they 'thrashed out a scheme which met with [the Prime Minister's] approval'.[33] In the end, according to Lloyd George, he thought they had reached a 'complete understanding',[34] which Asquith agreed to put in writing, but did not do so until later on Monday. The agreement was based on the compromise Lloyd George proposed on 1 December, that he would run the new small war committee, but subject to the ultimate direction of the Prime Minister, should he choose to intervene. There had been no agreement as to the personnel of the committee, other than that Lloyd George would be the working Chairman. Bonham-Carter recalled that before leaving, Lloyd George suggested to Asquith that Carson and the Labour leader Arthur Henderson[35] should also be members.[36] Once again, the Prime Minister had used his political skills to slow events down, in the hope that cool heads would prevail as the days progressed. He certainly thought he had put the 'crisis' to bed that evening, writing to Pamela McKenna that it 'shows every sign of following its many predecessors to an early & unhonoured grave'.[37] That night an official statement also confirmed that the King had accepted the recommendation of the Prime Minister for a reconstruction of the government, 'with a view to the most active prosecution of the War'.[38] George V recorded in his diary, 'The Prime Minister came and told me about the Cabinet crisis, started by Lloyd George who wants to run the War Committee. The Government will have to be reconstructed. I told the Prime Minister that I had the fullest confidence in him.'[39] The King's sympathy was certainly with Asquith, and he thought Lloyd George was behaving like 'a blackmailer, whom it is better to tackle and have done with'.[40] It was a sentiment shared by Margot Asquith as well, who believed the crisis had stemmed ultimately from the Prime Minister's decision to bow to the pressure to make Lloyd George War Secretary. In her opinion, that 'was the <u>first time</u> that Henry gave way to <u>blackmail</u>'.[41]

After leaving Asquith at Downing Street, Lloyd George went to the War Office where he saw Lord Northcliffe at 7 p.m., for a meeting that years later he denied ever took place.[42,43] The fact that it did was recorded by Ruth Lee in her diary, whose husband Arthur was with Lloyd George at the War Office that evening, and then the two men returned to 2 Abbey Gardens to dine at 8.30 p.m. Ruth also noted that Lloyd George told them Asquith had agreed 'to a small War Council (on which *he* is not to sit) consisting of four members: L.G., B.L., Carson and Arthur Henderson.'[44] Tom Clarke also noted in his diary, that after seeing Lloyd George on Sunday evening, Northcliffe 'wrote a two-column article on the political crisis. The burden of it is that there must be a small War Council consisting of Lloyd George, Carson, Bonar Law and possibly Arthur Henderson. Asquith, the Prime Minister, is to be left "free to devote himself to other matters."'[45]

In his *War Memoirs* Lloyd George recalled of that Sunday evening, 'I had not communicated any information as to the negotiations which were going on with Mr. Asquith or the agreement arrived at with him, to the proprietor or editor of [*The Times*], either directly or indirectly.'[46] It seems doubtful, though, given his meeting with Northcliffe, that he hadn't communicated 'any' information to him. Lloyd George also used C. P. Scott as a messenger to Northcliffe, encouraging him to seek the press baron out after they'd driven back to London from Walton Heath that afternoon. Scott recorded in his diary, 'Ll.G. told me Northcliffe wanted to see me, so after leaving him I called at N.'s house. I doubt if N. had asked to see me, or any way, if he remembered doing so. He was interested in some things I told him – he did not know, e.g. whom [Lloyd George] designed for his War Committee.'[47] Northcliffe's brother, the Liberal politician Cecil Harmsworth,[48] also wrote in his journal for 3 December after visiting him that afternoon, 'Alfred has been actively at work with Ll.G. with a view to bringing a change.'[49]

Yet, there was also a big misunderstanding between Asquith and Lloyd George as to what they had actually agreed. Lord Crewe recalled joining Asquith, Montagu and Reading at 10 o'clock that Sunday night where the Prime Minister believed that an accommodation with Lloyd George had been reached, 'without sacrifice of his own position as chief of the War Committee', and that 'no compromise of principle' could be given on that point.[50] This view was also reflected in the briefing given to the Liberal *Daily News*, which forecast in its morning edition, 'the reconstruction involves not so much a change in personnel as a shifting of offices . . . These will be accompanied by some revision of the functions of the War Council . . . There is no split, and the wild rumours which were circulated by a certain section of the Press on Saturday and yesterday are without foundation.'[51] However, Geoffrey Dawson's leader column in *The Times* that morning, 4 December, blew any such illusions out of the water.

Under the headline, 'Reconstruction', Dawson wrote:

> The gist of [Lloyd George's] proposal is understood to be the establishment forthwith of a small War Council, fully charged with the supreme direction of the war. Of this Council Mr Asquith himself is not to be a member . . . Certain of Mr Asquith's colleagues are also excluded on the ground of temperament from a body which can only succeed if it is harmonious and decisive . . . Mr Lloyd George, to the best of our knowledge, took his stand entirely alone so far as his colleagues in the Cabinet are concerned – a fact which itself refutes the tales of intrigue.

In a separate accompanying article *The Times* also reported that 'It was Mr Lloyd George who brought matters to a head by a direct demand for reform, and there can be no doubt that he will play a large and perhaps controlling part in the drama of reconstruction.'[52] The report claimed that a new four-man War Committee would be created and that it had been 'suggested' by Lloyd George that the members would be himself, Bonar Law, Carson and the Labour leader Arthur Henderson.[53] The front page of another Northcliffe paper the *Daily Mirror* proclaimed Lloyd George was 'The Man the Nation Wants'.[54] *The Daily Telegraph* also reported that day, 'We are unable to think of any statesman now in power in any of the combatant countries whose withdrawal from office would have such an effect of discouragement upon associated nations as would be caused by that of [Lloyd George].'[55]

Dawson himself had been at a weekend party at Cliveden, the Berkshire estate of fellow Cabal member Waldorf Astor, where Lord Milner was also a guest. After returning to London on Sunday afternoon, he met with Sir Edward Carson at Printing House Square, the offices of *The Times*, where they discussed the political situation before Dawson filed his explosive leader column. In his personal memorandum on the 'Political Upheaval of December', Dawson stated that it had been written 'entirely by myself',[56] but clearly reflected the articles that had been circulating in the press over the weekend, his conversations with Milner and Carson, who Dawson knew was 'in close touch with L.G.', and Northcliffe's discussion with Lloyd George on the Sunday evening.[57]

In response, an enraged Prime Minister wrote to Lloyd George complaining that 'the first leading article in to-day's *Times*, showing the infinite possibilities for misunderstanding and misrepresentation of such an arrangement as we considered yesterday, made me at least doubtful as to its feasibility. Unless the impression is at once corrected that I am being relegated to the position of an irresponsible spectator of the War, I cannot go on.'[58] Asquith clearly blamed Lloyd George for the article and would not accept such a public humiliation. Lloyd George himself, however, was relaxed about the situation. At 12.30 p.m. C. P. Scott visited him at the War Office and recorded in his diary that Lloyd George 'Congratulated himself on "a very good press" that morning.'[59]

That evening Asquith received a delegation of the Liberal ministers including McKenna, Runciman, Harcourt, Samuel and Grey, and according to Samuel, the Prime Minister explained 'Lloyd George's proposals, which were in effect that the War Committee of the Cabinet should consist of Ll.G., Bonar Law, Carson and Henderson, that the P.M. should see its agenda before its meetings, have a veto on its decisions, and, whilst not usually attending its sittings have the right to be present when he wished. He asked me . . . whether I thought his acceptance would be an abdication of his position and be inconsistent with his responsibilities. I said I thought it would. The others were all of the same opinion.'[60] As Lord Crewe described in a memorandum of the crisis, Lloyd George's attitude towards Asquith at this moment appeared to be, 'In the words of Gambetta[61] – of whom Mr. Lloyd George may regard himself as in some respects the reincarnation – "il faut se soumettre ou se démettre" [submit or resign]."[62]

At the regular Monday night meeting of the Cabal, Carson was entrusted by the members with the task 'to keep L.G. firm'.[63] Carson also wrote to Bonar Law that day, reaffirming his support for Lloyd George. 'I am convinced after our talk last evening that no patchwork is possible . . . The only solution I can see is for the P.M. to resign and for L.G. to form a Government – a very small one. If the House won't support it, he should go to the country and we would know where we are.'[64] Lloyd George held firm and resigned the following morning, 5 December, stating in his letter to Asquith, 'I am fully conscious of the importance of preserving national unity . . . but unity without action is nothing but futile carnage, and I cannot be responsible for that. Vigour and vision are the supreme need at this hour.'[65] After Bonar Law read Asquith's final letter of rejection of the proposals, he resolved that he had 'no longer any choice, and that I must back Lloyd George'.[66]

The game was now up, but what followed was the intricate process of dismantling the Asquith premiership and creating a new coalition, where multiple options appeared both possible and plausible. Despite their reservations about Lloyd George, the Conservative Cabinet ministers met with Bonar Law and agreed they should resign from the government; most, though, wanted to hedge their bets and see who came out on top. Asquith, who had been closeted with McKenna, met again with the Liberal members of the Cabinet at 5 p.m. on 5 December, and agreed that the whole government should resign, wrongly hoping, as Christopher Addison, now Lloyd George's unofficial Chief Whip, recorded in his diary, that 'neither Bonar Law nor L.G. would be able to form a Government, and that Asquith would have to be sent for by the end of the week'.[67] Yet Montagu cautioned Asquith that evening, 'McKenna's loyalty to you is above suspicion but always unwise, because he hates Lloyd George . . . as much if not more than he likes you. He can only see one object to be achieved, to drive Lloyd George out of the Government . . . Far be it from me to underrate McKenna . . . but he has irritated the Allies and the City and quarrelled with his best advisors, and if you have to choose between Lloyd George and McKenna, there is little doubt as to whom you could best do without, whichever is the best character.'[68]

Nevertheless, Asquith saw the King to tender his resignation at 7 p.m. George V recorded in his diary, 'He said he had tried to arrange matters with Lloyd George about the War Committee all day, but was unable to, all his colleagues both Liberal & Unionist urged him to resign as it was the only solution to the difficulty. I fear it will cause a panic in the City & in America & will do harm to the Allies. It is a great blow to me & will I fear buck up the Germans.'[69] George V needn't have worried, as rather than causing 'panic' on the international exchanges, the news of Asquith's resignation caused the pound to rise and the German Mark to fall in value.[70]

At about 8 p.m. Addison received a message from the War Office, that Lloyd George wanted to see him there immediately. On arriving in his room, he also found Bonar Law and Carson, and was told that the King had just sent for Bonar Law in order to ask him to form a government. After a discussion, they agreed that Bonar Law should go and tell the King that he would try, and the four men would then reconvene at Carson's house, at 5 Eaton Place in Belgravia, at 10 p.m. As Bonar Law had his audience with the King, Lloyd George went to dine at F. E. Smith's house at 32 Grosvenor Gardens, where he joined a party that included Churchill and Max Aitken. After Lloyd George left to meet Carson and Bonar Law, the conversation turned to the prospect of the new government. Then Aitken recalled that:

> Thus I conveyed to [Churchill] the hint that Lloyd George had given me . . . 'The new Government will be very well disposed towards you. All your friends will be there. You will have a great field of common action with them.' Something in the very restraint of my language carried conviction to Churchill's mind . . . he blazed into righteous anger. I have never known him address his great friend . . . in any other way except 'Fred' or 'F.E.' [F. E. Smith]. On this occasion he said suddenly: 'Smith, this man knows that I am not to be included in the new Government.' With that Churchill walked out into the street carrying his coat and hat on his arm.[71]

At 10 p.m. at 5 Eaton Place, Addison recalled that 'We met accordingly, and, after half an hour's discussion, decided that it was wise, as a preliminary, that Bonar Law should offer Asquith a post in his Government, preferably the Lord Chancellorship. Bonar Law went straight away to

No. 10.' He returned to Carson's house an hour later with the news that Asquith had declined. Addison noted that 'In order that no stone should be left unturned to secure, if possible, the inclusion of both L.G. and Asquith, it was decided to suggest to the King that there should be a conference on Wednesday [6 December] with Asquith, Balfour, Bonar Law, L.G. and Henderson, and a further endeavour made to arrive at an adjustment.'[72] Over at Carmelite House that evening, Lord Northcliffe personally approved a front-page splash headline for the *Daily Mail* that read 'Bravo! Lloyd George'. He also instructed Tom Clarke to 'Get a smiling picture of Lloyd George and underneath it put the caption "Do It Now", and [next to it] get the worst possible picture of Asquith and label it "WAIT AND SEE."'[73]

The following morning Asquith met with Harry Burnham at 10 Downing Street and told him that he had declined the offer to serve in a Bonar Law government, because he thought the man had 'no courage'. He also added, 'I don't think things will follow that course today.'[74] The Buckingham Palace meeting was held at 3 p.m. in the 1844 Room,[75] a sumptuous chamber of gold and royal blue where successive monarchs had held conferences and received important guests. Over the next hour and a half, King George recorded in his diary, 'We discussed the possibility of forming a National Govt. It was agreed that Mr Asquith should inform Bonar Law if he would come under him, as soon as possible, if he would not do this, then Bonar Law would not become Prime Minister & I should then ask Lloyd George to form a Govt.'[76] Asquith agreed to go away and consult with his colleagues as to whether he could serve in the new government if he wasn't Prime Minister. However, following a meeting just 45 minutes later at 5.15 p.m. at 10 Downing Street, with his Liberal Cabinet ministers and Arthur Henderson, Asquith sent a final message of refusal. The consensus was, Samuel recorded, that even if a Bonar Law or Lloyd George administration was possible, the Liberal leader would retain greater influence outside of it, and that they 'should form a possible alternative Govt. which it was to the interest of the country to have'.[77] At 7 p.m., after receiving Bonar Law, the King 'sent for Lloyd George & asked him to form a government, which he said he would endeavour to do'.[78]

Lloyd George had been due to dine at 8 p.m. with Riddell and Burnham at Queen Anne's Gate, but instead arrived just over an hour late. The owner of the *Daily Telegraph* recalled that he 'was rather white in the face, and refused anything to eat [apart from a plate of soup] and would not drink champagne'. Lloyd George told them that he would 'go on at all costs, even if I have to form a cabinet out of permanent officials. In case of trouble I shall appeal to the country.'[79] Burnham replied that he thought Lloyd George had 'a good chance of winning', but warned, 'The worst thing you have got against you is that you are supposed to be a Northcliffe creature, and the *Daily Mail* will call this another *Daily Mail* victory.' Lloyd George acknowledged the problem, replying, 'You need not tell me that', and adding, 'As to Northcliffe I have never told him anything he has not betrayed me in. He is a man with great power and that is how he uses it. He always looks simply for the advantage he can get for one of his papers.' However, when Burnham suggested that Lloyd George should meet with Northcliffe the following day, he responded, 'I have not had communication with him purposely, although he has been several times trying to make it up during the last week.'[80] Riddell recalled of this conversation that Lloyd George had said that 'He had not seen [Northcliffe] for three months till Monday, or yesterday, I forget which.'[81] Whereas the truth was that he had met with Northcliffe on four separate occasions during those crucial days from 1 to 3 December. After an hour Lloyd George left to join Bonar Law, and on the way out Riddell wished him luck, to which he replied, 'I shall do my best. The belief of these fellows that I shall fail will be an additional incentive.'[82]

While the wheels of power turned, the dining clubs of Pall Mall were buzzing with political gossip. Geoffrey Dawson recalled, 'No doubt there was a strong impression that the end of it would be the return of Asquith. The Athenaeum . . . was full of this foolish notion.' After dinner Dawson also 'ran Carson to earth again in the Carlton Club and drove back with him to Whitehall. He told me . . . Asquith and his friends had been asked whether they would take any part in the new Government and, after taking time for consideration, had definitely declined. Lloyd George, Bonar Law, and Carson had thereupon held a meeting and had agreed that Lloyd George should be put forward to the King as Prime Minister.'[83]

Meanwhile at the Liberal, Reform Club,[84] Addison:

> . . . found the place humming with excitement. The Whips were very busy and foolishly very jubilant. Some of them came to me and

evidently, more in sorrow than in anger, seemed to sympathise with me, as they thought I was the only man who at that time had decided out and out to support L.G . . . The fact was that on the Monday, Kellaway, Glyn Jones and I had gone through the list of Members of Parliament which had been made in the summer-time when a crisis was threatened. We divided them into 'doubtfuls' and those whom we thought to be 'for' L.G. and I arranged for a small band of men to canvass round and report through Kellaway. By Wednesday evening it was certain that L.G. was going to get a good deal of support, and that a large number of Members would support him if he succeeded in forming a Government . . . I had a preliminary list of them in my pocket all the time that I was being sympathized with at the Club as the only Liberal follower L.G. had.[85]

By Addison's calculations, 126 Liberal MPs would support Lloyd George if he could form a government. More than enough, if he had the backing of the Conservatives as well.

Later that night, Lloyd George worked in his room at the War Office to secure the key positions in the administration, along with Bonar Law and Carson, and the men who would be the joint Chief Whips of the new government, Freddie Guest and Edmund Talbot.[86] Bonar Law, who would become Chancellor of the Exchequer, had been sent out to offer the position of Foreign Secretary to Arthur Balfour, while Lloyd George had been with Riddell and Burnham. Bonar Law found the former Prime Minister, who had been ill at home, sitting in a chair at the bottom of his bed and wearing a dressing gown. Balfour jumped up instantly on receiving the invitation and replied, 'Well if you hold a pistol to my head – I must accept.'[87] As Winston Churchill later observed of Balfour, 'He passed from one Cabinet to the other, from the Prime Minister who was his champion to the Prime Minister who had been his most severe critic, like a powerful graceful cat walking delicately and unsoiled across a rather muddy street.'[88]

On the morning of 7 December, Lloyd George held a meeting at the War Office with Arthur Henderson and representatives of the Labour Party and Trades Unions. Henderson was loyal to Asquith and had also suffered the loss of his son David[89] during the Battle of the Somme, on the same day that Raymond Asquith had been killed, and at a location just three miles apart. Circumstances now dictated a different approach, so as Henderson would tell a conference of Labour Party members the following month, he was 'not concerned with the methods by which the old government was terminated. What I am concerned with . . . is the most expeditious way we can adopt to bring the war to a final success.'[90]

During their meeting, Lloyd George was challenged by Henderson, Ramsay MacDonald,[91] Philip Snowden,[92] and the young leader of the dock workers' union, Ernest Bevin,[93] over the role for Labour in the new government. Lloyd George proposed to include Henderson in the new small War Cabinet, plus two other Cabinet positions for the Labour Party, heading a new Ministry for Labour and a Ministry for Pensions. In addition, shipping and coal mining would be brought under government control for the duration of the war. Following the meeting, the Labour representatives withdrew and the party's National Executive Committee (NEC) voted by 17 votes to 14 to combine with Lloyd George.[94] This was a decision that he thought 'vital' to the establishment of his new national government.[95] According to the interview given to Robert Donald by Ramsay MacDonald the following week, Lloyd George had been 'exceedingly amiable, but excessively indefinite. He was like a bit of mercury; when you thought you had caught him he darted off to something else.'[96]

That evening, Edward Carson was with Lloyd George at the War Office when the summons came for the 'Cottage Bred' Welshman to go back to Buckingham Palace to give his answer to the King. 'Go,' said Carson grimly, 'and take what is coming to you.'[97] At 7.30 p.m. Lloyd George arrived at the Palace and George V afterwards wrote in his diary that 'he informed me that he is able to form an administration & told me the proposed names of his colleagues. He will have a strong Government. I then appointed him Prime Minister.'[98]

Lloyd George remembered a particular moment from his childhood, Frances Stevenson recalled, of Uncle Lloyd at their cottage in Llanystumdwy, 'standing in front of the gate one day when he (D.) returned from school. Uncle Lloyd looked at him for a long time & then said: "I wonder what will become of this lad!"' Lloyd George now wrote to his brother William[99] asking him to 'Tell Uncle Lloyd that he is responsible for putting me in this awful job.' The old man responded with the words, 'The man is greater than the office he holds.'[100] Uncle Lloyd may have nurtured the instinct that was within the new Prime Minister, but the impulse to act was his own. Winston Churchill, during his 1945 eulogy to Lloyd George in the House of Commons, described how in December 1916 he had 'seized the main power in the State and the headship of the Government'. When MPs audibly questioned his description of those events, Churchill stated once again, 'Seized. I think it was Carlyle who said of Oliver Cromwell:[101] He coveted the place; perhaps the place was his.'[102,103] Yet what other description could there be. Lloyd George had initiated the political crisis, with the objective of taking over the leadership at least of the War Council, and if required the whole government. Through his cultivation of the press, the Cabal, and the personal investment in his relationships with Bonar Law and Balfour, he had made possible the creation of this new administration. Searching for a constitutional precedent for such a government, without an election, and where the Prime Minister was not even a member of the largest party within it, Lord Stamfordham was required to look back to the brief premiership of Lord Aberdeen,[104] over 60 years before. That government had lasted barely two years and was broken by its handling of the Crimean War. Now the fate of the nation rested on the authority of Lloyd George, and if the fortunes of war also turned against him, how long would this new multi-party government hang together?

SIX

Gentlemen and Players

At 4.10 p.m. on 19 December 1916, Lloyd George rose to address the House of Commons as Prime Minister. For the first time in 11 years, he wasn't sharing the front bench with Asquith. His former colleague was now directly across from him, in the place reserved on such occasions for the Leader of the Opposition. Lloyd George, in tones today more familiar with the rhetoric of Winston Churchill in May 1940, told Parliament:

> I appear before the House of Commons to-day, with the most terrible responsibility that can fall upon the shoulders of any living man, as the chief adviser of the Crown, in the most gigantic War in which the country has ever been engaged – a war upon the event of which its destiny depends . . . What is the urgent task in front of the Government? To complete and make even more effective the mobilisation of all our national resources, a mobilisation which has been going on since the commencement of the War, so as to enable the nation to bear the strain, however prolonged, and to march through to victory, however lengthy, and however exhausting may be the journey.[1,2]

However, the challenge came not just from Germany. From the first hours of his premiership, Max Aitken assessed, 'Lloyd George knew himself to be surrounded by political enemies, Liberals he had worsted and driven from office, Conservatives whom he could never hope to placate. A combination of ambitious generals willing to take over control of the Administration in association with political figures who were in opposition to Lloyd George's Ministry would certainly be able to turn him out in a crisis of the war.'[3]

For them, Lloyd George was only necessary as long as he was useful in the lonely task of being Prime Minister. Victory was his mission, and to achieve it Lloyd George would hold great power and responsibility. The new Foreign Secretary, Arthur Balfour, was forthright on the matter, stating, 'If he wants to be a dictator, let him be. If he thinks he can win the war, I am all for him having a try . . . I have no prejudices in favour of Lloyd George. I have opposed every political principle that he holds . . . but I think that he is the only man who can, at this moment, break down the barriers of red tape and see that the brains of the country are made use of.'[4] Austen Chamberlain, who had retained his position as Secretary of State for India, was more critical, writing to his sister Hilda on 14 December, 'I take no pleasure in a change which gives me a chief whom I profoundly distrust – no doubt a man of great energy but quite untrustworthy; who doesn't run crooked because he wants to but because he doesn't know how to run straight; who has tired the patience of every man who has worked with him . . . You will see that I am sick of being told how beautiful the new world is and how pleased I must be to live in it. Still I hope it will be a better world and for the time being at least I will twang my harp in my own little corner.'[5] However, his half-brother Neville[6] was more realistic, writing to their sister Ida on 9 December, 'I don't know what to say about Austen . . . Indeed I felt very doubtful whether he would remain until I saw that Balfour was in and then concluded A. would feel that he ought to do the same, although some time ago he said to me none of us would serve under Ll. George. But of course, circumstances alter cases.'[7]

In a 1939 BBC radio broadcast Lloyd George reflected on the creation of his new government that, 'I had for some time come to the conclusion that to entrust the direction of the war to a Sanhedrin[8] of some 20 ministers, chosen largely for party reasons and all engaged with the administration of departments which demanded their whole attention, was worse than worthless.'[9] Instead, there was now the long-promised small War Cabinet, where Lloyd George and Bonar Law were joined by the Cabal leader Lord Milner, as well as Arthur Henderson for Labour, and Lord Curzon, a necessary concession to those establishment

Conservatives who were agnostic about the leadership of the government, as long as they were in it. Edward Carson joined the wider Cabinet as First Lord of the Admiralty, and Lord Derby replaced Lloyd George as War Secretary. Lloyd George's colleague Christopher Addison was rewarded with his appointment as Minister of Munitions, one of the few Liberals in the senior ranks of the government, but as Max Aitken had predicted, there was no place for Churchill. Lloyd George told George Riddell, 'I am sorry for some of my friends. They would not have Winston at any price. Had I insisted, the new Ministry would have been wrecked. The same remark applies to Reading.'[10] Aitken himself had to be content with being raised to the peerage as Lord Beaverbrook.

Maurice Hankey ran the new secretariat for the War Cabinet, as such becoming the first ever Cabinet Secretary, a role in which, according to Lloyd George, 'He discharged his very delicate and difficult function with such care, tact and fairness that I cannot recall any dispute ever arising as to the accuracy of his Minutes or his reports on the action taken.'[11] He was assisted by his deputy, Thomas Jones, ensuring that agendas were prepared for meetings, minutes taken, and action points followed up. George Adams,[12] a political scientist from the University of Oxford who had previously worked at the Ministry of Munitions, was also appointed as Lloyd George's principal private secretary. Thomas Jones remembered that 'A large clerical staff was engaged at the Cabinet office to deal expeditiously with the typing, printing, indexing, and filing of papers. This was the secret of the speed with which Hankey could produce any minute or memorandum required.'[13] Many of them were accommodated, along with other policy experts, in temporary offices in the garden of 10 Downing Street that became known as the 'Garden Suburb'. In addition to this new secretariat, Frances Stevenson and J. T. Davies followed Lloyd George from the War Ministry to run his private office, and at Milner's suggestion, Philip Kerr[14] was appointed as an additional private secretary with expertise on foreign affairs. He had also been a protégé of Milner's from the Imperialist 'Round Table'[15] movement. There were roles as well for other members of the Cabal, including Waldorf Astor who had become Lloyd George's parliamentary private secretary, alongside David Davies, and Leo Amery who joined the War Cabinet secretariat, along with Cecil Harmsworth. In April 1917, F. S. Oliver was also appointed to the war propaganda department at the Foreign Office, working under its Director, John Buchan,[16] another member of 'Milner's Kindergarten' in South Africa.

On 8 January 1917, Amery wrote to the Australian Prime Minister Billy Hughes about the new arrangements:

> We have ... swept away altogether the old system ... of twenty-three gentlemen assembling without any purpose and without any idea of what they were going to talk about, and eventually dispersing for lunch without any idea of what they had really discussed or decided, and certainly without any recollection on either point three months later. Under the new system the Cabinet has a definite agenda; there are no speeches but only short, business-like discussions between four or five Cabinet Ministers and the Departmental Ministers of professional experts brought in for the discussion ... Lloyd George is of course wonderfully quick and active ... But it is invaluable having Milner, with his steadiness and strength of mind alongside him.[17]

Milner quickly established himself as the leading administrator in the War Cabinet, as Christopher Addison recalled:

> ... it is the custom to refer questions affecting big problems belonging to a number of Departments to individual members of the War Cabinet ... With a man of Milner's capacity it works excellently ... Henderson is really not his best at a job like this ... Curzon does his share but is very slow, and Bonar, of course, is full with House of Commons work and the Exchequer, so that there is really only Milner of good administrative capacity to do this kind of thing.[18]

Lloyd George's treatment of Arthur Lee, though, was a further reminder that intimacy with the Prime Minister was always on his terms. From that night when at the peak of the Cabinet crisis on 3 December Lloyd George had dined with Arthur and Ruth Lee at Abbey Gardens, he didn't see or speak to Arthur again until 8 February, when he was invited to breakfast at 10 Downing Street. In frustration at having heard no news either way from Lloyd George as the new government was being formed, Arthur wrote in desperation to him in late December confirming that 2 Abbey Gardens remained available for his use whenever he needed it, and also offering his seat in Parliament for any new minister from outside of politics that the Prime Minister wished to create. He received neither a reply nor an acknowledgement. In early January, Lee also suffered the indignity of being invited to a weekend party at Cliveden, where he recalled, 'Several of L.G.'s new staff were of the party and, whilst I delighted in their keenness and enthusiasm, I found rather trying their tendency to explain his personality, merits and even peculiarities, to me – not realising apparently how intimately I knew them already.'[19] At breakfast on 8 February, Lee was greeted by Lloyd George 'most effusively', almost as if the absence of the two friends was a consequence of Arthur's distraction rather than the Prime Minister's neglect. Their meeting, though, led to Lee being appointed as Director General of Food Production at the Board of Agriculture. Arthur recorded in his memoirs that 'I was also inspired by the belief that the problem was the one which, in L.G.'s opinion, was the most vital to the success of the Allied cause.'[20]

The new regime also brought challenges to Lloyd George's domestic arrangements, with his wife Margaret running 10 Downing Street upstairs, while his mistress Frances held sway in the offices in the garden and basement. As the wife of the Prime Minister, Margaret would also be a more present figure in Westminster, and in her absences the household affairs were managed by Sarah Jones,[21] the family's formidable Welsh housekeeper, who had previously been nanny to the Lloyd George children. During wartime, Thomas Jones recalled, 'It was not necessary to urge the hostess of No. 10 to give evidence of a simple democratic way of life – from first to last she knew no other, either at Criccieth or in London. There was never any discrimination between high and low at that warm Welsh hearth in the heart of the metropolis.'[22] Lord Riddell also recalled after dining at 10 Downing Street in April 1917 that 'So far as the food, service, and appointments were concerned, it looked as if a small suburban household were picnicking in Downing Street – the same simple food, the same little domestic servant, the same mixture of tea and dinner. And yet with all that, an air of simple dignity and distinction pervaded the room – no affection, no pretension, nothing mean, nothing ignoble.'[23]

Frances Stevenson believed that for Sarah Jones, who had never married, 'L.G. was her "child" over whom she watched, unselfishly, devoted to his welfare, and often incurring the displeasure of his family by her fearless words.' She was also sympathetic to his relationship with

Frances, who noted that 'L.G. could depend upon her help for looking after me when he wanted me in Downing Street.'[24] While primarily focused on his own needs, Lloyd George wasn't totally insensitive to Margaret's feelings. Frances recalled in her diary in January 1917, after a weekend away from Lloyd George who'd been with his wife and family at Walton Heath, 'D. said he would have sent for me, only that he felt it would not quite be playing the game with Mrs. Ll.G. "She is very tolerant," he said, "considering that she knows everything that is going on. It is not right to try her too far."'[25]

The new Downing Street operation, which transformed the building from a stately residence into the pulsing heart of government, was designed around Lloyd George's working style. Thomas Jones remembered that:

He 'was born fresh every morning'.[26] He arrived in the Cabinet room with his batteries fully charged, with ideas which he wished discussed and, brushing aside irrelevant secretarial programmes, he issued a whirl of lightning instructions. Waking early, he had read the official memoranda and telegrams in the red boxes at this bedside, and had devoured the newspapers of all colours. At breakfast began the innumerable interviews which filled his days, cross-examined Ministers, experts, friends, visitors from the Front or on missions from abroad. He had a retentive memory for essentials, though he was apt to be inaccurate in detail, and there was no limit to his curiosity within the field of politics and war.[27]

Observing the political crisis of December 1916, Regy Esher had written to Douglas Haig astutely informing him what the change of government would mean. '[Lloyd George's] only chance of success is to govern for a time as Cromwell governed. Otherwise Parliamentarianism (what a word!) will be the net in which his every effort will become entangled. It is of no use to make a *coup d'état* unless you are ready with the whiff of grapeshot. The organising of our resources is the objective of Lloyd Georgeism. If he gets the power into his hands and . . . sweeps away all the old instruments and abolishes red-tape . . . we shall come into our own. I cannot believe that he will have the courage to tell the truth to the nation. This of course, must be the first step. We shall see.'[28] However, Esher also noted in his journal, 'I do not like the outlook. This man will think he has a "mandate" to override military and naval opinion.'[29]

Haig's private secretary, Philip Sassoon, was back in Westminster as the new government was formed and sent a letter to the commander-in-chief advising, 'I think by now all the appointments and disappointments have been arranged . . . I think Derby's is a very good appointment. Northcliffe said, "That great jellyfish is at the War Office. One good thing is that he will do everything Sir Douglas Haig tells him to do"! I think the whole week has been satisfactory.'[30] Haig wrote to Sassoon as well, that he thought 'The new Govt. is splendid and should devote all its energies to mobilising the resources of the Empire as soon as possible but . . . it must leave to the General Staff and the Sailors the decision as to how & where to employ troops & ships to attain that end.'[31] Northcliffe would also be keeping a close eye on relations between Lloyd George and GHQ, and the day after the new Prime Minister took office, the press baron informed Sassoon that he had 'told the *Daily Mail* to telephone you every night at 8pm, whether I am in London or not'.[32] That was the exact time each evening that Haig left the office to dine in the officers' mess, and as such he would be conveniently unaware of anything that was discussed.

Haig was confident of his position; he had been promoted to the rank of Field Marshal on 1 January 1917, enjoyed the confidence of the King, and the public backing of Northcliffe's newspapers. Senior Conservatives like Curzon and Chamberlain had also made the retention of Haig a condition of their joining Lloyd George's new government. Yet, as far as the new Prime Minister was concerned, it was time for a change. In his *War Memoirs*, Lloyd George set the scene, as he saw it, for the military campaign of 1917: 'Our great commanders, having refused or neglected to organise a breakthrough where and when it was feasible, and having made ineffective attempts on fronts where such rupture was impossible, thereby throwing away myriads of valuable lives and losing inestimable time and opportunity, being unable to think out anything more original, had fallen back on attrition – always the game of the poor player.'[33] Over the two months from Christmas 1916 to late February 1917, Lloyd George sought to challenge the orthodoxy that the war could only be won on the Western Front. On 4 January he met in Paris with the French Premier Aristide Briand and the French Minister of Armaments, Albert Thomas,[34] and they travelled together to the Inter-Allied conference in Rome, where the campaign plan for 1917 would be discussed. From his perch at the Hôtel de Crillon, Regy Esher observed, 'Lloyd George is absolutely heterodox on the question of the Western Front. He has no faith in a decision here. His active intelligence keeps casting about for solutions. Will he find one? Yes! – he has got one. He rushes at it. Then suddenly he has another idea. He switches off the great solution on to the greater. And so on. Anyway he is tremendously alive.'[35] Esher also noted the interactions of the new Prime Minister with his French counterparts: 'Lloyd George admired as he is, appears to these Frenchmen only a brilliant demagogue and not a statesman. Perhaps they are wrong. I hope so.'[36]

In Rome, Lloyd George wanted to revisit the conclusions of the Paris Conference the previous November and make the case again for investing in alternative fronts where the enemy's position was weaker. As he recalled in his *War Memoirs*, 'With each campaign, the opportunities for trying the policy of attacking the enemy where he was most vulnerable became bricked up by the enemy, and had now narrowed down to the extreme east and to the Italian Front.'[37] This included Salonika, and a proposal from General Cadorna[38] for a joint Allied attack on the Austro-Italian front, with the objective of taking Trieste and the Istrian peninsula. Yet, once again Lloyd George was rebuffed in favour of the proposal from the new French commander-in-chief, Robert Nivelle,[39] for an offensive in the Aisne Valley to seize the high ground to the north, along the route known as the Chemin des Dames.[40] Nivelle was the man of the moment, who had led the French defence of Verdun the year before, including the recapture of Fort Douaumont, and scored some notable counter-offensive victories against the Germans in December. These successes had also attracted the favourable attention of Sir William Robertson, who briefed the War Cabinet that 'The French success shows once more what can be accomplished at little cost, even by comparatively small numbers, if the attack is thoroughly prepared and organised, and especially if measures are taken to ensure surprise.'[41] Nevertheless, Lloyd George felt let down by Briand and Thomas in Rome, for supporting their generals instead of his ideas: 'Their action was incomprehensible to those who knew their previous attitude. They both were and always had been zealous advocates of the "way around." They never believed in the policy of attrition.'[42] Lord Northcliffe's newspapers, however, were delighted at the triumph of the Western leaders at Rome, with *The Times* proclaiming, 'The decisive front . . . We must run no risks of dissipating our efforts.'[43]

The Gare du Nord railway station in Paris was one of the great meeting places of the war. There, as William Orpen,[44] one of the official war artists, observed, were to be found 'masses of humanity, mostly British officers and men, each with their little "movement order" . . . in the heart of the Gay City. Yet that little slip of paper would, in a couple of hours, send them to Amiens, and a little later they would be at the front suffering Hell.' Yet amidst 'the blackness, smoke, smell and crush',[45] General Nivelle seized the opportunity for a quiet word with Lloyd George. The Prime Minister was waiting to depart for the Channel coast, on the journey back to London from Rome. Nivelle boarded Lloyd George's carriage and tried to persuade him that his planned offensive would not be another Somme, and that he was not another Haig. His proposal was audacious, a massive, concentrated attack uphill in the Aisne Valley against well-fortified German defences. Yet if they could take the Chemin des Dames, they would have the high ground of that plateau and could then drive home their advantage. The French general was confident and articulate; and he spoke perfect English. Nivelle's proposal was for a 'rupture of the front', led by French forces, that would surprise the Germans and with 'a single stroke' break their line in 24 hours.[46]

Impressed, Lloyd George invited Nivelle to London on 15 January, to discuss his battleplan in more detail. According to Duff Cooper,[47] the future Conservative Cabinet minister and official biographer of Douglas Haig, Nivelle 'had much to recommend him to a statesman like Lloyd George, who had always had something of the rebel's contempt for the rules of precedence and something of the self-made man's admiration for self-confidence in others'.[48]

On the morning of their conference with Nivelle, Lloyd George met with Haig and Robertson in 10 Downing Street. From Frances Stevenson's diary record of the meeting, the Prime Minister was clearly looking for a fight, and he duly found one. He began by asking Haig about the request from Nivelle that the British should take over some of the French front line, so that they could build up their reserves to support the Aisne offensive:

> 'Oh,' Haig said, 'that had already been decided by Nivelle & myself: no further discussion is needed.' D. turned on him. 'That is a question,'

> he said swiftly, 'to be decided by the War Cabinet; and it will be discussed by the War Cabinet.' . . . D. then raised the question of officers. 'The French,' he said, 'have of course a much higher percentage of trained officers. What's our percentage?' 'Oh, that is not to the point,' said Haig. 'I wish to know,' insisted D., 'what percentage of trained officers we have! Is it ten per cent?' 'Well,' said Haig insolently, 'supposing it is ten per cent?' 'There is no supposing about it,' said D. turning on him angrily, 'I ask you for a definite statement. I have a right to know & I will know.'

Haig then agreed to supply the Prime Minister with the figures requested and proceeded to talk down the French army in general:

> Haig said, they had no infantry, he said: their officers were just fat tavern-keepers, no good at anything. 'Well, all I can say,' broke in D. sharply, 'is that with no infantry & fat tavern-keepers for officers they have taken more guns and more ground than the British with half the casualties. And in that case their generals must be wonderful men.'[49]

At 3.30 that afternoon they were joined by Nivelle and the French commanders, who wanted the British to take over 15 miles of their front-line trenches, which would require them to deploy another four divisions of men. This would take away the reserves Haig needed for his planned spring offensive to the north, against Ypres and the occupied Belgian ports. The War Cabinet was impressed with Nivelle and backed his proposal. Lloyd George told Frances Stevenson that evening, 'Nivelle has proved himself to be a Man at Verdun; & when you get a Man against one who has not proved himself, why, you back the Man!'[50]

Although Lloyd George had been persuaded to support another major battle on the Western Front, the Nivelle offensive created the opportunity for him to advance the idea of a unified command for the Allied armies. In his *War Memoirs* he observed, 'My experience of life has taught me that men and women are not moved so much by arguments as by hidden motives which are never exposed in the interchange of words. Once the undisclosed impulses or prejudices are overcome the task of the persuader becomes simpler. The road has then been cleared for reason.'[51] In this case, Lloyd George believed that the generals always supported their own battle plans rather than considering on which front it was most likely that the decisive blow could be landed. Nivelle didn't want to send men and materiel to Italy, if that meant he lost the opportunity to win the war that spring on the Western front. Haig was reluctant to support Nivelle, to the detriment of his own plans for a breakthrough on the Ypres Salient.[52] Lloyd George suspected that Haig would fail to give Nivelle all of the support he had requested, and so conspired with the French, without consulting Haig or Robertson, to effectively place Nivelle in supreme command.

According to Lloyd George the idea of a unified command 'was resisted so viciously by Haig and Robertson that the delays caused by the time spent allaying suspicions and adjusting differences destroyed the effectiveness of the [Nivelle] plan'.[53] The conference that would be held in Calais on 26 February to agree the final requirements and timings for the Nivelle offensive was in fact 12 days after, according to the original plan, the attack was supposed to have commenced. Two days before the Calais conference a meeting of the War Cabinet authorized Lloyd George to act in order to 'ensure unity of command both in the preparatory stages of and during the operations'.[54] Robertson was not at this meeting and the minutes were not circulated until after the Calais conference. However, the real nature of the War Cabinet's discussions that day were recorded by Lord Stamfordham, after a conversation with Curzon on 4 March. According to Stamfordham, the persuading arguments for the unity of command under Nivelle had been not just that the French had the larger army, and that the war was being conducted on their soil. They believed 'Independent opinion shows that without question the French Generals and Staffs are immeasurably superior to the British Generals and Staffs.' Furthermore, 'The War Cabinet did not consider Haig a clever man. Nivelle made a much greater impression on the members of the War Cabinet.'[55]

Lloyd George arrived in Calais before lunch on 26 February and went straight to meet with Aristide Briand. There it was agreed that during the conference, upon Lloyd George's prompting, Nivelle should raise concerns as to how operations were to be co-ordinated between his armies and Haig's. When the moment came, according to Haig's private secretary, Philip Sassoon, 'It soon became apparent that something was on the *tapis* [carpet] and Geddes and the Transport Officers were sent out of the room when Ll.G. enquired of Nivelle if he was satisfied with the arrangements with the British army.'[56,57] Hankey recorded in his diary that Lloyd George added, 'he hoped that [Nivelle] would feel no delicacy or reserve in expressing his full opinion'. Briand also chimed in that 'General Nivelle and Field-Marshal Sir Douglas Haig should speak their whole minds and state exactly what they considered was required to ensure complete co-operation and the best possible dispositions of our forces.' Put on the spot, a somewhat flustered Nivelle, unwilling to offer criticism in front of Haig, turned red and he 'beat around the bush' before finally stating that 'there must be certain rules' to 'guide the relations of the generals'.[58]

At that point Sassoon recalled 'Ll.G. getting impatient said, "Well before dinner please formulate your demands." There was only one hour before dinner but in the interval, printed memoranda were produced by Nivelle demanding that the whole British Army should be placed under his orders.'[59] During that time Lloyd George and Hankey met with Briand and Nivelle, where they shared the rules that had been secretly prepared by the French the week before. When Lloyd George asked Hankey what he thought, he recalled, 'It fairly took my breath away, as it practically demanded the placing of the British army under Nivelle; [and] the appointment of a British "Chief of Staff" to Nivelle; who had powers practically eliminating Haig . . . I showed no emotion and said I wanted time to consider it.'[60] Robertson's reaction, however, when he first heard of the proposals as he was finishing dinner that evening, was more explosive. According to the British liaison officer Edward Spears,[61] his 'face went the colour of mahogany, his eyes became perfectly round, his eyebrows slanted outwards like a forest of bayonets held at charge – in fact he showed every sign of having a fit. "Get 'Aig" he bellowed.'[62]

Both Haig and Robertson quickly beat a path to Lloyd George's door. The commander-in-chief told the Prime Minister, 'Tommies[63] wouldn't stand being under a Frenchman', to which Lloyd George, standing his ground, replied, 'Well, Field-Marshal, I know the private soldier very well. He speaks very freely to me, and there are people he criticises a good deal more strongly than General Nivelle.'[64] When Haig retired for the evening he recorded in his diary, 'And so we went to bed, thoroughly disgusted with our Government and the Politicians.'[65] That night, though, Hankey prepared a face-saving compromise, which proved the following morning to be acceptable to all. Haig would only be subordinate to Nivelle for the duration of the planned offensive, and in relation to it. He would remain free to plan his own initiatives and could appeal against requests from the French High Command. Nevertheless, Lloyd George left Calais believing he had scored a tactical victory over his generals, and they were left smarting from the experience. Robertson wrote to Haig of Lloyd George, 'I can't believe that a man such as he can remain for long head of any Government. Surely *some* honesty and truth are required.'[66]

Almost immediately, Haig took exception to the demands of Nivelle, and his request that General Sir Henry Wilson act as the chief liaison officer between their commands. On 28 February, Haig wrote to Robertson complaining, 'this is the type of letter which no gentleman could have drafted . . . I intend to send a copy of the letter to the War Committee with a request to be told whether it is their wishes that the Commander-in-Chief of this British Army should be subjected to such treatment by a junior *foreign* commander.'[67]

On 2 March, Haig also wrote privately to his ally in the War Cabinet, Lord Curzon, thanking him for his assurances that he 'still possess the confidence of the War Cabinet', and complaining that this 'should be made known to the French government and to General Nivelle, because proceedings at Calais did much to shatter such opinion'. Haig also warned that 'there can never be any idea entertained even, much less give effect to, of putting the British army under a French Commander in Chief . . . I told Mr Lloyd George that to attempt to give effect to such an organisation would be madness.'[68] Yet there was no outright dissent from the War Cabinet. Hankey recalled after debriefing Bonar Law back in London, that while he didn't much care for the arrangements agreed in Calais, 'he regarded Ll. George as dictator, and meant to give him his chance'.[69]

Buckingham Palace was different terrain altogether, where general distrust of Lloyd George reigned. According to his son Edward, Prince of Wales,[70] the King 'disliked [Lloyd George] . . . But he did like Asquith – a great intellectual . . . 100% Liberal but not the reformer L.G. wanted to be . . . [Asquith] was exceedingly tactful, and handled my father in a tactful and clever manner . . . L.G. . . . [had] amazing charm, even if he was a scamp.'[71] When Lloyd George was appointed War Secretary in 1916, Hankey recalled being at a meeting where the King launched into 'a most violent diatribe against him'.[72] The King also felt slighted by Lloyd George's new system, whereby instead of receiving a weekly handwritten bulletin from his Prime Minister, he now had to be content with a typed copy of the Cabinet minutes, when 10 Downing Street remembered to send them to him. Lloyd George maintained, though, the tradition of regular audiences with the King, including travelling to meet him at his Norfolk estate at Sandringham on 10 January, to debrief him on the Inter-Allied conference in Rome. On that occasion they met at York Cottage, where George V had lived with his family since 1893, rather than in the main house. It was a large villa by a small lake, filled with bulky furniture in cramped rooms, and despite the name, was far grander than the humble four-room dwelling that had been Lloyd George's childhood home. Yet it provided a simpler life than many would have expected for the head of the British Empire, and according to the Prince of Wales, Sandringham represented his father's 'private war with the twentieth century'.[73]

Douglas Haig was quick to exploit his friendship with the King in the days following the Calais conference. He delivered to a 'furious'[74] George V the worst possible interpretation of the meeting and the King also recorded in his diary for 1 March, 'Had a long talk with Sir W Robertson, the P.M. makes things very difficult for him.' The following day he noted that the War Secretary, 'Eddy Derby came & I discussed with him various matters connected with the Army & the P.M. I am very worried about it all.'[75] General Rawlinson[76] also recalled a meeting on 12 March with an hysterical Clive Wigram,[77] the King's assistant private secretary, who told him that 'L.G.'s reason . . . is based on his ultimate intention of breaking up the Monarchy and introducing a republic with himself at the head and that he foresees the loyal adherence of the Army to the Monarch is his chief obstacle – For this reason he desires to weaken it by breaking it up and distributing it amongst the French Armies.'[78] This strength of feeling was no doubt shaped by the poor relations between Lloyd George's personal advisors and the King's. Bonar Law's private secretary J. C. C. Davidson recalled that 'Lord Stamfordham, Clive Wigram and other members of the Palace staff were treated like dirt by William 'Bronco Bill' Sutherland[79] and J. T. Davies. They did not even get up from their chairs when Stamfordham . . . came into the room . . . Lloyd George was a republican, and not a monarchist, at heart. He was a demagogue, very radical, and he disliked any show of pomp and dignity on the part of the Crown and its servants.'[80]

On 12 March the King had also held a heated audience with the Prime Minister, where he told him that he 'objected to being in ignorance of matters affecting the welfare of the Army', and that the 'whole army' was certain to 'strongly resent' being placed 'under the command of a foreign General'. He added that if this state of affairs 'were known in the Country it would be equally condemned'. To this Lloyd George told the King, 'in the event of any such public expression of feeling, he would go to the country and would explain matters and very soon have the whole Country on his side'.[81] Frances Stevenson recalled in her diary Lloyd George's recollection of his disagreement with the King, and that he'd told George V, 'The most important thing seems to me that the lives of our gallant soldiers should not be squandered as they were last summer, but that they should be used to the best advantage. It seems to me that General Haig's prestige is a very minor consideration compared with this!'[82] Nevertheless, Lloyd George did make some concessions in favour of Haig and Robertson, in particular providing assurances that there would be no amalgamation of the French and British armies, and that while General Wilson would be the British liaison officer at Nivelle's headquarters, he'd also report directly to Haig. Yet even if Bonar Law was content for Lloyd George to become a 'dictator', there were also limits to the support of the War Cabinet. Haig's lobbying of Curzon had a practical effect when at the meeting on 9 March, they required that Lloyd George demonstrate his 'full confidence' in Haig as the British commander at his next conference with the French.[83] The Prime Minister might have been able to clip Haig's wings, but he couldn't replace him, or be responsible for his resignation. Neville Lytton,[84] the head of Haig's press staff, remembered a conversation with Lord Northcliffe in February 1917 where the press baron told him, 'The little man [i.e. Lloyd George] came to see me some weeks ago and told me that he would like to get rid of Haig, but that he could not do so as he was too popular. He made the proposition to me that I should attack him in my group of newspapers and so render him unpopular enough to be dealt with. "You kill him and I will bury him." Those were his very words.'[85] Northcliffe, though, remained loyal to Haig and his staff officers. On 14 March the War Cabinet further agreed that should the Nivelle offensive fail, then Haig could continue with plans for his northern offensive in Flanders for later in the year.

With his view from Paris, the éminence grise Regy Esher wrote to Lord Stamfordham:

> The fact is that Lloyd George and some others are labouring under illusions as regards the French leading. They believe Nivelle to be Napoleon, whereas here the man in the street knows that he is a good average soldier, but does not believe him the superior in any way of Micheler[86] or Pétain,[87] and do not compare him to Castelnau[88] or Foch . . . Whether Lloyd George or the Frenchman in the street is right remains to be seen. No one here would wink an eyelid or show any surprise if Nivelle were superseded in four months' time by Micheler. You can therefore imagine the stupefaction of soldiers, French soldiers, when they find the English Ministers proposing to hand over two million British soldiers to the command of Nivelle. The idea is naturally not unwelcome, as immediately there become obvious all sorts of advantages present and future. Still, you cannot help the French sceptical mind from enquiring whether Lloyd George is aiming at popularity here even greater than he already possess (and it is enormous) and what 'M. Lloyd George fera quand il sera Roi de France [what Mr Lloyd George will do when he is King of France].'[89]

SEVEN

The Valley of the Shadow of Death

With Lloyd George on board, the *Irish Mail* train[1] left Euston Station in London and raced through the night of 2 March 1917, headed for north Wales. At 2 a.m. it made a special stop at Bangor, where the Prime Minister was met by the motorcar of his friend Sir Thomas Roberts[2] and driven to the Carnarvon home of his brother William George. From there they made the journey together to Criccieth to complete their solemn duty. In the midst of his battle with the generals, the Prime Minister was also concerned by the bulletins he had been receiving from home. When Lloyd George had returned to London from the Calais conference, he finally received the news he'd been dreading for the past few weeks. On the evening of 28 February his 82-year-old uncle, Richard Lloyd, had died. Frances Stevenson feared that when the news came, Lloyd George would be 'very upset',[3] and that he 'often says that he owes everything to him & that it is he who has kept him up to the mark during the whole of his career, writing him every day a letter of encouragement'.[4] In 1910, after Lloyd George's 'People's Budget' had finally been passed by the House of Lords, he sent a bound copy of the Finance Act to his uncle, inscribed 'To the real author of this budget with his pupil's affectionate gratitude'.[5]

The old man's health had been failing fast since the turn of the year, due to the bowel cancer that would ultimately take his life. Frances recalled that the family had 'begged him to try & keep his strength & pull himself together, for Dai's[6] sake'.[7] On 11 February, after 50 years of service, Richard Lloyd had preached what was to be his last sermon at the Chapel of the Disciples of Christ in Criccieth, taking as his inspiration Psalm 23: 'The Lord is my shepherd'. The significance of the lines, 'Yea, though I walk through the valley of the shadow of death I will fear no evil, for thou art with me; thy rod and thy staff they comfort me', would not have been lost on that small congregation.[8] At 11 a.m. on 3 March, a dark, damp day when the mist from the mountains shrouded the town and obscured the grey waters of Cardigan Bay, a simple funeral service was held at the family home in Criccieth. Afterwards, Lloyd George followed the hearse on foot, bareheaded in the rain with wind ruffling his hair. He was accompanied by his brother, and eldest son Richard, along the 300-yard route to the town's cemetery. When the casket was lowered into the ground, the booming of the sea was the only gun salute, as Lloyd George's uncle took his rest alongside the grave of his sister Elizabeth,[9] Lloyd George's mother. One onlooker observed, 'The whole attendance at the cemetery was not above a hundred people, and so simple was the ceremony that a stranger, coming on it unawares, would have missed its real significance. It was the very keynote of democracy. Here was the most highly placed man in the world's greatest Empire burying his foster-father and uncle, the village cobbler.'[10]

In the parlour of the cottage in Llanystumdwy where Lloyd George grew up, his uncle had created a schoolroom where his nephews could study. It was there he taught them the foreign languages they would need for their law examinations, and which the old man had only just learnt himself for the purpose of educating the boys. On the walls of that room were two portraits, one of their father William George,[11] and the other of Abraham Lincoln. The former American President had been a hero to Richard Lloyd, as he was to many people in Wales, where anti-slavery feelings had been very strong, particularly amongst the non-conformist communities. In 1853 the American abolitionist novel, *Uncle Tom's Cabin*, had become the first novel ever to be translated into Welsh.[12] For Lloyd George too, Lincoln was one of the past leaders that he most admired, recognizing that he was also a cottage-bred man, turned country lawyer, who was called to lead his nation in a war for its very existence.

Just over two weeks before his uncle died, Lloyd George had written a Lincoln Day[13] message for the American people, which was published in the *New York Times* on 12 February 1917. Lloyd George wanted the United States to join Britain and France in a great democratic front against militarism. When the Cunard liner the *Lusitania* was sunk by a German submarine in May 1915, leading to the deaths of 128 Americans including the theatrical impresario Charles Frohman and the enormously wealthy Alfred Gwynne Vanderbilt, Lloyd George's friend the former President Theodore Roosevelt wrote that 'Unless we act with immediate decision and vigour we shall have failed in the duty demanded by humanity at large, and demanded even more clearly by the self-respect of the American Republic . . . For many months our Government has preserved between right and wrong a neutrality which would have excited the emulous admiration of Pontius Pilate, the arch-typical neutral of all time.'[14] He also considered that 'If Lincoln had acted after the firing of Sumter[15] in the way that Wilson did about the sinking of the Lusitania, in one month the North would have been saying they were so glad he kept them out of the war.'[16]

Unfortunately, President Wilson believed serendipity would bring a peaceful solution to the crisis in Europe, and successfully sought re-election in November 1916, as the man who had kept America out of the war. Lloyd George hoped that Roosevelt would stand again for the Presidency and seek a then unprecedented third term in office, but in a letter to Arthur Lee, which he asked to be shared with Lloyd George, Roosevelt advised, 'I don't believe there is any chance of my being nominated . . . unless the country was in heroic mood. If they put "Safety First" ahead of honour and duty, then they don't want me.'[17] On 1 November, six days before the presidential election, Lloyd George had also confided in Harry Burnham that 'he was anxious that Mr Hughes[18] should win . . . because he thought that it would make a great difference in the moral attitude of America. Hughes represented the Eastern interests of capitalist companies, many of them engaged in munition work and transport, and, bound to be favourable to the Allies.'[19]

Yet the events of early 1917 would shake Wilson's conviction for peace at any price, when on 1 February, Germany declared unrestricted submarine warfare on all shipping in the Atlantic Ocean. The Royal Navy also decoded a secret German message to the government of Mexico, offering support should they declare war on the United States. Against this background Lloyd George wrote in the *New York Times* on Lincoln Day:

> The American people under Lincoln fought not a war of conquest, but a war of liberation. We today are fighting not a war of conquest,

but a war of liberation – a liberation not of ourselves alone, but of all the world, from that body of barbarous doctrine and inhuman practice, which has estranged nations, has held back the unity and progress of the world, and which has stood revealed in all its deadly iniquity in the course of this war . . . Through all the carnage and suffering and conflicting motives of the civil war, Lincoln held steadfastly to the belief that it was the freedom of the people to govern themselves which was the fundamental issue at stake. So do we today . . . the German people, too, will find that in losing their dream of an Empire over others, they have found self-government for themselves.[20]

In his first parliamentary speech as Prime Minister, Lloyd George had told the House of Commons, 'our fight is not a selfish one, and that it is not merely a European quarrel, but that there are great world issues involved'. This argument was not just directed at the United States, but also to bind closer to the war leadership the Empire dominions of Australia, Canada, South Africa and New Zealand, as well as the government of India, who collectively had already provided one million fighting men towards the effort. In the same speech Lloyd George declared:

. . . the time has come when the Dominions ought to be more formally consulted as to the progress and course of the War, as to the steps that ought to be taken to secure victory, and as to the best methods of garnering in the fruits of their efforts as well as of our own. We propose, therefore, at an early date to summon an Imperial Conference, to place the whole position before the Dominions, and to take counsel with them as to what further action they and we can take together in order to achieve an early and complete triumph for the ideals they and we have so superbly fought for.[21]

In January 1917, in an exclusive interview for Keith Murdoch's Australian United Cable Service, Lloyd George gave a further explanation of his intentions for the Imperial War Council:

The people of the Dominions know that I am not a jingo. My record contains no journeys into flamboyant Imperialism. Yet I regard this

Council as marking the beginning of a new epoch in the history of the Empire ... Of this I am certain: the peoples of the Empire will have found a unity in the war such as never existed before it – a unity not only in history but of purpose ... The terms of the peace will be only a beginning. After they are satisfactorily arranged, we shall have to set to work to build up that ordered freedom and fraternity which is the only security for human peace and progress, and which militarism has destroyed.[22]

When the Council first met in London on 20 March 1917, Lloyd George addressed the assembled leaders, using language similar to his Lincoln Day appeal to the American people, that amongst the war aims of the Allies must be 'the democratisation of Europe. It is the only sure guarantee of peaceful progress.' He also claimed that 'with all its faults, the British Empire is the truest representative of freedom – in the spirit even more than the letter of its institutions'.[23] Lloyd George, it would seem, could appreciate the importance of that caveat to the millions of His Majesty's imperial subjects who lived without democratic government. The Council would also bring Lloyd George into contact with the South African Minister for Finance and Defence, Jan Christian Smuts,[24] who became not only an important ally but the only representative of the Empire to become a full member of the War Cabinet. Lloyd George was at once impressed with Smuts's 'rare gifts of mind and heart', which 'were strengthening elements in this hour of savage temper and pitiless carnage', and believed he possessed 'that fine combination of intellect and human sympathy which constitutes the understanding of man'.[25] For his part, Smuts found that 'Lloyd George is more than fascinating. He has genius. His mind is brilliant, energetic, resourceful, and courageous without limit ... History will show him the biggest Englishman of them all.'[26] Smuts's son noted in his biography of his father that 'it was not until 1943 that he was prepared to put Mr. Churchill on an equal footing with the Welshman'.[27]

The Imperial War Council was held five days after the abdication of Tsar Nicholas II[28] of Russia on 15 March 1917, in favour of a Provisional Government intent on holding elections to a Constituent Assembly. Lloyd George seized on this event to further strengthen his case that the war had become a struggle for democracy against militarism. In optimistic terms he told the Imperial Council that 'The democratisation of Europe has come nearer within the last few days. In fact, if there is wisdom amongst the democratic rulers of Russia, not merely will Russia become a great democratic State, but Germany must follow her example inevitably.'[29] The following day, 21 March, he also wrote to Prince Lvov,[30] head of the Russian Provisional Government, that 'the revolution whereby the Russian people have placed their destinies on the sure foundation of freedom is the greatest service which they have yet made to the cause for which the Allied peoples have been fighting since August 1914. It reveals the fundamental truth that this is at bottom a struggle for Popular Government as well as for liberty.'[31]

The Times declared of the revolutionaries in Russia that 'All lovers of liberty must sympathise with them and wish them success.'[32] C. P. Scott also thought it a 'wonderful and glorious event',[33] and cabled his congratulations on behalf of the *Manchester Guardian* to the President of the Russian Parliament. On 28 March, King George V hosted a lunch for members of the Imperial War Conference at Buckingham Palace, and two days later Lord Stamfordham wrote to the Foreign Secretary, Arthur Balfour, raising concerns as to whether, on reflection, Britain should accept the request from the Provisional Government in Russia to provide sanctuary for the Tsar and his family, who were also closely related to the British Royal Family.[34] Stamfordham observed, 'His Majesty cannot help doubting not only on account of the dangers of the voyage, but on general grounds of expediency, whether it is advisable that the Imperial Family should take up their residence in the country.'[35] On 5 April the London evening newspaper, *The Globe*, owned by Lord Beaverbrook, published an editorial entitled 'A Respectful Protest', which argued against granting asylum to the Russian royals. In particular, it protested that Empress Alexandra[36] was 'a German Princess' who had 'wrecked the dynasty of the Romanoffs by attempts to betray the country of her adoption to the country of her birth'. There had been rumours in St Petersburg that Alexandra had tried to arrange a dishonourable peace with her German cousins. *The Globe* then added that 'The English people will not endure that she shall be given refuge in England, from which to resume her dangerous activities . . . We speak plainly because we must, and because the danger is great and imminent. The British Throne itself would be imperilled if this thing were done.'[37] The following day Stamfordham wrote again to Balfour, that the King 'must beg you to represent to the

Prime Minister that from all he hears and reads in the press, the residence in this country of the ex-Emperor and Empress would be strongly resented by the public, and would undoubtedly compromise the position of the King and Queen . . . Buchanan[38] ought to be instructed to tell Milyukov[39] that the opposition to the Emperor and Empress coming here is so strong that we must be allowed to withdraw from the consent previously given to the Russian government's proposal.'[40] The invitation was effectively withdrawn on 10 April and while that final decision rested with the King, it suited Lloyd George as well. His rhetoric about the triumph of democracy over autocracy might have sounded a little hollow, if the Imperial Russian Royal Family were also lodging rent free in the Surrey countryside.[41]

On Friday 6 April 1917 the United States of America formally declared war on Germany, and in his address to the Congress, President Woodrow Wilson declared, in terms echoing the sentiments expressed by Lloyd George in his Lincoln Day article, 'We are glad, now that we see the facts with no veil of false pretence about them, to fight thus for the ultimate peace of the world and for the liberation of its peoples, the German peoples included; for the rights of nations, great and small, and the privilege of men everywhere to choose their way of life and of obedience. The world must be made safe for democracy.'[42] Ten days later, Lloyd George joined Ambassador Walter Hines Page at the American Luncheon Club at the Savoy Hotel in London. In the opulent splendour of the Lancaster Ballroom, Lloyd George, standing beneath the entwined flags of Great Britain and the United States, gave a rallying speech to the 500 guests. He told them:

> I am in the happy position, I think, of being the first British Minister of the Crown who, speaking on behalf of the people of this country, can salute the American nation as comrades in arms [*Cheers*]. I am glad. I am proud. I am glad not merely because of the stupendous resources which this great nation can bring to the success of the Alliance, but I rejoice as a Democrat.

Then, referring to the recent success of the Canadian forces at the Battle of Vimy Ridge between 9 and 12 April, he said, 'it was written of those gallant men that they attacked with the dawn. Fitting work for the dawn to drive out of forty miles of French soil those miscreants who had defiled it for nearly three years. They attacked with the dawn. It is a significant phrase.' As Uncle Lloyd had no doubt taught him, the phrase was used in the Old Testament Book of Samuel[43] to describe David's victorious attack against an invading army. Lloyd George continued:

> ... the freeing of Russia from the oppression which has covered it like a cloud for so long, the great declaration of President Wilson [Cheers], coming with the might of the great nation he represents in the struggle for liberty, are heralds of dawn. 'They attacked with the dawn', and those men are marching forward in the full radiance of that dawn, and soon Frenchmen and Americans, British, Italians, and Russians, yea, Serbians, Belgians, Montenegrins, and Rumanians will march into the full light of perfect day [Loud cheers].[44]

A reporter from the Daily News who attended the lunch observed 'Youth was everywhere – in faces, in speeches, in each scrap of racy casual table talk. An incubus of doubt had lifted. Even through the tobacco smoke America's clear young eyes shone with that utter faith in a just cause which is the assurance of victory.' It was further noted that Lloyd George's speech was 'democratic in tone, eloquent in terms, and fervid in delivery . . . It had a magnificent reception.'[45] That lunch had effectively become the wedding breakfast for what would later be known as the 'special relationship'[46] between the United States and the United Kingdom, and the organizing idea in international affairs for much of the rest of the twentieth century; that America and Britain were and should be brothers in arms, as the defenders of freedom against tyranny. Yet the fervent hopes of that afternoon, much like those of the cheering crowds of August 1914, had more false dawns to face.

Four days after the conclusion of the Battle of Vimy Ridge, on 16 April,[47] the long-anticipated Nivelle offensive began in earnest. The Battle of Vimy Ridge, which Lloyd George had spoken of in his speech, had been one of the pre-planned diversionary attacks from the British Empire forces, which saw Canadian success against the Germans. This was an early phase of what became the Battle of Arras (9 April–16 May), where despite making some significant advances, the British were ultimately unable to break the German lines. Lloyd George's reference to the Germans being driven 'out of forty miles of French soil' was actually a tactical withdrawal to the pre-prepared defensive fortifications, which became known as the Hindenburg Line.[48] In their wake the Germans had left a wasteland full of booby-traps, where every building had been demolished, every water well poisoned and bridge destroyed. While the Allies had delayed, the Germans had reorganized and withdrawn from most of the vulnerable defensive positions Nivelle had intended to attack, with the exception of the trenches along the Chemin des Dames, which they had reinforced. In addition to arguments between the British and French commanders about logistics and supplies, the early spring weather had been appalling, and in trench raids the Germans had captured documents that gave them a good idea of exactly when and where the new offensive would occur. In Lloyd George's *War Memoirs* he even suggests there may have been treacherous motives behind the loss of these documents, so unlikely was it that such sensitive material should have been found in the front line. All of this had led to a growing lack of confidence in Nivelle's plans.

On 15 March the French Minister of War, General Lyautey,[49] had resigned after an incident at the French National Assembly where during a presentation on military strategy, he was shouted down by Socialist parliamentarians, angry about the heavy losses at the front. According to Edward Spears, he responded in kind, directing 'at the gesticulating mob three words which the official stenographers did not take down, very military words which described exactly what he thought of his audience'.[50] Lyautey's departure then brought on a political crisis that resulted in Aristide Briand's resignation as Prime Minister on 19 March. He was succeeded by his 75-year-old Finance Minister, Alexandre Ribot,[51] with Paul Painlevé[52] becoming the new Minister of War. Painlevé was, as Lloyd George observed, 'a man of high intelligence and considerable charm', but he 'was something of the academician in politics, and war is the most cunning of all pursuits'.[53] Ribot and Painlevé were also sceptical about Nivelle and preferred the more cautious Philippe Pétain as commander-in-chief of the French forces. Pétain had also warned them that he thought Nivelle's planned offensive would only lead to slaughter.

General Sir Henry Wilson, now in post at French GHQ as the British Chief Liaison Officer, recalled in his diary an important meeting on 6 April between the military and political leaders of France, held at Compiègne on board the train of the President of the Republic, Raymond Poincaré.[54] 'I hear that the Government, aided by Pétain, wanted to force

Nivelle to abandon his great offensive, and have a small one instead. Nivelle stood firm and won.'[55] It was a moment where, as Winston Churchill recalled in *The World Crisis*, 'Nivelle was actively planning the most ambitious offensive ever undertaken by the French; and Painlevé was the Minister who had to take responsibility before Parliament . . . Had Painlevé acted upon his convictions, which in this case were proved right, he would have dismissed Nivelle . . . But practical difficulties and many valid considerations dissuaded him . . . He temporized. He made the best of the situation as he found it. He bowed – who in great position has not had to do so? – before the day-to-day force and logic of circumstances, before the sullen drift of events.'[56]

On 17 April, Wilson recorded in his diary, 'the great attack has been a failure. Of course, all this will greatly shake confidence in Nivelle, and my opinion is that unless the Fourth and Fifth Armies pull off a real success Nivelle will fall and that we shall have Pétain here. Painlevé will certainly aim towards that . . . Foch was clear that Nivelle was done.'[57] Wilson visited Haig at GHQ in Montreuil on 19 April and noted, 'I told him that my feeling was that Lloyd George and Painlevé were determined to take a more active command of the major operations of the war, and that Painlevé was determined to get rid of Nivelle, and so replace him with Pétain, whose mental attitude was to sit and do nothing and wait for the Americans.'[58] Regy Esher also wrote to Lord Derby from Paris, that the political and military crises in France had acted to strengthen the position of Lloyd George as the leading statesman of the Allied cause: 'If Lloyd George would recognise his phenomenal influence and almost uncanny position he holds in France he would cease to think of Albert Thomas or Nivelle or Ribot or indeed any of these French politicians or soldiers super-anything, and would fix his attention solely on the French people. They are the most intelligent people in the world, and it is one of the signs of their cuteness that they have contrasted so favourably Lloyd George's (1) desire to win the war and (2) capacity to get things done, with the extraordinary lack of similar qualities in French politicians . . . Get the War Council firmly and decisively and promptly to take command of the French.'[59]

Lloyd George recalled in his *War Memoirs* that 'A fortnight after the Nivelle attack there was a perceptible slackening in the French offensive.'[60] The War Cabinet met on 1 May and agreed that they should 'press the French to continue their offensive', and failing that, 'insist on our entire freedom of action and on the French army to re-occupy the trenches recently taken over by the British forces'.[61] On the morning of 4 May, Lloyd George arrived in Paris, with the encouragement of Haig, in order, as Hankey described it, to 'ginger-up the French'.[62] Hankey noted, 'Ll. G.'s methods much amuse me. Scarcely had he set foot in Paris than his scouts were out to try and pick up all the political gossip, particularly with regard to the status of the principal ministers . . . His scouts included Col. David Davies, Mantoux[63] the interpreter, Lord Esher and others.'[64] Before Lloyd George's arrival, however, Esher had warned him of the mood in Paris, that 'There is a general *malaise* or ferment of uneasiness here among the people, the shopkeepers, and in the faubourgs. They are so intelligent and well-informed that they realise perfectly the failure of their offensive.'[65]

That afternoon, at the conference at the French Foreign Ministry on the Quai d'Orsay, Lloyd George urged his French counterparts that 'We must go on hitting and hitting with all our strength until the German ended, as he always did, by cracking.'[66] During a break in the talks he was confronted in the corridor by Philippe Pétain, now Chief of Staff to the French army, who seemed 'strangely reserved' and addressed Lloyd George in an almost teasing tone: 'I suppose you think I can't fight.' To which the Prime Minister responded, 'No General, with your record I would not make that mistake, but I am certain that for some reason or other you won't fight.' To this remark Pétain did not respond, but instead 'passed it off with a good-humoured smile'.[67] Yet unknown at that moment to Lloyd George was the extent of the severe strain on the French army. The day before, its 2nd Colonial Infantry Division, which was about to be sent to the front line, appeared on parade without rifles and shouted, 'We're not marching . . . Down with the War',[68] and the mutinies soon spread. The French offensive was officially ended on 9 May at the cost of 187,000 casualties for the Nivelle attack along the Chemin des Dames, with a further 150,000 dead or wounded at the accompanying Battle of Arras, led by Douglas Haig. One week later, Nivelle was replaced as commander by Pétain.

Lloyd George's expectations of Nivelle had been 'doomed to disappointment',[69] for which he blamed in part 'the workings of a divided command',[70] but also the predictability of the tactics of the Allied generals. 'When Joffre, Nivelle and Haig commanded on the Western Front,' he wrote, 'it needed no special genius to discern the trend of their one-way minds.'[71] As far as the Prime Minister was concerned, the failure of the offensive was the responsibility of Nivelle and Haig. For as Siegfried Sassoon wrote in his war poem 'The General'[72] about the Battle of Arras, in which he himself had been wounded on 16 April, the troops were cursing the 'incompetent swine' of the staff officers at GHQ for the failure of the 'plan of attack'.[73] Even the German general, Erich Ludendorff,[74] wrote in his war memoirs of the Battle of Arras, 'no doubt exceedingly important strategic objects lay behind the British attack but I have never been able to discover what they were'.[75]

This defeat was also, as Lord Beaverbrook described it, a 'bitter blow'[76] for Lloyd George. Frances Stevenson noted in her diary that Nivelle had 'let D. down badly after the way D. had backed him up at the beginning of the year. Sir Douglas Haig has come out on top in this fight between the two Chiefs, & I fear D. will have to be very careful in future as to his backings of the French against the English.'[77] The Western Front was not the only source of setback for Lloyd George's government. On 2 April the War Council had authorized the commander-in-chief of the Egyptian Expeditionary Force, Sir Archibald Murray,[78] to press forward to end the control of the Ottoman Empire in Palestine with the ultimate aim of occupying Jerusalem. This was one of the few romantic ideas about the war held by Lloyd George; that the British Empire should capture, as in the Bible, 'the stronghold of Zion: the same is the city of David.'[79] He had written to his brother a few days before, 'We are not far from Jerusalem and although it is not going to fall yet, I am looking forward to my Government achieving something which generations of the chivalry of Europe failed to attain.'[80] Yet reports on the strength of Murray's position had been exaggerated and the result was a disastrous second attempt to occupy the city of Gaza in a battle from 17 to 19 April. This failure led to the recall of Murray and his replacement by General Allenby.[81] Andrew Bonar Law would also receive news from Gaza on 19 April that his son Charles[82] was missing, later confirmed to have been killed in action.

Yet the greatest risk confronting Lloyd George in the spring of 1917 came from the war at sea. The German declaration of unrestricted submarine warfare in the Atlantic had helped bring the United States into the war but provoked a real sense of crisis in London, that supplies of food and materiel could run critically short. As Lloyd George observed in his *War Memoirs*, 'The second half of the War brought home to all the belligerents the fact which ought to have been obvious before, that an adequate supply of food, not only for the troops, but for the civilian population, was an essential condition of their continuance in the War. The final event depended more on food than on fighting.'[83] It had been the deciding factor in the collapse of Tsarist Russia as well, where a lack of food and fuel had left the men at the front, and their families in the great cities, shivering and starving during the winter of 1916–17. When he became Prime Minister, Lloyd George had created new ministries for Shipping and Food to improve supply and distribution, but the critical issue had become, as the former First Sea Lord Jacky Fisher described, a question of 'Can the army win the war before the navy loses it?'[84] In January 1917, 153,512 tons of British merchant shipping was lost to enemy action and by April the figure had risen to 545,282 tons sunk in that single month alone.[85] By then one merchant ship in four that left British ports never returned, and new building only replaced one ton of shipping for each ten that was lost. Such were the risks, ships from neutral countries refused even to set course for British ports. Lloyd George recalled of this time that 'The new submarine monster was gliding everywhere through the deep in search of prey – defenceless prey. Allied ships were being stricken down in increasing numbers. We seemed impotent to protect our ships and their devoted mariners.'[86]

Just over a month before Lloyd George became Prime Minister, Admiral Jellicoe[87] assessed that there was 'a serious danger that our losses in merchant ships, may, by the early summer of 1917, have such a serious effect upon the import of food and other necessaries into the Allied countries as to force us into accepting peace terms . . . which would fall short of our desires'.[88] Yet despite the gravity of the situation, Jellicoe confessed that there was 'absolutely no solution that we can see'.[89]

Sir Edward Carson as First Lord of the Admiralty, however, put his faith in the navy commanders. Lloyd George was growing frustrated that despite Carson's great qualities as an advocate, 'he had neither the natural gift nor the experience to make a good administrator'. He was, the Prime Minister considered, an 'Aginner', of 'unmanageable contrariness', who opposed the ideas of others but did not bring forward solutions of his own.[90] On 8 March, Carson told a luncheon of members of the Aldwych Club,[91], presided over by Lord Northcliffe in the Grand Hall of the Connaught Rooms,[92] 'I advise the country to pay no attention to amateur strategists, who are always impatient and ready for a gamble', a statement that clearly sounded like an intentional criticism of men like Lloyd George and Churchill. Carson then added, 'As long as I am at the Admiralty the sailors will have full scope. They will not be interfered with by me and I will not let anyone interfere with them.'[93] Tom Clarke saw Northcliffe that afternoon at Printing House Square, who, reflecting on the speeches and the lunch, told him vehemently, 'the faint-hearts are talking again of peace. There's far too much talk of peace – far too much of it in the newspapers. It's creating a peace atmosphere. There can be no peace yet.'[94] He was also concerned that the German successes in the Atlantic were creating shortages of paper and driving up prices, so that his newspapers were barely breaking even.

Determined to find an answer to the U-boat menace, Lloyd George was assisted by Northcliffe, who had a young naval staff officer, Commander Joseph Kenworthy,[95] smuggled into 10 Downing Street through the garden gate, and under the cover of darkness. Kenworthy was the son-in law of the former Liberal MP, Sir Frederick Whitley-Thomson,[96] and had used his political contacts to befriend journalists at *The Times* and the *Daily Mail*. After impressing the press baron, Kenworthy recalled that Northcliffe asked, 'if I dared go with him to . . . tell the Prime Minister himself some of the things we had been discussing, face to face. He was good enough to warn me that the visit would be known and reported to the Admiralty, that there were spies everywhere, and that the arm of the [Navy] Board was long.' At the meeting, Northcliffe introduced Kenworthy to Lloyd George, saying, 'Here is an officer . . . who is not afraid to tell you the true state of affairs.'[97] The Prime Minister challenged him, 'Now tell me who are the good men. I want to use any men with brains.'[98] Kenworthy, along with the younger officers of the Admiralty War Staff, favoured the convoy system, whereby merchant ships sailed together with the protection of Royal Navy destroyers. This had already been tried with success for coal convoys into western France, and indeed troopships and the Grand Fleet itself only sailed as convoys. Sir Maurice Hankey was also in touch with another junior officer from the anti-submarine department at the Admiralty, Reginald Henderson,[99] who broke service rules to brief him on the convoy system, and helped the Cabinet Secretary prepare a memo for Lloyd George on 11 February, which recommended it.

Yet Jellicoe and the senior admirals were against the system for merchant vessels, as they believed it created a larger target for the German U-boats. What they overlooked, as Winston Churchill later explained, was that:

> The size of the sea is so vast that the difference between the size of a convoy and the size of a single ship shrinks in comparison almost to insignificance. There was in fact nearly as good a chance of a convoy of forty ships in close order slipping unperceived between the patrolling U-boats as there was for a single ship; and each time this happened, forty ships escaped instead of one . . . The concentration of ships greatly reduced the number of targets in a given area and thus made it more difficult for the submarines to locate their prey. Moreover, the convoys were easily controlled and could be quickly deflected by wireless from areas known to be dangerous at any given moment. Finally, the destroyers, instead of being dissipated on patrol over wide areas, were concentrated at the point of hostile attack.[100]

On 30 April 1917 the situation was perilous and with the backing of the War Cabinet, Lloyd George strode across Horse Guards Parade from Downing Street, and descended on Jellicoe at the Admiralty. There he recalled that 'The High Admirals had at last been persuaded by the "Convoyers" not perhaps to take action, but to try action.'[101] They agreed that the convoy system would be trialled, and the first left Gibraltar on 10 May, arriving safely in England ten days later. That month Lloyd George placed his administrator par excellence, Sir Eric Geddes, at the Admiralty as Navy Controller and also put him in charge of shipbuilding. From 4 June, the convoy system was used for all trans-Atlantic shipping, and such was its success that by November, the losses at sea were less than a quarter of the levels in April and a greater tonnage of ships were being launched than the U-boats could sink.

On the day the Gibraltar convoy set sail, the Prime Minister faced a trial of his own, at a secret session of the House of Commons on the government's war strategy. Lord Beaverbrook recalled, 'If the sky of war was overcast, the scene of domestic politics was troubled and stormy. A gathering combination of forces threatened the administration of Lloyd George.'[102] Since the new government had been formed, Russia had collapsed, the French army was in mutiny, and the losses at sea had grown immeasurably worse. Although the Americans had now entered the war, it could be another year before they had a trained and equipped army of any significant size in Europe. There was no party machine to turn the political wheels of the government and in Parliament it had to contend with Asquith and the Liberal Party old guard, Winston Churchill full of restless ambition, the Irish party still frustrated at the lack of settlement on Home Rule, and many Conservative and Labour MPs who had never really supported Lloyd George. Beaverbrook later wrote that 'Lloyd George's position while the war continued to go badly was therefore immensely precarious. A great speech by Churchill, a cunning move by the generals, a direct thrust by the Asquith group – each of these or all together – might carry the day against the Government . . . Seeing the whole picture with the eye of a master of political tactics, Lloyd George was frightened.'[103]

From the end of April, Lloyd George started to dine again with his old allies in the Monday Night Cabal, a sure sign that parliamentary matters were back on his agenda. It was Winston Churchill, however, who suggested to Freddie Guest, the Coalition Liberals Chief Whip, the idea for a secret session debate in the House of Commons, where the Prime Minister would be able to set out the government's war strategy. Lloyd George agreed, and as the debate hadn't been formally requested by the Opposition, Asquith was not prepared for it, so Churchill opened for them instead. He gave a commanding speech, but one that urged caution, reflecting the mood of French commanders like Pétain. 'Is it not obvious,' Winston told the House of Commons, 'that we ought not to squander the remaining armies of France and Britain in precipitate offensives before the American power begins to be felt on the battlefields? . . . Let the House implore the Prime Minister to use the authority which he wields, and all his personal weight, to prevent the French and British High Commands from dragging each other into fresh bloody and disastrous adventures. Master the U-boat attack. Bring over the American millions. And meanwhile maintain an active defensive on the Western Front, so as to economize French and British lives, and so as to train, increase and perfect our armies and our methods for a decisive effort in a later year.'[104] In response, Lloyd George made no firm commitments for the Western Front, only to reiterate his support for a continued offensive spirit in the war against Germany. He also confirmed that Germany's overseas colonies would not be returned to her after the war, and that it was the intention of the Allies that the Ottoman Empire should lose both Palestine and Mesopotamia. Freddie Guest wrote to him after the debate that 'The impression in the House, lobby and smoking room is that you have made a great speech. It has been a good day's work in more ways than one. Winston's speech is also considered to be a fine statesmanlike effort.'[105]

Recognizing Churchill's success, though, Lloyd George decided to try and neutralize opposition voices by bringing them inside the government. He could see, as Beaverbrook observed, that 'Churchill could not be left out of the Government. He must be fenced in and forthwith.'[106] Winston recalled after their exchanges in the House of Commons, a brief and intimate conversation with Lloyd George behind the Speaker's Chair, where 'In his satisfaction at the course the Debate had taken [the Prime Minister] assured me of his determination to have me at his side. From that day, although holding no office, I became to a large extent his colleague. He repeatedly discussed with me every aspect of the war and many of his secret hopes and fears.'[107] Lloyd George encouraged Churchill to make an immediate visit to the front, with letters of endorsement from the government, and to report back to him over Sunday lunch at Walton Heath on 19 May. The evening before, Churchill sought out Lloyd George's confidant, Lord Riddell, at a dinner of The Other Club,[108] where he relayed his opinion that 'LG was fighting the battle practically single-handed', adding, 'He made a terrible mistake in cutting himself adrift from me.'[109] After their lunch at Walton Heath, Frances Stevenson noted in her diary, 'D. is seriously contemplating some changes in his Ministry. He says he wants someone in who will cheer him up and help & encourage him, & who will not be continually coming to him with a long face and telling him that everything is going wrong. At present, he says, he has to carry the whole of his colleagues on his back . . . I think D. is thinking of getting Winston in in some capacity. He has intense admiration for his cleverness, & at any rate he is energetic and forceful.'[110] From Paris, Lord Esher was also picking up the signals of Churchill's likely return, writing to warn Haig, 'The degree to which his clever but unbalanced mind will in future fulfil its responsibilities is very speculative . . . The power of Winston for good and evil is, I should say, very considerable. His temperament is of wax and quicksilver, and this strange toy amuses and fascinates L. George who likes and fears him.'[111]

Lloyd George was also keen to understand the lie of the land with Asquith, and over a Whitsun weekend party hosted by the Asquiths at The Wharf, the Prime Minister's trusted emissary Lord Reading sounded out the former leader about a possible return to government. Yet Asquith told him in no uncertain terms that he thought the Lloyd George coalition with its small War Cabinet was 'a hopeless and unworkable experiment'. Furthermore, he recalled informing Reading that 'Under no conditions would I serve in a government of which Lloyd George was the head. I had learned by long and close association to mistrust him profoundly. I knew him to be incapable of loyalty and lasting gratitude. I had always acknowledged, and still did, to the full his many brilliant and useful faculties, but he needed to have someone over him. In my judgement he has incurable defects, both of intellect and character, which totally unfitted him to be at the head.'[112]

If Lloyd George was unable to reunite the Liberals by bringing back Asquith, he could weaken their force in Opposition by recalling Churchill. Another powerful voice he sought to pacify was Lord Northcliffe, whose dislike of Winston and support for the generals meant his support couldn't be taken for granted. Northcliffe believed that for some time Britain had been losing the propaganda war within the United States. Of particular concern was William Randolph Hearst,[113] the American news magnate, who was not only fiercely against the United States entering the war, but had actively opposed support for the Allies against Germany.[114] The chief foreign correspondent for Hearst newspapers, Karl von Wiegand,[115] was seen in official circles in America as being 'very strongly pro-German',[116,117] and the war reporting from Hearst's International News Service was considered so bad that it was banned in Britain, France and Canada. Even after President Wilson had declared war on Germany, Hearst urged the American government to 'Keep every dollar and every man and every weapon and all our supplies and stores AT HOME, for the defense of our own land, our own people, our own freedom, until that defense has been made ABSOLUTELY secure. After that we can think of other nations' troubles. But till then, America first!'[118]

On 30 January, Northcliffe met with Lloyd George to discuss a report he had commissioned from Pomeroy Burton,[119] an American-born journalist who was then the manager of his Associated Newspapers group. Burton recommended establishing the War Intelligence Department that would be run by John Buchan of the Foreign Office in order to deliver the 'vital duty of keeping millions of neutrals correctly and promptly informed about the progress of the war'.[120] The American journalist Isaac Marcosson also discussed with Northcliffe and Lloyd George in February 1917 his concerns 'about the failure of British propaganda in the United States and the inroads made by the German secret service'.[121]

In late May 1917 the Foreign Secretary, Arthur Balfour, recommended to the Cabinet that a permanent war mission to the United States should be established, in addition to the embassy, and Lloyd George thought that Northcliffe would be an excellent choice, not only to lead this but also to spearhead British propaganda in that country as well. There was significant resistance from the Foreign Office, including the ambassador in Washington D.C., Sir Cecil Spring-Rice.[122] The Liberal MP David Davies also warned Lloyd George that if he went ahead with the appointment, 'you will raise a devil of a storm in the Liberal Party, which is just what you want to avoid just now. Northcliffe is one of the biggest intriguers and most unscrupulous people in the country . . . If you are sending him there to be rid of him, you are making a huge mistake . . . Here it will be said that you are afraid of the Harmsworth Press.'[123] The disagreement led to a breach between the two men that resulted in Davies, who had been one of the Prime Minister's key lieutenants in the House of Commons, leaving Downing Street and returning to the army in France.

Nevertheless, Lloyd George offered the post to Northcliffe over lunch at 10 Downing Street on 30 May. The press baron accepted immediately and set sail for America on 2 June. On arrival he was determined to make his mark straight away. Spotting William Randolph Hearst at a welcoming lunch at the St Regis Hotel[124] in New York, he brazenly told him, 'I have known you for a long time, you are a poor journalist, you know.'[125]

At the dinner of the Monday Night Cabal on 4 June, Leo Amery recalled that 'The P.M. was in great form, chaffing Robin [Dawson] about the service he had rendered him in despatching Northcliffe to

America.'[126] Maurice Hankey believed that Lloyd George's motivation behind the mission was 'really a dodge to get rid of Northcliffe, of whom he is afraid'.[127] Yet this was only partly true, for Lloyd George also believed Northcliffe was well suited to the task and told Riddell over lunch, the day that the press baron departed, 'Don't you think it is a good idea? He was getting unbearable, jumpy and dangerous. It was necessary to give him something to do and I think he will do the job well.'[128] Northcliffe too seemed to accept that now he was busy elsewhere, he would have to be content with observing the political scene in England from a distance. On 13 June, in anticipation of Winston Churchill's return to government, he sent him a telegram from New York reading 'Many congratulations on your appointment.'[129]

Lloyd George may have 'squared'[130] Northcliffe, as Lord Beaverbrook later put it, but he knew there would still be fierce Conservative opposition to Churchill's return. Lord Curzon and Austen Chamberlain had insisted that Churchill be excluded from the government when they joined. Lloyd George sounded out Bonar Law on the prospect, by asking him whether he thought Winston was 'more dangerous when he is FOR you than when he is AGAINST you?' To which the Conservative leader replied, 'I would rather have him against us every time.'[131] Churchill's great friend Freddie Guest was lobbying on his behalf, and he encouraged Lloyd George that 'Your will and influence with your Tory Colleagues is greater than you have credited yourself with and . . . sooner or later you will have to test it – why not now? I have the strongest reasons to believe that the Tories mean to support your leadership even at the expense of their personal feelings.'[132] On 11 June, Lloyd George also dined with George Riddell and Robert Donald. Riddell recalled that Donald thought 'LG ought to rope Winston into the Government as otherwise he might join Mr A who, Donald thought, was growing in popularity. LG agreed about the roping in, but not about Mr A.'[133]

Lord Milner was also encouraging Lloyd George to make further Cabinet changes including, following the problems with the Navy Board and the convoy system, removing Carson, First Lord of the Admiralty. On 26 June, Milner wrote to the Prime Minister reassuring him that:

> It may seem a rather startling proposition, but I think it would be the best plan to bring Carson into the War Cabinet, where he will be excellent, and to make [Eric] Geddes First Lord. In that case, with

> a really first-rate administrator at the Head of the Board, the great requisite in the First Sea Lord would be courage and knowledge of men, and intimate acquaintance with the best men in the service and a determination to bring them on and put them into their right places regardless of seniority and red tape. Such a First Sea Lord can be found more easily than a naval man, who is a great administrator. That quality must be imported from outside.[134]

Lloyd George agreed and tried to soften the blow with Carson by urging him to accept the position in the War Cabinet, telling him, 'I wanted you in the Cabinet from the start. My plans were then thwarted for reasons you know. The time is now ripe for reverting to my original idea . . . We need your insight, courage and judgement.'[135] Carson reluctantly accepted, but told one of the Sea Lords, 'I never wanted to leave the Admiralty. I am sorry to leave the Admiralty.'[136]

Lloyd George was required to make a further change with the resignation of Austen Chamberlain as Secretary of State for India, following the inquiry of a special commission into failings of the military campaign in Mesopotamia,[137] for which he had ultimate if not direct responsibility. Austen wrote to his sister Ida, 'It is curious that most of the men of the Cabinet would say there was no need & indicate some surprise; whilst to others it is clear I was right. I ask curiously: Would they have known it was right if I had not done it?'[138] His departure stood in stark contrast to Winston Churchill's ambition to return, despite the interim report of the Commission on the Dardanelles, which while not exonerating him for the failure of the campaign did concede it believed that he had acted in 'good faith'.[139] The loss of Chamberlain created a vacancy that Lloyd George filled by recalling his Liberal colleague Edwin Montagu, thus depriving Asquith of another potential ally.

The Cabinet changes were announced on 18 July 1917, including Winston Churchill's appointment as Minister of Munitions; Christopher Addison was moved to accommodate him, to the new Ministry of Reconstruction. The Prime Minister was unable to bring himself to tell Bonar Law in person, so instead sent Lord Beaverbrook as his messenger. Upon receipt of the news, the Conservative leader said 'Lloyd George's throne will shake.'[140] His prediction was correct. Lloyd George recalled of the reaction of the Conservatives that 'the insensate fury they displayed . . . surpassed all my apprehensions, and for some days it swelled to the dimensions of a grave ministerial crisis which threatened the life of the Government.'[141] Yet the Prime Minister had also calculated accurately, and while he had spent political capital in the process, the gamble of recalling Churchill had been made. The throne may have tottered, but it did not fall. In the process, though, the first loosening of the bonds of alliance that had carried Lloyd George into 10 Downing Street had been made. Carson was disappointed to have been moved, Bonar Law frustrated at the return of Churchill, and Northcliffe sent out of the way to America.

Yet Lloyd George had also paid a debt of honour to Churchill for his support during the Marconi affair, an act of friendship that Winston would never forgot. After his return to the government, the two men dined at 10 Downing Street, and afterwards Lloyd George took Winston into another room and showed him a framed *Daily Express* newspaper placard from the time of Marconi, which read 'Churchill defends Lloyd George.'[142]

EIGHT

Mud Sticks

Lloyd George was woken at home in Walton Heath in the early hours of the morning of 7 June 1917, in order to hear the greatest explosion in the history of warfare. One hundred and forty miles away, 19 mines dug under the German front line at Messines Ridge, six miles south of Ypres in Belgium, were detonated with the combined force of nearly one million pounds of explosive power. They were followed by the co-ordinated firing of over 2,000 artillery guns across the front. The Press Association was briefed that Lloyd George 'gave orders that he wished to be called at three o'clock [that] morning, evidently in anticipation of the explosion . . . he and others heard clearly the tremendous shock'.[1,2]

The attack, planned by General Sir Herbert Plumer,[3] took the Germans by complete surprise and led to the capture of the strategically important ridge, which commanded unbroken views across the Ypres Salient, a necessary step before Douglas Haig's long-planned assault on the front in Flanders could be launched. Haig had been patient while the indignities were meted out to him during the Nivelle offensive. Its failure had ended the career of that commander and weakened the position of Lloyd George as the man who'd backed it. Haig now wanted his offensive with the objective of smashing through the German lines at Ypres and capturing the Belgian coast.

In late April, as the French army had stood on the brink of mutiny, Sir Henry Wilson set out over dinner with Paul Painlevé the three strategic options for the Allies as he saw it. These he named 'Somme, Verdun, Pétain', explaining that 'Somme was *usure*; Verdun was a whirlwind and a crash through; Pétain was squat, do little and have small losses. I said that Verdun had been tried and failed, and there remained Somme and

Pétain. I urged that the proper course was Somme, with variations, and that "squat" was fatal.'[4] Somme II would mean another broad attritional offensive to wear down the strength of the German army.

Lloyd George liked Wilson, and what the deputy Cabinet secretary Thomas Jones called his 'clear, black-board fashion'[5] of presenting complex problems. Maurice Hankey believed that 'We must do the enemy all the damage we can. This can best be done by fighting a great battle with the object of recovering the Flanders coast.'[6] Jellicoe had also warned in the early summer of 1917, before it had been established that the convoy system would be successful in countering the threat from the German U-boats, that a campaign was needed to capture their bases at Zeebrugge and Ostend, without which he warned it would 'be improbable that we could go on with the war next year for lack of shipping'.[7] On this matter, Jellicoe's opinion would be proven by events to have been completely wrong.

Yet, while Wilson believed that a 'Somme, with variations' was the best course of action for the summer of 1917, he had severe misgivings about an offensive in Flanders, and wasn't alone. Pétain thought Haig was embarking on an 'impossible task',[8] which was 'certain to fail' and 'hopeless'.[9] Foch told Wilson that 'he wanted to know who was the fool who wanted Haig to go on a duck's march through the inundations to Ostend and Zeebrugge'.[10] Wilson also noted in his diary that Foch 'thinks the whole thing futile, fantastic & dangerous, and I confess I agree & always have'.[11] The 'duck's march' was a reference to the flat marshy terrain of the Ypres Salient, which before the war had been maintained by a complex network of drainage ditches, but by 1917 as a result of heavy shellfire was quickly reduced to a boggy swamp when it rained. Haig's chief intelligence officer, Brigadier-General John Charteris,[12] also noted there was anxiety 'about the weather conditions that were to be anticipated. Careful investigations of the records of more than 80 years showed that in Flanders the weather broke early each August with the regularity of the Indian monsoon: once the autumn rains set in the difficulties would be greatly enhanced.'[13] None of these concerns were conveyed to the British War Cabinet at the time, and as Lloyd George later wrote in his *War Memoirs*, 'If the whole truth, as it was known at the time to the military staffs, had been exposed before the members of the War Committee, the Flanders offensive would have been turned down.'[14]

Regardless of these facts, however, Lloyd George was instinctively against Haig's proposal. He wanted a version of 'Pétain' in which limited objectives would be pursued on the Western Front until the Americans arrived in greater numbers in 1918. In addition, he continued to propose supporting the Italians with a view to knocking Austria out of the war and pushing ahead with the campaign against the Ottoman Empire in the Middle East. On 19 June, Douglas Haig made his presentation on the Flanders campaign to the War Policy Committee of the Cabinet, to which Lloyd George responded with a 5,000-word memorandum setting out his reservations. He was concerned that:

> ... we should rush into the greatest battle of the War, against an enemy almost equal in number, quite equal in equipment, still the greatest army in Europe . . . with larger reserves than our own . . . holding formidable defensive positions which he has taken three years to strengthen and to perfect; and we are to launch this attack with doubtful support from our most powerful and important ally . . . if it pulls less than its full weight we shall be attacking the strongest army in the world with an actual inferiority of numbers . . . curious indeed must be the military conscience which could justify an attack under such conditions.[15]

Haig offered no compromise and held fast with strong support from Sir William Robertson as Chief of the Imperial General Staff, who told him 'Argue that your plan is the best plan – as it is – that no other would even be *safe* let alone decisive, and then leave them to reject your advice and mine. They dare not do that.'[16] This was their ace card, and reluctant as they were to support another major offensive neither Lloyd George nor Bonar Law was prepared to overrule Haig, which would cause his resignation and undermine public confidence in the war. This time it was the politicians who were boxed in and forced to accept a proposal they neither wanted nor agreed with. Lloyd George's questioning of the Field Marshal did make clear, though, that this decision was based on his personal confidence in the plan of attack. Its failure would therefore be Haig's failure. Approval from the War Cabinet was given on 25 July, after the preliminary bombardment had already started, and the offensive, the 3rd Battle of Ypres, later known as Passchendaele, would begin on 31 July.

On Saturday 28 July, Siegfried Sassoon, who as a serving officer had been awarded the Military Cross for gallantry at Mametz Wood, published a declaration critical of the war, 'in wilful defiance of military authority'.[17] This first appeared in *The Woman's Dreadnought*, a newspaper edited by Sylvia Pankhurst,[18] to coincide with a pacifist assembly that day of 250 people at the Brotherhood Church in Hackney,[19] organized by the Workers' and Soldiers' Council.[20] A pro-war protest march of 800 people, many recruited from local pubs, had also gathered outside. Some of the protestors then broke through a police cordon and invaded the meeting by kicking through the church windows to enter the building and wreck the interior. The philosopher and pacifist Bertrand Russell,[21] whom Lloyd George had previously accused of delivering 'poisonous speeches . . . to interfere with this country achieving a victory',[22] was among those in the church. In a letter that day to his friend Lady Ottoline Morrell,[23] Russell described how 'A vast crowd of roughs and criminals (paid) led, or rather guided from behind, by a few merely foolish soldiers (Colonials) broke in . . . It was really very horrible . . . The crowd outside as we were leaving was very fierce.' In his autobiography Russell also recalled how 'two drunken viragos began to attack me with their boards full of nails . . . one of the ladies among us went up to the police and suggested that they should defend me. The police however merely shrugged their shoulders. "But he is an eminent philosopher," said the lady, and the police still shrugged . . . "But he is the brother of an Earl," she finally cried. At this the police rushed to my assistance.'[24]

George Lansbury,[25] editor of the *Daily Herald*, the newspaper of the labour movement, wrote of the riot at the Brotherhood Church, 'Those who imagine that because of the opposition and violence with which the new movement has been met, it will therefore lie down, are very much mistaken. Things don't happen that way in this country. The Boer War made Mr. Lloyd George one of the best-hated men in Britain.'[26] The incident was raised in the House of Commons the following Monday by the Asquith-supporting Liberal MP, Henry Chancellor,[27] who was also the constituency Member of Parliament for the Brotherhood Church. He stated that a 'mob of public house loafers, engaged in nefarious work, was led by Canadian and Australian troops, accompanied by an officer . . . One soldier told a lady he knew that they had orders to break up the meeting.'[28] The leading Labour MP Philip

Snowden, whose wife Ethel[29] had been due to address the meeting, called the incident 'the worst riot seen in London for years'.[30] Another Asquith Liberal, Hastings Lees-Smith,[31] read out Siegfried Sassoon's statement in the House of Commons, including a charge that directly challenged the war aims as set out by Lloyd George in his Queen's Hall Speech in 1914. 'I believe this War,' Sassoon declared, 'which I entered as a war of defence and liberation, has now become a war of aggression and conquest.' He added that he was 'not protesting against the military conduct of the War, but against the political errors and insincerities for which the fighting men are being sacrificed'.[32] The army High Command attributed Sassoon's behaviour to shell-shock, and he was sent to convalesce at Craiglockhart in Edinburgh.[33]

The incident at the Brotherhood Church in Hackney occurred as the Labour leader Arthur Henderson was returning from Russia, where he had represented the War Cabinet in a delegation of Allied Socialist leaders, sent to build relations with the new Minister-Chairman of the Provisional Government, Alexander Kerensky.[34] Henderson shared the final leg of his journey back to Britain, onboard a ship crossing the North Sea from Bergen in Norway to Aberdeen, with a delegation of moderate Russian Socialists who called themselves the 'Argonauts of Peace'.[35,36] Their mission was to persuade Socialist leaders in Britain and France to join them in Stockholm in September for an international peace conference, which would also include representatives from Germany and Austria. Lloyd George recalled that Henderson was 'Fresh from the glow of that atmosphere of emotionalism and exaltation which great Revolutions excite ... When he came back from Russia the fine steel of his character was magnetised by his experiences. He was in an abnormal frame of mind. He had more than a touch of revolutionary malaria.'[37] Without informing the War Cabinet, Henderson decided, along with his pacifist Labour colleague Ramsay MacDonald, to accompany the Russians to Paris in order to persuade the French Socialists to join them all in Stockholm. Upon his return to London on 1 August, Henderson was summoned to 10 Downing Street, and made to wait outside the Cabinet Room for an hour while his colleagues discussed his behaviour; a situation that became known as the 'doormat' incident.[38] It was made clear to Henderson that he could not attend the Stockholm conference and remain a member of the War Cabinet. The French government was also anxious that any informal attempt to agree and publish peace terms could undermine public confidence in continuing the war. On 11 August, following the endorsement of the Labour Party that Henderson should go to Stockholm, he resigned from the Cabinet before he could be fired by a 'furious'[39] Lloyd George, and was replaced by his colleague George Barnes.[40] It was ultimately an empty gesture, as the seamen refused to sail the ship that was to convey the Labour Party delegation to Stockholm, but this affair had long-term consequences. Henderson from then on determined that Labour should organize across the country and seek to be a party of government in its own right, rather than the minority supporters of Lloyd George and the Liberals. A. G. Gardiner, editor of the *Daily News*, wrote the following year of Henderson, 'It may be said that he was made great by his fall. No man in public life certainly ever grew more sensibly in stature as the result of resignation. The Russian episode converted him from a commonplace figure on the political stage into a man of capital significance.'[41] The Fabian social reformer Sidney Webb[42] also noted of Henderson's transformation that 'a certain doormat . . . is now being very effectively used as an altar-cloth'.[43]

During August 1917, Lloyd George decided for a personal change of scene, by resting and working at Great Walstead, a mansion house next to an idyllic old farm near Lindfield, in East Sussex, that Lord Riddell rented for his use that summer. There, surrounded by meadows, woods and parkland, the Prime Minister could indulge his love for rural living; rising early, walking, chopping wood for the fire, and engaging in all matters concerning the running of the farm. One of the Land Girls[44] remarked of Lloyd George, 'There's no side about him, and when he visited us at the dairy he was just like one of us. He took a hand at churning and asked a great many questions.'[45] An old man working on the farm recalled asking Lloyd George about the progress of the war, and that he replied, '"Oh France is doing this and Russia's doing that and England's doing the other things," he says, and when I read the *Daily Mail* I said to my Missus, blewed if I don't think Lloyd George had been reading the *Daily Mail* too!'[46]

Despite the enormous pressure that the Prime Minister was under, Riddell observed of him at Great Walstead that:

> His energy, capacity for work, and power of recuperation are remarkable. He has an extraordinary memory, imagination, and the art of

> getting at the root of a matter . . . He is not afraid of responsibility, and has no respect for tradition or convention. He is always ready to examine, scrap or revise established theories and practices. These qualities give him unlimited confidence in himself . . . he is one of the craftiest of men, and his extraordinary charm of manner not only wins him friends, but does much to soften the asperities of his opponents and enemies. He is full of humour and a born actor . . . He has an instinctive power of divining the thoughts and intentions of people with whom he is conversing. His chief defects are: (1) Lack of appreciation of existing institutions, organisations and stolid, dull people . . . their ways are not his ways and their methods are not his methods. (2) Fondness for a grandiose scheme in preference to an attempt to improve existing machinery. (3) Disregard of difficulties in carrying out big projects . . . he is not a man of detail.[47]

The South African minister Smuts too had come to the conclusion, according to Leo Amery, that Lloyd George could 'only think while he is talking, and is incapable of clear sustained thought which alone can see daylight through a complicated and big situation. This is more fatal because he fancies himself as a strategist.'[48]

Lloyd George now found himself caught between growing calls for a negotiated peace with an undefeated enemy, and Haig's battle plan to win the war, neither of which he believed in. As War Secretary the previous autumn he'd told Hankey that he was not prepared to stay in office to oversee another bloody and disastrous campaign in 1917, akin to the Battle of the Somme. Now as Prime Minister, he was about to see it all happen again. From the start of the Battle of Passchendaele the conditions in Flanders were appalling. For three weeks it rained, during what turned out to be one of the wettest Augusts on record. Soldiers struggled in the heavy mud, tanks sank, and it was almost impossible to manoeuvre heavy artillery into new positions. However, in his bulletin to the War Cabinet on 4 August, Haig reported that progress had been 'most satisfactory'.[49] Five days later, Brigadier-General Charteris recorded in his diary, 'The rain keeps on and with each day's rain our task gets more difficult . . . the front area now baffles description . . . It is just a sea of mud churned up by shellfire.'[50] The objectives for the early weeks of the campaign were not secured and the hope of breaking through the German front and capturing the Belgian ports was abandoned for the more limited objective of taking the Passchendaele Ridge. As Lloyd George observed in his *War Memoirs*, 'Attrition was an afterthought of beaten Generals to explain away their defeat, and perhaps to extract some residue of credit out of a bad scheme badly handled.'[51]

By mid-August the situation was so bad that, unknown at the time to the War Cabinet, General Gough,[52] the commanding officer for the offensive, recommended to Haig that they should call it off. In his memoirs Gough recalled, 'The state of the ground was by this time frightful . . . I informed the Commander-in-Chief that tactical success was not possible, or would be too costly, under such conditions, and advised that the attack should now be abandoned. I had many talks with Haig during these days and repeated this opinion frequently, but he told me that the attack must be continued.'[53] Lloyd George was not made aware of these concerns, and his *War Memoirs* declared in great frustration, 'It must seem incredible to those who have no experience of the tyrannical repression imposed on honest men by professional etiquette, that Gough's entreaty to the Commander-in-Chief that he should break off the attack was never reported to the War Cabinet.'[54]

However, even without this intelligence it was clear that Haig had failed to make the progress that had been promised. Hankey recalled finding the Prime Minister at this time 'obviously puzzled, as his predecessor was, as to how far the Government is justified in interfering with a military operation'.[55] The Cabinet Secretary also confided in Lord Riddell that 'Ministers are so overwhelmed with work that they cannot follow the naval and military operations in detail from day to day.'[56]

If, to use Siegfried Sassoon's phrase, 'political errors' were sending men to their deaths for no tangible gain, Lloyd George's solution was now the removal of Sir William Robertson as Chief of the Imperial General Staff, so that there might be more of a challenge to and scrutiny of Haig's strategy. However, the Prime Minister did not yet have a strong enough position of authority to achieve this. On 23 August, Lloyd George expressed his concerns to Henry Wilson, who recorded in his diary that the Prime Minister 'was quite clear in his mind that we were not winning the war by our present plans, and that we never should on our present lines; but he did not know how, or what we should do, and he had no means of checking or altering Robertson's and Haig's plans though he knew they were too parochial. He said he was not in a position nor had he the knowledge to bring out alternative plans & to insist on their adoption as it would always be said that he was over-ruling the soldiers.'[57]

Lloyd George put to Wilson his idea of creating a three-man military committee, comprising Wilson himself, in addition to Sir John French and another general to oversee the work of Robertson and Haig. Wilson countered with a proposal of his own, namely, the creation of an inter-Allied command to prepare for the military campaign of 1918. This Lloyd George supported and he encouraged Wilson to discuss his proposal with the other members of the War Cabinet, who put forward no objections. In a secret letter to the American President Woodrow Wilson, dated 3 September 1917, which was hand delivered to the White House by Lord Reading, Lloyd George also stated that 'At the forthcoming Conferences, which will assemble as soon as the results of the present offensives have become clear, I shall urge the imperative importance of establishing more effective unity in the Allied strategy . . . In my opinion it will be necessary to establish some kind of Allied Joint Council, with permanent military and probably naval and economic staffs attached to work out the plans for the Allies, for submission to the several Governments concerned.'[58]

Italian success against Austro-Hungarian armies in the Battle of the Isonzo in late August also reopened the question of diverting resources from France to that front, in the hope of delivering a knockout blow against Austria. On 30 August, Lloyd George met for an hour with Geoffrey Dawson, who noted of their conversation that the Prime Minister believed 'The plan of going for the enemy at his strongest point was all very well in a war of movement and of comparatively small armies; but this was virtually a siege, and in a siege one looked for the weakest spot. That spot was Austria or perhaps Turkey . . . Now we should do better if we were effectively helping Italy with heavy guns and shells.'[59] However, at a meeting between Lloyd George, Haig, Robertson and Foch on 4 September, the British commander stood firm on insisting that nothing should detract from the manpower and artillery he needed to continue with his offensive in Flanders. Hankey recorded of the meeting that 'L.G. had been very truculent about the idea of overruling the soldiers, but, when he came to the point, he funked it.'[60] Robertson also complained to the newspaper editor H. A. Gwynne about the Prime Minister, that 'Each day brings a proposal more wild than its predecessor, regardless of time & space . . . interference is constant.'[61]

By September 1917, Lloyd George was physically and mentally at his lowest point of the war. Frances Stevenson thought he was 'desperately tired and overworked'.[62] For the nation as well, the privations were felt at home, as well as grief for the losses at the front. People had grown used to shortages of food and fuel, trains were slow and overcrowded, and everywhere there was evidence of a new British institution, the queue. Robertson also warned Haig that 'There are gradually accumulating in the country a great many wounded and crippled men who are not of a very cheery disposition; there are others who are mere wasters and without patriotism; and finally, there are the various Labour Unions etc. On the whole there is a fairly formidable body of discontented or half-hearted people.'[63]

On 5 September the Prime Minister left London to attend the National Eisteddfod at Birkenhead in Merseyside, with the intention of travelling on afterwards for a rest at home at Criccieth. Hankey noted in his diary, 'I was very glad to see him go. He has been restless and neurotic, unstable and rather infirm in purpose, neuralgic and irritable, exacting and difficult to please.'[64] Lloyd George, accompanied by his wife Margaret and daughter Megan, stayed overnight with Lord Leverhulme[65] at Thornton Manor on The Wirral, before driving on to the Eisteddfod at Cannon Hill in Birkenhead Park the following afternoon.

As with the previous year in Aberystwyth, cheering crowds lined the route as he approached the great pavilion of the Eisteddfod, but behind the smiles the atmosphere was already more sombre. Earlier in the day the crowds had risen to greet Lance-Corporal Samuel Evans, the conductor of the choir of the 17th Battalion of the Royal Welsh Fusiliers, which had competed at the Eisteddfod in Bangor two years before. Since then, they had sustained heavy losses at Mametz Wood during the Battle of the Somme, and in the opening stages of the Passchendaele offensive, so that Evans, himself crippled for life, was the only surviving member of the choir. The families of two of the dead soldiers had sent a black-and-white rosette to be presented to the Lance-Corporal; white representing the honour of the men, and black for those who remained to mourn. With a trembling hand Brigadier-General Sir Owen Thomas[66] pinned it to his breast.

When Lloyd George reached the pavilion, he was received by a packed audience standing and cheering, but as soon as he rose to speak, silence fell on that great gathering. The Prime Minister told his audience that 'This ancient institution has its special lessons for this tremendous hour. The first is a lesson of national unity for a national purpose . . . What is the second great lesson? That an intense love for Wales is compatible with the most fervent British patriotism.'[67] He also warned them, 'We have many dangerous marshes to cross; we will cross them. We have steep and stony paths to climb; we will climb them. Our footprints may be stained with blood, but we will reach the heights; and beyond them we shall see the rich valleys and plains of the new world which we have sacrificed so much to attain.'[68] Lloyd George then stated:

> Humanity at the end of this war will know that it largely owes its freedom to the fact that the British Empire had proved to be a reality and not a sham . . . [it] is made up of many nations some great, some small; but today we are one people, one in purpose, one in action, one in hope, one in resolve, one in sacrifice and soon we shall be one in triumph.[69]

One reporter observed that 'the delivery of the speech mainly in English but partly in Welsh was marked by great impressiveness of style, and the speaker's voice which has late grown in mellowness and fullness was heard in almost every part of the enclosure. The audience listened with the closest attention, punctuated the telling points with lusty cheers, and at the close the Premier sat down amid a perfect hurricane of acclamation.'[70]

The arrangements were then made for the highlight of the Eisteddfod, the Chairing of the Bard for the writer of the winning entry of the *awdl* (ode); a long Welsh poem written in strict metre. A specially designed bardic chair[71] was placed like a throne in centre stage, and as was the tradition, Dyfed the Archdruid[72] announced the *nom de plume* of the winning entrant, which was 'Fleur de Lys'. At that moment, the winning bard should have revealed themselves, and be escorted to the chair, but instead there was silence. Twice more, the name 'Fleur de Lys' was called without response, then Dyfed raised his arm and announced that the bard had instead been called to a greater choir. Ellis

Humphrey Evans,[73] the 30-year-old shepherd-poet from Trawsfynydd in Snowdonia, better known by his Bardic name of Hedd Wyn, had won the competition with his poem, 'Yr Arwr' ('The Hero'). This had been written on home leave in July and submitted to the Eisteddfod as Evans departed for France to rejoin his regiment. The stunned audience was then informed that on 31 July, Hedd Wyn, whose name meant 'blessed peace', had been killed in action at Pilckem Ridge on the first day of the Battle of Passchendaele.

The Archdruid then declared, 'the festival in tears and the poet in his grave',[74] and the bardic chair was draped with a black cloth. Spontaneously, the audience rose as one and sang the Welsh funeral hymn 'Bydd Myrdd o Ryfeddodau' ('There will be many wonders'), and the poet, Silyn Roberts,[75] an eyewitness at the meeting recalled, 'The wave of emotion that swept over the vast throng is indescribable and can never be forgotten.'[76] Lord Leverhulme also thought that it was 'the most impressive service I have ever witnessed'.[77] It was observed that 'Lloyd George . . . looked sad and stern, as if controlling with difficulty the emotion which surged in the hearts of everyone in the hall.'[78] Another noticed the Prime Minister's 'face expressing deep feeling'.[79]

In his poem 'The Hero', Hedd Wyn had written:

I was a shield to the weak
When battlefields would redden;
And on my breast was borne
The blood of every Armageddon.[80]

There was no shield though for Lloyd George, who was filled with emotion and standing on the stage with the parents of the slain young poet. Hedd Wyn had been a pacifist brought up in the Welsh mountains just 20 miles from the Prime Minister's childhood home. Then conscripted into the army by Lloyd George's legislation, the poet had been struck down in a battle the statesman had been unable to prevent. The blood of that Armageddon was now represented by the Black Chair of the Eisteddfod, which became a symbol for the loss of the people of Wales in the war. The event also left a lasting impression on Lloyd George, and after the war Austen Chamberlain recalled the Prime Minister telling the story again at a private dinner in Paris during the peace conference.[81]

Twenty-four hours after the Eisteddfod, Lloyd George's health failed, and he wrote to Frances from Criccieth the following week, 'Since I left you I have had a really bad time. Saturday I felt ill. Sunday worse and Sunday night I had a high temperature – the highest I have had for years – & I felt I was in for a serious illness.'[82] Hankey, only given a few days' respite in London, was summoned to Wales on 14 September where he found Lloyd George 'quite seriously ill' and 'rather despondent at the failure of the year's campaigning' and 'disgusted at the narrowness of the General Staff and the inability of his colleagues to see eye to eye with him'.[83]

Riddell, who had also accompanied Lloyd George to the Eisteddfod, noted that he was becoming increasingly depressed with the war. 'L.G. says that the Western offensive looks like being a failure and that he has received a letter from Burnham, who has been in France, telling him that there is much dissatisfaction in the Army on the subject.'[84] Bonar Law also wrote to Lloyd George in Wales on 18 September that 'he had lost absolutely all hope of anything coming of Haig's offensive . . . It is evident, therefore, that the time must soon come when we will have to decide whether or not this offensive is to be allowed to go on.'[85] Three days later, Bonar Law would lose another boy at the front, when his son James[86] was killed in action with the Royal Flying Corps at Arras. It was, his private secretary J. C. C. Davidson recalled, a 'terrible blow', which left Bonar Law 'very broken'.[87]

Lord Milner had joined Lloyd George in Wales on 17 September, and Riddell observed that:

> Both LG and Milner consider the continuation of the offensive a mistaken policy. Asquith has been visiting Haig, and LG and Milner are disposed to believe that the soldiers are preparing to defend their position by engaging the sympathies of the Opposition and the Press. LG and Milner spoke strongly regarding the loss of life involved in a continuation of the offensive and the inadequate results achieved. They say that the soldiers have no plan but to continue to batter the German front of the West.[88]

However, despite the weight of responsibility, Lloyd George's political position was more secure than perhaps even he realized. If he took on Haig and Robertson and ordered them to stop the offensive, who else had the prestige to challenge him, especially with Bonar Law now favouring some kind of intervention. The situation was as Balfour set out to his cousin, the Conservative minister, Lord Robert Cecil:[89]

> You must not expect perfection. You see Lloyd George's faults, and they are not difficult to see. But do you think he can be improved upon out of our existing material? Is there any one of his colleagues in the present War Cabinet you would like to see in his place? Do you believe there is in the House of Commons any genius on the Back Benches fit for the place? Do you think there is somewhere in the undistinguished mass of the general public, some unknown genius to whom, if we could find him, we might entrust the most difficult, and the most important task with which British statesmanship has ever been confronted?[90]

As the grief of war grew, the 'knockout blow' Lloyd George had spoken of the year before looked as far away as ever. Peace feelers were also being extended, over the summer from Pope Benedict[91] and that September from the German Foreign Minister, Baron Richard von Kühlmann,[92] who was proposing the restoration of Belgium, a German withdrawal from France, and the hint of a return of territory in Alsace and Lorraine. However, there was no suggestion of peace terms for the Eastern Front. On 20 September, Balfour sent a 'secret' memorandum to Lloyd George at Criccieth advising that it was 'beyond question that the German Foreign Office is desirous of entering into conversations with the British Government; *probably* with a view to arriving at some basis of discussion as regards the terms of peace, *possibly* with the amiable purpose of sowing dissensions among the Entente Powers.'[93] Bonar Law urged Lloyd George to return to London, which he did immediately, and the situation was discussed on 24 September in Downing Street by the War Cabinet who, according to Hankey's notes, concluded that it was 'in favour of seeing the proposals and deciding whether the Germans meant business or not'.[94] It was also agreed that Lloyd George should discuss the German initiative with the French, before informing the other Allies.

At 8 p.m. that evening Lloyd George left London with Maurice Hankey for France, but German air raids delayed their journey, and they dined precariously on board their train while it was suspended on Hungerford Bridge over the River Thames, just outside Charing Cross Station. The following morning they met for breakfast on board a train at Boulogne with Foch and Paul Painlevé, who had succeeded Alexandre Ribot as Prime Minister on 12 September. While the British believed the German peace offer was serious, Painlevé's position was too politically vulnerable for him to consider it. Lloyd George observed that 'what M. Painlevé seemed to fear was not that the approach was not bona fide, but that it was bona fide. He evidently doubted whether France would continue fighting if it were known that the Germans had offered both nine-tenths of Alsace-Lorraine and the whole of Belgium. French Ministers took the same general view about the desirability or otherwise of peace *pourparlers* with Germany as we did – that it was undesirable to enter into any negotiations until German military power was broken.'[95] To that end, Lloyd George also used the occasion to secretly raise with his French counterpart the idea of establishing an Inter-Allied command for the Western Front, with Foch as its chief, but advised that he would need time to prepare British public opinion for such a change.[96]

After the conference Lloyd George motored with Robertson and Hankey to meet with Haig at GHQ in Montreuil-sur-Mer. The commander-in-chief's personal office and accommodation was the nineteenth-century Château de Beaurepaire, in the nearby hamlet of Saint Nicolas, and, as one staff officer recalled, if he 'decided to think out his problems over a round of golf', a 'little bungalow was maintained at Le Touquet for his convenience'.[97] The communications nerve centre of GHQ was based in the seventeenth-century Citadel at Montreuil which dominated the town. The Officers' Club in the Rue du Paon was believed to have one of the best wine cellars in Europe, and tennis courts had also been constructed between the ramparts that surrounded the Citadel.[98] Montreuil had also been one of the settings for Victor Hugo's 1862 novel, *Les Misérables*,[99] and that significance would not have been lost on Lloyd George. Thomas Jones noted in his memoir of the Prime Minister that as a young man, 'he never went anywhere without putting in his bag a shilling paper-cover translation'[100] of the book. Frances Stevenson also recalled how Lloyd George 'admires tremendously Victor Hugo's understanding of human nature and his descriptions of human impulses. He says *Les Misérables* is one of the greatest stories ever written. He described the play in the mind of Valjean when a poor wretch is arrested for a crime, he himself committed, the struggle between conscience and reason.'[101]

For Lloyd George, walking along the high ramparts of Montreuil, looking across at what Victor Hugo had called the 'upper city' now with the British Officers' Club, and then below at the people in the 'lower city',[102] historically the poorer part of the town, it was a reminder that in wartime, as in peace, his duty was to speak for those who had no voice; in this case, the servicemen at the front. His sense of responsibility too had become a struggle between conscience and reason. As much as he wanted the slaughter to stop, he knew that peace without victory would be a betrayal of those who had given their lives in the cause of freedom. Lloyd George was determined, though, that the generals should never again be given such a free hand in military strategy, and that the tragedy of Passchendaele must not be repeated in 1918.

Haig remained confident in the outcome of the Flanders offensive, and Hankey noted he told them at Montreuil 'that the right course for us was to go on hammering now, and to make the French fight without delay. He believed that the Germans were in a bad way.' To which 'The Prime Minister said they [Germany] were not in such a bad way as to not be able to fight.' Haig responded 'that the Germans were now very worn out and had some very poor material in the fighting line'.[103]

At 5.50 a.m. on 26 September the British had launched another attack, the Battle of Polygon Wood. Hankey also observed that throughout their meeting that morning 'messages were coming in from the front. Haig has a great map showing the line we wanted to reach, and it was very interesting the way first one bit was filled in, then another... the whole picture was complete like a jigsaw puzzle.'[104] Step by step, following Haig's battle plan, the British forces slowly made their way to the summit of the Passchendaele Ridge, and the shattered remains of the village of the same name. Impervious to criticism, the generals stuck to their guns.

On the Italian front, however, disaster struck. On 24 October the Austrian and German forces launched a devastating attack breaking the Italian defensive lines at Caporetto.[105] More than a quarter of a million Italian soldiers were taken prisoner and General Cadorna's army was forced to retreat nearly 100 miles. The government fell when the news of the disaster became clear, with Vittorio Orlando[106] replacing Paolo

Boselli[107] as Prime Minister on 29 October. This compounded Lloyd George's frustration at the failure to send more soldiers and equipment to the Italian front. Not only had an opportunity to attack been missed, but the Central Powers had now punched through with an offensive of their own. Caporetto, though, provided Lloyd George the opportunity he needed to press for the inter-Allied command.

The day after Orlando's appointment, Lloyd George wrote to Painlevé:

> As compared with Germany the fundamental weakness of the Allies is that the direction of their military operations lacks real unity . . . If we are to win the War, it will only be because the Allied nations are willing to subordinate everything else to the supreme purpose of bringing to bear upon the Central Empires in the most effective manner possible, the maximum pressure military, economic, and political which the Allies can command. There is, I am sure, only one way in which this can be done and that is by creating a joint council – a kind of Inter-Allied General Staff – to work out the plans and watch continuously the course of events, for the Allies as a whole. This council would not, of course, supersede the several Governments. It would simply be advisory to them.[108]

Upon receiving the letter, Painlevé came immediately to London with Pétain to discuss the proposal, whose acceptance Lloyd George made conditional on the British taking over a greater proportion of the front line in France. On 2 November the British War Cabinet endorsed Lloyd George's plan and authorized the Prime Minister to attend a conference with the French and Italian governments to agree the new Inter-Allied Supreme War Council. This would be held at Rapallo on the Italian Riviera on 7 November.

Lloyd George left for the continent on the morning of 3 November, crossing the Channel in just 45 minutes on board a destroyer. In Paris at the Hôtel de Crillon he met Lord Esher, who found the Prime Minister 'frightened and "rattled" by a sense of failure. It is not surprising that, having "taken military advice" for three years that often ran contrary to his own; that having found his fears and prognostications justified by events, he should wish to obtain some other working system and fuller defined responsibility.'[109] Lloyd George also briefed Haig in Paris on the agenda for Rapallo, in particular the creation of the Inter-Allied

Lloyd George with his uncle Richard Lloyd in the garden at Downing Street in 1915.

The Lloyd George family in 1904 – from left to right, Megan, Margaret, Mair and Lloyd George.

Published in *The Illustrated War News*, 9 August 1916.

LG walking by the sea in Llanystumdwy with
Lord Milner and Philip Kerr.

LG at the News of the World golf match play
competition at Walton Heath in 1913.

Golf at Cannes in 1922 with Aristide Briand.

LG conferring with Joffre and Haig at Méaulte near Albert during the Battle of the Somme, August 1916.

LG accompanied by Lord Reading at the edge of a mine crater on the western front in France, 1916.

LG chats with Sir Henry Wilson and Ferdinand Foch at Folkestone Harbour in 1920.

LG speaking at the Queen's Hall in London, August 1917.

LG speaking at the Welsh National Eisteddfod
in Aberystwyth in 1916.

LG with Bonar Law at
Cannes, 1922.

LG confers with Austen Chamberlain
at Lympne, 1920. Behind them stands
Philip Sassoon and on the right is the
French Ambassador to Great Britain,
Paul Cambon.

LG and Winston Churchill outside
the War Office, 1914.

LG and Asquith at Buckingham
Palace, 1914.

The Hall of Mirrors for the signing of the Treaty of Versailles. Seated at the table we can see, one place in from the left, Colonel House, followed by (from left to right) Henry White (US Ambassador to France), Robert Lansing (US Secretary of State), Woodrow Wilson, George Clemenceau, LG, Arthur Balfour, Lord Milner and George Barnes.

LG in Paris with Clemenceau and Wilson.

Anglo-French conference at Port Lympne 1921, pictured left to right, Ralph Wigram, George Riddell, Philip Kerr, Philip Sassoon, Basil Blackett, Maurice Hankey, Robert Vansittart, LG, Lady Sybil Cholmondeley, Gustave Camerlynck, Philippe Berthelot and Aristide Briand. Final two unknown.

Lloyd George, by William Orpen at Port Lympne, 1920.

Cartoons by David Low for *The Star*, London evening newspaper, published in 1921.

Supreme War Council. The commander-in-chief wrote in his diary of their encounter, 'I told him that the proposal had been considered for 3 years and each time had been rejected as unworkable ... The PM then said the two Governments had decided to form it. So I said there is no need saying any more then!'[110]

Haig also observed that 'L.G. is feeling that his position as PM is shaky and means to try and vindicate his conduct of the war in the eye of the public and try to put the people against the soldiers! In fact, to pose as the saviour of his country, if he had not been hampered by bad advice given by the General Staff! One important point to bear in mind is that he has never taken the soldiers' advice and *concentrated all resources* on the Western Front.'[111] A few days later Esher wrote to Lord Stamfordham that Lloyd George was 'in a curious mood. Bad-tempered would perhaps describe it. He thinks that he has been misled by his military advisors. It is his own fault. Over and over again he has been warned that the political factors in this war were the grave danger; that unless he gripped the situation hard for England, the Allied vessel would drift on to the rocks. He never realised the peril. It is now a bit late.'[112]

The Western Allies gathered for the Rapallo conference at the luxurious Excelsior Palace Hotel, while the Winter Palace in St Petersburg, once the official residence of the Tsar, but now the headquarters of Kerensky's government, was stormed and occupied by Bolshevik revolutionaries. The establishment of a Communist government under Lenin's control was the final blow that would knock Russia out of the war. Whatever victories the military commanders believed they were winning on the Western Front, the consequences of defeats in the east were self-evident. Serbia and Romania had been lost, Russia had collapsed, and Italy was suffering from a crushing defeat. Lloyd George was accompanied by Hankey and Smuts to Rapallo, where they were also joined by Sir William Robertson. The principle of unity of command had already been agreed by the Allied governments, and when this became apparent to Robertson, he walked out, telling Hankey, 'I wash my hands of this business.'[113] The Supreme War Council was created with General Sir Henry Wilson as the British military representative.

As the Rapallo conference concluded, the final push of the Passchendaele offensive was being executed. By the time the battle finally ended on 10 November, 300,000 British servicemen were killed or missing, compared to 200,000 for Germany, for a total advance of four miles.[114] Lloyd George recorded in his *War Memoirs*, 'During the whole battle we recovered less ground, we took fewer prisoners, we captured fewer guns than we did in the despised Nivelle offensive, and that with nearly three times the casualties we sustained in that operation, which was always alluded to by the Staff as a "failure".'[115]

General Gough had wanted to stop in August, and by early October believed that 'Every day conditions grew worse. What had once been difficult now became impossible.'[116] Brigadier-General Charteris had also become overwhelmed by 'the awfulness of it all', and believed that while Haig was 'still trying to find some grounds for hope that we might still win through here this year', in his opinion there was 'none'.[117] Even Robertson would write in his memoirs, 'It is difficult to deny that the campaign was protracted beyond the limits of justification.'[118] After the battle had concluded, Haig's chief of staff, Lieutenant-General Sir Launcelot Kiggell,[119] was driven to the front for the first time. He broke down at the scene, crying 'Good God, did we really send men to fight in that?', only to be told by the officer accompanying him, 'It's worse further on up.'[120]

NINE

The Man Who Won the War

In the old banqueting hall of the Hôtel de Brienne, once the Paris residence of the mother[1] of Napoleon Bonaparte, members of the French National Assembly, Army Council and government gathered for lunch, and to listen to David Lloyd George. This grand eighteenth-century mansion was now home to the French War Ministry, but on 12 November 1917, unknown to the British Prime Minister or anyone else in his audience that day, the countdown to the end of the conflict had begun. In one day less than a year, victory would be at hand, but no such prognosis would have been believed at that moment. For the speech Lloyd George gave was not that of a leader on the eve of a famous victory, but instead of the careworn statesman, bloody but unbowed by the travails of total war. The British Prime Minister had though, as he told the assembled dignitaries, the 'advantage in speaking of this war in that I am almost the only Minister in any land on either side who has been in it from the beginning to this hour'.[2]

In that time, Lloyd George stated, thinking of the loss of men like Hedd Wyn, the Williams boys from Criccieth, the brothers of Frances Stevenson and Maurice Hankey, and the sons of Asquith, Henderson, Bonar Law and Lord Plymouth, 'We have won great victories. When I look at the appalling casualty lists I sometimes wish it had not been necessary to win so many.' The Prime Minister then took direct aim at Haig and Robertson by contrasting the Flanders offensive with the Italian defeat at Caporetto. 'When we advance a kilometre into the enemy's lines, snatch a small shattered village out of his cruel grasp, and capture a few hundred of his soldiers, we shout with unfeigned joy . . . But what if we had advanced 50 kilometres beyond his lines, made 200,000 of his soldiers prisoners, and taken 2,500 of his best guns with enormous quantities of munitions and stores?'[3]

Lloyd George believed that Allied strategy had become 'a collection of completely independent schemes pieced together', but warned, 'Stitching is not strategy. So it came to pass, when these plans were worked out in the terrible realities of war, the stitches came out, and the disintegration was complete.' That was why, at the Rapallo conference, 'we have come to the conclusion that for the cumbrous and clumsy machinery of conferences there shall be substituted a permanent Council, whose duty it will be to survey the whole field of military endeavour, with a view to determining whether and how the resources of the Allies can be most effectively employed'. Then, adding his own bombshell, he announced, 'Personally, I had made up my mind that unless some change were effected I could no longer remain responsible for a war direction doomed to disaster for lack of unity.'[4]

The Times reported that Lloyd George's speech, 'bristling as it was with harsh frankness has made a profound impression. The Press comments are full of gratitude to the man who has had the courage, in speaking for the Alliance, to dare to confess the faults of the Alliance.'[5] The French newspaper, *Écho de Paris*, also declared that 'The Prime Minister's wholehearted sincerity calls for admiration. From start to finish he went straight ahead, heedless of the personalities, roughly handled, on his path.'[6] It was the response he had hoped for, later telling Riddell, 'It was necessary. I had to speak strongly to secure attention both here and in France and Italy.'[7]

The speech was not just a programme to win the war, but the first draft of his history of what had gone before. As Thomas Jones later observed of Lloyd George's *War Memoirs*, their assessment of the Passchendaele campaign was, for over 100 pages, the 'vitriolic outpouring of the prosecuting counsel in a criminal court, outpourings in which the most scornful, blistering epithets are hurled at the two defendants, Haig and Robertson. These generals are condemned for their inexhaustible vanity, their narrow and stubborn egotism, their muddle-headedness, their misrepresentations, their lack of flair and flexibility.'[8]

After Lloyd George's speech, Painlevé paid tribute to 'his energy, eloquence and imagination, ever brilliantly active, sustained, developed and stimulated unceasingly the magnificent effort of Great Britain and her Dominions'.[9] He also stated that the conclusions at Rapallo meant that 'The Allies are fighting not each for himself, but each for all . . .

The Allies must share in common all their resources and all their energies, and there must be one front, one army and one nation to assure victory.'[10]

Back in London, the Cabal member Leo Amery was appointed as the liaison between the War Cabinet and the new Supreme War Council. But attending the Cabinet meeting on the day of Lloyd George's Paris speech, he noted in his diary that there was a general feeling 'L.G. had carried them further than they were quite willing to go. Derby and the CIGS [Chief of the Imperial General Staff] both in rather a touchy and contentious state of mind.'[11] Lord Derby later told Riddell that he thought the speech had been 'a great mistake' and that as a result the army had 'lost confidence in their leaders and in the politicians'.[12] Lloyd George's enemies, on the General Staff, and amongst the Opposition members of Parliament, saw a moment to strike against the government. On 15 November, Hankey wrote in his diary after lunch with Asquith, that the former Prime Minister 'let the cat slip out of the bag, mentioning that he had seen Robertson that morning. I have no doubt that Robertson is intriguing like the deuce. Last night [Colonel] House let slip that Robertson was coming to see him this morning . . . Why does Robertson cut the War Cabinet and see House and the Leader of the Opposition? Was it in order to intrigue against the Council? Carson told me this afternoon that he was very sick with Lloyd George's speech and opposed to the Supreme War Council but meant to stick with him because he was the only man to win the war.'[13]

To compound matters further, while Hankey lunched with Asquith, Lloyd George entertained Lord Northcliffe at 10 Downing Street, the press baron having just returned from his work promoting the Allied war effort to the American people. Keen to keep Northcliffe occupied and on side, the Prime Minister sounded him out about the idea of joining the government, in order to head a new Ministry of Air. What followed was an act of supreme crassness on the part of the press baron. In an open letter to Lloyd George, prominently published without warning the following day on the editorial page of *The Times*, he announced not only that the offer had been made, but the reasons for his declining to serve. Northcliffe declared, 'I have given anxious consideration to your repeated invitation that I should take charge of the new Air Ministry. The reasons that have impelled me to decline that great honour and responsibility are in no way concerned with the office which is rightly to be set up.' He went on to complain about the lack of 'fervour and enthusiasm' of some members of the government, adding that 'There are still in office here those who dally with such urgent questions as that of unity of war control . . . I feel that in present circumstances I can do better work if I maintain my independence and am not gagged by loyalty that I do not feel towards the whole of your administration . . . I have none but the most friendly feelings towards yourself.'[14]

Austen Chamberlain thought the letter was 'insolent and offensive'.[15] Lloyd George also considered it to be 'one of those lapses into blundering brutality to which his passion for the startling gesture sometimes led him'.[16] During a round of golf with Lord Riddell at Walton Heath on Saturday 17 November, Lloyd George complained of Northcliffe, 'I did not see the letter until I saw it in the newspapers. You cannot rely on him. He has no sense of loyalty and there is something of the cad about him. You can see it in his face. He is angling for the Premiership. His object is plain.'[17] Northcliffe's letter also enraged Lord Cowdray,[18] President of the Air Board and owner of the *Westminster Gazette*, who had assumed that he would be asked to lead the new Ministry, and now promptly resigned from the government.

Lord Beaverbrook later observed that 'The tragedy of Lord Northcliffe was that, in his hour of political pre-eminence, he cast himself down. Never again was he invited to take high office.'[19] While that was true, dangerous and unpredictable as he was, Northcliffe would remain a factor in events, whether he was in the government or not. Colonel House dined with Lloyd George and Lord Reading on 20 November and noted, 'We talked of Northcliffe. He [Lloyd George] is evidently afraid of him and, unfortunately, Northcliffe knows it.'[20] This attitude was perhaps exemplified by the Prime Minister's decisions to appoint Northcliffe's brother Lord Rothermere as the new President of the Air Board, and to grant Northcliffe himself a Viscountcy for his work in the United States.

Herbert Asquith sought to exploit these new tensions between Lloyd George, the generals and Northcliffe by tabling a motion in the House of Commons for debate on 19 November, which would require Lloyd George to come to Parliament to explain the meaning behind his speech in Paris. Austen Chamberlain noted that 'Under the circumstances some people were using Asquith to make a serious effort to turn Lloyd George out, on the ground that he had become a public danger.'[21] There was open speculation in the foreign press about the imminent fall of the government, with the German newspaper *Vorwärts*[22] declaring, 'Peace will not emerge suddenly from Mr Lloyd George's resignation but a particular system will go with the British Prime Minister, and at last the pacifists will have their say.'[23] The evening before the debate, Chamberlain saw Lloyd George with Bonar Law, where Chamberlain 'took up with him very seriously his Paris speech. He repudiated eagerly, and I have no doubt, sincerely the interpretation which I attached to it; but I impressed upon him that . . . I myself had been shocked and dismayed by the tone of the speech, & that I thought it vital that he should remove the unfortunate impression it had created.'[24]

As was often the case in the House of Commons, Lloyd George rose to the occasion, while Asquith disappointed with his motion, and the Prime Minister thought the debate had 'cleared the air'.[25] Chamberlain considered the Prime Minister's speech was 'a prodigious personal triumph – almost too great a triumph I am inclined to say for our safety'.[26] Yet, Lloyd George had been required to issue a clarification as to whether his Paris speech had called for 'the appointment of a Generalissimo . . . of the whole of the forces of the Allies'. He answered stating, 'Personally I am utterly opposed to that suggestion, for reasons into which it would not be desirable to enter. It would not work. It would produce real friction, and might really produce not merely friction between the Armies, but friction between the nations and the Government.'[27] Instead, he told the House of Commons that what had been agreed was the creation of 'a Council representative of all Allied countries with technical advisers drawn from all the Allied Armies to help the various Governments to co-ordinate their efforts'. Furthermore, he added, 'the Council will have no executive power, and that the final decisions in matters of strategy and as to the distribution and movements of the various Armies in the field will rest with the several Governments of the Allies'.[28] These statements had correctly gauged the mood of the House, but were certainly disingenuous. Foch as Generalissimo was what he wanted, and in a few months that was what he would get. However, Asquith's motion was withdrawn, and the government lived to fight another day, without a vote being called.

The political situation of France had been even more dramatic in the days following Lloyd George's speech at the War Ministry. On 13 November, Painlevé's government lost a vote of confidence in the National Assembly, which forced him to resign as Prime Minister. Lloyd George observed of his French counterpart that while 'he was penetrating and shrewd in his judgements. He had a real insight into the heart of the problem. What he lacked was the manoeuvring skill and the force necessary to convert his ideas into the action which sweeps aside obstacles, cuts through entanglements and bears down the intrigues of parliamentary and military cliques.'[29] In his place, Lloyd George wrote in his *War Memoirs*, 'There was only one man left, and it is not too much to say that no one wanted him. The President, Poincaré disliked him. He had insulted every prominent politician in France and conciliated none. He had no party or group attached to him . . . He was nevertheless much the most arresting and powerful personality in the arena of French politics during the Third Republic.'[30] That man was the fearless radical, Georges Clemenceau.[31]

In 1893, Clemenceau had fought a mercifully unsuccessful duel with another member of the National Assembly, Paul Déroulède,[32] who had accused him of being an English spy. Clemenceau was a journalist as well as a politician, and it was his newspaper *L'Aurore* that in 1898 had famously published 'J'Accuse', the article by Émile Zola[33] castigating the French military authorities for obstruction of justice and antisemitism, in their handling of the prosecution of Alfred Dreyfus[34] on the false charge of spying for Germany. Winston Churchill was in the French National Assembly on 20 November to see Clemenceau address the chamber as Prime Minister, observing how 'without a note or book of reference or scrap of paper, barking out sharp staccato sentences as the thought broke upon his mind. He looked like a wild animal pacing to and fro behind bars, growling and glaring; and all around him was an assembly which would have done anything to avoid having him there.'[35]

Lloyd George and Clemenceau had first met in 1910, because of a chance encounter in Carlsbad, Germany, and the younger British statesman recalled that it 'was not a success'.[36] Clemenceau had a general contempt for politicians, an interpretation of which Lloyd George set out at length in his memoirs, perhaps because he felt some of his contemporaries in the House of Commons also fitted the description.

He believed Clemenceau thought, on the whole, that his colleagues in the National Assembly were:

> ... merely adept at all the arts and crafts of the political game, either in or out of Parliament. They talked jargon that won or held votes or *applaudissements*. They could manoeuvre themselves or their groups into Ministerial offices. But they were not doers. When they got into office, the most hard-working amongst them only toiled at Minutes or despatches submitted to them by bureaucrats whose main purpose was not so much to solve the problem as to get it disposed of for the time being. When they attended Conferences these parliamentary leaders regarded it as a triumph if at the end they were able to say there was an *accord complet*, and could get an agreed *communiqué* to the Press which implied a great deal to the general public but meant nothing to the initiated. Clemenceau knew them all well – too well – and held them in utter disdain.[37]

Lloyd George's first encounter with Clemenceau as the French Prime Minister was in preparation for the opening meeting of the Supreme War Council at Versailles on 1 December. Then, in order to show the 'Tiger'[38] Clemenceau that he too was a force to be reckoned with, Lloyd George 'chose a topic upon which there was some difference of opinion, but as to which I felt assured that we were entirely in the right. When he rather curtly and in his roughest manner tried to sweep me aside, I protested with an emphasis – perhaps a deliberate over-emphasis – which completely astonished him. He very adroitly gave in. After that his temper, which could be savage, never ruffled our intercourse.'[39] Lloyd George at a later conference also admired the 'courage' of Foch in standing up to the 'redoubtable Clemenceau'.[40] The French Prime Minister also respected the combative character of his British counterpart. In his memoirs Clemenceau would write, 'Mr Lloyd George, that complex personality whose Welsh astuteness could by turns assume the most varied aspects, has not always shown himself the intractable man of legend. He knows that there are times for being reasonable, and when the moment appears to him to have come he does not always refuse to compromise. I have every right to say this, for never have two men in critical debates looked more like going down one another's throats.'[41]

On 30 November, while Lloyd George was in Paris, the Germans launched a large counter-attack against the British, reversing the losses they had sustained over the previous ten days at Cambrai. The initial Allied attack, led by the Third Army under the command of General Byng,[42] had featured the largest assembly of tanks so far in the war. The result had been a major advance of five miles, including breaching the Hindenburg Line, and bulletins of the success were enthusiastically briefed to the press by GHQ. The public excitement at the news was such that on 23 November crowds had gathered at St Paul's Cathedral in London, and other churches across the country, to hear the bells rung for the first time since the outbreak of the war. Yet as a result of the heavy casualties at Passchendaele, and the need to reinforce the Italian front, there were no reserves for Byng to draw on in order to fully exploit this opportunity.

At the Hôtel de Crillon in Paris, Lord Esher briefed Lloyd George on the full extent of what had happened at Cambrai, which produced a furious reaction from the Prime Minister. Esher recalled in his diary that Lloyd George:

> ... launched out against 'intrigues' against him. Philip Sassoon was the delinquent conspiring with Asquith and the press. I expressed doubt and said that Haig had no knowledge of such things if they existed, but Lloyd George replied that every one of the journalists etc. reported interviews and letters to him. He was kept informed of every move. He then used most violent language about Charteris ... Haig had been misled by Charteris. He had produced arguments about German 'morale' etc. etc. all fallacious, culled from Charteris. The man was a public danger and ruining Haig. Haig's plans had all failed. He had promised Zeebrugge and Ostend, and then Cambrai. He had failed at a cost of 400,000 men. Now he wrote of fresh offensives and asked for men. He would get neither. He had eaten his cake, in spite of warnings.[43]

Even within GHQ there were now concerns about Charteris. When Esher relayed to Philip Sassoon the details of his meeting with the Prime Minister, Sassoon wrote back that he had 'never agreed with these foolish optimistic statements which Charteris has been putting in DH's [Douglas Haig's] mouth all year but what they [the war Cabinet] ought to know is that morale is a fluctuating entity and there is no doubt that events in Russia and Italy have greatly raised the enemy's spirits'.[44]

The reversal at Cambrai also shook the confidence of Lord Northcliffe in Sir William Robertson and the senior staff at GHQ. On 11 December, Northcliffe wrote to Charteris that he had 'been informed indirectly that members of [the] Government consider that you have misled them by exaggerated statements as to [the] decline of German morale and the number of German reserves . . . I am convinced that unless examples are made of those responsible and changes at once made in Headquarters Staff the position of the Commander-in-Chief will be imperilled.'[45] The following day an editorial in *The Times*, under the headline 'A Case for Inquiry', made the complaint that 'The merest breath of criticism on any military operation is far too often dismissed as an "intrigue" against the Commander-in-chief.' It further stated of Haig himself that 'His weakness, if it be a weakness, is his inveterate devotion to those who have served him longest – some perhaps too long', and demanded a 'prompt, searching and complete' inquiry into the fiasco of Cambrai.[46] Lord Northcliffe also warned Philip Sassoon. 'I ought to tell you frankly and plainly, as a friend of the Commander in Chief, that dissatisfaction, which easily produced a national outburst of indignation, exists in regard to the Generalship in France . . . Outside of the War Office I doubt whether the High Command has any supporters whatever. Sir Douglas is regarded with affection in the army, but everywhere people remark that he is surrounded by incompetents.'[47] This was also an important personal matter for Northcliffe, as his nephew Vyvyan Harmsworth[48] had been seriously injured at Cambrai and would later die from his wounds.

Cambrai and Passchendaele also stood in stark contrast to the success of General Allenby's forces in Palestine, where despite being starved of the reinforcements he had requested, the Allies had driven the Ottoman Empire from Gaza and then forced them into surrendering Jerusalem on 9 December. Two days later Allenby fulfilled the request made by Lloyd George, that Jerusalem should have fallen to the British forces before Christmas, when at noon he walked through the Jaffa Gate, accompanied by a few staff officers, to take command of the City of David. Before his arrival the British had distributed pamphlets publicizing the Balfour Declaration,[49] which promised a national home for the Jewish people in Palestine. On 12 December in the House of

Commons, Lloyd George read out to great cheers the telegram he had received from Allenby the previous day reporting that, 'The population received me well. Guards have been placed over the Holy Places . . . The Mosque of Omar and the area around it has been placed under Moslem control, and a military cordon composed of Indian Mohammedan officers and soldiers, has been established round the mosque. Orders have been issued that no non-Moslem is to pass this cordon without the permission of the Military Governor and the Moselm in charge of the mosque.' Lloyd George then read from the proclamation issued by Allenby to the population of Jerusalem from the steps of the Tower of David, confirming that:

> . . . your city is regarded with affection by the adherents of three of the great religions of mankind and its soil has been consecrated by the prayers and pilgrimages of multitudes of devout people of these three religions for many centuries, therefore do I make known to you that every sacred building monument, holy spot, shrine, place of prayer of whatsoever form of the three religions will be maintained and protected according to the existing customs and beliefs of those to whose faiths they are sacred.[50]

To Lloyd George however, the news was 'a Christmas present for the British people'.[51]

Emboldened by this success, the Prime Minister was now agitating for the dismissal of both Haig and Robertson, but came up against resistance from the War Secretary, Lord Derby. Instead, the removal was demanded and achieved from GHQ of Charteris, and Major-General Maxwell,[52] the Quartermaster General. Sir Launcelot Kiggell also left GHQ, suffering from nervous exhaustion. Over lunch on 16 December at 10 Downing Street with Amery, Smuts and C. P. Scott, Lloyd George was still, according to Amery, 'very outspoken in his denunciation of the stupidity and obstinacy of Haig and Wully [Robertson]'.[53] A week later, Riddell recalled the Prime Minister telling him over dinner at Walton Heath that 'the military position is serious and that Robertson and Haig have mismanaged matters'.[54] For good measure the following day, on Christmas Eve, Admiral Jellicoe was also sacked as First Sea Lord by Lloyd George's favourite, Sir Eric Geddes; a delayed reckoning for Jellicoe's hesitancy over adopting the convoy system. When Geddes telephoned the Prime Minister on Christmas Day with the news, Lloyd George said, 'It is a good thing, as Jellicoe has lost his nerve.'[55]

Just as he had done during the political crisis that followed the failure of the Nivelle offensive in May 1917, in early 1918 Lloyd George stayed close to the members of the Cabal, using them as a sounding board for his private thoughts and intentions. On New Year's Day he hosted a dinner at 10 Downing Street that was attended by Milner, Kerr, Oliver, Dawson and Sir Henry Wilson. When Wilson returned to the Supreme War Council secretariat in Paris, Amery, who was also there, noted from their conversation that the Prime Minister was 'evidently hankering after getting Henry back to London as CIGS'.[56] Amery, back in Downing Street on 9 January, saw Lloyd George before a meeting of the War Cabinet and recalled that he was 'very impatient with the soldiers, whose figures he swore were always cooked, incomprehensible and wrong'.[57] Over lunch at Walton Heath three days later, the Prime Minister further confided in Amery, who wrote in his diary of their discussion, 'On the soldiers he fairly let himself go: he told me that in his opinion the two men who had done most to lose us the war were Asquith and Robertson: that R hadn't the faintest grasp of the very meaning of the word strategy, that he hadn't the slightest confidence in his judgement and that R now realised this.'[58] On 14 January, Sir Edward Carson hosted a dinner of the Cabal at his home in Eaton Place, which was also attended by Lloyd George. However, the relations between these two men were now much more strained. An announcement was made six days later that Carson would be leaving the War Cabinet. The official reason given was disagreements over policy towards Ireland, but as Carson would later say in a personal statement to the House of Commons, 'For the whole time that I was First Lord of the Admiralty one of the greatest difficulties I had was the constant persecution – for I can call it nothing else – of certain high officials in the Admiralty, who could not speak for themselves . . . I had the most constant pressure put upon me – which I need hardly say I absolutely resisted – to remove officials, and among them Sir John Jellicoe.'[59] Now that Jellicoe was gone, Carson saw no reason to stay.

Lloyd George was also careful, as he had been before, to square off Northcliffe before making a big decision on personnel. The press baron was still loyal to Haig, but had now abandoned Robertson. On

17 January he told Philip Sassoon, amidst rumours of the imminent removal of the Chief of the Imperial General Staff, 'the War Council will take matters into their own hands. I believe that it will have the support of ninety-five per cent of the people. The fall of Jellicoe has not produced a murmur of disapproval, and Parliament and the public are in a mood that will not brook the support of incompetence.'[60] On 10 February, Lloyd George asked Northcliffe to become the Director of Propaganda in Enemy Countries, reporting to the Prime Minister directly, and with the mission to undermine public confidence in Germany and Austria. Lord Beaverbrook was also appointed Chancellor of the Duchy of Lancaster and Minister for Information at home. When C. P. Scott challenged Lloyd George over lunch at 10 Downing Street about Northcliffe's new position, the Prime Minister responded that *The Times* had been 'quite reasonable' when he was in America and it was 'necessary to find occupation for his abounding energies if he were not to run into mischief'.[61]

Two days after Northcliffe's appointment there was also a great showdown in the House of Commons where Asquith challenged Lloyd George in the King's Speech debate, on the powers of the Supreme War Council. At its meeting in Versailles on 2 February, Lloyd George had recommended that the Council should place the inter-Allied reserve under the command of Foch, effectively making any new offensive impossible without the approval of that body. The idea had been presented to him at breakfast that morning by Wilson, and discussed with Hankey and Milner who were also present. Clemenceau had from the start believed in the idea of a Generalissimo and at an Allied conference on 23 December he had called for the creation of an Anglo-French reserve 'under a single command'.[62] When the decision was made by the Council, Sir William Robertson was observed 'sitting alone in his place, motionless, his head resting on his hand, glaring silently in front of him'.[63]

In supporting this proposal Lloyd George gave a furious Robertson the choice of either remaining in London as Chief of the Imperial General Staff or being the British military advisor to the Supreme Council. Either way, his power would be curtailed, and the War Council in London would have alternative advice with which to challenge Haig's proposals. Robertson now wrote to Lord Derby to complain of the 'impossible, unfair and unpractical position'[64] that British officers could now be placed in, as he saw it, required to take orders from a foreign commander rather than the ministers of their own government. Robertson also warned King George that the army could be placed under the effective control of the 'Versailles Soviet'.[65]

Press speculation about the agreement in Versailles was timed to increase the pressure on the government ahead of the debate on 12 February. In particular, the day before the debate Colonel Repington writing in the *Morning Post*, in defiance of the military press censor, revealed both the creation of the Allied general reserve, and that it was to be placed under the command of Foch. The article rounded off that 'by approving a decision which deprives our Commander in France of his full command, Mr Lloyd George has clearly and finally proved his incapacity to govern England in a great war. This is the situation which Parliament must clear up in such a manner as it thinks best.'[66]

Repington had resigned as *The Times* war correspondent the previous month due to what he believed was an 'intrigue'[67] by that newspaper against Haig and Robertson, and he was, in Lloyd George's opinion, the 'favoured confidant of the General Staff'.[68] From his articles it also appeared that Repington had been given direct access to the English translation of the classified minutes of the Supreme War Council. In response to what the Prime Minister called the 'treachery'[69] of the *Morning Post*, Repington and his editor H. A. Gwynne were prosecuted by the government, under the terms of the Defence of the Realm Act, for publishing an article that had been vetoed by the official censor. The hearing was attended at Bow Street Magistrates' Court in London, according to the *Daily Mail* by 'a number of fashionably attired ladies'.[70] These included Lady Bathurst,[71] the proprietor of the *Morning Post*, the first woman ever to hold such a position on Fleet Street, and whom Northcliffe regarded as 'the most powerful woman in England without exception, other than Royalty'.[72]

In the House of Commons on 12 February, Asquith spoke with the loud, roaring approval of the Opposition benches. Lloyd George sat low on the bench in front of him flanked by Bonar Law and George Barnes as the blows rained down on him. Asquith challenged the Prime Minister as to whether 'any change' had been made or was being 'contemplated' to the 'personnel, or the functions of the Commander-in-Chief or the CIGS'. Also, how could the proposed new function for the Supreme Council be consistent with the promise given by the Prime Minister to the House in November, that this body would have no 'executive' function?[73]

Lloyd George responded to a stormy Chamber, 'I stated that it was not the intention of the Allies that this body should have any executive functions. What has happened since then? Russia has gone out of the War. [HON. Members: "She was out then!"] In effect, Russia has gone out of the War. [An Hon. Member: "When?"] The House will allow me to follow that up.' The Prime Minister then composed himself and explained:

> Since then a very considerable number of German divisions have actually left the Eastern Front, and been brought to the West. The situation has become very much more menacing than it was at that time. The Allies met at Versailles to consider the best methods of meeting that menace during 1918 . . . Up to this year, there was no attack which the Germans could bring to bear upon either our Army or the French Army which could not, in the main, be dealt with by the reserves of each individual Army. The situation is completely changed by the enormous reinforcements brought from the East to the West; and the Allied representatives at Versailles had to consider the best method of dealing with the situation, which was a completely different one from any situation with which they had been previously confronted.[74]

On the specific questions posed by Asquith about the nature of the executive functions that the Supreme Council was taking on, Lloyd George, as one observer noted, 'point blank refused to answer',[75] and seemed to insinuate that by asking for such information, Asquith was in danger of pressing 'the Government to give information which any intelligence officer on the other side would gladly pay large sums of money to get'. This led to loud cries from MPs for him to withdraw this accusation and they gave roars of approval when Asquith successfully rose from his seat to challenge the Prime Minister to do so.

Lloyd George responded with wounded pride by rounding on his critics, stating that 'When you are conducting a war, there are questions which a Government must decide. The House of Commons, if it is not satisfied, has in my judgment but one way of dealing with the situation; it can change that Government . . . There is only one way when we go to councils of war – you must leave it to those who are there to decide, and if you have no confidence in them, whether they be military or whether they be civil, there is only one way, and that is to change them.'[76]

The day after these bad-tempered exchanges, Lloyd George met with Lord Stamfordham, who told him that 'the King strongly deprecated the idea of Robertson being removed'.[77] George V also wrote in his diary for that day, 'I am much worried as the P.M is trying to get rid of Robertson, if he doesn't look out his Govt will fall, it is in deep water now.'[78] Feeling the pressure, Lloyd George confided in Hankey that 'he had come to the conclusion that he could not sack Robertson',[79] but Milner upon hearing of this change of heart rushed to Downing Street and persuaded him not to capitulate. He had earlier counselled the Prime Minister that 'Haig will, I believe obey orders, if he once clearly understands that your mind is made up. And if he were to stick his toes in the ground, which I do not anticipate, it would be better to lose both Haig and Robertson than to continue at the mercy of both or either of them. The situation is much too critical for that and no time should be lost.'[80]

What followed was two days of negotiations with Derby and Robertson where it became clear that the Chief of the Imperial General Staff was not prepared to accept any compromise that would lessen his authority. On the evening of 15 February, Milner and Wilson joined the Prime Minister at Walton Heath, where, as Wilson recorded in his diary, 'At last I found Lloyd George in real fighting trim. He sees now, and fully admits, his weakness up to now, and how instead of leading he has balanced one interest against another.'[81] The following day Lloyd George had an audience with George V for over an hour to discuss the situation, but beforehand he spoke with Stamfordham, who noted of their discussion that 'the question of Sir William Robertson had now reached a point that if His Majesty insisted upon his (Sir W.R.) remaining in office on the terms he laid down the Government could not carry on, and the King would have to find other Ministers. The Government must govern, whereas this was practically military dictation. I assured the Prime Minister that His Majesty had no idea of making such an insistence.'[82] After the audience the King wrote in his diary, 'The Prime Minister came to see me, he is in difficulties & I regret to say Robertson is to go & Derby too, Henry Wilson will be the new C.G.S. I don't trust him.'[83] Lloyd George then saw Haig and Lord Derby at Walton Heath, where, as Milner had predicted, Haig threw over Robertson and pledged his support to the government. Lord Derby said he would resign, but later withdrew his request. At 5 p.m., Sir Henry Wilson received a telephone call from the Cabinet Secretariat Office, informing him that he was now Chief of the Imperial General Staff. That evening, without Robertson's knowledge, the government announced that he had resigned.

Lloyd George dined with Riddell at Walton Heath at the end of that week, where he confessed:

> Haig has acted well. He will not resign. He says that he is out to beat the Germans. If he had resigned I should have been in an awkward position. As it is we have to face a very serious crisis, and the Government may fall. This is the first real test we have had; and although I know that the country is with me, I am not sure what line the House of Commons will take.[84]

On 19 February, Lloyd George returned to Parliament to account for the resignation of Robertson and the powers given to the Versailles council. As had always been the case in Parliament, a sense of crisis guaranteed a full Chamber. Every seat was taken and members filled the side galleries, gangways, and packed in standing behind the Speaker's Chair. The parliamentary reporter for *The Times* noted that 'The Prime Minister, on rising to make his statement . . . was greeted with a general cheer, which conveyed the impression that the House had only one anxiety, and that was to be convinced of the soundness of his case.'[85] In a carefully worded statement he reassured members that 'none of the Ministers or Generals dissented from the plan adopted', and that Douglas Haig 'said that he was prepared to work under the arrangement'.[86] Lloyd George had originally wanted to say that Haig thought the scheme was 'workable', but changed the text of his statement following objection from the commander-in-chief.[87]

In closing his statement, Lloyd George made the acceptance of the Versailles plan a question of confidence in his premiership, telling members that:

> The Government are entitled to know, and I say so respectfully, to know to-night whether the House of Commons and the nation wish

that the Government should proceed upon a policy deliberately arrived at, with a view to organising our forces to meet the onset of the foe. For my part – and I should only like to say one personal word – during the time I have held this position, I have endeavoured to discharge its terrible functions to the utmost limits of my capacity and strength. If the House of Commons to-night repudiates the policy for which I am responsible, and on which I believe the saving of this country depends, I shall quit office.[88]

As Lloyd George sat down, the 'loud cheers, long sustained' that he received gave him his answer.[89] Whereas when Asquith tried to respond with questions about perceived discrepancies in Lloyd George's speech of the previous week, he was heckled by members with cries of 'You are not a cross-examining counsel', and 'Men are dying at the front while this is going on.'[90] The overall result was, according to *The Times*, 'a great Parliamentary success' for the Prime Minister.

Six days later, Robertson wrote to Repington, looking back on the 'whole sordid business of the past month'. He continued, 'Like yourself, I did what I thought was best . . . and the result has been exactly as I expected . . . The Country has just as good a Government as it deserves to have. I feel that your sacrifice has been great . . . But the great thing is to keep straight on a course.'[91]

Despite Lloyd George's success in removing Robertson, Northcliffe was concerned that the pressure of work was beginning to tell on the Prime Minister. On 18 March he wrote to Lord Reading in Washington D.C. Reading had taken up his position as British ambassador, and so was fulfilling the same function of prime ministerial alter ego as Colonel House performed for President Wilson in London. Northcliffe told Reading that:

Lloyd George was whiter and older looking than he was when you left. He has wonderful recuperative power; has the faculty of auto-stimulation by conversation, to a degree I have never seen in anybody else . . . Walton Heath is nominally golf on Saturday, but really dispatch boxes, telephones and visitors. Downing Street is a public breakfast, with thirty minutes' walk with someone who is trying to get something out of him. The War Cabinet right up till lunch; Americans and other foreigners at lunch; deputations and interviews in the afternoon, and perhaps another War Cabinet; boresome and intense people like me at about six; very often people at dinner.'[92]

Yet the greatest moment of trial of the whole war was yet to come.

At 4.40 a.m. on 21 March the anticipated German offensive was launched. Sir Henry Wilson recorded in his diary, 'The Boches started their big attack this morning. Two hours intense artillery, and then an infantry attack on an 85 kilometre front from the Scarpe to the Oise. This is a big affair.'[93] In fact, it was the biggest offensive of the war, on either side. The German objective was simple; to smash the British, drive them back to the sea, and then force the French to surrender, before the American forces could arrive in sufficient numbers to win the war for the Allies. The General Staff had been confident that they were ready for the German assault, and eight days before the offensive began, Lloyd George noted that Major-General Maurice,[94] the Director of Military Operations at GHQ, briefed the War Cabinet that there was a 'total of enemy rifle strength of 1,370,000 and an artillery strength of 15,700 guns, while the total Allied rifle strength on the Western Front numbered 1,500,000 infantry and 16,600 guns'. What's more, 'The average strength of the British divisions was larger than that of the German divisions.'[95] This was consistent with the view of Haig, who had told a conference of his army commanders on 2 March that he was 'only afraid that the enemy would find our front so strong that he will hesitate to commit his army to the attack with the almost certainty of losing very heavily'.[96]

On that first day Lloyd George recalled, 'The news that arrived . . . was very confused and gave us no clear idea of what had happened in the fighting. But there was nothing in the reports recorded to excite alarm . . . When we met the following morning . . . the information conveyed to us by the C.I.G.S. on reports from G.H.Q. was not much more definite.'[97] Writing in his diary that evening, however, Wilson could clearly see that the situation was grave. 'I don't understand why we are giving ground so quickly, nor how the Boches got through our battle zone apparently so easily. Our casualties yesterday are estimated at 30,000 by G.H.Q. and I am afraid will have been heavy again today, and we have no reserves beyond 50,000 men on which to draw.'[98]

On the morning of Saturday 23 March, Lloyd George wrote in his memoirs, 'the War Office seemed to be either bewildered or stunned by the reports. I therefore decided to postpone the Cabinet and to take matters in hand at the War Office itself. I invited the Staff to meet me there in order to see what could be done to throw all available reinforcements into France.'[99] However, Wilson had a clearer view of the problems at the front. He wrote in his diary that 23 March was 'An anxious day. The Fifth Army seems beaten, and has fallen back behind the Somme.'[100] On the same day from GHQ, Philip Sassoon wrote to Lord Esher:

> This is the biggest attack in the history of warfare I would imagine. On the whole we were very satisfied with the first day. There is no doubt that they lost very heavily and we had always expected to give ground and our front line was held very lightly. We have had bad luck with the mist, because we have got the supremacy in the air, fine weather wd. have been in our favour . . . The situation is a very simple one. The enemy has fog, the men, and we haven't. For two years Sir DH has been warning our friends at home of the critical condition of our manpower; but they have preferred to talk about Aleppo and indulge in mythical dreams about the Americans . . . We are fighting for our existence.[101]

At the War Office, Lloyd George was astonished to discover that there were 88,000 soldiers on home leave in Britain, when before an Allied offensive any such absences were cancelled. Arrangements were made to increase the shipping of soldiers to the front from 8,000 per day to up to 30,000, reserves were sought from other theatres of war, including the Middle East, and the decision was made to comb out as many men as possible from war production at home, to fight at the front. By the end of the month, 170,000 reinforcements would be committed to counter the German offensive. Lloyd George wanted to introduce conscription in Ireland for the first time in the war, in return for concessions on Home Rule, a dual proposal that offended both the nationalist and unionist communities in the island and proved unenforceable. By the end of the month the Prime Minister would also secure the agreement of President Wilson that he would send 120,000 men a month for the next three months toward the Allied cause, so long as they could be transported and equipped by Britain and France.

On the evening of 24 March, Lloyd George had dined with Winston and Clementine Churchill at their London home at 33 Eccleston

Square in Pimlico. Sir Henry Wilson was also there, and Hankey joined them after dinner. Winston would later write in The World Crisis, 'I never remember in the whole course of the War a more anxious evening. One of the great qualities in Mr. Lloyd George was his power of obliterating the past and concentrating his whole being upon meeting the new situation . . . The resolution of the Prime Minister was unshaken under his truly awful responsibilities.'[102] Later Lloyd George returned to Walton Heath where he saw Riddell and told him 'things look very bad'.[103] Wilson also recorded in his diary that night, 'A moving day. We are very near a crash. Lloyd George has on the whole been buoyant.'[104]

Lord Milner and Wilson were sent to France for an emergency conference with the military and political leaders of France. This was held on 26 March in the imposing town hall of Doullens in the Somme, which was barely 20 miles from the front line. This proved to be a pivotal moment in the war, where the decision was made as to how and where the Allies should respond to the German attack. Clemenceau remembered:

> We were in the courtyard of the mairie, under the eyes of a public stricken with stupefaction, which on every side was putting the question to us, 'Will the Germans be coming to Doullens? Try to keep them from coming.' Among us there was silence, suddenly broken by an exclamation from [Pétain], who pointing to Haig close by us, said to me in a low voice, 'There is a man who will be obliged to capitulate in open field within a fortnight, and very lucky if we are not obliged to do the same.' . . . [Then] there was a bustle, and Foch arrived, surrounded by officers and dominating everything with his cutting voice, 'You aren't fighting? I would fight without a break. I would fight in front of Amiens. I would fight in Amiens. I would fight behind Amiens. I would fight all the time.'[105]

In his personal record of the meeting, the French President Raymond Poincaré described how Clemenceau took him to one side 'to confide in me sadly that General Pétain was contemplating the retreat of the French army to the south while the British Army retired to the north. Pétain, added Clemenceau, had given orders on this basis. Foch confirmed this last piece of information and told me of the order to retreat which Pétain had given.' Poincaré recorded that Foch explained to him, 'Common sense indicates that when the enemy wishes to begin making a hole, you do not make it wider. You close it, or you try to close it. We have only got to try and to have the will; the rest will be easy. You stick to your ground; you defend it foot by foot. We did that at Ypres, we did it at Verdun.'[106] The formal proceedings of the Doullens conference were held in a large wood-panelled room on the first floor of the town hall where Wilson clashed with Pétain, 'for contemplating retreat'.[107] Milner then proposed, with the support of Wilson and Haig, that Foch be empowered to co-ordinate the actions of the Allied armies. Clemenceau agreed and signed the document with Milner that put this into effect. On 14 April, Foch would be named as commander-in-chief across the Western Front. Confronted with the prospect of defeat, and in dire need to co-ordinate their defence, the unity of command that Lloyd George had strived for was eventually achieved. Four days later the Prime Minister further consolidated his position at home by appointing Lord Milner to replace Lord Derby as Secretary of State for War. Derby had been sent to Paris as the new British ambassador. To quiet potential discontent on the Conservative benches, Austen Chamberlain was recalled to join the War Cabinet to fill the vacancy left by Sir Edward Carson.

The significance of Foch's appointment to the supreme command was also recognized by the post-war inquiry of the German parliament, which stated in its report that 'The phenomenon which appears in almost all coalition wars had been repeated: in a moment of acute danger, each of the Allies thinks of his own interests . . . it marked a turning point in the War, that in this extremity the Entente was successful in setting up unity of command. The Entente has to thank General Foch for successfully subordinating the divergent interests of the Allies to a higher, united purpose, for closing the gaps and organising resistance to the separation of the English and the French.'[108]

The Germans launched the second phase of the great offensive on 9 April, prompting Haig to issue his special 'order of the day' that was distributed to all ranks. The British commander wrote, 'There is no other course open to us but to fight it out. Every position must be held to the last man: there must be no retirement. With our backs to the wall and believing in the justice of our cause each one of us must fight on to the end. The safety of our homes and the freedom of mankind alike depend upon the conduct of each one of us at this critical moment.'[109] The British lines held. Haig's army had been beaten back, but not broken, and as each week passed, the Allied forces grew stronger, and the problems the Germans faced with supplying their tiring army increased. As Lloyd George observed in his *War Memoirs*, 'Our military advisers, in their computation of the relative strengths of the armies, always ignored the immense advantage which our undoubted mechanical superiority gave us in fighting strength . . . not merely in tanks but in guns, in ammunition and in aeroplanes.'[110] With the failure as well of the unrestricted U-boat campaign to starve Britain and France into submission, and the imminent arrival of hundreds of thousands of Americans, it looked as though Germany's last roll of the dice had failed.

In the House of Commons, on 9 April, Lloyd George sought to reassure MPs by stating:

> What was the position at the beginning of the battle? Notwithstanding the heavy casualties in 1917, the Army in France was considerably stronger on the 1 January 1918, than on the 1 January 1917 . . . Owing to the growth of the strength of our Armies in 1917, when this battle began, the combatant strength of the whole of the German Army on the Western Front was only approximately, though not quite, equal to the total combatant strength of the Allies. In Infantry they were slightly inferior; in Artillery they were inferior; in Cavalry they were considerably inferior; and what is very important, they were undoubtedly inferior in aircraft.[111]

This speech would, though, lead to the final great offensive against Lloyd George's premiership, launched by a man he described as 'the fizzling cracker that was chosen to blow up the Government'.[112]

Major-General Frederick Maurice was, in Lloyd George's opinion, Sir William Robertson's 'right-hand man and the architect of his downfall'.[113] After Wilson replaced Robertson as Chief of the Imperial General Staff, Maurice would lose his job as Director of Military Operations. On 7 May 1918 *The Times* published a letter from Maurice questioning 'misleading' statements made to parliament by both Lloyd George and Bonar Law, relating to the strength of the British armed forces on the western front. In particular Maurice claimed Lloyd George's assertion on 9 April that 'Sir Douglas Haig's fighting strength on the eve of the great battle which began on March 21 had not been diminished', was 'not correct'. In writing the letter, Maurice stated, he hoped that 'Parliament may see fit to order an investigation into the statements I have made.'[114]

Leo Amery was dismissive of this intervention, writing in his diary that 'When I got to the War Office I found it all buzzing over Maurice's foolish letter . . . There is no doubt that Maurice has been got hold of by Repington and the whole thing is a plant aimed at creating a Parliamentary situation in which Asquith, by the help of disgruntled Unionists, may climb back to power.'[115]

Repington had continued to go after Lloyd George and the government in his *Morning Post* columns, complaining of 'the failure of our War Cabinet, and particularly of the present Cabinet, to maintain the strengths of our Armies in the field . . . Our soft-hearted Premier's idea of not sacrificing men was to keep them at home . . . The one question which concerns most deeply every man, woman and child in the United Kingdom is whether Sir Douglas Haig's armies will now be sufficiently reinforced to enable them to compete with the enemy on fair terms.'[116] On 2 April, Repington had also written to Philip Sassoon at GHQ that 'The Cabinet view seems to be that the F.M. [Field Marshal Sir Douglas Haig] guaranteed that he could hold on if he were attacked & that he has misled them . . .but you can tell me the truth. My personal opinion of the War Cabinet is that they deserve hanging.'[117]

Lloyd George joked with Bonar Law's close parliamentary colleague, Stanley Baldwin,[118] 'Poor old Bonar, he felt it very much. He doesn't like being called a liar. I don't mind. I've been called a liar all my life.'[119] Bonar Law's initial response to Maurice's allegations was to suggest the appointment of a judicial inquiry, but Lloyd George instead recommended to the War Cabinet that this should be dealt with swiftly and on the floor of the House of Commons, in effect as a question of confidence in the government itself. On 9 May, Herbert Asquith tabled a motion calling for the appointment of a special select committee, 'to inquire into the allegations of incorrectness in certain Statements of Ministers of the Crown to this House'.[120] In response, Lloyd George told the House that it was 'absolutely without precedent . . . this is the first time, as far as I can discover, that it has ever been suggested – even in a period of peace, when there is more time – that a Select Committee of the House of Commons should examine the question whether a Minister has made a correct statement or not in the course of a speech'.[121] Then turning on Maurice personally, he thought it was outrageous that he had been put in this position, given that the General Staff had briefed the War Cabinet on 13 March, that they had superiority over the Germans on the Western Front. 'The figures that I gave,' he said, 'were taken from the official records of the War Office, for which I sent before I made the statement. If they were incorrect, General Maurice was as responsible as anyone else.'[122]

Maurice Hankey thought the Prime Minister's statement was 'not the speech of a man who tells "the truth; the whole truth; and nothing but the truth"'.[123] Bonar Law's private secretary, J. C. C. Davidson, who also watched the proceedings from the official's box in the House of Commons chamber, observed, 'there were very genuine doubts in the minds of both Liberal and Conservative members of Parliament about Lloyd George's position. There was a tradition in the Conservative Party – founded out of bitter experience – of strong mistrust of Lloyd George's statistics from the days when he was Chancellor of the Exchequer, when his statistics had been more in line with his enthusiasm than with actual facts.'[124] Davidson believed that clearly 'the last thing that Lloyd George wanted was to have his figures questioned. They were undoubtedly exaggerated, if not actually untrue, and the impression which he conveyed to the House was that everything in the garden was lovely, which in fact was not true . . . I never thought very highly of Maurice, but he was the responsible official, and he was supposed to know all the figures.'[125]

In terms of the 'actual facts' Maurice was correct. The combatant strength of the British armies in France in January 1918 was just short of 1.2 million, about 86,000 fewer than they had been 12 months before. Lloyd George's error, though, was because he had been supplied with inaccurate figures from the War Office, which initially wrongly added 300,000 non-combatant Allied servicemen, including members of the labour corps. This was not discovered until after the debate, but no attempt was made to correct the record. However, given that at the start of the German offensive it was readily identified that 170,000 men could be brought to France at speed to reinforce the front lines, it was not so much a question of whether the commanders had the manpower they needed, but how they had used the resources at their disposal. As the military historian and serving officer of the First World

War, Basil Liddell Hart, later wrote, 'The whole matter has been blown out of all proportion to its military importance . . . The very slight deficiency in numbers was due to the fact that 113,000 of the troops in France had gone to Italy to buttress the Italian collapse at Caporetto . . . The whole argument about figures is trivial and irrelevant compared with two principal facts . . . The much criticised decision to hold the General Reserve in England was taken by the General Staff, for reasons of convenience, and not by the War Cabinet . . . [and] Haig was amply confident of repelling the German offensive.'[126]

Lloyd George had correctly gambled that the House of Commons wasn't going to throw over the government based on inaccurate briefing from the reports of a disgruntled staff officer. It was ultimately a question of confidence, and whether they'd rather see him as Prime Minister than Asquith. As Lord Esher wrote to Hankey on the day of the debate, 'Soldiers are so stupid. They never understand that politics are a tournament and not a battle. Maurice will be let down by all those who have used him. It is inconceivable that the House of Commons should at this juncture swop horses.'[127]

At the end of his speech, Lloyd George sought to rise above Maurice's specific allegations and make a wider 'appeal to all sections of the House and to all sections of the country'. He continued:

> These controversies are distracting, they are paralysing, they are rending, and I beg that they should come to an end. It is difficult enough for Ministers to do their work in this War. We had a controversy which lasted practically for months over the unity of command. This is really a sort of remnant of it. The national unity is threatened – the Army unity is threatened – by this controversy . . . I really beg and implore, for our common country, the fate of which is in the balance now and in the next few weeks, that there should be an end of this sniping.[128]

The Times reported that 'the Prime Minister's case was overwhelming'.[129] In the debate Amery thought that Asquith 'opened very hesitatingly and made the poorest speech I have ever heard from him . . . L.G. followed in great debating form and, thanks to an admirable case worked up by Hankey, was able to completely pulverise the attack . . . I am more than inclined to think that this finishes Asquith as a possible Prime

Minister. People won't follow a man who has shown to such a degree both bad judgment and lack of courage.'[130] Even Sir Edward Carson, speaking from the Opposition benches, implored Asquith to withdraw his motion, asking, 'Does he really mean to go on and insist on an inquiry before a Committee of this House? Anything more disastrous I cannot contemplate.'[131]

Asquith's motion was defeated by 106 votes for to 293 against, but it had a wider political significance, for as Davidson observed, 'From the point of view of the Liberal Party, the division in the Maurice debate was a fatal blow to its corporate existence.'[132] Two days later Riddell told Lloyd George, 'you smashed them this week'. To which the Prime Minister replied, 'Yes, I think we did pretty well. Old A. looked very sick. He crouched low down on the bench and kept moistening his lips, a habit of his when excited. He made a great mistake.'[133]

Thomas Jones also considered this episode as an exemplar for F. E. Smith's maxim on Lloyd George; 'The man who enters into real and fierce controversy with Mr Lloyd George must think clearly, think deeply, and think ahead. Otherwise he will think too late.'[134] Northcliffe wrote to Lord Reading in Washington D.C. of Lloyd George's handling of the Maurice affair. 'You have no doubt read of the ridiculous attempt of the Old Gang to unseat him . . . Robertson, Maurice, Jellicoe and all the rest of them have absolutely no following in the country, or in the Army and Navy.' Of the Prime Minister himself Northcliffe added, 'He is complete master of the country if he only knew it.'[135]

At dawn on 8 August, having withstood all that the Germans could throw at them over the previous months, the Allies launched their own counter-offensive. British, French, Australian and Canadian forces broke through the German lines at the Battle of Amiens, in what Erich Ludendorff called 'the black day' of the German army.[136] News from the front was still unclear, however, at 3 p.m., when Lloyd George departed from London's Paddington railway station with Margaret and Megan, heading for south Wales and the National Eisteddfod at Neath where he was due to speak the following day. At Cardiff Central station the Prime Minister left the train to receive a telegram from the War Office. As he returned to his carriage, he then announced to the crowd gathered on the platform, 'We are smashing through . . . We have won a great victory.'[137]

The following day in Neath, Lloyd George received the Freedom of the Borough at a ceremony in Gwyn Hall, where large crowds greeted him. The Prime Minister inspected a parade of the Fifth Volunteer Battalion of the Welsh Regiment, met munitions workers, and spoke with some wounded soldiers. Inside, he told the assembled dignitaries:

> Some friends of mine complain occasionally that I am rather optimistic. I do not think that I am. I was not one of those who thought in August 1914, that it would soon be over. I thought it was a long job and a terrible job. I have, however, always been confident we should get through. I knew the spirit of this land, its strength of purpose and the quality of its people . . . All the conditions made it unlikely that you could bring this conflict to an end in a short time. Nevertheless, we are getting on. It is a long tunnel. Now and again you have a shaft of light that comes down from above, and you go on plunging into further darkness, and then comes another shaft of light. People say, 'We had this before and were plunged into darkness again.' Never mind: you are getting through. Full steam ahead. [Loud cheers] With all the might of the Empire put into it we shall be through the tunnel into perfect daylight.[138]

The meeting concluded with an emotional rendition of the Welsh anthem *Hen Wlad Fy Nhadau* (*Land of my Fathers*).

To attend the Eisteddfod that afternoon, Lloyd George and his party travelled by motorcade, and the *Western Mail* reported that 'The many miles of the road traversed by the journey were thronged with the populace, who had made holiday in order to greet and do honour to our Welsh Prime Minister.'[139] These scenes were also captured by the film director, Maurice Elvey,[140] for the biopic he was making of the life of David Lloyd George,[141] in anticipation of victory in the world war. At the Eisteddfod itself a marquee had been put up to accommodate 8,000 people, but over 12,000 attended. The emotion of the previous year's Chairing of the Bard was not repeated. The winner, the Calvinist Minister J. T. Job,[142] too old to serve at the front, was present to receive his award. But now, instead of the Eisteddfod being held in the pit of grief, there was hope that victory and peace would soon come.

The changing fortunes on the Western Front meant that for the rest of that summer the Prime Minister could turn his attention to the prospect of a general election, in order to seek a personal mandate to continue the task of winning the war, and to demonstrate the strength of his personal appeal to the country. In February the new election regulations, agreed after the Lloyd George government had taken office, became law, meaning that for the first time all men over the age of 21 would be able to vote, whether they owned property or not. They also delivered on the promise Lloyd George had made to Christabel Pankhurst at the Ministry of Munitions in 1915, as women over the age of 30 who owned property were included in the franchise for the first time.[143] The new electoral register would come into force from 1 October 1918, with the best prospects for a general election, the first in nearly eight years, coming after that date.

On 13 and 14 August at Danny House,[144] the estate near Hassocks in West Sussex that George Riddell had rented for the summer, Lloyd George discussed with his friend and confidant the 'forthcoming election'. Riddell wrote in his diary that 'Sir Henry Norman[145] is to organise the campaign. LG says that Norman has written quite a good memorandum. LG absolutely exuding energy and enthusiasm. He has a wonderful way of getting things moving; a sort of all-pervading energy. He is going to Criccieth for a few days, after which he returns to Danny, which he has enjoyed very much, so he says. While he is away he is going to read up on reconstruction, and prepare his opening speech, which he will make at Manchester.'[146]

The finances for the election campaign were being organized by Lloyd George's political fixer, William 'Bronco Bill' Sutherland. On 15 August, Riddell met with Sutherland at the Carlton Club, where he found him:

> An amusing cynical dog. He was engaged as usual in supping and wining, being entertained to dinner by a Tory magnate who is coming over to LG. A few days ago Sutherland dined with Lord Charles Beresford,[147] who has £100,000[148] for party purposes and proposes to utilise it for LG's campaign. Sutherland says they want cash. I gave him some likely names, including Sir Howard Spicer,[149] who came to me the other night to say that he and nineteen friends of his can put up £250,000. The Asquithians are busy hunting for cash and the Tories are doing the same, so not withstanding all the pious protestations against the party system, it is still in reality as strongly entrenched as before.[150]

Hankey had also observed in his diary back in February that he could 'only suppose that Ll.G. put [Beaverbrook] in the Government in order to induce him to finance the new party machine, which he tells me he is about to found. A shady business.'[151]

In Criccieth on 22 August, Lloyd George held a general election planning meeting with Norman, Christopher Addison and Philip Kerr. Freddie Guest was represented by another senior Liberal whip, William Dudley Ward.[152] The question that faced Lloyd George was whether to make a personal appeal to the nation or for the Coalition members to stand together in a re-election campaign. Guest had written to Lloyd George earlier in the month that 'Reports from the constituencies indicate that the bulk of the Electors do not want any issue put before them at the next election of a domestic character, but that if they could be appealed to purely on the issue and conduct of the War, it is certain that you and your Government would be returned by an overwhelming majority.'[153] Norman believed, 'If the decision is for a personal appeal from the P.M. my own opinion is that he can win, but the fight will be more complicated and difficult than if the decision is for a Coalition appeal.'[154]

From Norman's notes of the Criccieth meeting there also remained the unanswered question as to whether the Asquithians, now a named and numbered grouping following the House of Commons vote on the Maurice debate, were to be 'defied, conciliated or ignored'. Lloyd George agreed, though, to pre-empt any negotiation with Bonar Law by accepting protection and preference within the Empire for certain key industries, a question that had been one of the main dividing lines between the Conservatives and Liberals since the turn of the century.[155] The Prime Minister would set this out in his speech in Manchester, which would be followed by pre-election rallies in Newcastle and Leicester, to demonstrate the strong personal rapport that Lloyd George enjoyed with the people.[156]

Back at Danny House in late August, Riddell recorded that Lloyd George was:

> ... strongly in favour of an appeal to the country in November ... LG proposes to hold a meeting of the Liberal Party to ascertain who is prepared to support him. He also proposes to make an arrangement with the Tories as to the seats which are to be left to their candidates.

He says that the Tories have loyally supported him, and he proposes to be equally loyal to them. He hopes to carry with him 120 of the Liberals. The issue at the election will really be who is to run the war. Is it to be LG, Bonar Law and their associates, or Asquith, McKenna, Runciman and others who act with them? . . . He is to make all this plain in his speech at Manchester on September 12.[157]

Lloyd George's visit to Manchester was a major civic occasion, where accompanied by his wife Margaret, the Prime Minister was to receive the Freedom of the City. It was the start of an arduous three-day tour of the north-west of England, where similar honours were also to be bestowed in Salford, Bolton and Blackpool. However, its political nature was evident from the presence of William Sutherland in the Prime Minister's entourage. According to the *Manchester Evening News* a 'huge crowd' had assembled in Albert Square in Manchester to see Lloyd George leave the town hall, departing with the Lord Mayor[158] for the citizenship service, which was to be conducted at the 3,000-seat Manchester Hippodrome theatre.[159] The Prime Minister acknowledged the crowd, 'by raising his silk hat, and his shock of hair, which is now distinctly white, waved in the breeze'.[160] During the open-carriage procession from the Town Hall to the Hippodrome, the 'rain fell heavily'. It did not, however, 'damp the ardour of the crowd which lined the streets, at some places to a considerable depth'.[161] It was nevertheless observed that as 'the rain came down in torrents', the crimson gown of the Lord Mayor was soaked while the Prime Minister's overcoat 'suffered severely'.[162]

This was also a kind of homecoming for Lloyd George, as he had been born in the city, during the brief period his father worked there as a teacher.[163] In his introductory remarks at the Hippodrome the Lord Mayor said, 'We are proud of the fact that you are the first Manchester man who has become Prime Minister.' Lloyd George replied, 'I am proud of it, that I was born here among the humble homes of the people. All my life I have done my poor best to fight for them and to this end I consider that every effort I have put forth is an effort for the real, deep, permanent interests of the people of this and other lands.'[164]

Then addressing the situation in the war, Lloyd George gave his audience hope that the end was in sight. The news from the front was, he said, 'Really good. There are some more steep gradients to climb.

There may be tunnels dark, but they will be short. The worst is over . . . Our casualties in the last offensive were less than one-fifth of what they were in 1916 when we advanced over the same ground.'[165] The Prime Minister was keen to remind his audience the role his own leadership had played in this change of fortune. 'When I came to Manchester in 1915,' he said, referring to the first major speech he had given as Minister for Munitions, 'there is no doubt that our army was deplorably ill-equipped for . . . this war . . . I am glad that through the national effort which was initiated in Manchester the balance has been redressed.' Then concerning the leadership of the army, Lloyd George asked his audience, 'What is the difference between 1916 and 1918? Undoubtedly the main difference is the unity of command . . . I am proud of nothing more in the whole of my public life than the troublous part I took in achieving unity of command – [cheers] and I am prouder of nothing in that struggle than the fact . . . I proposed Marshal Foch should take the lead in this direction.'[166]

Looking ahead to the prospect of peace, Lloyd George emphasized that this could only be secured if the Allies maintained a position of strength. 'The German people must know', he said, 'that if their rulers outrage the law of nations the Prussian military strength cannot protect them from punishment. [cheers] . . . do not let us be misled into the belief that the establishment of a league of nations without power will in itself secure the world.'[167]

The war had brought great changes to society, and advances in science. Lloyd George wanted to harness these forces to change Britain in the post-war world. 'There are times in the history of the world when nations take such a great leap forward. This is such a time . . . there were things that we tolerated before the war that cannot be tolerated any longer.' In particular, he believed the war had demonstrated the need to improve the health and fitness of the nation. He told his audience, 'A war, like sickness, lays bare the weakness of a constitution . . . we have used our human material in this country prodigally, foolishly, cruelly. I asked the Minister of National Service how many more men could we have put into the fighting ranks if the health of the country had been properly looked after. I was staggered at the reply. It was a considered reply; it was "at least one million."' Then, referring to the grades used to assess the health of men when they entered the armed forces, Lloyd George warned, 'You cannot maintain an A1 Empire with a C3 population (cheers).'[168] Speaking for just over an hour and a half he listed his priorities for driving up educational standards, providing the people with better homes and places to work, and increasing productivity in agriculture, as well as in the factories. There was also included, as discussed at Criccieth, his support for 'the shielding of industries which have been demonstrated by the war to be essential to the very life of the nation . . . There does not seem to be I am very glad to say, any difference of opinion amongst any party in the State that these essential industries shall be preserved after the war.'[169] The speech was well received, but it was observed that the Prime Minister wasn't quite on top form and for that reason perhaps spoke for a little longer than he usually would have.

Lloyd George then proceeded with the Lord Mayor from the Hippodrome, through streets of cheering crowds, to a luncheon in the theatre at the Midland Hotel.[170] That afternoon, and by this time feeling distinctly feverish, he spoke with members of the Welsh community at Albert Hall,[171] then Manchester's Methodist Central Hall. Afterwards his health collapsed, and a speaking engagement that evening at the city's Reform Club[172] was cancelled. The following day a bulletin was published from the Town Hall by Lloyd George's doctor, William Milligan,[173] that 'The Prime Minister is suffering from an attack of influenza,[174] accompanied by high temperature and complicated with a sore throat, and is at present confined to bed, and is therefore obliged to cancel all appointments.'[175] That month marked the start of a major new wave of the Spanish Flu pandemic, and hundreds of people a week in Manchester would lose their lives to it. For those first few days the Prime Minister's condition was considered so serious that he was too ill to be moved. Hankey was later told by Lloyd George's valet, George Newnham,[176] that it had been 'touch and go'.[177] The Prime Minister stayed at the Town Hall and received treatment in a converted committee room, with medical support brought in from local hospitals, under the supervision of Dr Milligan. This included being placed on a respirator to help with his breathing. Lloyd George's only other visitors during this time were his wife Margaret and his political secretary William Sutherland. On 21 September, accompanied by Milligan, Margaret, their daughter Megan, Sutherland, and the Liberal Chief Whip Freddie Guest, the Prime Minister went back to London by train in a special carriage. The *Manchester Evening News* reported on the quiet departure from the Town Hall of 'the familiar figure in the unfamiliar garb of a greatcoat, a large white muffler, a respirator, and a soft hat turned down over the face'.[178] From London, Lloyd George was transferred straight to Danny House in Sussex, along with Milligan and Bonar Law, for a working convalescence. When he arrived Frances Stevenson recalled being 'horrified at the mark that the illness had left upon him', concluding that 'He must I fear have been at death's door.'[179] Lord Riddell also observed in his diary that evening, 'LG has had a nasty illness which has shaken him a good deal.'[180] Certainly the planned-for autumn general election would now have to be delayed. At Danny House, when Bonar Law had tried to raise with Lloyd George the need for them to decide upon their 'policy' for the next election, the Prime Minister had responded, 'Well, next week we can have a talk.'[181]

While Lloyd George had been recovering in Manchester, on the Eastern Front, General Allenby had won a decisive battle on 19 September against the Turkish forces at the Battle of Megiddo (19–25 September), opening the road to Damascus, which was captured on 1 October, effectively bringing about the end of the Ottoman Empire. At the same time in Salonika, a combined offensive led by Serbian,[182] French and British forces defeated Germany's ally Bulgaria, forcing her to sign an armistice on 29 September. General Ludendorff advised the German government that no men could be spared from the Western Front to support their Eastern allies, and that overall their military situation was hopeless. On 4 October the new German Chancellor Max von Baden[183] approached the American government with a view to agreeing an armistice to end the war, based on President Wilson's 'Fourteen Points'.[184] Wilson's peace plan had been set out in a speech on American war aims delivered to the United States Congress on 8 January 1918, though it had been the subject of some private mockery between Lloyd George and Clemenceau. The Prime Minister confided in Riddell that 'Clemenceau says that the Almighty was content with ten, but ten are not enough for President Wilson, who wants to surpass all records.'[185]

On 8 October, President Wilson replied to the German government, seeking to clarify their position, before giving a final response, 'as candid and straightforward as the momentous interests involved require'.[186] In particular the President wanted to be 'assured that the German armies will everywhere be withdrawn to German territory and explicit assurance is given that the terms of peace outlined in his address to the Congress . . . are accepted by the Imperial German Government.'[187]

Five days later, on Sunday 13 October, Lloyd George walked before breakfast with Reading and Riddell to the top of Wolstonbury Hill, next to Danny House, taking in its panoramic views of the South Downs. From the privacy of that summit, Riddell recalled, Lloyd George set about 'declaiming all the time against Wilson's action in replying without consultation with the Allies'.[188] 'The Germans have accepted the terms,' the Prime Minister said, 'as I prophesied they would. We are in a serious difficulty. Wilson has put us in the cart and he will have to get us out . . . The time is coming when we shall have to speak out. We have borne the heat and burden of the day and we are entitled to be consulted. What do the fourteen points mean? They are very nebulous.'[189] Yet this lack of definition would work to the advantage of Lloyd George. The fourteen points required Germany to surrender territory it had conquered, but otherwise made no specific commitments to how the boundaries of Europe were to be redrawn or how the former colonies of the defeated powers were to be administered. Wilson had sought to establish principles concerning disarmament and the freedom of the seas, but there were also exemptions given that could be open to wide interpretation in the minds of clever lawyers like Lloyd George.

The Prime Minister's party was joined for lunch at Danny House by Balfour, Bonar Law, Milner, Churchill and Sir Henry Wilson, and later by the First Sea Lord, Sir Rosslyn Wemyss,[190] and Maurice Hankey. There they agreed that mere acceptance of the Fourteen Points alone could not be the basis of an armistice, and that it 'would be fatal to the interests of the Allies unless the armistice with the Central Powers was based upon such naval and military conditions as would prevent Germany reopening the war in the event of a breakdown in negotiations'.[191] This message was telegrammed to the British Embassy in Washington D.C. that evening, and agreed by the War Cabinet the following day. There, Lord Curzon also stated that 'unless it was quite clear from the terms of the armistice that Germany was defeated, it would be fatal to commence negotiations'.[192] The requirement for Germany's unconditional surrender was included in a further note sent by President Wilson on 14 October, to which he added nine days later the abdication of the German Emperor.[193] That day Lloyd George also had lunch with George V, who noted in his diary, 'we had a good talk about everything & he thinks Germany will be ready for peace very soon'.[194]

Events unfolding in Europe would now drive the war to its conclusion. The German navy mutinied at Wilhelmshaven on 29 October and on 4 November, Austria withdrew from the war and an armistice with its defeated empire came into effect. On 8 November, Germany received the armistice terms from the Allies, and was given 72 hours to accept them. The following day, revolutionary unrest in Germany led to the abdication of the Kaiser, and the appointment of the Social Democratic Party leader, Friedrich Ebert,[195] as the first Chancellor of the German Republic. That evening, Lloyd George addressed the Lord Mayor[196] of London's Banquet at the Guildhall, the glittering annual event where the people who run the country report back to their investors, creditors and adjudicators. *The Times* described the scene:

> In the Great Hall . . . set with the customary splendour . . . The procession of the Lord Mayor[197] and his chief guests around the hall to their seats at the head of the table was stately and full of variety and colour. When all were seated, the khaki, navy blue, and light blue of the Services, the Court dress of Ministers, the scarlet robes of Judges, the darker stuff of civic gowns, the stars and sashes and ribbons blended with the softer colouring of women's dresses into a picture which could hardly be reproduced outside the grey walls of the Guildhall.[198]

Frances Stevenson recalled as well, 'I shall never forget the triumphal procession that filed into the Guildhall to take their places at the high table. It was one of the peaks of L.G.'s career, for it was clear that although the Armistice had not actually been signed, the war was as good as over.'[199]

At the same occasion, exactly 113 years before, and three days after the news of Nelson's victory at the Battle of Trafalgar[200] had first reached London, the Prime Minister, William Pitt the Younger, had told his audience that 'England has saved herself by her exertions, and will, as I trust, save Europe by her example.'[201] Now, Lloyd George, this cottage-bred man on the brink of leading his nation to its greatest ever triumph, was introduced by a loud fanfare of trumpets to the brokers, bankers and merchants, whose investments drove the commerce that empowered the British Empire. There was 'much cheering and waving of handkerchiefs',[202] as the Prime Minister took to his feet. To loud and prolonged cheers he told his audience, 'The potent Empire that threatened civilization is now tonight headless and helpless. Its head the Kaiser, and the Crown Prince, have abdicated.'[203] Frances Stevenson also remembered of this moment that 'the jubilant applause . . . was almost overwhelming'.[204]

Lloyd George continued, 'Events have marched on the wings of a hurricane growing in force and momentum month by month, week by week, day by day, hour by hour. We have never lived in such days.' Then, speaking of the recent conference at Versailles to discuss the terms of the Armistice to be offered to Germany and her allies, he said:

> Walking through the beautiful forests of Versailles – the leaves were falling but these were not alone. Empires and Kingdoms and Kings and Crowns were falling like withered leaves before a gale. It was a remarkable week. Bulgaria had just gone. Turkey went at the beginning of our Conference. Then followed Austria. You may ask why we delayed sending our terms to Germany, the most formidable of our foes. It was due to no disagreement among the Allies. We thought it better to begin by knocking the props from under her. [Laughter] It is an old policy that some of us have advocated for years, and it has come off at last.[205]

As to the question of whether Germany would accept the Allies' armistice, Lloyd George made clear the choice that she faced. 'She is enveloped in ruin. She has ruin encircling her. It is getting nearer to her day by day and hour by hour. She has ruin tearing at her vitals, ruin outside and ruin inside. There is but one way she can avert it, and that is by immediate surrender.' Then looking to the future he proclaimed:

> This nation has accomplished greater things in the last four years than it has ever achieved in the whole story of its glorious past, and I say without hesitation that the British Empire never stood higher in the councils of the world than it does today. That is due in the main to the valour, the sacrifice, the skill and the resource of her sons; but it is also due to the fact that wisely, we sank all sectional interests, all partisan claims, all class and creed differences in the pursuit of one

common purpose which Providence in its mysterious decrees had called upon the British Empire to help to effect. That task is not at an end when the treaty of peace is signed; it will only be beginning . . . I appeal that as we united in war to achieve victory so we shall unite in peace, and lift up this country by our common efforts to a position such as it never held in all its history. [Loud cheers][206]

The following day at Walton Heath, on the eve of the Armistice, as they waited for news as to whether the German government would accept the terms of the Allies, Lloyd George was locked in conference with Bonar Law. Later he told Riddell, 'Bonar Law said to me, "Do you want to go down to history as the greatest of all Englishmen." I replied, 'Well, I don't know that I do . . . But tell me your prescription! Do you mean retire into private life now that the war has been won?' Bonar Law said, "Yes!" He is right.'[207]

That evening Lloyd George returned to Downing Street where he dined with his wife Margaret, Churchill and Smuts. During their meal the Prime Minister received a message that he was needed for a telephone call with the War Office. Margaret remembered, 'The three of us that were left never spoke a word. Mr Churchill paced restlessly up and down the room. General Smuts and I sat in silence. He was not gone many minutes, but to us sitting there it seemed an age. When he returned he was smiling and said only, "They're going to sign."'[208]

TEN

Prime Minister for Life

At 5.10 a.m. on 11 November 1918, onboard a railway carriage parked in an isolated clearing of the dark and misty Compiègne forest some 80 kilometres north of Paris, the Supreme Allied commander, General Foch, and the First Sea Lord, Admiral Wemyss, signed the armistice agreement with Germany, which would come into effect six hours later. There were four signatories for Germany: Matthias Erzberger, who led the delegation and was a politician from the Catholic Centre Party; Count Alfred von Oberndorff from the Foreign Ministry; Major-General Detlof von Winterfeldt, representing the army; and Captain Ernst Vanselow, from the navy. In return for the termination of hostilities, the German government had agreed to immediately leave conquered territories and withdraw their troops to the east of the River Rhine. The Allies would then establish defensive bridgeheads at Mainz, Koblenz and Cologne. Germany was to surrender her submarines and surface fleet, as well as large quantities of war materiel. All Allied prisoners were to be released without reciprocation. There was no question that Germany had not been defeated.

Leo Amery recalled his journey into Whitehall on that historic day:

Came up this morning on the 24 Bus and was presently passed by a lorry full of shouting soldiers saying it was finished. When we got near Downing Street, I saw a crowd running across, so I got off and was in time to see L.G. at his doorstep telling them (being then about five minutes to eleven) that the war was over at eleven o'clock and that they could cheer with a good will. They did so and also started singing 'God Save the King', a performance politically though not musically quite satisfactory.[1]

At the door of Number 10, Lloyd George had announced to the assembled crowd, 'At 11 o'clock this morning the war will be over. We have won a great victory, and are entitled to a bit of shouting.'[2] Winston Churchill remembered at that hour, standing at the window of Lloyd George's old office in the Ministry of Munitions, looking towards Trafalgar Square, and 'waiting for Big Ben to tell that the war was over'. As the first chimes struck, the streets were deserted, but he then noticed emerging from one of the government offices:

> ... the slight figure of a girl clerk, distractedly gesticulating while another stroke sounded. Then from all sides men and women came scurrying into the street. Streams of people poured out of all the buildings. The bells of London began to clash. Northumberland Avenue was now crowded with people ... All bounds were broken. The tumult grew. It grew like a gale, but from all sides simultaneously. The street was now a seething mass of humanity ... Almost before the last stroke of the clock had died away, the strict, war-straitened regulated streets of London had become a triumphant pandemonium. At any rate it was clear that no more work would be done that day.[3]

Later, Lloyd George appeared at the window on the first floor of 10 Downing Street, accompanied by Bonar Law and Winston Churchill, and told the thousands standing below, 'The people of this country and the people of the Dominions and of our Allies have won such a victory for freedom as the world has never seen. You have all had a share in it, and this is their hour for rejoicing.'[4] A reporter from the *Evening Mail* observed that 'A rousing cheer, which will long be remembered by those who heard it, greeted the speech, and then the crowd swollen by this time to enormous proportions, surged into Whitehall to begin a day of rejoicing unequalled within the memory of man.'[5]

Just before three o'clock that afternoon Lloyd George entered the chamber of a crowded House of Commons where he was greeted by 'loud cheers, members rising in their places and waving their order papers'.[6] Then, after being called by the Speaker,[7] Lloyd George rose to more cheers to announce the terms of the Armistice with Germany, and concluded, 'at 11 o'clock this morning came to an end the cruellest and most terrible war that has ever scourged mankind. I hope we may say that thus, this fateful morning, came to an end all wars.'[8]

That evening, Lloyd George dined at 10 Downing Street with Sir Henry Wilson, Winston Churchill and F. E. Smith. Wilson wrote in his diary that 'We discussed many things, but principally the coming General Election. Lloyd George wants to shoot the Kaiser. F.E. [F. E. Smith] agrees. Winston does not; and my opinion is that there should be a public *exposé* of all his works and actions.' After dinner, Wilson walked home from Downing Street to Eaton Place, passing 'Wonderful crowds in the streets showing wonderful loyalty.' As he made his way along Buckingham Palace Road he came upon a well-dressed lady in mourning black, all alone and weeping. Wilson approached her asking if she needed help, to which she replied, 'Thank you. No, I am crying, but happy, for now I know that all my three sons who have been killed in the war have not died in vain.'[9]

The newspapers were full of notes of personal congratulations to the Prime Minister, including from President Wilson's representative Colonel House, who wrote, 'No one has done more to bring about this splendid victory than you.'[10] While no one person or single act could claim credit for winning the war, Lloyd George had played a leading role in many of the most significant decisions – from resolving the crisis over the supply of shells, to the drive for conscription, the adoption of the convoy system to counter the U-boat menace, and establishing the unity of command on the Western Front. Each of these challenges faced substantial institutional resistance and required Lloyd George's leadership to see them through. Yet the greatest lesson, one that he had learned before any other senior government minister, was that winning a world war would require every ounce of courage, resilience, tenacity and vigour that the nation and its leaders could bring forth. It was not the one thing you did, but everything. In the late 1920s, when Winston Churchill was Chancellor of the Exchequer, and completing *The World Crisis*, he met with Lloyd George to discuss questions about the war that only he would be able to answer. After the meeting Churchill told his parliamentary private secretary, Bob Boothby,[11] 'Within five minutes the old relationship between us was completely re-established. The relationship between Master and Servant. And I was the Servant.'[12] The example of Lloyd George's wartime premiership was one that, as Churchill would later state when he held that office during the Second

World War, 'forever abides with me, and to which I have often recurred in thought during our present second heavy struggle against German aggression'.[13]

Thomas Jones observed of Lloyd George when the Armistice was signed that:

> His prestige as the architect of victory was at this supreme moment unparalleled in British political history, and had he been able to rely on a referendum his majority against any conceivable rival candidate would have been overwhelming. But he underrated his unique power to sway the country, of which his wife and some of his secretaries sought in vain to convince him: he could not ignore the mechanics of party warfare, he had to provide a programme and to endorse candidates.[14]

The tragedy for Lloyd George was that the political decisions he felt compelled to make when his power was at its greatest would continue to constrain him. He remained the head not of a party or movement, but a team of competing rivals, who were his out of convenience rather than conviction.

Lloyd George believed that the old party structures had been broken by the challenges of war and reconstruction, as well as the rise of revolutionary Socialism in Europe. Therefore, progressive politicians on the centre and right should combine. Lloyd George was a Liberal who had championed illiberal methods like conscription in order to win the war. He'd done more than any previous British statesman to alleviate the conditions of the poor, but was not a Socialist, and certainly had no sympathy for the leading Labour Party pacifists like Ramsay MacDonald. His own personal politics did not fit neatly into the ideologies, such as they were, of any of the parties. Lloyd George thought of himself, 'incongruous as it may appear', he would tell Riddell, 'as a Nationalist-Socialist.[15] I was and am a strong believer in nationality, and I believe in the intervention of the State to secure that everyone has a fair chance and that there is no unnecessary want and poverty. Of course, there are wasters who must suffer the penalty of their own misconduct; but every member of the community who behaves properly and does his best should be secured a fair chance. That has always been my creed.'[16] Even the use of the term 'Nationalist-Socialist' demonstrated that Lloyd

George was thinking of new formations that crossed the pre-war political boundaries. Earlier in the year, Riddell had recorded in his diary that 'L.G. thinks that the Liberal Party in its old form is a thing of the past and cannot be galvanised into life . . . He thinks that it may come to a fight between him and Henderson, and that all Parties, including Labour, will be split and reconstituted.'[17]

Bonar Law's political secretary Davidson 'was convinced' from the early days of the Coalition 'that Ll.G had made up his mind that somehow or other he would create a united Centre Party . . . of which he would be the head'.[18] He even thought that should the opportunity arise either from Bonar Law's retirement or resignation that Lloyd George had 'set himself out to lead the Tory Party, and integrate his Liberals into the government to win the war, and convert the non-party into a party which would have been a national party after the war. That might have had an appeal to a Conservative, because there is one repetitive sentence which you will find in all Conservative leaders' speeches, namely that the Conservative Party is not a party of factions; it is a national party . . . Lloyd George was clever enough to make that appeal in order to get the leadership of the Tory Party.'[19]

Yet Lloyd George was understandably cautious about placing his future prospects in the hands of a Conservative Party that had before the war been his principal opponent. As early as August 1917, Geoffrey Dawson wrote after meeting with him that:

> . . . he didn't want either to relapse into the old Liberal Party . . . or to be left entirely with the old Unionists. He kept recurring to the fate of [Joseph] Chamberlain,[20] who (according to L.G.) had placed himself in a false position when he joined the Conservatives and abandoned his old non-conformist backing . . . His own view was that the old Unionist and Liberal Parties both contained elements with which it was impossible to work for reconstruction . . . What he hoped to do was to get together soon a private meeting of some half-dozen friends from each of the old parties – say, his own friends and Lord Milner's – to see whether they could agree upon a basis of reconstruction policy and if not, then agree to carry on for the period of the war and part afterwards. He repeated that he had found nothing in Lord Milner's views to which he would not himself subscribe.[21]

The election preparations over the previous months had persuaded Lloyd George, however, that the only real prospect for an early campaign was to seek the re-election of the Coalition government with the broadest possible base of support. In time though, Lloyd George believed the Coalition MPs could come together to form a new centre or national party. In early November, Lloyd George and Bonar Law had agreed the text of a letter in the name of the Prime Minister, which would be the basis of their co-operation in a future government. This set out the need for a 'fresh Parliament' where candidates could be returned to support the Coalition government 'not only to prosecute the War to its final end and negotiate the peace, but to deal with the problems of reconstruction which must immediately arise directly an armistice is signed'.[22] The commitment was made to 'the imperative need for improving the physical conditions of the citizens of this country through better housing, better wages, and better working conditions', without going into details as to how this would be funded.[23] These were all issues that Lloyd George had championed in his Manchester speech in September. Similarly, the Prime Minister's support for the protection of vital industries, also voiced at that time, was restated, along with a promise that there would be no new taxes on imported food. This was a compromise on the old pre-war divisions between the Liberals and Conservatives on free trade versus tariff reform. On Home Rule for Ireland, there was a commitment not to support any 'settlement which would involve the forcible coercion of Ulster'. It was also recognized that any future decision 'must be postponed until the condition of Ireland make it possible'.[24] Again, what that would mean in reality was open to wide interpretation.

Co-operation with the Conservatives was a necessity for Lloyd George, as the Liberals remained divided and unreconciled since the coup that had brought down Asquith two years before. In late September there had been overtures from Lords Rothermere and Murray to George Riddell, that Asquith should be brought into the Coalition as Lord Chancellor, the offer he had turned down in 1917. Although Rothermere's brother Lord Northcliffe gave Riddell a message to pass on to Lloyd George that 'the few people to whom I have mentioned the matter seem outraged by the idea'.[25] As before, the question never really arose, as Asquith would not accept a subordinate position to Lloyd George. The Liberal President of the Board of Education, Herbert Fisher,[26] noted after seeing the Prime Minister on 6 November, 'L.G. says Asquith had definitely decided not to join. He is too proud. The Coalition must go on.'[27] Furthermore, Asquith and his followers would decline, as the former Prime Minister noted in his memoirs, 'to bind themselves' to the Coalition, 'by a blind pledge in advance, to become items in what was called a "reliable majority"'.[28]

On 12 November, Lloyd George sought to rally the Liberal MPs who were loyal to his cause, at a meeting at 10 Downing Street. There he asked them of the post-war world:

> Are we to lapse back into the old national rivalries and animosities and competitive armaments, or are we to initiate the reign on earth of the Prince of Peace? . . . We must not allow any sense of revenge, any spirit of greed, any grasping desire to override the fundamental principles of righteousness . . . I was reared in Liberalism . . . I am too old to change. I cannot leave Liberalism . . . Now is the great opportunity of Liberalism! Let it rise to it! Don't let it sulk. If there are personal differences, in God's name what do they count compared with the vast issues and problems before us? Let us help to regenerate the people, the great people who have done more to save the world in this great crisis than any other nation.[29]

At the same time, at the Connaught Rooms in Covent Garden, Bonar Law and Balfour addressed a meeting of 1,000 Conservative representatives, including MPs, parliamentary candidates and members of the party's Central Council. There they endorsed the letter from Lloyd George as the basis for renewing their commitment to the Coalition. On 14 November the Labour Party voted to leave the government and to stand as an opposition party at the general election. As the meeting closed, George Bernard Shaw[30] remarked, 'Go back to Lloyd George and say nothing doing.'[31] The same day, Bonar Law announced to the House of Commons that Parliament would be prorogued on 25 November for a General Election on Saturday 14 December. The Coalition Liberal and Conservative candidates each received a letter of endorsement from Lloyd George and Bonar Law, along with a guarantee that neither party in the government would challenge each other's representatives. Asquith derisively referred to this as a process where 'seats are bartered and candidates ticketed and political coupons distributed'.[32] However, the balance of power in this election greatly favoured the Conservatives, who had 364 'Coupon' candidates compared to 159 for the Coalition Liberals.

In public the election campaign was a triumphal procession for Lloyd George, starting in Wolverhampton on Saturday 23 November, where he was given the Freedom of the Borough and in a famous speech at the Grand Theatre told his audience, 'What is our task? To make Britain a fit country for heroes to live in (cheers). There is no time to lose. I want us to take advantage of this new spirit. Don't let us waste this victory merely in ringing joy bells.'[33] However, in the background, there was a great dispute raging between Lloyd George and Lord Northcliffe over the position the government would adopt in the peace negotiations with Germany.

At a meeting at 10 Downing Street shortly after the Armistice, Lloyd George claimed that Northcliffe insisted on being amongst official delegates from the British government to attend the peace conference. The Prime Minister also informed him that George Riddell would be in charge of news and information during the negotiations. The meeting, according to Lloyd George, left Northcliffe 'visibly astonished and upset at my declining to accede to his request', and ended with him telling the great press baron to 'Go to Hell.' The two men never met again.[34]

When the election was announced on 14 November, Northcliffe presented himself at Printing House Square, where according to Dawson's diary, he told his editors that 'he'd served notice on LG that he could no longer support him'.[35] Lloyd George would later tell Tom Clarke of his meeting with his chief. 'I broke with Northcliffe. I refused absolutely to have him at the Peace Conference. I put up with him for four years. The break had to come – when he wanted to dictate to me. As Prime Minister I could not have it. Northcliffe thought he could run the country. I could not allow that.'[36] He recounted a similar story to Riddell at Walton Heath at the end of the month, adding that Northcliffe 'asked that I should tell him what was to be the composition of my Government, should I become Prime Minister again. Of course I would never agree to give such information.'[37] Lloyd George also told Riddell that Northcliffe had tried to 'blackmail' him, adding that 'Northcliffe does not seem to realise that if I quarrel with him I shall raise a great accession of support in many quarters, and that I really have little to fear from his opposition . . . I would rather cease to be Prime Minister than be at the beck and call of Northcliffe, Rothermere, Beaverbrook & Co.'[38]

The personal impact of the victory on Lloyd George would seem to have released him from two of the bonds that friends and observers had previously believed had held him back; fear of Northcliffe, and not realizing the immense power that his standing amongst the British people gave him. Yet as news of his row with Northcliffe spread, it brought to the surface again the old blackmail rumours. Moreton Frewen,[39] an uncle of Winston Churchill, wrote to John Strachey,[40] the editor of *The Spectator*, on 23 January 1919 that he'd been told by Gilbert Parker[41] in strict confidence that 'There are two Marconi letters of the PM's in Northcliffe's hands and to a degree they are compromising. These letters are about to come out in a libel action now ripening.'[42] On the same day, Walter Long also wrote to tell Lloyd George that:

> The talk of the town is that Northcliffe is out to destroy you, and rumours are going about that he has some Marconi letters of yours. I knew nothing about these, perhaps you would care to instruct your solicitors to make inquiries. Of this I am perfectly certain, that if he attempts anything of the kind, public opinion will be unanimous in condemning him as a blackmailer and supporting you, and speaking for a moment for my own Party, I am absolutely certain that they will be behind you and outspoken in their condemnation of such cowardly and un-English tactics.[43]

These letters, if they existed, never came to light, but for the reasons set out by Walter Long, if Lloyd George was ever going to test Northcliffe's resolve, that moment had now come.

The Times adopted a more critical tone of Lloyd George and the coalition campaign, based on Northcliffe's concern that the coupon system would give too much authority to the 'Old Gang'[44] Conservative politicians. On 4 December the paper commented that 'Nobody, we imagine, has any doubt that Mr. Lloyd George would have been wiser if he had frankly gone to the country on his own great war record and his own views on social reform without any attempt at securing pledges or making bargains over candidates.'[45] *The Times* also observed that the Conservative Party 'is anxious for a true Coalition, and is bent on doing all it can to prevent the revival of party politics. It has seen a definite reassertion of the old party position by the Asquith Liberals, and frankly it does not like the spectacle.'[46] Although it would certainly seem that the compliments were returned. John Simon, for example, complained that during the election, 'Liberal candidates, who regarded Asquith as their leader, were effectively proscribed, as though they had not supported the prosecution of the war!'[47] Asquith himself recalled in his memoirs that 'As I drove round the voting stations in Fife on the polling day, I saw, amongst other specimens of the electioneering appeals of my Conservative opponent, huge placards with the inscription "Asquith nearly lost you the War. Are you going to let him spoil the Peace?"'[48]

Despite Lloyd George's hope when he addressed the Coalition Liberal MPs in Downing Street on 12 November, that Britain should avoid imposing a peace motivated by 'revenge' against Germany, the mood in the country was that their enemies must be made to pay. Although personal relations had broken down between the two men, on 7 December Northcliffe sent the Prime Minister a telegram stating that 'The public are expecting you to say definitely [the] amount of cash we are to get from Germany. They are very dissatisfied with [the phrase] "limit of her capacity" which [may] mean anything or nothing. They are aware France has an amount. I am apprehensive of serious trouble in the country on the matter.'[49] To which Lloyd George responded, 'You are quite wrong about France. No ally has named [a] figure. Allies in complete agreement as to demand for indemnity. Inter-Allied Commission will investigate on behalf of all on identical principles. Don't be always making mischief.'[50]

Two days later though, Eric Geddes told an election meeting at the Drill Hall[51] in Cambridge that as far as extracting reparations from Germany was concerned, 'I will squeeze until you can hear the pips squeak.'[52] On 11 December, two days before the poll, Lloyd George gave a speech in Bristol where he stated that the former Kaiser should be put on trial. When he was asked about the costs of the war, 'Who is to foot the bill?', someone in the crowd responded 'Germany' and another 'In full', to which the Prime Minister responded 'Certainly in full, if they have got it.'[53] To Northcliffe's criticism, Lloyd George's commitment could have meant anything or nothing, but the inference was reported as a commitment to make them pay. In the same speech he also suggested that the Imperial Committee of experts had calculated that the total cost of the war to the Allies had been £24 billion.

For the first time in a British general election, all of the votes were cast on the same day, 14 December, but were not counted until 28

December, to allow time for the ballots of soldiers serving overseas to be returned. That evening George V wrote in his diary, 'The results of the General Election are coming in fast Lloyd George & his coalition party have got a great majority.'[54] It was an overwhelming expression of support for the Coalition candidates. Some 379 Conservatives and 127 Lloyd George Liberals were elected, giving them a total of 506 MPs out of a House of Commons of 707 seats. In reality, their advantage within the Parliament was even greater as the old Irish Parliamentary Party had been reduced to a rump of just 7 members, their places having been taken by 73 members[55] elected for the Sinn Féin[56] republicans, who refused to take their seats and swear allegiance to the King. Asquith, McKenna, Runciman, Simon and Samuel all lost their elections, and only 36 of the old Liberals had been returned. For the first time, the Labour Party would be the largest present opposition party with 59 MPs. Overall, 260 new MPs were elected to Parliament, but the average age of the House of Commons was higher. Perhaps this was not surprising as many of the younger men who might have stood for election were yet to be demobilized from the armed forces. These new arrivals were businessmen and shop-stewards who had largely fought the Germans on the home front, leading Stanley Baldwin to famously comment that Parliament contained a lot of 'hard-faced men who looked as if they had done well out of the war'. Lloyd George too told Riddell, 'It is a curious assembly. Quite different from any other House of Commons I have known. When I was speaking, I felt, as I looked in front of me, that I was addressing a Trade Union Congress. Then when I turned round, I felt as if I were speaking to a Chamber of Commerce.'[57]

Lloyd George had the mandate he needed to negotiate the peace and begin the task of reconstructing Britain after the war. However, the 'Coupon Election' had made the Conservatives the dominant party in the House of Commons. In the absence of the Sinn Féin members, on their own they had a majority of 124 members over all of the other parties combined. If they chose, at any moment they could force Lloyd George and his Coalition Liberals out of power and govern by themselves. The shattering of Asquith and his supporters now meant that there was in effect no Liberal Party of any great standing to reunite, with their combined strength still being the lowest number elected since the creation of the party in the 1830s. There was no question that the Prime Minister's personal standing in the eyes of the nation had never been greater, but in his moment of triumph he had also placed his fate in the hands of his rivals.

On 5 January 1919, Northcliffe descended on Dawson at Printing House Square and complained, according to the editor's diary, that '*The Times* has not spoken with his voice! He held me entirely responsible for LG's great majority!! . . . In future he was going to take a more direct hand in the conduct of the paper.'[58] Five days later, Lloyd George made changes to the Cabinet following the election; this included appointing F. E. Smith as Lord Chancellor, and being made Lord Birkenhead as part of the process. Churchill replaced Milner as Secretary of State for War, and Milner was moved to the Colonial Office. Balfour remained Foreign Secretary, and Bonar Law stayed as Leader of the House of Commons, but decided not to retain the position of Chancellor of the Exchequer, which was given to Austen Chamberlain. Lord Curzon was Lord President of the Council and Leader of the House of Lords, whilst Walter Long became First Lord of the Admiralty and Eric Geddes stayed in the Cabinet as Minister without Portfolio, later becoming Minister for Transport. Christopher Addison was moved from heading the Ministry of Reconstruction to lead the Local Government Board, but in June would be appointed as Great Britain's first ever Minister for Health. There was no return, however, for Edward Carson.

Chamberlain seemed underwhelmed, though, by his return to the Treasury and the top echelons of British politics, telling his sister Ida, 'I enter an office which I dislike with no circumstance omitted that could help increase my distaste for it. I do not feel sure that I shall get any help or backing from the P.M.; the financial situation is full of difficulty & the normal working of the Treasury control of finance has been utterly overthrown first by Lloyd George as Chancellor & afterwards by four years of war. So I have a heavy heart & not very much pleasure in prospect.'[59] He was also frustrated that he was not to have the use of 11 Downing Street, which would remain with Bonar Law. Lloyd George also intended to carry on with the small, three-man War Cabinet model established in 1917, of which Chamberlain would not be a permanent member. However, dissent from within the government would see a return to the peacetime model of Cabinet government by the autumn of 1919. Northcliffe also felt his concerns about too much power resting with the Conservative 'Old Gang' had been vindicated. He wrote to Dawson, 'I am not given to saying . . . "I told you so", but I saw the possibilities of the present deplorable Cabinet when I asked you to begin that campaign last summer. I blame myself greatly for my lack of vigour in regard to The Times when I was ill at Elmwood[60] in November and December.'[61] This was almost the last straw for Dawson, and by 6 February he left his position as editor of The Times by mutual consent.

On 11 January 1919, leaving domestic concerns behind him, Lloyd George led the British Empire Delegation to Paris for the start of the peace conference. He departed though, as Churchill would later write, 'somewhat dishevelled by the vulgarities and blatancies of the recent General Election. Pinned to his coat-tails were the posters, "Hang the Kaiser", "Search their Pockets", "Make them Pay"; and this sensibly detracted from the dignity of his entrance upon the scene.'[62] The British official representatives, led by the Prime Minister, were Balfour, Bonar Law, Sir Henry Wilson and Edwin Montagu, the Secretary of State for India. Lord Curzon would remain in London, but in the absence of Balfour would become responsible for the work of the Foreign Office, outside of the peace conference. In Paris they would be supported by Maurice Hankey and a team of over 400 officials. The Hotel Astoria at 133 Avenue des Champs-Elysées became the offices of the British Foreign Office in Paris.[63] For accommodation the delegation took over the Hotel Majestic at 19 Avenue Kléber, close to the Arc de Triomphe, with a large annex to the rear, the Villa Majestic in Rue La Pérouse, which was home to Hankey and the senior officials. According to Harold Nicolson,[64] one of the resident diplomats, the Majestic was a 'vast caravanserai . . . constructed almost entirely of onyx for the benefit of the Brazilian ladies who, before the war, could come to Paris to buy their clothes'.[65] For reasons of security the Hotel Majestic had been entirely staffed from England, from the concierge to the chambermaids, giving it the flavour of a large railway hotel, rather than a Parisian salon.

One of the British officials, Clement Jones,[66] remembered spending an evening in 'the ballroom in the basement of the Hotel to watch the young things dancing. J. T. Davies surprised me by coming up at once and introducing me to his party, which consisted of Megan Lloyd George, Miss Stevenson and the Downing Street typists . . . The room was nearly full and the dancing marvellous to behold, fox trots and what-not!'[67] On another evening, Lloyd George arranged for them to be entertained at the Majestic by the singer Leila Megáne,[68] who performed for the Paris Opera House, but was originally from north

Wales, born less than 30 miles from Criccieth, but with the support of the Prime Minister had established herself as a star in the French capital. Clement Jones recalled that 'the concert was a personal triumph for Lloyd George in that marvellous way he had of getting hold of all the thunder and limelight that may be going'.[69]

Lloyd George stayed in a 'palatial'[70] apartment a short walk from the Hotel Majestic, at 23 Rue Nitot.[71] Located on a quiet cobbled street with a clear view of the Eiffel Tower, it had been the Paris home of Lord Michelham,[72] who'd died the week before, and whose widow offered its use to the Prime Minister. The Michelhams had furnished the apartment with the help of the famous art dealers, the Duveen brothers,[73] and on walls of the Drawing Room there were 'Gainsboroughs, Lawrences, and other old English masters, along with rich tapestries – exquisite pieces'.[74] There the Prime Minister was accommodated with the Michelhams' resident French cook, and Newnham, his valet from 10 Downing Street. Frances Stevenson would later write that, 'L.G. used to say that the happiest time of his life was the six months he spent in Paris during the conference. The worry of the war was finished . . . the framing to the peace brought out all his arts and skill as a negotiator – he enjoyed the fray of the conference table: and in addition, he was able to indulge to his heart's content in entertaining, which he loved and for which, almost for the first time in his life, he possessed complete and unrestricted facilities.'[75]

The Paris Peace Conference formally opened on 18 January 1919 at the French Ministry of Foreign Affairs, the Quai d'Orsay. The date was chosen to mark the proclamation of the German Empire by Kaiser Wilhelm I[76] in the Hall of Mirrors at Versailles in 1871. For Clemenceau, this was not history but memory. As a 29-year-old politician and Mayor of Montmartre, he had stayed in Paris during the siege of the city at the end of the Franco-Prussian War.[77] As a young member of the National Assembly, he had resigned rather than support the confiscation of Alsace and Lorraine by a victorious Germany, as a condition for peace. Lloyd George had read Victor Hugo as a young man, whereas Clemenceau had campaigned alongside him for a reprieve for the revolutionary leaders of the Paris Commune.[78]

Woodrow Wilson's early life had also given him a different perspective on war to the British Prime Minister. Wilson, eight years old at the end of the American Civil War, was the first former citizen of the Confederate States to be elected as President of the United States. He remembered seeing his mother care for wounded Confederate soldiers in a hospital established at the Presbyterian church in Augusta, Georgia, where his father was the pastor. Unlike any other President, Wilson knew from his childhood what it was like to live in a defeated nation.

Yet for all of these three leaders, the challenge of the Paris Peace Conference was something completely new. As Lloyd George remembered, 'We were all feeling our way, and I had a sense that we were each of us trying to size up our colleagues, reconnoitring their respective positions, ascertaining their aims and how they stood in reference to the desiderata in which each of them was most deeply interested and involved.'[79]

The full conference consisted of delegates from 32 nations, including separate representation for Australia, New Zealand, Canada, South Africa and India.[80] When it had originally been suggested that the dominions should share one representative as part of the British Empire Delegation, the Canadian Prime Minister, Robert Borden,[81] reminded Lloyd George that his nation 'had lost more men killed in France than Portugal [which had two delegates] had put in the field'.[82] Overall, the task facing them, as Lloyd George would tell the House of Commons, was 'a gigantic one. No conference that has ever assembled in the history of the world has been confronted with problems of such variety, of such complexity, of such magnitude, and of such gravity . . . There has never been in the whole history of this globe anything to compare to it.'[83] The Congress of Vienna, which had redrawn the boundaries of Europe at the end of the Napoleonic Wars, had sat for 10 months in 1814–15; In Paris they would reorganize the world in half that time.

The empires of Austria and the Ottomans had collapsed and would give rise in Paris to the new European states of Czechoslovakia, Hungary, Yugoslavia, and the requirement to organize the territories of Mesopotamia, Syria, Lebanon and Palestine. German colonies in Africa and East Asia were also to be administered by the victorious powers. The revolution in Russia had seen the emergence of independent states in Estonia, Finland, Latvia, Lithuania and Ukraine. The redrawing of the boundaries of Russia and Germany would allow the restoration of an independent Poland. Yet for the big three of Lloyd George, Clemenceau and Wilson, there were also fundamental issues to be resolved relating to the terms to be given to Germany.

On 1 December 1918, Clemenceau and Foch had visited London, and the greeting they received could hardly have been more cordial.

When their train arrived at Charing Cross Station they were welcomed by Lloyd George and members of the Cabinet, a great red carpet ran the length of the platform and the band of the Grenadier Guards played 'La Marseillaise'. The station was full of flags, dressing the entrance and the concourse, including the French tricolor and those of the other Allied nations. A large crowd of Londoners had gathered to cheer their arrival, and they rode in open carriages along Pall Mall to Piccadilly and Hyde Park Corner; cries of 'Vive Clemenceau' were heard clearly.[84] When the two premiers met in private in Lloyd George's rooms at the House of Commons, Clemenceau asked, 'Well, what are we to discuss?', to which his host replied, 'Mesopotamia and Palestine.' 'Tell me what you want,' said Clemenceau and Lloyd George answered, 'I want Mosul.'[85] 'You shall have it,' responded Clemenceau, asking, 'Anything else?' 'Yes, I want Jerusalem too,' said Lloyd George, and the French Premier responded again, 'You shall have it.'[86] When Clemenceau was told that British troops would be staying in Mesopotamia and Palestine, he simply replied, 'All right, I don't care.'[87]

But later in their discussions, Clemenceau challenged Lloyd George, stating, 'From the very day after the Armistice, I found you an enemy of France.' To which the British Prime Minister replied, 'Well, was it not always our traditional policy?'[88] Recalling this exchange in his memoirs Clemenceau wrote, 'Great Britain has not ceased to be an island defended by the waves, which is why she believes herself obliged to multiply causes of dissension among the people of the Continent, so as to secure peace for her conquests. This policy has brought her many a day of triumph, in opposition to us.'[89] What he would care about at the conference would be securing the defence of France from future attack, by making Germany too weak to fight. Wilson's principal aim was the creation of the League of Nations as the forum that would prevent another world war; but Clemenceau held a healthy scepticism for its practical assistance in a time of crisis. However, the French Premier could see that Britain had already achieved much, before even the stroke of a pen at the Paris Peace Conference. As Lloyd George told Riddell during the negotiations:

> The truth is that we have got our way. We have got most of the things we set out to get. If you had told the British people twelve months ago that they would have secured what they have, they would have laughed you to scorn. The German navy has been handed over; the

> German mercantile shipping has been handed over, and the German colonies have been given up. One of our chief trade competitors has been most seriously crippled and our Allies are about to become her biggest creditors. That is no small achievement.[90]

Britain could afford to think of restoring the balance of power in Europe and helping to get Germany back on her feet, because the threat she presented to British trade and shipping had vanished.

Lloyd George would spend the Paris Peace Conference, as he later described, 'seated . . . between Jesus Christ and Napoleon Bonaparte',[91] yet he did not always seek an equilibrium in this balancing act. Clemenceau would complain of his British counterpart, 'All arguments are good to him when he wishes to win a case, and if it is necessary, he uses the next day arguments which he had rejected or refuted the previous day.'[92] On one occasion Clemenceau even called out, 'You have told me seven lies this morning, this is the eighth.'[93] At which point the French Premier remembered, 'Lloyd George, fresh and pink, coming forward with a bright, two-fisted smile, and gesticulations now and then so violent that . . . President Wilson had to interpose between us with outstretched arms, saying pleasantly, "Well, well! I have never come across two such unreasonable men!" which allowed us to end the angry scene in laughter.'[94] Lloyd George then responded, 'Well! I shall expect an apology for these outrageous words!', to which Clemenceau replied, 'You shall wait for it as long as you wait for the pacification of Ireland.'[95]

For most of the first month of the conference, the delegates discussed and agreed the covenant of the League of Nations. Following this, in mid-February 1919, Wilson returned briefly to the United States. While he was away, on 19 February, Clemenceau was shot as he left his apartment in Avenue Benjamin Franklin[96] to meet with Balfour and Colonel House at the Hôtel de Crillon. His assailant, Émile Cottin,[97] a French anarchist with Bolshevik sympathies, fired seven times at the French Prime Minister, only hitting him once. Although he was not seriously injured, the bullet lodged so close to Clemenceau's heart that the doctors declared it was unsafe to remove it. As a consequence of this attack, there was a significant increase in security for all of the delegates at the conference. However, Lloyd George believed that for Clemenceau that attack left a lasting legacy. Frances wrote in her diary that he 'is not the man he was. D. says that he is breaking up, & that the old Clemenceau was killed by Cottin'.[98]

Lloyd George was also called back to Britain in February to help settle major industrial unrest across the country. In Glasgow, on 27 January, the shipbuilding unions had gone on strike calling for a reduction in the working week from 47 hours to 40. They were soon supported by local power-station workers and coal miners. This culminated in violent scenes in George Square in the city, where government troops and tanks were brought in to try and control a major riot. In February the national unions of the miners, railwaymen and transport workers came together to threaten a general strike over pay and conditions. This challenge was repulsed by the offer of a special government commission on the future of the coal industry, which Lloyd George personally introduced the legislation in the House of Commons to establish. This was an often used negotiating strategy of the Prime Minister. It kept things moving, made a concession to the complainants that they had a grievance worthy of consideration, but delayed a final decision to a later date, when the heat of the moment might have reduced. However, a fearful Austen Chamberlain wrote to his sister Hilda that 'I have no expectation of getting through the year without some very serious trouble . . . Smillie[99] the Miner's leader, is a Bolshevik at least, pacifist abroad & at one moment it looked very ugly for us & everyone.'[100]

President Wilson returned to Paris on 14 March, and for the remainder of the conference would reside at a grand house at 11 Place des États-Unis, directly opposite Lloyd George's apartment at 23 Rue Nitot. In fact, from the drawing room of the apartment you could look straight down onto the ground-floor reception rooms of Wilson's house. For the weekend of 22 and 23 March, Lloyd George took key members of the British delegation to stay in Fontainebleau, 55 kilometres south of Paris, with the intention, as he told Riddell, 'to put in the hardest forty-eight hours thinking I have ever done'.[101] The result was a memorandum setting out considerations for the Paris Peace Conference before the final terms to be offered to Germany were drafted. Lloyd George's concern was that a Germany deprived of its great coalfields in the Saarland and Upper Silesia, and humiliated by the permanent removal of its lands to the west of the Rhine, would be unable to recover and vulnerable to revolutionary forces taking over the country. In the memorandum, dated 25 March, he wrote:

> The greatest danger I can see in the present situation is that Germany may throw in her lot with Bolshevism and place her resources, her brains, her vast organising power at the disposal of the revolutionary fanatics . . . They offer to free the German people from indebtedness to the Allies . . . They offer complete control of their own affairs and the prospect of a new heaven on earth . . . If Germany goes over to the spartacists[102] it is inevitable that she should throw in her lot with the Russian Bolsheviks. Once that happens all Eastern Europe will be swept into the orbit of Bolshevik revolution.[103]

With regard to French occupation of the Rhineland, or even the question of whether it should become an independent buffer state to protect France from German aggression, Lloyd George would also tell Clemenceau, 'We must not make a second Alsace-Lorraine for Germany. We are at one with France as to the end to be attained; we are not at one with her as to the means.'[104] Although Lloyd George had supported calls to make Germany pay during the British general election, he could also see that 'We cannot both cripple her and expect her to pay.'[105] The armistice agreement stated that Germany would pay reparations to the Allies, but not how much or what for. On 28 March, Lloyd George introduced John Maynard Keynes to Wilson and Clemenceau. As the leading official from the UK Treasury at the conference, Keynes explained that 'Our uncertainty chiefly concerned Germany's capacity to pay. We proposed to tell the Germans: "Here is what you owe; but we haven't yet determined how much you are able to pay." It is this second point that we will have to discuss with them.'[106] The great coup that Lloyd George executed against President Wilson would, though, be in using the South African Minister Jan Smuts, whom the American greatly admired, to persuade him that British war pensions and family allowances should be included in the reparations bill. It was an example of the great psychological difference between the two men. Wilson stood alone. He had left the leaders of the Republican Party in the United States Senate, whose support he would need to ratify the Treaty, behind in Washington DC. The President trusted his own judgement but isolated himself in the process. He developed almost a martyr complex in seeking complete acceptance or rejection of his judgements. Whereas Lloyd George was prepared to use any tactic that would deliver the result he wanted. By consulting and working with his rivals, he bound them into the decisions that the peace conference would reach.

After the Paris Peace Conference, Keynes would write of Lloyd George, 'How can I convey to the reader any just impression of this extraordinary figure of our time, this siren, this goat-footed bard, this half-human visitor to our age from the hag-ridden magic and enchanted woods of Celtic antiquity.'[107] Then adding in lines he left out of his published portrait of the Welshman, 'One catches in his company that flavour of final purposelessness, inner irresponsibility, existence outside or away from our Saxon good and evil, mixed with cunning, remorselessness, love of power, that lend fascination, enthralment, and terror to the fair-seeming magicians of North European folklore.'[108] Yet Keynes considered that Lloyd George used his powers to full effect to 'bamboozle'[109] President Wilson. Keynes observed:

> What chance could such a man have against Mr. Lloyd George's unerring, almost medium-like, sensibility to everyone immediately round him? To see the British Prime Minister watching the company, with six or seven senses not available to ordinary men, judging character, motive, and subconscious impulse, perceiving what each was thinking and even what each was going to say next, and compounding with telepathic instinct the argument or appeal best suited to the vanity, weakness, or self-interest of his immediate auditor, was to realize that the poor President would be playing blind man's buff in that party.[110]

Wilson certainly conceded that he 'wished that he had a less slippery customer to deal with than L.G for he is always temporizing and making concessions'.[111] Of Wilson himself, though, Keynes noted, 'The President's slowness amongst the Europeans was noteworthy. He could not, all in a minute, take in what the rest were saying, size up the situation with a glance, frame a reply, and meet the case by a slight change of ground; and he was liable, therefore, to defeat by the mere swiftness, apprehension, and agility of a Lloyd George. There can seldom have been a statesman of the first rank more incompetent than the President in the agilities of the council chamber.'[112] It was an observation that Austen Chamberlain later wrote that he'd read with 'malicious pleasure'.[113]

Yet the secret workings of the Paris Peace Conference remained cloaked in mystery back in England, leading to wild rumours and speculation in Lord Northcliffe's newspapers that Lloyd George was planning to go soft on Germany. On 28 March, Riddell discussed the situation with Lloyd George, noting his diary, 'He says Wickham Steed,[114] Editor of *The Times*, has a personal animus against him because he snubbed him. I said the whole world is asking for peace. They want to get to work. All eyes are turned to Paris. The people do not understand the delays. They do not appreciate the difficulties because they have not been explained. They are nervous and critical. They think civilisation may be shattered.'[115] This was also starting to put a personal strain on Riddell's relationship with Lloyd George. He noted in his diary that the Prime Minister told him that he 'really must try to get the papers to be more reasonable',[116] and that 'he used strong language about some of the journalists and rather indicated that the Press had not been properly handled. He said he rather thought about getting Sutherland to come over.'[117]

On 5 April, Lloyd George again exclaimed to Riddell, 'What do you think of the disgraceful attacks upon me in *The Times* and *Daily Mail*? They call me pro-German. That is a libel. I have a good mind to bring an action. I shall certainly say in public what I think about Northcliffe. His action is due to vanity and spleen . . . I should like to ask him (N) this question, "By whom would you replace me? Bonar Law and Balfour both agree with me, so they would be equally objectionable."'[118] However, a few days later Riddell also observed in his diary of Lloyd George that, despite the criticism, 'it is useless to deny that he has become more autocratic, more intolerant of criticism, and more insistent upon secrecy. Thus he has given Northcliffe his opportunity.'[119] Other ministers too, at that time, in particular Milner, Curzon and Birkenhead, had cause to complain at Lloyd George's curtness of manner, or some public rebuke aimed at them from an irritated Prime Minister.[120]

Lloyd George would made good on his promise to 'say in public' what he thought of Northcliffe in an extraordinary speech in the House of Commons on 16 April. The occasion was ostensibly to update Parliament on the progress of the Paris Peace Conference, and he told the members that 'the real danger' to peace was 'The gaunt spectre of hunger is stalking throughout the land. The Central Powers and Russia have overtaxed their strength in the conflict. They are lying prostrate, broken, and all these movements of Spartacists, and Bolsheviks, and revolutionaries in each of these countries are more like the convulsions of a broken-backed creature, crushed in a savage conflict. It is in these conditions, and with this material, that we are making peace.'[121] Referring to the Armistice he said, 'There were peace terms published in November as a model for us to proceed upon. In those peace terms there was not a word about indemnities, not a word about the cost of the War. Reparation – yes, in the strictest and narrowest sense of the term, but no reparation for lost lives, no reparation for damaged houses, not even at Broadstairs.'[122,123] Later, though, Lloyd George turned his fire directly at Northcliffe, stating:

> I am prepared to make some allowance – even great newspapers will forgive me for saying so – and when a man is labouring under a keen sense of disappointment, however unjustified and however ridiculous the expectations may have been, he is always apt to think the world is badly run. When a man has deluded himself, and all the people whom he ever permits to go near to him help him into the belief that he is the only man who can win the War, and he is waiting for the clamour of the multitude that is going to demand his presence there to direct the destinies of the world, and there is not a whisper, not a sound, it is rather disappointing; it is unnerving; it is upsetting . . . but let me say this, that when that kind of diseased vanity is carried to the point of sowing dissension between great Allies, whose unity is essential to the peace and happiness of the world, and when an attempt is made to make France distrust Britain, to make France hate America, and America to dislike France, and Italy to quarrel with everybody, then I say that not even that kind of disease is a justification for so black a crime against humanity . . . They still believe in France that *The Times* is a serious organ. They do not know that it is merely a threepenny edition of the *Daily Mail*. On the Continent of Europe they really have an idea that it is a semi-official organ of the Government. That shows how long these traditions take to die out. I want them to know what all this means. I am doing this in the interests of good will. That is my only apology for taking notice of that kind of trash, with which some of these papers have been filled during the last few weeks.

Neville Chamberlain, now a Member of Parliament, remembered how Lloyd George 'turned to the [government] benches below the gangway' and tapped his head as he said 'diseased vanity'.[124] His half-brother Austen also wrote to their sister Ida of Lloyd George's speech, 'I never liked him better . . . I thoroughly enjoyed the wit & sarcasm of his attack on that mischievous, vain & unscrupulous man.'[125]

On 7 May 1919, the fifth anniversary of the sinking of the *Lusitania*, the peace conference presented its terms to the representatives of Germany. They were aghast at their severity and responded in detail with a 434-page counter-proposal on 29 May. The following morning at Rue Nitot, Lloyd George had breakfast with President Wilson's advisor Bernard Baruch,[126] who remembered 'He said to me that he had taken the opinion of his Cabinet on the German reply and that unless the Conference agreed to modify the treaty in accordance with the German observations, neither the British fleet nor the British army will move to enforce the terms.'[127] Baruch then returned later that day with Wilson, and Lloyd George repeated what he'd said before. The advisor observed that 'Wilson sat there twiddling his thumbs in his lap, as he so often did. His thumbs did not miss a twirl, but his jaw grew white and forehead grew red and he said, "Mr. Lloyd George, now after months of making difficulties, you take the position that I have been taking all along. We have to have some treaty. The world needs it. Now when we are facing the enemy and need a united front you say this. I wish truly to you that you can persuade the French to agree with your new position. I will agree also.'[128]

Lloyd George would achieve moderation to a degree. A Reparations Commission would determine how Germany could afford to compensate the Allies, the Rhineland was to be a demilitarized zone but still part of Germany, referenda would decide the ultimate national home of the Saarland and Upper Silesia, and at a future date Germany might be allowed to join the League of Nations. But most importantly, the conference agreed terms that both the French and German governments would sign up to, meaning that there would be no resumption of the conflict.

On 28 June 1919, the fifth anniversary of the assassination of the Archduke Franz Ferdinand in Sarajevo, the delegates of the Paris Peace Conference met in the Hall of Mirrors at the Palace of Versailles to sign the treaty. That great room, whose 300 reflecting panels had captured the admiring glances of Louis XIV,[129] Kaiser Wilhelm I and now David Lloyd

George, was witness to another great moment of history. On that hot summer afternoon 1,000 people were packed into the Hall to witness the signing. Lloyd George and Bonar Law had to push their way through the crowd in order to reach their seats. Frances Stevenson observed that 'Almost half the room was taken up with representatives of the Press. The Press is reducing everything that is noblest and impressive in modern life into terms of Press photographs and Press interviews. In fact they try to dominate everything. How can you concentrate on the solemnity when you have men with cameras in every direction?'[130]

Sir Henry Wilson recalled, 'The room was much too full, a crowd of smart ladies, constant buzz of conversation, the whole thing unreal, shoddy, poor to a degree.'[131] At 3 p.m. the German signatories were, according to Henry Wilson, 'sort of half marched in by some six Allied officers. The moment that they sat down, Clemenceau rose, and said they would be asked to sign . . . This was translated into Boche for the Boches. They said nothing, but rose and walked over to the table where the book was, and then straight back to their seats.' The Germans had signed the treaty at 3.12 p.m. Then it was the turn of President Wilson, followed by Lloyd George and the British Empire Delegation, then Clemenceau and the remaining delegates. Henry Wilson wrote in his diary, 'I have never seen a less impressive ceremony . . . It only took 45 minutes from 3.10 to 3.55pm.'[132] Yet while the British were underwhelmed by the mechanics of the signing, the old 'Tiger' Clemenceau was long enough in the tooth to see the true symbolism of the occasion. In his memoirs he compared the German signatories in the Hall of Mirrors to those individuals and that event in the same room in January 1871 when their nation's Empire had first been proclaimed:

> The Great King's mirrors now sent back nothing but the will-o'-the-wisps of the big round spectacles like crowns about administrative skulls, whose sour, set faces belied the vague gestures of a frigid courtesy. A tragic silence. Suddenly there was a stir among the silent throng. Upon a velvet-covered bench between two windows there had just been placed in full view three ghastly masks of the hellish tragedy, with eyes unsocketed, with twisted jaws, their faces ploughed with scars – three grievously wounded men, invited to the place of honour, a reminder of hideous torments heroically borne.[133]

Now, at the stroke of a pen, across Europe the lands of old states would be divided into new territories marked by concrete posts bearing the legend, 'Versailles 28.6.1919'.[134]

The following morning Lloyd George departed from the Gare du Nord for London, on a special train for the British delegation. As they pulled out of the station he said to Riddell, 'There is always a sense of sadness in closing a chapter of one's life. It has been a wonderful time. We do not quite appreciate the importance and magnitude of the events in which we have been taking part.'[135] Later, when the steamer that carried them from Boulogne to Folkestone docked on the harbour arm, a large crowd was there to receive them, and Lloyd George told the mayor, Sir Stephen Penfold,[136] 'I think it is a good peace, good for everyone except the Germans, and really it is good for them.'[137] Then, walking across to the train waiting to take the delegates back to London, the Prime Minister learned that the King would take the unprecedented step of waiting to receive him at Victoria Station when he arrived.

Clement Jones remembered that 'the size of the crowds in the streets outside Victoria Station and the warmth of the welcome extended had certainly not been anticipated'.[138] The King wrote in his diary, 'At 6.30 I went with David[139] to Victoria station to meet the Prime Minister on his return from Paris after the signature of peace, he drove with me to B.P. & got a splendid reception from large crowds; Mrs Lloyd George also came.'[140] Frances Stevenson recalled that as Lloyd George departed with the King along Buckingham Palace Road, 'Everyone threw flowers at D. & a laurel wreath was thrown into the Royal carriage. It fell on the King's lap but he handed it to D. "This is for you", he said. D. has given it to me[141] . . . I know better than anyone how well he deserves the laurels he has won.'[142]

On 12 August, George V presented Lloyd George with the Order of Merit,[143] traditionally the personal gift of the Sovereign, and given, as the King wrote in his diary that evening, 'for the great services he has rendered to his country'.[144] Years later, Lord Beaverbrook would recall of this time that 'it is not now possible to realise the immense position of this man Lloyd George'.[145] Even Bonar Law then believed that Lloyd George could be 'Prime Minster for life if he likes'.[146]

ELEVEN

The Rules of the Road

In the 1920s Maundy Gregory,[1] a former bankrupt theatre impresario, would have been considered an unlikely tenant of 38 Parliament Street in Westminster. This smart office was conveniently located for Downing Street, the House of Commons and New Scotland Yard,[2] the headquarters of the Metropolitan Police. The liveried messengers coming and going from the building created a sense of respectability and importance, and the framed signed photograph of Prince Albert, the Duke of York,[3] implied social acceptance. The *Whitehall Gazette* that Maundy Gregory published was seen in the libraries of all the leading gentlemen's clubs, even though they didn't subscribe to it. That was his front, but not the way he'd afforded such plush premises. Out the back, he was running the biggest brokerage for honours and titles ever known.

In 1910, Gregory had bounced back from insolvency by publishing the *Mayfair Society Journal*, a magazine that covered the social life of London's elite. That, and his previous career fundraising for London theatre productions, had taught him that there were a lot of people with new money who were happy to spend it in order to mix with the higher echelons of society. He was unscrupulous, and years later Arthur Askew,[4] once head of the Metropolitan Police's Criminal Investigation Department, said of him, 'I have met many villains in my lifetime but none whom I distrusted more than Maundy Gregory.'[5] Yet in late 1918, Gregory came to the attention of Lord Murray of Elibank, who in turn introduced him to Freddie Guest and William Sutherland. Lord Birkenhead too would become an acquaintance of Gregory, whom he nicknamed 'the cheerful giver'.[6]

Murray believed that as a consequence of the results of the 1918 general election, Lloyd George would have to create a new Centre Party to survive. This would require bringing together the Conservatives with the Coalition Liberals as a single organization, and the establishment of a large political fund to finance future elections. By Murray's estimation they would need to raise £4 million to achieve this and the only sure way to make such a sum was by selling honours.[7] The trade of treasure for title to support the political campaigns of a Prime Minister was nothing new. Over a century before, William Pitt the Younger had let it be known that he believed 'Any man who is master of £10,000 has a right to a Peerage.'[8] Gladstone had sanctioned the sale of peerages for party funds,[9] and in 1895 Lord Salisbury wrote to Queen Victoria's[10] private secretary,[11] that he felt 'distressed at being obliged to lay so large a list of honours before her Majesty. If she comments on it, pray remind her that this is a Coalition Government; that we have an exceptional number of supporters, and consequently an exceptional number of candidates for honours.'[12]

Lloyd George, who cared little for honours himself, would even tell Bonar Law's private secretary, J. C. C. Davidson, that he thought:

> ... it was a far cleaner method of filling the Party chest than the methods used in the United States ... In America the steel trusts supported one political party, and the cotton people supported another. This placed political parties under the domination of great financial interests and trusts. Here a man gives £40,000 to the Party and gets a baronetcy ... The attachment of the brewers to the Conservative Party was the closest approach to political corruption in this country. The worst of it is you cannot defend it in public, but it keeps politics far cleaner than any other method of raising funds.[13]

Yet what Lord Murray and Freddie Guest envisaged for the Lloyd George Fund was on a completely different scale than had been employed before. For the first time they would establish a rate card of cash for honours: £10,000 would secure a knighthood, £30,000 a baronetcy, and if someone wanted a peerage and seat in the House of Lords that would require offers above £50,000.[14] Maundy Gregory would later tell friends that 'Freddy's only concern was that he should not get his hands soiled. That is why he consented to the brokerage system so readily. It eliminated the necessity of him dealing directly with touts who fastidious Freddy described as grubby little men in brown bowler hats. From now on the touts would be my responsibility.'[15] Another Coalition Liberal MP, Colin Coote,[16] who also wrote articles for the *Whitehall Gazette*, described the relationship between Guest and Gregory as that of a 'sportsman [who] employs a retriever . . . to bring the game into the bag'.[17]

While Lloyd George himself kept a safe distance from these shady dealings, Freddie Guest certainly made sure he was appraised of the progress they were making. In May 1919, while Lloyd George was in Paris, Guest wrote to advise with regards to the 'Honours List' that he was 'hoping that you will rely to a certain extent upon my discretion. I think that I should be able to come over to you, if you so desire . . . as it is almost impossible to communicate the details of my recommendations over the telephone.'[18] Overall, between December 1916 and July 1922, Lloyd George would approve the awarding of 1,500 knighthoods and 91 peerages, twice as many as had been granted in the previous 20 years.

Fundraising, though, was only addressing part of Lloyd George's political problems. Even during the peace negotiations in Paris, there was evidence that the lustre of the new government was beginning to lose some of its shine. On 14 March 1919 a Coalition Conservative was heavily defeated by a Liberal in the Leyton West by-election,[19] losing the seat with a swing of more than 24 per cent against the government. A result, Lloyd George told Birkenhead, that was 'a warning to those who have drawn wrong deductions from the overwhelming majority of the last election'.[20] The declaration of another by-election in Hull Central on 11 April, following the death of the Conservative MP, Sir Mark Sykes,[21] produced a similar swing against the government, with another Asquith Liberal defeating the Coalition Conservative. Lord Birkenhead had become strongly convinced of the need for fusion between the Conservatives and Lloyd George Liberals, because of the inherent weakness of Coalition governments as a political force. He believed not only that 'Pre-war politics have disappeared. They no longer divide men's minds or afford the material for acute antagonisms', but that they now had to organize themselves in recognition of this fact. 'Political parties,' he wrote, 'are maintained under democratic conditions in office and retain influence in opposition so long, and only so long, as they can excite enthusiasm and add to, or at least maintain, the number of their adherents in the country. Mere merit

– even if it be assumed – never maintained the vitality of a political party . . . if the Coalition is to remain powerful it must organise itself with a degree of thoroughness comparable to that which is shown by the parities, or the party, which challenge its existence.'[22]

This would become one of the first political issues to which Lloyd George would return after the signing of the Treaty of Versailles. In July, Riddell stayed with the Prime Minister in Wales, where Winston Churchill also came to visit. He noted afterwards in his diary that Lloyd George and Churchill 'must have decided upon joint action as W, after this return to London from Criccieth, made a carefully prepared speech, proposing the formation of a Central Party'.[23] The speech in question was delivered by Churchill at a dinner on 15 July at the Criterion restaurant in London, to a group of parliamentarians who were members of the 'Centre Coalition Group'. Significantly, Birkenhead and the Conservative Chairman Sir George Younger[24] also spoke at the same event.

In his speech Churchill declared that 'party organization must in these serious times be definitely subordinated to national spirit, national interests, and national organization. At the present time it would be a folly and a crime to revert to the ordinary party basis. That would be a crazy game to play.'[25] The *New York Times* also reported 'it was suggested that Churchill had spoken at the instigation of Lloyd George, who, in some quarters was represented as pulling political wires with the object of strengthening his own hand and weakening the influence of Bonar Law'.[26]

The great external threat was presented as revolutionary Socialism, as exemplified by the Bolsheviks in Russia. The immediate challenge to the Coalition in Britain would come from Labour and the trades unions. There were ongoing disputes with the coal miners, particularly after the publication of the report of the Sankey Commission[27] on the future of the mining industry, when in August 1919, Lloyd George ruled out nationalization, an action that was for many years seen by the miners as a great betrayal. In September the Prime Minister would have to personally intervene to settle a national strike of the railway workers over pay, giving in to their demands. Overall, in 1919, 34 million working days were lost due to strikes. On 6 December, Lloyd George addressed the issue directly in a speech at the Reform Club in Manchester, to mark his third anniversary as Prime Minister. There he was greeted with much applause and a standing ovation and told the members, 'There are some moderate men in the Labour Party, but there are also Bolsheviks, Syndicalists, Direct Actionists and Sovietists. There is a new challenge to civilisation.'[28] To this he added his own call for fusion between Conservatives and Liberals. 'What was the alternative to the Coalition?' he asked. 'The alternative was confusion. If there was a dissolution, was there anyone who would pretend that there was a single party which could get a majority. There was no reason why the best elements of the Liberal and Unionist parties should not work together where there was ground for agreement.'[29]

One young Conservative MP who had surprisingly come within the close orbit of Lloyd George at this time was Sir Philip Sassoon, a man he'd previously accused of intriguing against him. Sassoon had recently been appointed as parliamentary private secretary to Eric Geddes at the new Ministry of Transport, both of them having worked under Douglas Haig at GHQ. He was also the heir of the Sassoon banking and trading house, one of the wealthiest Jewish families of the nineteenth century, and his French mother Aline[30] was the daughter of Baron Gustave de Rothschild.[31] In November 1919 Philip gave a dinner party for Geddes in his mansion at 25 Park Lane,[32] which Lloyd George had attended with Frances Stevenson and 'enjoyed himself immensely'.[33] A couple of weeks later, Frances noted in her diary that Philip had 'just dropped in for a chat. He has been very attentive lately, I think probably because he wants to get an under-secretaryship, or something of the kind. Nevertheless he is an amusing person and as clever as a cartload of monkeys.' She also observed that Philip 'is quite good company. Very ambitious though, which he admits. D has asked him to come to Paris with us after Xmas purely D says because he has been nice to me! He certainly has and very attentive – almost embarrassing, in fact. He seems to be fabulously rich, but is clever also and can be most amusing. But one of the worst gossips I have ever come across.'[34]

The result of the Spen Valley by-election[35] in West Yorkshire on 3 January 1920 would prove to be another blow to the government where John Simon, standing for the Asquith Liberals, split the vote with the Coalition Liberal candidate, allowing the Labour Party to come through the middle and win. H. A. L. Fisher recorded after meeting with the Prime Minister, 'L.G. agitated about a new party. Thinks we can't go on losing by-elections.'[36] He further noted that Lloyd George thought it would be 'Impossible to reunite Liberals. Liberalism not enough anyhow to govern the country.'[37] On 10 January, Riddell noted of a dinner with 'Birkenhead and Bonar Law, and others' that there was 'Much talk about the political situation, etc. It was generally agreed that unless the Liberals and Conservatives join forces and present a united front, they will find themselves in serious difficulties. Birkenhead was all for this, but B.L. said very little, and it is obvious that the older section of the Conservatives are not disposed to give up their organisation and place themselves unreservedly in L.G.'s power.'[38] Lloyd George believed that 'all the younger Conservatives are strongly in favour of fusion – men like Horne,[39] Worthington-Evans[40] etc.'[41] Another young Conservative MP in whom Lloyd George confided was the future Coalition minister Philip Lloyd-Greame.[42] In private the Prime Minister told him that 'Some of your people want to tie me to the Tory Party pure and simple. I want a National Party, but I want Liberals in it. I should be quite content if I got such a party by dropping some of the people at both ends who would not agree. I want strong government.'[43] Yet the strong sense of Liberal identity that his parliamentary colleagues held, and their commitment to traditional policies like free trade and Home Rule for Ireland, would not melt away. Asquith's return to Parliament at the Paisley by-election in Renfrewshire, Scotland, on 25 February,[44] and the resumption of his position as Leader of the Opposition in the House of Commons, would only strengthen the divisions within Liberalism. Ultimately, it was Liberal dissent rather than Conservative reluctance that would prevent the creation of a National Party in 1920. In two separate meetings on 16 and 18 March, Lloyd George would put the proposal for closer co-operation with the Conservatives to the Coalition Liberal ministers, and then the backbench MPs, and both groups resisted. There was growing Conservative opposition to fusion now as well, including from men like Lord Robert Cecil and Neville Chamberlain, who had never been admirers of Lloyd George, and some younger Members of Parliament like Sam Hoare,[45] who had not had preferment in government under the Coalition. Their position was also strengthened by the Wrekin by-election result in Shropshire on 20 February where an independent Conservative candidate easily beat the Coalition Liberal into a poor third place. Two days after the meeting with his Liberal MPs, a weary Prime Minister confided in George, now Lord Riddell, 'Was there any stage at which I could, with honour, have broken up the Coalition and thrown over my Conservative colleagues?

I cannot think of one. Now I should like some rest. For many reasons I should like to resign and take a good holiday. But I feel there is work for me to do. Fate. Providence, or what you will, has ordained me for the purpose. It is my destiny and I must fulfil it.'[46]

Throughout these months Lloyd George's thoughts had also been drifting back, beyond the fog of industrial disputes, by-elections and party politics, to the Paris Peace Conference, when the delegates had redrawn the boundaries of the western world. Woodrow Wilson was now in failing health after a serious stroke in October 1919, and a political lame duck in the last year of his Presidency. The Republican Party controlling the Senate of Congress had even blocked ratification of the Treaty of Versailles on the grounds that membership of the League of Nations could commit the United States to intervene in future European wars. Rather than accept their proposed amendments, in the end Wilson asked his own Democrats to vote down the treaty he had negotiated. In June 1919, Vittorio Orlando's government had been swept from power in Italy after the Paris Peace Conference, for failing to secure the annexation of the port of Fiume on the eastern Adriatic.[47] Clemenceau had resigned as Prime Minister in January 1920 following a failed bid to be elected President of France. After a final meeting with the French Premier in Paris before he left office, Lloyd George told Clemenceau, 'I envy you. You are going off to rest and quiet & freedom from worry, whereas I am going back to the same old attacks, which will probably succeed eventually in downing me, as they have you.' 'Ah,' the Frenchman replied, 'but your people will do it in a cleaner way!'[48] The British Prime Minister was now the last of the big four of Lloyd George, Wilson, Clemenceau and Orlando, still effectively active on the political stage. This sentiment was captured in Lloyd George's favourite cartoon by David Low[49] for *The Star* evening newspaper in London. The Prime Minister was depicted peering from a window in Downing Street at a dishevelled deputation of unemployed 'Versailles veterans' including Clemenceau, Wilson and Orlando, above a caption which read, 'You're Next!'[50] Lloyd George purchased the original drawing and Low recalled, 'I had promised him at the time that if ever there were a sequel in which his likeness was added to the others he should have that, too, and I was working on it.'[51]

On 12 February, Lloyd George attended a dinner party given by Philip Sassoon at 25 Park Lane for the Prince of Wales, which was highly reminiscent of his evenings in Paris at the Rue Nitot. The drawing room was hung with exquisite Flemish tapestries alongside paintings by Thomas Gainsborough, Sir Joshua Reynolds and the German neoclassical painter Johann Zoffany, and Philip's French chefs prepared endless courses of delicious food. Three days later, Lloyd George golfed with Riddell at St George's Hill in Surrey and reflected:

> I shall never forget the day I left Paris after the Peace Conference. I opened the windows at the Rue Nitot and gazed on Wilson's house, shorn of all its pomp – no guards, no detectives and the windows all shuttered. I felt I was closing a book that would never be reopened – a book of intense interest. It was an anxious time, but a pleasant time. I enjoyed it. I doubt if I shall ever spend such another. It was all so vivid. I felt as I looked at the empty house with its closed shutters that I should never see Wilson again and that these historic scenes had passed away never to return. I don't mind confessing that a feeling of sadness crept over me.[52]

That same weekend Frances Stevenson enjoyed an 'interesting and enjoyable'[53] time at Philip Sassoon's estate at Trent Park,[54] where they were joined by the Prince of Wales and his younger brother Prince Albert. Frances had also come with a gift from Lloyd George for her host, the offer that he should become his parliamentary private secretary. Sassoon was an unusual addition to the Prime Minister's entourage, being neither Welsh nor a Liberal Party fixer, but Philip was wealthy and well connected. Lloyd George may have also believed that having a Conservative MP as his parliamentary private secretary would help with his longer-term hopes for political fusion. But most importantly, Philip could offer him the resources to entertain and relax without any thought or care, as he'd enjoyed in Paris. With his appointment Sassoon effectively placed 25 Park Lane and Trent Park at the Prime Minister's disposal, as well as his other home, the Port Lympne estate in his constituency on the south Kent coast.

For the next few months international conferences, rather than domestic affairs, would dominate Lloyd George's attention. In April 1920, along with Lord Curzon, who had replaced Arthur Balfour as Foreign Secretary the previous autumn, Lloyd George joined the new French Prime Minister, Alexandre Millerand, and the Italian Premier Francesco Nitti, in San Remo on the Italian Riviera, to finalize the dissolution of the Ottoman Empire and the new borders for Syria, Iraq, Palestine, Lebanon and Jordan.[55] There they also agreed to meet in England in May, to discuss German reparations, ahead of a further conference with the German government at Spa in Belgium in July. Returning from San Remo by train via Paris, Lloyd George had a prolonged conversation with the British Ambassador Lord Derby on a chilly platform at the Gare du Nord. As a result, the Prime Minister caught a severe cold, but Maurice Hankey believed that he was 'really suffering from nervous exhaustion . . . this is about the fourth time I have known him beaten to a frazzle'.[56] Remembering the physical impact of the influenza he had contracted in September 1918, Lloyd George was advised by his doctors to have a working convalescence away from London, just as he'd then done at Danny House. Philip Sassoon suggested that he should stay at Port Lympne, and that this would also be an ideal location for the conference with the French government planned for May.

Port Lympne was set in 600 acres of woods and farmland, secluded by a natural amphitheatre created by the former cliff line of an ancient silted-up bay. The estate commanded excellent unbroken views of the Romney Marsh below and the English Channel beyond. Its coastal location was reminiscent of the salt marshes at Porthmadog, near Criccieth, and its commanding views were even more panoramic than those enjoyed from Lloyd George's home, Brynawelon. This was also a part of Kent that Lloyd George knew well, having spent a month convalescing at Beachborough Park, at the mouth of the Elham Valley, during the spring of 1911. Beachborough, which was just five miles from Lympne, was then the home of the Liberal MP, Sir Arthur Markham, and it was there in its summer house that Lloyd George had written his National Insurance Bill.[57]

The Port Lympne mansion, however, was like its owner, luxurious, mysterious and exotic. One contemporary, Henry 'Chips' Channon,[58] believed that Sassoon was 'homosexual but there was never an open scandal, although much amused speculation on the subject'.[59] The house was a modern structure, but aged bricks gave it more of the appearance of a large English manor. For the interior, striking works had been commissioned from leading contemporary artists, including Josep Maria Sert,[60] who before the war had designed sets for the Ballets Russes.[61] He had painted a full wall and ceiling mural for the drawing room, which was an allegorical depiction of the war, where France was shown as a draped and crouching female figure being attacked by two German eagles. The dining room was lined with lapis lazuli, with a frieze above painted by Glyn Philpot,[62] depicting a scene from ancient Egypt of loin-clothed men, working with oxen and other animals.[63] Philip Sassoon took personal charge of the arrangements for Lloyd George, and Frances Stevenson was also safely installed. Secluded from the real world the Prime Minister could set to his work, with senior ministers and officials shuttling back and forth from London to Sandling on the Charing Cross train. Yet there was a danger that prolonged absences would make him more distant from his colleagues. There were no more dinners with the Monday Night Cabal, he saw less of political friends like Riddell and Reading, and relations with previously close Cabinet colleagues like Milner and Addison were more distant.

The unresolved question of Ireland, though, was the looming cloud on the otherwise unbroken horizon to be enjoyed from the terrace of Port Lympne. Any commitment to Home Rule at the general election had been left open-ended and dependent on a settled peace on the island, but the leaders of Sinn Féin, unlike the old Irish Parliamentary Party, were prepared to take matters into their own hands. On 19 December 1919, Irish nationalists had attempted to assassinate Sir John French, now 1st Earl of Ypres and Lord Lieutenant of Ireland, on his way back to the Viceregal Lodge in Dublin's Phoenix Park. It was an incident that caused Lloyd George to reflect on the 'path of fatality'[64] that characterized the relations between Great Britain and Ireland. There was a growing escalation in republican nationalist violence, and General Nevil Macready,[65] commanding the British military forces on the island, came to Lympne to ask for Lloyd George's support for more resources to be put at his disposal – in particular, five more battalions and a large number of motorized armoured vehicles. This prompted the Prime Minister to ask the War Secretary Winston Churchill to 'help' and come down to Lympne to discuss the situation, adding 'We cannot leave things as they are. De Valera has practically challenged the British Empire and unless he is put down the Empire will look silly. I know how difficult it is to spare men and material, but this seems to me to be the urgent problem for us.'[66] The Cabinet in London under Andrew Bonar Law's chairmanship was due to consider Macready's request the following day, and Lloyd George also fired off another missive to

Bonar Law stressing that 'we are bound to give him [Macready] all the support in our powers . . . in order to crush rebellion. Unless we do any measure of home rule is in my judgement bound to fail. I beg you not to allow delays to occur.'[67] Bonar Law wrote back to Lloyd George to confirm the Cabinet's acceptance of Macready's request for supplies, and also to convey the suggestion that 'a special body of ex-servicemen here in England should be enlisted on special terms, as gendarmerie to be used in Ireland'.[68] This 'gendarmerie' would become the 'Black and Tans', who would make themselves notorious for their reprisal actions following attacks from the republicans.

Maurice Hankey arrived at Lympne for the Anglo-French conference early on 14 May and found Lloyd George and Churchill in the drawing room. He noted that even though it was before lunch, 'Winston was drinking and he looked very bloated and bleary.' Hankey also thought the Prime Minister was 'looking old and ill, but he had just had 24 hours of Winston which is enough to make anyone look old and ill'.[69] Hankey could see the appeal of Port Lympne for Lloyd George, noting 'Everything [is] of the very best and most expensive. The best beds, linen, baths, food, wine, cigars, Rolls Royce motor cars etc. There was a pool and fountain in the hall; a swimming bath and more fountains in the terrace.'[70] He also acknowledged that it was 'a very lovely place . . . If I were convalescent and comfortably settled here, nothing would induce me to budge.'[71] But Hankey 'had a rather disagreeable feeling that the P.M. is getting too fond of high-living and luxury'.[72]

At 7.30 on the evening before the conference opened, Alexandre Millerand arrived at Folkestone accompanied by Lord Derby. The French tricolor and the British Union Jack flew one above the other from the same flagpole at Port Lympne, and Lord Riddell had arranged for cinema newsreel cameras to record Lloyd George welcoming Millerand, and for photographers to take informal pictures of the conference. The *Daily Mail* commented that 'Gossip is naturally rife as the reason for thus settling the affairs of Europe, or trying to, at an overcrowded house party.'[73] Riddell thought Sassoon's organization was on a 'lavish scale', and that he'd 'made hospitality an art'. He wrote in his diary that it was 'the most informal conference I have seen. Most of the talking was done by Millerand and LG when walking about the grounds.'[74] The society architect Philip Tilden[75] was also there in the background working for

Sassoon and remembered the Prime Minister 'pacing up and down on the south terrace at Port Lympne, enveloped in his perennial cloak. His gleaming hair was blown about by the wind from the sea. His walk was solid and full of assurance, now halting for a moment, now proceeding, as he pressed his points home in conversation with his companion.'[76]

The conference discussions were dominated by the issues of Allied debt and German reparations. Lloyd George rejected the French proposal not to agree a fair divide in the reparations from Germany between the Allies, but rather to prioritize projects that needed urgent financial support wherever they occurred – most of which would have been in France. Instead, Lloyd George got Millerand to agree that experts from their respective countries would prepare 'immediately for examination . . . a minimum total for the German debt which will be acceptable by the Allies and at the same time compatible to Germany's capacity to pay'.[77] This formula accorded much more closely with the terms set out in Lloyd George's Fontainebleau memorandum presented at the Paris Peace Conference, and Clemenceau was aghast when he heard what had been agreed. In his memoirs he noted that 'Mr Lloyd George . . . had no great difficulty in winning over our Prime Minister, M Millerand, to the thesis of the fixed sum for reparations. This was the first surrender. M Poincaré resigned his position as President of the Reparation Commission.'[78]

A couple of weeks after the conference, Lord Derby told Sassoon to pass on to Lloyd George that he thought Millerand was politically 'shaky and will probably have to go after Spa [the forthcoming conference in Belgium] . . . we could save him if we wished to by wiping off one third of the French debt as a contribution to the devastated areas. If Millerand goes Poincaré will probably come in.'[79] Things were worse, however, for the French President, Paul Deschanel.[80] He had only been in post since February but suffered a complete breakdown at the end of May. Things came to a head when, dressed only in a nightshirt, he'd fallen out of a large window of the presidential train near Montargis, about 70 miles south of Paris. Deschanel was found wandering by the tracks and was taken to the nearest level-crossing keeper's cottage where he apparently remonstrated with his hosts: 'Can't you see I'm a gentleman as I've got clean feet?' Philip Sassoon told Lloyd George that 'All Paris reviews are full of skits on him.' According to Lord Derby, Clemenceau thought it was 'not surprising that [Deschanel] had come off his head as he had after all very little brains to lose, adding "The world is divided into two clans – those who don't get what they want and those who do and find it is not what they expected."'[81]

The Spa conference was held in the Villa Fraineuse on 9 July, where Wilhelm II of Germany had spent his last night as Kaiser before his abdication and flight to Holland. The British delegation stayed at the Hôtel Britannique, which had been the General Headquarters of the German military command in the last months of the war. The conference itself was bad-tempered and not a success. The Germans stated that there should be a plan for the 'partaking of the Allied governments' in the improvement of economic and financial conditions in Germany, and that any agreement on reparations could 'only' be based on the country's ability to pay.[82] This led to an ultimatum from the British and French that unless the deliveries of coal they had been due to receive as part of the first £1 billion of the reparations package were made up within 72 hours, they would occupy the Ruhr and take it for themselves. The ultimatum was later withdrawn, but the crisis remained unresolved. The Germans offered a schedule for deliveries of coal for the next six months, but nothing more was agreed other than a resolution on how the reparations should be divided amongst the Allies.[83] Philip Sassoon observed the German delegation closely and thought their Chancellor, Constantin Fehrenbach,[84] 'a very respectable old man [who] looks like the father of the prodigal son', whereas the Defence Minister, Otto Gessler,[85] was 'very truculent'. But overall, Sassoon considered that in conference against a 'master hand like LG they are like very poor amateurs'.[86]

Illness and international conferences kept Lloyd George away from parliament for long periods in 1920. In April that year he only spoke in the House of Commons on one occasion, to give a report on the San Remo conference, and not at all in either May or July. Arthur Lee blamed these absences in part, for a major row that had broken out about the dismissal of Brigadier-General Dyer,[87] for his responsibility for a massacre in Amritsar on 13 April 1919. Fearing a popular uprising against British rule in the Punjab, the authorities had declared martial law, banning public gatherings of more than two people. Dyer had ordered his men without warning to fire on a crowd that had peacefully gathered at the enclosed Jallianwala Bagh garden, to mark the Sikh festival of Vaisakhi. Dyer's men fired 1,650 rounds in ten minutes, killing 379 people including women and children, and injuring a further 1,208. An independent commission chaired by Lord Hunter,[88] which reported in May 1920, found that Dyer had directed the fire at places where the crowd was thickest, continued to fire as the crowd dispersed and noted that, 'it was his intention to create a moral effect throughout the Punjab and they condemn this as a mistaken conception of his duty.'[89] On 14 May, Winston Churchill returned to the War Office after visiting Lloyd George at Lympne and confronted Sir Henry Wilson about Dyer. Wilson noted in his diary, 'Winston made a long speech, prejudging the case and in effect saying that the Cabinet, and he, had decided to throw out Dyer, but that it was advisable for the Army Council to agree. It appeared to me, listening, that the story was a very simple one. The Frocks[90] have got India (as they have Ireland) into a filthy mess. On that the soldiers are called in, and act. This is disapproved of by all the disloyal elements, and the soldier is thrown to the winds.'[91]

Churchill would go on to describe the Amritsar massacre in the House of Commons as, 'an episode which appears to me to be without precedent or parallel in the modern history of the British Empire . . . It is an extraordinary event, a monstrous event, an event which stands in singular and sinister isolation.'[92] In the same debate, Edwin Montagu, the Secretary of State for India, aroused fierce criticism from Conservative MPs, many of whom believed Dyer was doing his duty, when he asked, 'Are you going to keep hold of India by terrorism, racial humiliation and subordination, and frightfulness . . . or are you going to rest it upon the goodwill, and the growing goodwill of the people of your Indian Empire?'[93] After the debate William Sutherland wrote to Lloyd George that, 'Montagu thoroughly roused most of the latent passions of the stodgy Tories and many of them could have assaulted him physically, they were so angry. It was not so much what Montagu said as the way he said it that roused them. Under interruption, Montagu got excited when making his speech and became more racial and more Yiddish in screaming tone and gesture, and a strong anti-Jewish sentiment was shown by shouts and excitement among normally placid Tories of the backbench category.'[94] A press report duly appeared, stating that, 'when Mr. Lloyd George returns he intends to take up the question of General Dyer and the situation that has arisen from the controversy. He is aware of the bitterness that has been aroused. His intention is to do what he can to ameliorate the situation.'[95]

Lloyd George's response to the massacre in Amritsar and the removal of General Dyer was consistent with the government's approach to India, which was creating opponents on both sides of the debate. Conservatives believed that too many concessions were being made, whilst leading Indian nationalists like Mohandas K. Gandhi[96] wanted equal status for India in the Empire, and considered that the reforms[97] introduced by Montagu and the Viceroy, Lord Chelmsford,[98] fell a long way short of the self-government they wanted. In an open letter to the British people that autumn Gandhi wrote, 'the treachery of Mr Lloyd George and its appreciation by you, and the condonation of the Punjab atrocities have completely shattered my faith in the good intentions of the Government and the nation which is supporting it . . . You can compel Mr Lloyd George to redeem his promises. I assure you he has kept many escape-doors.'[99]

Another international crisis would bring Lloyd George back again to Port Lympne for a conference with Millerand and Marshal Foch on 8 August, this time concerning the worsening situation in the war between Poland and the Soviet Union. It would also mean, for the second year running, that he would be unable to attend the National Eisteddfod to be held at Barry in south Wales. Although the Poles had started the war by invading Ukraine in November 1918, the Soviet Red Army now had the upper hand and was set to cross the River Vistula and take Warsaw. This war could be the first real test of the Treaty of Versailles as the new state of Poland was regarded as the 'lynch-pin' to peace in the east.[100] On 4 August 1920 at 10 Downing Street, Lloyd George told the Russian representatives Lev Kamenev[101] and Leonid Krasin,[102] 'If the Soviet armies advanced further into Poland, a rupture with the Allies would be inevitable.' It was six years to the day since Britain had entered the Great War and Winston Churchill recalled that his 'mind's eye roamed back over the six years of carnage and horror through which we had struggled. Was there never to be an end? Was even the most absolute victory to afford no basis for just and lasting peace? . . . Again it was August 4th, and this time we were impotent. Public opinion in England and France was prostrate. All forms of military intervention were impossible. There was nothing left but words and gestures.'[103]

At the conference itself, Lord Riddell recalled, Lloyd George was 'in wonderful spirits. When I arrived he was crossing the lawn to speak to Millerand. He came over to me and shielding his mouth with his hands as if he were telling me a secret, whispered, "We have decided to go to Warsaw for another conference. Will you come with us?" In the evening there was a cinema show at the villa, which produced roars of laughter from the PM, Millerand and Foch.'[104] There was to be no conference in Warsaw and the Soviets also rejected the idea of a conference in London, opting instead for peace talks with Poland in Minsk. Foch was greatly concerned about the situation and told Lord Riddell, 'It is serious. If Poland fails, Germany and Russia will combine. You will have a worse position than in 1914.' To which Riddell replied, 'Are you willing to say that publicly?' Foch answered, 'Yes, it is a serious position which the world should understand. Events are on the march.'[105] The crisis was averted, however, by a surprise and decisive military victory for the Poles in the Battle of Warsaw (12–25 August 1920). This brought to an end any chance of further Russian military operations in Poland, and a peace treaty was successfully concluded. Nevertheless, it had forced the Allies to consider how far they were prepared to go to uphold the terms of the Treaty of Versailles. There had also been considerable public protest against British involvement in the war, with some dock workers even refusing to load ships of ammunition to be sent to the Polish government.

Lloyd George was determined to take a break in August, but instead of returning to Wales, took a holiday party to Switzerland, to stay at Horw on the shores of Lake Lucerne in Villa Haslihorn, which had been lent to him by the King of Belgium.[106] He was accompanied by his daughter Megan and son Gwilym, J. T. Davies, Frances Stevenson, Maurice Hankey and Lord Riddell, who suspected that 'L.G. said he wanted a holiday amongst the mountains and was absolutely bent on Switzerland, but I think his real reason is that he is anxious to meet Giolitti,[107] the Italian Prime Minister, in order to make a combination with him on the Russian and Polish questions. L.G.'s antipathy to the French is very marked.'[108]

The meeting with Giolitti duly took place in the garden of the villa on the morning of 22 August, with the Italian Prime Minister finding Lloyd George to be 'very intelligent and acute', but adding, 'I am a bit of a fencer myself.'[109] The purpose of their discussion was to explore whether there was a more constructive common ground between Britain and Italy in their attitudes towards Germany, in contrast to the hard-line position of France. Lloyd George told Giolitti that 'It would be a good idea to get our representatives in Berlin to urge Germany to meet the protocols of Spa', then, 'Germany could help Britain and Italy to restrain France.'[110] A draft communique for the press was prepared following the meeting, and before lunch Lloyd George asked Riddell's opinion of it. He recalled responding that 'the memorandum was undesirable and dangerous in its present form, that it would accentuate difficulties between France and ourselves, and might lead to a reorientation of world power, with France and America on one side, and Gt Britain, Italy, Greece and the rag-tag of Europe on the other.'[111] This brought forth a 'very angry' response from Lloyd George, who accused Riddell of being 'pro-French'. The argument continued over lunch, where Riddell also told the Prime Minister, 'I think it is right to say that there is a strong feeling that we are devoting too much time to international and not enough to home affairs. We cannot be the arbiters of Europe. We have no power to enforce our decisions, and the result of our continued interference is that we make enemies all round.'[112] This disagreement did not mark the end of Lloyd George's friendship with Riddell, but they were never on such intimate terms again. One by one, the men who had helped to project Lloyd George to the premiership were breaking away.

TWELVE

Solver of the Insoluble

They have immortalised another day
Who struck you down. And oh, we burn with pride
Because of you, our peerless one, who died
In the old proud, unbending, Irish way.[1,2]

So wrote the poet Lord Mayor of Cork, Terence MacSwiney,[3] about the executed Irish nationalist Roger Casement,[4] but the words made a fitting epitaph for him as well. MacSwiney died in Brixton prison in south London on 25 October 1920, after a 74-day hunger strike. He had been arrested in Cork on Thursday 12 August under powers given to the police by the new Restoration of Order in Ireland Act, which allowed the internment of suspected members of Sinn Féin and the IRA.[5] The following Monday, after a 15-minute court martial, MacSwiney was convicted and ordered to serve a custodial sentence, but told the presiding officer, 'I will put a limit to any term of imprisonment you may impose. I have taken no food since Thursday . . . Whatever your government may do, I shall be free, alive or dead within a month.'[6] The outcry of support for the Lord Mayor of Cork was immediate and on 25 August, Lord Stamfordham sent a telegram from Balmoral Castle to the Home Secretary Edward Shortt,[7] stating that if MacSwiney was 'allowed to die in prison results would be deplorable from every point of view. His Majesty would be prepared to exercise clemency if you so advise and believes this would be a wise course.'[8]

Lloyd George was still on holiday at Lake Lucerne where Lord Riddell recalled, 'Evidently the matter is causing L.G. deep anxiety.'[9] The Prime Minister had stood to account for the death of Hedd Wyn at Passchendaele, now he would once more have to face the responsibility of putting a poet in his grave. Yet the official statement he felt compelled to release on 25 August showed no sign of remorse, stating that while he did 'deeply regret', MacSwiney's 'decision to starve himself . . . If the Lord Mayor were released, every hunger-striker, whatever his offence, would be let off . . . The release some weeks ago of hunger-strikers in Ireland was followed by an outburst of cruel murder and outrage, one defenceless man being shot within sight of the altar of his church, and no expression of protest or regret ever came, even in that case, from the political organisation to which the Lord Mayor belongs.'[10] This message triggered a further telegram from Balmoral, this time from the King, stating, 'I am receiving appeals from many quarters, including the editor of the *Manchester Guardian*, to exercise my prerogative. The government knows my views and while appreciating the difficulty of their position, I still advocate clemency.'[11] Yet Lloyd George was contemptuous of his concern, writing to his wife Margaret, 'The King is an old coward. He is frightened to death and is anxious to make it clear that he has nothing to do with it.'[12]

Yet the issue of personal safety of public figures was real. In Ireland in the past year nearly 300 policemen had been shot and over 100 killed. The security services considered it likely that the IRA would take reprisal actions in England, including against senior members of the government, should MacSwiney lose his life. Lloyd George told Margaret that 'it will rouse fierce feelings if he dies. You & Megan need not be anxious. There has never been a case of assassination of wives & daughters. Of course they will try to kill me & may succeed. I must do my duty.'[13] The Prime Minister's personal security was increased and once back home he was encouraged to change his routine by staying from time to time at Philip Sassoon's Trent Park estate. Michael Collins,[14] who directed the Republican military campaign in the Irish War of Independence, was a Cork man and close to Terence MacSwiney; they'd met in Dublin less than two weeks before he was arrested. Collins sent four men to London, including Frank Thornton[15] and Seán Flood[16] from his assassination 'squad',[17] to identify opportunities to take hostage senior British politicians. Thornton remembered a particular incident when Flood was running for a train at Westminster Underground station, he heard a 'terrific crash' and in pursuit fell over two men lying on the ground. One of them was Seán Flood, and the older gentleman they helped to his feet was to their great astonishment Lloyd George. The two security officers accompanying the Prime Minister, on hearing the Irish accents of the other men, drew their guns and told Flood and Thornton to put their hands up. At this, and unaware of their real identities, Lloyd George intervened. 'Well, Irishmen or no Irishmen, if they were to shoot me I was shot long ago.'[18] At that, they went their separate ways.

At Carnarvon on 9 October, Lloyd George accepted the Freedom of the Borough and gave a speech on the government's response to the crisis in Ireland. His solution, which would soon pass as the Government of Ireland Act 1920,[19] was to create two new devolved 'Home Rule' parliaments with limited powers, for 'Northern' and 'Southern' Ireland. However, such a settlement had been completely rejected by the supporters of Sinn Féin, who wanted full independence and an Irish Republic. Lloyd George also addressed reports of the growing number of reprisals against the IRA. 'Policemen and soldiers do not go burning houses and shooting men down wantonly without provocation,' he said. 'There is no doubt that at last their patience has given way and there has been some severe hitting back. But take the conditions whilst these murders were going on. I never read or heard a word of protest from Sinn Féiners in Ireland, not a single syllable.'[20] While there were reported cries of 'hear, hear'[21] from the audience at these lines, Lloyd George's increasingly strident tone on Ireland was at odds with some senior Liberals. Asquith responded to the speech saying, 'An attempt to answer murder and outrage by terrorism is not government, but anarchy.'[22] Even the Prime Minister's brother William, who was at Carnarvon for his speech, later wrote that he thought Lloyd George 'was mistaken in his public utterances at this time when he said the trouble in Ireland was to do with the machinations of a "murder gang" which was about "to meet its doom." It is an instance of how the wielding of supreme power, with the terrible decisions it entails, particularly in time of war, clouded the clearer vision which characterised his utterances during the Boer War.'[23]

When Terence MacSwiney died from his hunger strike on 25 October 1920, there was a great public outpouring of grief, just as the King had feared there would be. Members of London's Irish community arranged for the former Lord Mayor's coffin, wrapped in the republican tricolour flag of Ireland, to be placed on public display at Southwark's Catholic Cathedral, where over 30,000 people queued to pay their respects. The scene of MacSwiney's requiem mass on 28 October was painted by the Irish artist John Lavery,[24] and afterwards in a great funeral procession a horse-drawn hearse carried his coffin through London to Euston Station for its journey home to Ireland. An unrepentant Lloyd George made Ireland the central theme of his annual address at the Lord Mayor of London's banquet at the Guildhall on 9 November, committing to do whatever it took to suppress the actions of the IRA, telling his audience 'we have murder by the throat'.[25] Then adding, 'These men who indulge in these murders say it is war. If it is war they at any rate cannot complain if we apply some of the rules of war. [Loud cheers] You must break the terror before you can get the peace.'[26]

Yet the violence continued to escalate, culminating 12 days later in brutal attacks and reprisals in Dublin on 'Bloody Sunday', 21 November 1920. That morning, under orders from Michael Collins, 12 British intelligence officers, known as the 'Cairo Gang',[27] were assassinated. Then at around 3.20 p.m. the Royal Irish Constabulary (RIC) and the auxiliary force, the Black and Tans, burst into Croke Park stadium during a Gaelic Football match,[28] firing without warning indiscriminately for about five minutes. Thirteen spectators and one of the players[29] were killed and between 60 to 100 others were injured. As a consequence of the auxiliaries blocking the exits of the stadium while the firing took place, two people were crushed to death as the crowd tried to escape in the panic. In the House of Commons the following day, while condemning the murder of the officers, the Chief Secretary for Ireland, Sir Hamar Greenwood, claimed that the match at Croke Park had been attended by 'Sinn Féin gunmen' and that the auxiliaries were engaged in a 'search for arms' at the stadium when they were 'fired upon and they fired back'.[30] The secret official British investigation into what happened maintained the disputed charge that the first shots came from within the crowd, but also concluded that the firing from members of the RIC was 'carried out without orders, and was indiscriminate and unjustifiable'.[31]

At London's Euston Station on the morning of 26 November nine gun carriages, each bearing a coffin of one of the murdered intelligence officers covered in the Union flag, were escorted to Westminster by soldiers from the Guards regiments, and members of the Black and Tans. This procession through streets lined with mourners was, according to the *New York Times*, 'a great military display, the most imposing seen in London since the war'.[32] The funeral of six of the men would be conducted at Westminster Abbey, and for the three Catholics their service was held at nearby Westminster Cathedral. Sir Henry Wilson attended the Abbey funeral and noted in his diary that it was 'a most pitiful sight'. When Lloyd George walked up the aisle behind the coffins, along with Winston Churchill and Hamar Greenwood, Wilson recalled, 'I wondered they did not hide their heads in shame.'[33]

The London press had condemned the attack on these men, but there was also criticism of the actions of the British forces in Ireland, with *The Times* reporting, 'an army already perilously indisciplined, and a police force avowedly beyond control, have defiled, by heinous acts, the reputation of England . . . who can doubt that the strength of the Irish Executive would in this grave emergency be ten times greater had its record entitled it to appeal for the moral support of all those Irishmen to whom murder is an abomination.'[34] The procession for the British officers also shared an appalling symmetry with the arrival at Euston Station of the coffin of the Lord Mayor of Cork less than a month before. *The Times* asked in its report of these two mournful journeys east and west along the Euston Road:

> Who that stood in those two crowds and heard and saw what passed among them, could help but hope, and even believe, that if nothing else at least the mingled tears of the English and Irish peoples might do what legislation and violence have failed to achieve.[35]

Following Bloody Sunday, Sir Henry Wilson was shocked at what he saw as the intransigence of the British government, writing in his diary on 24 November, 'there was again no Cabinet today! It is simply past belief; a matter of 17 murders in 48 hours is considered of no importance by Lloyd George and his amazing Cabinet.'[36] Wilson believed that full martial law should be introduced in Ireland, everywhere except in Ulster. This the Cabinet initially refused to do, but on 8 December it did authorize full martial law for the counties of Cork, Kerry, Limerick and Tipperary in the west of Ireland, and then on 30 December for the rest of the province of Munster. The following day, in a further diary entry to mark the end of the year, Wilson's assessment of the government's record was damning. He wrote, 'Lloyd George and his Cabinet have lamentably failed, whether in England where Lloyd George has given in every time to the Trades Unions . . . or in Ireland, where ever since the spring he has handed over the Government to the "Black and Tans" . . And when I remember all the speeches of Lloyd George and others two years ago about England being a land of heroes, etc., it makes me all the more contemptuous . . . Lloyd George's foreign policy has been beneath contempt . . . He has made enemies of all countries and friends of none.'[37]

In different spirits that same New Year's Eve, Lloyd George enjoyed Philip Sassoon's party at Port Lympne, where Lord Riddell recalled that 'LG sang "cockles and mussels"[38] and one or two other songs with great effect. He would have made a fortune on the music hall stage. Winston sat watching him with the keenest admiration and the eye of an artist.'[39] Lloyd George stayed at Lympne until 8 January 1921, when he hosted a house-warming party at Chequers to mark the transfer of the property to the nation for the use of the holder of the office of Prime Minister. This large Elizabethan manor set in 1,500 acres of Buckinghamshire countryside had belonged to his friends Arthur and Ruth Lee. The Lees had no children and had decided to make this gift back in 1917. Lloyd George thanked them now, adding that 'Future generations of Prime Ministers will think with gratitude of the impulse which has thus prompted you so generously to place this beautiful mansion at their disposal. I have no doubt that such a retreat will do much to alleviate the cares of state which they inherit along with it.'[40] Frances Stevenson remembered of Chequers that:

> . . . although L.G. appreciated the facilities which this beautiful country house afforded him, he was never entirely happy there. For one thing, there was no view.[41] The house – like so many old houses – was built in a hollow, and one had to climb up the hill behind to get the superb view of the Buckinghamshire plain. L.G. liked a view from his window. Moreover, he did not care for old houses. His spirit resented the atmosphere of preceding generations which seemed to cramp and encroach upon the essential independence of his nature which refused to be contained. It was something instinctive and innate and primeval which made him recoil from anything resembling the shackles of the past.[42]

For four years the Coalition had been held together by the relationship between Lloyd George and Bonar Law. Just before Christmas 1920, Lord Derby had warned Philip Sassoon that the Conservative MPs were tied to the Coalition because of their 'extreme loyalty' to Bonar Law, and there would not be a problem 'as long as Lloyd George and Bonar Law stick together'.[43] Yet the Conservative leader was mentally and physically shattered from the immense pressure of work since he'd joined the first coalition government nearly six years before, not to mention the loss of two of his sons in the war. On 13 March, after suffering from influenza, he collapsed and four days later on the advice of his doctor, resigned from the government and as Leader of the Conservative Party. Bonar Law then left England immediately for a holiday at Cannes in the south of France. A few weeks before, Lord Milner had also retired from the Cabinet as well as Walter Long. In anticipation of these departures, Riddell recalled discussing the situation with Lloyd George, writing in his diary, 'We talked of the vacancies in the Cabinet. L.G. said it was very difficult to find men to fill them, there were so few of outstanding ability.'[44]

Winston Churchill would succeed Milner at the Colonial Office, and Sir Laming Worthington-Evans joined the Cabinet, replacing Churchill at the War Office. Arthur Lee became the new First Lord of the Admiralty, finally achieving the full recognition from Lloyd George for his invaluable support over many years. The Prime Minister also appointed his great friend Lord Reading as Viceroy of India, which led to an anonymous antisemitic article in *Blackwood's Edinburgh Magazine* stating, 'The real danger is that another Jew is added to the many Jews who are taking part in the government of our empire. Behind all of Mr [Lloyd] George's actions is the hidden hand of Sir Philip Sassoon.'[45]

Yet the biggest problem for Lloyd George was the departure of Bonar Law. He was succeeded as leader of the Conservative Party by Austen Chamberlain, who also took his predecessor's position in government as Leader of the House of Commons, with Sir Robert Horne appointed to replace him as Chancellor of the Exchequer; the job that Churchill had hoped for. Austen Chamberlain has been famously described by contemporaries as a man who 'always played the game and he always lost it'.[46] Although a great statesman, he was a poor politician, unsuited to anchoring the Conservative Party in coalition with Lloyd George. It was a task, Chamberlain told his sister Hilda, that 'I accept as an obvious duty but without pleasure or any great expectations except of trouble & hard labour. For we are no longer an independent Party with a clearly defined & perfectly definite policy but part of a coalition bound necessarily to much compromise & and as such coalitions must be, largely opportunist . . . I wonder whether I can cultivate pleasant colloquial habits. To be hail fellow well met with all my "followers". I must try but I haven't shown much ability that way so far!'[47] His first mistakes would be in rejecting the help offered by the key Bonar Law lieutenants, George Younger and J. C. C. Davidson, now also a Member of Parliament. Both had made it their business to know intimately the workings of the Conservative Party in Westminster and out in the country, and such men tend not to retire when a chief no longer needs them. Instead, they find other leaders to help, so as to exercise the power that such knowledge commands.

Bonar Law's resignation came at a bad time for the government, as in addition to the problems in Ireland and Europe, there was growing economic pressure at home. The immediate post-war economic boom had turned to bust with the unemployment rate rising from less than 3 per cent in May 1920 to more than 23 per cent a year later.[48] In June 1921 the unemployment rate passed two million and in the industrial towns more than half of the people registered for social insurance were out of work. *The Economist* called 1921 'one of the worst years of depression since the industrial revolution'.[49] There was growing pressure for cuts in government spending from the Anti-Waste League, a new political movement created in January 1921 by Lord Rothermere, which defeated government candidates in a series of by-elections in the first half of that year. Coalition Liberal ministers in particular were targeted in Rothermere's *Weekly Dispatch*, which stated that 'Our difficulties have arisen out of the absence of Cabinet Government . . . Each minister goes his own way . . . Dr Addison, Mr. Fisher, Sir Eric Geddes spend what they please.'[50] There was particular criticism of Christopher Addison, the Minister for Health, whose housing schemes were considered costly and ineffective. High costs for materials, combined with a lack of budgetary control, meant that in 1921 he was paying £910 for homes that a year later could be built for £385 each.[51] Yet Addison was still responsible for building 213,000 new homes and establishing the unchanged principle of local government responsibility for the availability of decent affordable homes.

Similarly, the 1918 Fisher Education Act had raised the school leaving age from 12 to 14 and removed all fees from state elementary schools; reforms that would be built on by future governments rather than reversed. Lloyd George had expanded the availability of unemployment benefit to most of the workforce that needed it, and he'd settled pay demands from the unions, but he had also avoided a national general strike. Coalition certainly required compromise, as Chamberlain had complained, but that meant between full-blown socialism and pre-war laissez faire, and most people in Britain would have agreed with that.

Nevertheless, on 1 April, to ease the political pressure on the government, Lloyd George moved Addison to become Minister without Portfolio, a clear demotion. He was succeeded by another long-term ally of the Prime Minister, Sir Alfred Mond.[52] When three months later Addison resigned from the government altogether following a decision to halt his home-building programme, his position was not even replaced. That August, Lloyd George asked Eric Geddes to chair a special committee on national expenditure to identify savings that could be made across government, a process that became known as the Geddes Axe. He too, though, would resign as Minister of Transport in November 1921, as a consequence of political disputes over whether the railways should continue to be run by the state, as they had been in wartime, or by private companies. Geddes was the exemplar of Lloyd George's men of 'push and go', but he became yet another true believer that the Prime Minister was going to have to manage without. His successor was Viscount Peel,[53] an experienced politician but not a man of business like Geddes.

In Ireland, despite the Prime Minister's promise to grab 'murder by the throat', the situation was worsening, and there was concern that the government shouldn't hold the elections to the new southern Ireland parliament that were due in May. Lloyd George had based his support for Britain's entry into the First World War on the need to defend small nations from aggression. In his speech at The Queen's Hall in 1914 he had accused the Germans of being the 'road-hog' of Europe, crushing all who stood in their path. Now the same accusation was levelled at his government by, amongst others, the Irish poet W. B. Yeats.[54] In February 1921 Yeats had spoken in a debate at the Oxford Union Society in favour of the motion, 'This house would welcome complete self-government in Ireland and condemns reprisals.' According to the report of the *Freeman's Journal*, Yeats was 'loudly cheered' and told his audience that 'Everything being done by Germany in Belgium is being done by England in Ireland . . . We speak of liberty and law but there is truth in the jibe that the war "made the world safe for hypocrisy".' The motion was carried by 219 votes to 129.[55]

In March, Lloyd George met with Lord Midleton,[56] the leader of the Unionists in southern Ireland, who suggested bringing in businessmen along with representatives of the Catholic Church to establish a 'small conclave' that could be joined by someone from Sinn Féin and a 'member of the Cabinet whom they would be prepared to trust', in order to see if some 'middle way' could be found.[57] It was an approach that Sir Henry Wilson rejected, telling a friend later that month, 'Where our politicians fall into the mess in which they are always floundering over Irish affairs is that they will neither come away nor will they govern. They are always attempting some middle course which is fatal to the continued prosperity of Ireland herself and the safety of the Empire.'[58] Yet governing as Wilson intended would now mean the subjugation of the whole of southern Ireland under martial law. Even if such an action was achievable it would be condemned around the world.

On Sunday 3 April, Lloyd George invited Lords Riddell and Burnham to lunch at Chequers, and making the first leap asked them, 'The question is whether I can see Michael Collins. No doubt he is the head and front of the movement. If I could see him, a settlement might be possible. The question is whether the British people would be willing for us to negotiate with the head of a band of murderers.' Riddell replied, 'It is a pretty strong order for the Prime Minister of the British Empire to have such an interview. But it might be done by a third party.' To which Lloyd George responded, 'I don't think that would do . . . I must see him myself.' Both Riddell and Burnham thought this would be 'difficult'.[59] In order to test the water in Ireland, Lloyd George sent Lord Derby on a secret mission to Dublin. Unfortunately, his cover was blown by the local correspondent of *The Times*, who reported that 'Some excitement has been caused in Dublin by the report that Lord Derby was in the city . . . wearing dark spectacles and disguised under the name of "E. Edwards".'[60] In a secret meeting that it was later denied had taken place, Lord Derby saw Éamon De Valera,[61] who later recalled telling his English visitor 'that the Republic had been declared and that it would have to be accepted as a basic fact. My recollection is that he stressed the difficulties from the British point of view, but I pointed out that the position of the Republic was fundamental.'[62] De Valera thought that the meeting had been a 'useful . . . breaking of the ice'.[63] Derby also helped to broker a future private conversation for the leader of Sinn Féin with Sir James Craig,[64] head of the Ulster Unionists, which took place in Dublin on 5 May. This was an important symbolic engagement, though, as far as Lloyd George's interests were concerned, for if Craig was prepared to meet De Valera, why shouldn't he? Despite these first contacts the general situation in Ireland continued to deteriorate. On 25 May the IRA attacked the Custom House in Dublin, and a few days before some unarmed Sinn Féin supporters were found in the grounds of Chequers, while the Prime Minister was in residence. The elections to the southern Ireland parliament went ahead as planned, but they were reduced to farce with Sinn Féin winning 124 of the 128 seats unopposed and declaring that they didn't recognize the new assembly. Highlighting the difference in the north, the Unionists won 40 of the 52 seats.

On 31 May, Philip Sassoon hosted a dinner for Lloyd George and the Cabinet at 25 Park Lane, to discuss the general political situation. Such occasions, Lord Beaverbrook remembered, were where the Prime Minister 'exerted his charms' on his colleagues, 'that was the object of the Sassoon parties'.[65] Frances Stevenson noted that Lloyd George was 'Very pleased with the talk, which he says was most useful. Geddes stated that there was only one person that people cared about & would listen to and that was D. D said that when Geddes said this Winston could not conceal his anger & irritation & others noticed this too. D says he is going to detach F.E. [F. E. Smith] from Winston. He (D) wants a general election in the autumn, as he thinks it would be useful then.'[66]

Over dinner Lloyd George set out his case for a negotiated settlement in Ireland, an approach Churchill described as leading to the most 'complete and sudden . . . reversal of policy' in the modern history of the British government. 'In May the whole power of the State and the influence of the Coalition were used to "hunt down the murder gang": in June the goal was a lasting reconciliation with the Irish people.'[67] Lloyd George also asked General Smuts to act as an unofficial mediator with the Irish. He had the unique distinction of having been a rebel leader against the British in the Boer War, and then a member of the War Cabinet during the First World War. Smuts told the Prime Minister bluntly that the situation in Ireland was 'an unmeasured calamity; it is in negation of all the principles of Government which we have professed as the basis of Empire, and it must more and more tend to poison both our Empire relations and our foreign relations'.[68] Lloyd George shared these observations with the Cabinet and also asked Smuts to brief the King.

On 18 June the Prime Minister visited George V at Windsor Castle, following a very hot week of horse racing for Royal Ascot. Four days later the King, accompanied by Queen Mary,[69] would step into the inferno of Irish politics when making a speech in Belfast to open the new Northern Ireland parliament. It would be his first visit to the city in 24 years; there would be large crowds and a mile-long ride in an open carriage, with all of the associated security risks. There was certainly no cowardice in their Majesties' decision to go. Afterwards, the Queen told her lady-in-waiting, the Countess of Airlie,[70] 'They could have got any of us.'[71] The King considered, according to Lord Stamfordham, that 'he had been kept in the dark'[72] about the speech he was to give and wished to know the views of the Cabinet. After seeing Lloyd George at Windsor, the King noted in his diary that they had 'discussed Ireland & what I should say in my speech at the opening of the new Parliament in Belfast next week'.[73] The result of their deliberations was a bold offer that would have an immediate effect. King George told the packed assembly meeting in the Ulster Hall that he wished for 'all Irishmen to pause, to stretch out the hand of forbearance and conciliation, to forgive and forget and to join in making for the land which they love a new era of peace, contentment and goodwill'.[74] The following day Lloyd George told the Cabinet that De Valera was prepared to discuss a settlement, and he sent a message to George V exalting that 'None but the King could have made that personal appeal; none but the King could have evoked so instantaneous a response.'[75] On 11 July a truce in Ireland came into effect and three days later Lloyd George met De Valera, for the first of a series of discussions on how a permanent peace settlement might be reached. Crowds gathered around Downing Street ahead of De Valera's arrival and many sang and said the rosary prayers. Frances Stevenson remembered that she'd never seen Lloyd George 'so excited . . . He kept walking in and out of my room & I could see he was working out the best way of dealing with Dev. . . . He had a big map of the British Empire hung up on the wall in the Cabinet Room, with its great blotches of red all over it. This was . . . to impress upon Dev. The greatness of the [British Empire] & the King.'[76]

At their first meeting Lloyd George told De Valera, 'The British Empire is a sisterhood of nations – the greatest in the world. Look at this table: There sits Africa – English and Boer; there sits Canada – French, Scotch and English; there sits Australia, representing many races – even Maoris; there sits India; here sit the representatives of England, Scotland and Wales; all we ask you to do is to take your place in this sisterhood of free nations.'[77] The deal that Lloyd George was offering, as Thomas Jones summarized in a letter for the benefit of a convalescing Bonar Law, was '"Dominion status" with all sorts of important powers, but no Navy, no hostile tariffs, and no coercion of Ulster. There is a Territorial Force for Ulster, and for the South.'[78] This would give Ireland independence within the Empire, but no republic, and would also lead to the partition of the island. During another meeting the Prime Minister picked up a sheet of notepaper from a letter he had previously received from De Valera, which was headed 'Saorstat na hEireann'. He asked the Irishman with mischievous innocence what the word 'Saorstat' meant, to which he replied, 'Free State'. At this Lloyd George triumphantly responded, 'Must we not then agree Mr De Valera that the Celts never were republicans and have no native word for such an idea.'[79] Yet these talks made no progress, with De Valera telling Lloyd George that he would accept either dominion status for the whole of the island of Ireland, or complete independence for southern Ireland, but not the offer being made by the British government. Lloyd George complained after their talks that 'Negotiating with De Valera is like trying to pick up mercury with a fork.' De Valera's response when told this was, 'Why doesn't he use a spoon?'[80]

For Lloyd George, conceding either on the idea of all Ireland being a Republic outside of the jurisdiction of the Crown and Empire, or forcing Ulster to come under a Dublin government, were political impossibilities. Both would be blocked by the Conservative Party and would lead to the resumption of hostilities. At one point Lloyd George told De Valera what the consequences of failing to reach an agreement would be, telling him, 'Do you realise that this means war? Do you realise that the responsibility for it will rest on your shoulders alone?' To which De Valera replied, 'No Mr. Lloyd George, if you insist on attacking us it is you, not I, who will be responsible, because you will be the aggressor.' The Prime Minister then told De Valera, 'I could put a soldier in Ireland for every man, woman and child in it', to which the Irishman responded, 'Very well. But you would have to keep them there.'[81]

In late July, Lord Northcliffe gave permission for the editor of The Times, Wickham Steed, to give an interview in his name to the New York Times, which implied that the government's new approach to Ireland was due to the intervention of the King, rather than the initiative of the Prime Minister. From this, Northcliffe's Daily Mail attributed some of Steed's comments directly to Northcliffe, who was at that time in America on a world tour to recover his failing health. This included a statement that:

> 'At the last meeting he had with Mr Lloyd George before leaving for Ireland, King George asked him, "Are you going to shoot all the people in Ireland?" "No your Majesty," the Premier replied. "Well then," said King George, "you must come to some agreement with them. This cannot go on. I cannot have my people killed in this manner."'[82]

Frances Stevenson remembered that:

> D. was simply furious & said to Stamfordham: 'This means that the King's secretary is seeing the Editor of the chief Opposition newspaper, & gives the impression that there is a difference of opinion between the King & his Prime Minister. I cannot allow this happen again.' D. said S. was very frightened, as he is evidently the culprit.

In the House of Commons on 29 July, Lloyd George made a statement on behalf of himself and the King, that the newspaper reports in question were a 'complete fabrication. No such conversations as those which are alleged took place.' Instead, he attributed their origin to the 'criminal malignity which for personal ends is endeavouring to stir up mischief'.[83] This led to Northcliffe denying any involvement with the interview. 'I know nothing about it,' he stated, 'I never said that King George had said any such thing to Mr. Lloyd George nor have I given out anything with even a remote suggestion of the idea.'[84] Yet Steed had given the interview in his name, neither man had sought to retract it, and the Daily Mail had reported on it. The New York Times stood by their story, stating that it 'was written by a trustworthy reporter who believes that he reported accurately what Mr. Steed said. Mr Steed has since told *The Times* that it contained matter that should not have been published.'[85] Not the same thing of course as a denial of the facts. Yet this whole incident highlighted once more the general distrust that existed between Stamfordham and Lloyd George, and the continuing bad blood between Northcliffe and the Prime Minister.

On 4 August, Lloyd George enjoyed a great homecoming at the National Eisteddfod, his first appearance for three years, and held in his constituency at Carnarvon. Thirteen thousand people filled a huge pavilion to greet him with ovation when he arrived, accompanied by Margaret and Megan, for the ceremony of the Chairing of the Bard. During his speech he reflected that:

> Throughout the war the Eisteddfod was singing, 'Is there peace?' and the answer was being drowned in the sound of cannon. At Birkenhead there was an empty chair: the winner was slain on the battlefield. At Neath the armies of the enemy were advancing everywhere, but Peace ultimately triumphed. The Eisteddfod will remain from age to age a voice above all voices, to cry above the echo, 'Is there peace?' and continue to proclaim it, and the heart and conscience of humanity will answer, 'Peace!' There will be heavenly peace on earth and goodwill [Loud and continued applause].'[86]

Yet at the forefront of the Prime Minister's mind that summer was, would there be peace or war in Ireland. Despite the breakdown in talks in July, communications between Lloyd George and De Valera continued, seeking to establish terms for starting formal negotiations on a treaty of settlement. These approaches also failed, but in September, Lloyd George secured the approval of the Cabinet to invite the Irish to send representatives to a conference anyway, in the hope that a solution could be found. This invitation was sent on 29 September, with the talks to begin on 11 October. For the British negotiating team Lloyd George included Austen Chamberlain, so binding in the Conservative leadership. A now-revived Bonar Law was being assiduously briefed in the background at every step of the process by Thomas Jones, and Lloyd George also met with Bonar Law to discuss Ireland, at Philip Sassoon's Port Lympne estate that August. Lord Birkenhead and

Winston Churchill, both manoeuvring in the background for a position of advantage should the government fall, would also be included. De Valera chose to remain in Dublin, perhaps sensing from his previous exchanges with Lloyd George that whatever the outcome would be, the Irish negotiators would not return with the Republic he wanted. Instead, the Irish plenipotentiaries would be led by Arthur Griffith,[87] with Michael Collins, Robert Barton,[88] Eamonn Duggan[89] and George Gavan Duffy.[90]

The negotiations brought Lloyd George face to face for the first time with Michael Collins, another cottage-bred man. The young Irishman thought the Prime Minister was 'all comradely, all craft and wiliness – all arm around the shoulder . . . not long ago he would have had me joyfully at the rope end.'[91] Whereas Lloyd George considered Collins to be 'vivacious . . . highly strung, impulsive, but passing readily from gaiety to grimness and back again . . . full of fascination and charm – but also of dangerous fire.'[92] After the initial discussions Lloyd George decided that more would be achieved in small side conferences and identified Collins and Griffith as the two most influential of the Irish representatives. He also placed himself in the pivotal position of being the only person who was speaking directly to leading Unionists like James Craig and Bonar Law, as well as to the Irish negotiators.

Some of the most crucial of these meetings were held in the days leading up to the Conservative Party conference in Liverpool on 13 November, where there was expected to be heavy criticism of the Irish negotiations. The day before, Lloyd George had a private lunch with Arthur Griffith at Philip Sassoon's 25 Park Lane mansion, where he set out new terms for an agreement. The constraints the Prime Minister had explained to De Valera in the summer still applied. He could offer Dominion status within the Empire, so an Irish 'Free State' but not a republic. There would be no coercion of Northern Ireland, and Ireland would have to accept the King as head of state. But Lloyd George now said that he could make some concessions on economic policy, in particular giving Ireland control of customs and tariffs. In return the Prime Minister asked whether Griffith would accept that the people of Northern Ireland should be free to decide whether or not they wanted to come under a government led from Dublin. He also proposed the creation of a Boundary Commission taking into consideration the preferences of local people, to determine where the border between northern and southern Ireland might be. To this, Griffith said he would make no objection if that offer were made to the Ulstermen, but he believed they were unlikely to accept it. That evening at Trent Park, Lloyd George used a dinner with Bonar Law to try and secure his support for such a proposal. Frances Stevenson recorded in her diary that 'D told him quite plainly that he was not playing the game. Bonar flared up and said that if that was the case he would refuse to discuss the matter any further and for a short time there was real unpleasantness. However D eventually talked him round and they sat up discussing till nearly one o'clock. D thinks that Bonar has agreed not to oppose his new proposals for the All Ireland settlement.'[93]

Ahead of the Conservative Party conference, Austen Chamberlain wrote to his sister Hilda in despairing tones, 'Sinn Fein and Ulster in front, the Diehards on my back and the National Union[94] meeting on Thursday in Liverpool, the stronghold of Orange Toryism . . . And I might add to my catalogue of troubles Bonar Law, an Ulsterman by descent and in spirit, a very ambitious man now astonished at . . . his own complete recovery and itching to be back in politics where he is disposed to think that the first place might and ought to be his. I am fighting for my political life.'[95] However, Bonar Law was sufficiently reassured that he did not even attend the Liverpool conference. There would be one motion tabled to be debated at the conference by the Die-Hard Conservative MP, John Gretton,[96] which was critical of the Irish talks. However, after senior figures like Derby, Birkenhead and Austen Chamberlain urged the conference to support the continuation of the negotiations, on the principle that there would be no coercion of Ulster, Gretton's motion was overwhelmingly defeated by 1,730 votes to 70. Lloyd George also sent another intermediary, Sir Robert Bruce,[97] editor of the *Glasgow Herald*, to speak with Sir Edward Carson and Bonar Law about Ireland. In late November, Bruce reported back from a dinner that Carson told him 'The Little Man has betrayed Ulster and I'll have nothing to do with him.' However from Bonar Law, Bruce secured the commitment that he could 'tell the Little Man that in my own way and time I shall work for a Settlement'.[98] On 15 December, about three weeks later, Bonar Law duly used his first speech back in Parliament since his resignation to support the government's Irish policy, telling the House that it was an approach 'I should have presented, if it had been my responsibility'.[99]

The Unionists may have believed they were being clever, in trying to avoid making Ulster the issue that would bring down the Treaty negotiations, and instead wanting the fault for failure to be due to Sinn Fein refusing membership of the British Empire along with an oath of allegiance to the King. Yet Lloyd George knew that Griffith was not prepared to break with the negotiations on that question alone, and that he and Collins could both see that the deal being offered was the best that could be achieved. It would deliver the Irish Free State and might be the first big step towards achieving their ultimate ambition of a unified and fully independent Ireland. Also, if Lloyd George was forced to resign as a consequence of the failure to reach an agreement, his successor would most likely be Bonar Law at the head of a fully Unionist government, and they would not get a better settlement then. As Frances Stevenson observed in her diary, 'D. says that if the Ulster men accept they will do so in the hope that the S.F.'s [Sinn Féiners] would refuse it. They (the Ulstermen) are quite ignorant of the fact that the S.F.'s have already agreed. It is a very subtle plan & . . . D. is quite determined that it shall go through.'[100]

Yet there remained deep divisions on both sides. For many in Sinn Féin, the failure to secure the Republic, the division of the island of Ireland, and the recognition of the King were unforgiveable concessions that would ultimately lead to civil war. Leading Unionists like Carson and Sir Henry Wilson believed that although the proposed settlement would keep Northern Ireland in the United Kingdom, it would be under constant threat, both economic and military, from a hostile neighbour. The Boundary Commission could also mean further territory along that frontier being lost to the Irish Free State.

On 30 November, Lloyd George presented the Irish delegation with a draft treaty to which he said he would require their assent within one week, or else it would be assumed that the talks had broken down and the truce would be at an end. On 2 December, Arthur Griffith returned to Dublin, ahead of the rest of the delegation, to brief De Valera and the Irish Cabinet on the British offer. The Sinn Féin President recalled telling Griffith that he would 'never consent to or sign such an agreement', and that in response Griffith stated that 'he would not break on the Crown. We parted at that.'[101] At the Cabinet meeting the following day the members were split on whether or not to accept the treaty being offered, which Duggan said he believed to be 'England's last word'.[102]

De Valera declined to return to London with the Irish delegates, and instead sent them back with further requests for amendment. To bring matters to a close, however, at a meeting at 10 Downing Street on the evening of 5 December, Lloyd George insisted that unless the treaty was signed that night it would mean war. Barton recalled that Lloyd George 'shook his papers in the air, declared that we were trying deliberately to bring about a break on Ulster because our people in Ireland had refused to come within the Empire and that Arthur Griffith was letting him down where he had promised not to do so'.[103] The paper the Prime Minister was waving was a minute of their discussion at 25 Park Lane on 12 November, and in response, Austen Chamberlain remembered, Griffith replied 'I said I would not let you down on that, and I won't.'[104] Then, believing his honour was being impugned, the Irishman indicated that he would sign the treaty. Chamberlain recalled Lloyd George exclaimed that would not do, the whole Irish delegation would have to decide whether or not they were going to add their names to the treaty. 'I have to communicate with Sir James Craig to-night,' stated Lloyd George. 'Here are the alternative letters which I have prepared, one enclosing the Articles of Agreement reached by His Majesty's Government and yourselves, and the other saying that the Sinn Féin representatives refuse the oath of allegiance and refuse to come within the Empire. If I send this letter, it is war – and war within three days! Which letter am I to send?'[105]

It was nearly 8 p.m. and Arthur Griffith stated 'I will give the answer of the Irish delegation at nine to-night; but, Mr Prime Minister, I personally will sign this agreement and will recommend it to my countrymen.' Lloyd George then responded, 'Do I understand, Mr Griffith, that though everyone else refuses you will nevertheless agree to sign?' To which the Irishman stated, 'Yes, that is so, Mr Prime Minister.'[106] The conference adjourned, but the Irish delegation did not return until just after midnight. After discussing a number of small technical amendments, with great reluctance and led by Griffith and Collins, they all signed the treaty in the Cabinet Room of 10 Downing Street at 2.10 a.m. When it was done, for the first time the British ministers walked around the table and shook hands with their Irish counterparts. Lord Birkenhead told Michael Collins, 'I may have signed my political death warrant tonight', to which the young Irishman prophetically responded, 'I may have signed my actual death warrant.'[107]

For Lloyd George it had been an extraordinary day, starting at 5 a.m. and concluding nearly 22 hours later, with only a snatched 25-minute nap between meetings. Thomas Jones noted of the Prime Minister's performance, 'His patience and alertness have been extraordinary, even for him.'[108] At Sandringham, the King recorded in his diary:

> I got the joyful news first thing this morning from the Prime Minister that at 2.30 this morning articles of agreement were signed between the British representatives & the Irish delegates . . . complete acceptance of the British Govt's proposals, allegiance to the Throne & membership of the Empire. They sat from 11.0 to 2.30 before the agreement was arrived at. It is mostly due to the P.M.'s patience & conciliatory spirit & is a great feather in his cap & I trust that now after seven centuries there may be peace in Ireland. Ulster has got the option of coming in within a year, if they wish, but they will not be coerced.[109]

Lord Beaverbrook also recalled of this moment:

> The achievement of the Irish Treaty revealed in full what it was that LG possessed which other men lacked, in the understanding of human nature, in the art of tenacious negotiation, to a degree which few men in history have exhibited. If one way closed, he opened up another; he was, in the words of one of his friends, who presented him with a lovely piece of silver to mark the signing of the Treaty, 'the solver of the insoluble'.[110]

THIRTEEN

Things Fall Apart

Turning and turning in the widening gyre
The falcon cannot hear the falconer;
Things fall apart; the centre cannot hold;
Mere anarchy is loosed upon the world,
The blood-dimmed tide is loosed, and everywhere
The ceremony of innocence is drowned;
The best lack all conviction, while the worst
Are full of passionate intensity.[1]

From *The Second Coming* by W. B. Yeats

W. B. Yeats's great poem, first published in November 1920, was an apocalyptic vision of the chaos and turmoil of Europe after the war; a world where the voice of moderation was lost against a storm of radical fervour. As a supporter of the Irish Free State, Yeats would tell a friend of the treaty, 'I am by constitution a pessimist & never thought they would get so much out of Lloyd George & so am pleased.'[2] Yet he was fearful of the divisions it would bring, stating 'I am in a deep gloom about Ireland for though I expect ratification of the treaty from a plebiscite I see no hope of escape from bitterness, and the extreme party may carry the country. When men are very bitter, death and ruin draw them on as a rabbit is supposed to be drawn on by the dancing of the fox.'[3] For Lloyd George, while he had overcome great obstacles since becoming Prime Minister, solved problems which no one else had been able to answer, and still had great prestige in the eyes of the British people, by 1922 he too found it harder to control events. He was making the transition from dancing fox to weary falconer.

The luxurious resort town of Cannes was, though, a restful location for a New Year's international conference. In the first week of January, Lloyd George would escape the fog and rain of London for the warm breezes of the French Riviera and a reunion with his old friend now returned to high office, the French Premier Aristide Briand. The magnificent Villa Valetta,[4] owned by the British financier Sir Albert Stern,[5] was put at his disposal, and Lloyd George was joined by the Foreign Secretary Lord Curzon, Robert Horne, Winston Churchill and the War Secretary Sir Laming Worthington-Evans. The conference itself started on 6 January and had been called to discuss the payment of reparations owed by Germany to the Allies and the agenda for a meeting of all the European powers at Genoa in the spring. The Genoa summit was Lloyd George's great diplomatic initiative, and he wanted it to be a second Versailles, addressing all the outstanding issues facing Europe. This would bring together Britain, France and Italy with Germany and for the first time include the Soviet Union.

The Cannes conference, like so many others since the war, would prove to be an inconclusive disappointment. Years later, Lloyd George recalled that it was 'remarkable for the able, impressive and tenacious fight put up by Herr Rathenau[6] to save his country from being driven into insolvency by exactions beyond her capacity to bear. A few months later he was shot down like a wolf in the streets of Berlin by one of his own fellow countrymen.'[7] Aristide Briand would also be a victim of Cannes, from where he was recalled to Paris and forced to resign on 12 January. A motion was moved against his government in the National Assembly, a consequence that Lloyd George believed was of distrust at 'the concessions he was rumoured to be making to the Germans'.[8] The trigger, though, for this vote was an ill-fated photo-opportunity, which was also captured on film, of Briand playing golf with Lloyd George. Their match at the Cannes Golf Club had followed an informal lunch between the two leaders where, as A. J. Sylvester, Lloyd George's political secretary, remembered, 'As usual, L.G. wanted to create the "right atmosphere" to ensure success . . . So after lunch that day, the fun commenced.'[9] However, the Frenchman had never played the game before, and the scene made him look both ridiculous and subservient to the British Premier.

The loss of Briand and his replacement by Raymond Poincaré was a disaster for Lloyd George's foreign policy and everything he had been working to achieve with the French since the Treaty of Versailles. Ten years later, Lloyd George would write that compared to Briand, Poincaré was:

> ... cold, reserved, rigid, with a mind of unimaginative and ungovernable legalism. He has neither humour nor good humour. In conference he was dour and morose ... he is the most un-French Frenchman I ever met ... He wanted to cripple Germany, and render her impotent for future aggression ... The fall of M. Briand sent the world rolling towards the catastrophe which culminated in 1931.[10] Had he remained in office, European appeasement from the Urals to the Rhine might have been reached in 1922.[11]

In the wings of the conference at the Villa Valetta, Lloyd George had also convened a separate political meeting with Horne, Churchill, Sir Laming Worthington-Evans and Lord Beaverbrook to discuss whether the Coalition should seek to exploit the public support for the Irish agreement and call a general election. It was well known within political circles that the Lloyd George political fund had been swollen from the selling of honours to pay for an election campaign, but only a few senior Conservatives were also aware that their Treasurer, Horace Farquhar,[12] had transferred large sums of money from the party's account into the Prime Minister's fund. During their discussions this point was brought to farcical attention by Sir Albert Stern's parrot, perched in a cage nearby. At one point it suddenly called out, A. J. Sylvester recalled, 'so plainly that it was difficult to believe the voice was that of a bird,[13] "Stop it, Horace!"'[14] This, Beaverbrook recalled, gave those present 'a moment of embarrassment, amusement and delight'.[15] Later, in response to an impassioned speech from Worthington-Evans in favour of an early election, the parrot again interjected, 'You bloody fool! You bloody fool!'[16] Yet it wasn't just a sceptical parrot that the Prime Minister had to overcome. Beaverbrook arranged for Lloyd George and Bonar Law to meet in Cannes, at the Carlton Hotel on the Boulevard de la Croisette where the press baron was staying. It was just over five years since the two men had met in Beaverbrook's suite at the Hyde Park Hotel in London, where they agreed to support each other in the action that led to the fall of Asquith's government. Now, Lloyd George asked Bonar Law to rejoin the Cabinet as Foreign Secretary in return for his support for an early election in which the Coalition would stand as a single political force. Bonar Law declined.

The Conservative leader Austen Chamberlain was against an election, writing in January 1922 to his sister Hilda: 'Of politics I know nothing except what you may read in the papers – that the P.M. and Lord Chancellor want a dissolution and that I am opposed to it on many grounds, amongst which two stand out. 1st we have no right to go till we have carried through our Irish policy (not merely started it) and secondly I think that it will find my party in a very bad temper and a very difficult position.'[17] Sir George Younger, the Conservative Chairman, had been on political manoeuvres, and without consulting his leader sent an open letter to all of the local Conservative Associations, warning that an early election would split the party between those who supported the Lloyd George Coalition and those who were against it. Younger had commissioned research as well, suggesting that more Conservatives would be elected if they stood on their own and separate from the Coalition Liberals. He had also written to Lloyd George on 4 January, stating that he believed it would be 'a disaster to the best interests of the country if an election were held in the present circumstances. I see no justification for it . . . I believe it would be a most risky operation . . . it would be my duty to use what influence I could to oppose it.'[18] Lloyd George told Austen Chamberlain that he thought Younger had 'behaved disgracefully . . . His action has caused serious damage which it will be difficult to repair.'[19] Nevertheless, for the first time since the formation of the Coalition, Lloyd George lacked the political power either directly, or through his colleagues, to exercise political control over the government. The idea that he might become leader of a new Centre Party, which would be a fusion of moderate Conservatives and Coalition Liberals, seemed as remote as ever.

After an unsuccessful meeting with Poincaré at Boulogne on Saturday 25 February, Lloyd George returned to Philip Sassoon's Port Lympne estate in low spirits, weighed down by political pressures at home and abroad. Riddell, who was also staying with Sassoon, recalled that after lunch on Sunday, 'LG went to the writing-table, obtained a bundle of notepaper and sat down by the fire busily writing in pencil. He covered sheet after sheet . . . Later in the evening he sent for me to go to his bedroom and then handed me the result of his labours to read.' It was a long letter to Austen Chamberlain, stating that the country needed a strong, unified government and that if he or Bonar Law thought they were better placed to deliver this, Lloyd George would retire in their favour and offer his full support. Riddell noted in his diary that 'He asked my opinion on the letter. I said I thought he was taking the right course . . . If Chamberlain or Bonar Law accepted his proposal, well and good. If not, then he, LG, could reply that if he were going on, it would be necessary that he should have united support. In short the letter was a step in the direction of a fused party.'[20] The following morning, Lloyd George summoned A. J. Sylvester and told him 'I've given serious and earnest thought to the matter of retaining the Premiership, and have decided that I should give the Tories a chance. Chamberlain should have the opportunity.'[21] Sylvester remembered, 'Having dictated the letter to Chamberlain he entered his waiting car and told me to get it typed out and follow him to London in another car. Sir Philip had several cars which were at the disposal of the Premier, and so, leaving me at Lympne to type out the letter . . . LG drove away. It did not take me long to complete the typing, and as I finished it, a fast open car was driven round to the front door. Without any regard to speed limits, the chauffeur drove after the car conveying the Prime Minister, and soon we had overtaken it. The two cars stopped and I handed LG the letter.'[22]

Chamberlain declined Lloyd George's offer, knowing that it would not be easy for him to lead a government and a divided Conservative Party; 60 'Die Hard' Conservatives had, for example, voted in the House of Commons against the Irish Treaty. His state of mind was clear from a letter he wrote to his sister Ida on 26 February, 'I know what I want. My colleagues are agreed with me & Younger intends to carry out my policy; yet they all seem to conspire to prevent it. Younger humiliates the P.M. publicly, F.E. [F. E. Smith] attacks Younger personally; Bonar Law tries on the crown but can't make up his mind to attempt to seize it, won't join us & share the load but watches not without pleasure the trouble of his friends, & the Die Hards, instead of responding to my advances, harden their resistance.'[23] Chamberlain also had little sympathy for grassroots opinion in his party and confided to his sister Hilda, 'Our local Associations are full of old prewar Tories who have learned nothing and forgotten nothing and who are I am quite convinced unrepresentative of the bulk of the electorate. They are a positive danger to us and may easily be our ruin.'[24] The trouble for Lloyd George was less that he couldn't lead the Conservative Party, but that nor could Austen Chamberlain. An increasingly concerned Philip

Sassoon told his old friend and mentor Lord Esher, 'I feel in my bones that LG ought for his own sake to go at once. No patch up will avert the coming smash & he has a chance of jumping clear. But Winston (whose views are always personal) advised him to hang on because Winston does not want to give up his job and I am sure he means to join the Tories at the earliest possible moment. I hope LG will do something for me in any event, but I am not counting on it too much – for I know his nature. It is thrilling & heart breaking at the same time.'[25]

On 9 March, Edwin Montagu, one of the few leading Liberal members left in the Cabinet, was compelled to resign by Lloyd George, for authorizing the publication of a sensitive diplomatic telegram from the Viceroy of India, without the approval of the Cabinet. The telegram implied support from the British government in India for Turkey in its war with Greece, in order to appease Muslim opinion on the Indian subcontinent. This was contrary to the policy of Lloyd George and the Foreign Secretary Lord Curzon and the terms of the peace treaties at the end of the war. Montagu's resignation was followed by a bitter speech in his Cambridgeshire constituency on 11 March where he told his audience, 'The head of our Government at the present time is a Prime Minister of great, if eccentric genius . . . whose achievements are so well known, but who had demanded the price which it is the power of every genius to demand, and that price has been total, complete, absolute disappearance of the doctrine of Cabinet responsibility ever since he formed his Government. The wizard, as he is, from the cupboard where he has locked his doctrine, brings it out conveniently, and makes me the victim of his new creed.'[26]

On the same day, Lloyd George returned to Criccieth for rest and recuperation, but Philip Sassoon, as his eyes and ears in the House of Commons, wrote to tell him that:

> . . . it is a thing inevitable that the difficulties of the current administration will increase from week to week. It is enough in politics for the rumour to get about that the ship is sinking not only for the rats to leave it but for someone or other to lend the elements a helping hand by scuttling the vessel. If you do not now make sure of the moderate Conservatives and moderate Liberals, guiding both along the path of a really national policy, I fear that you may inevitably be led to resign by events. In that case, I am convinced that Winston

will find a way to form an alliance with the Conservatives himself. I feel more strongly than I can express in words that definite action by you should not be postponed longer than the period necessary to see the Irish Bill through parliament . . . it cannot be easy for you at Criccieth to keep in proper touch . . . Need I say that Lympne is open to you. The sea breezes of Kent are from the point of view of health no bad substitute for the winds and mountains of Wales.[27]

Lloyd George stayed in Criccieth enjoying the rough weather and writing to Frances Stevenson of the 'Heavy snow showers all day. I love them & I am lying outside now with the snow whirling around.'[28] The storm clouds in Westminster were brewing around the Genoa Conference due to start on 10 April. Lloyd George wrote to Frances again from Wales on 22 March telling her that 'The fat is well in the fire again. Austen writes to say that Winston says he will resign if I am to recognise the Bolsheviks at Genoa & that he (Austen) cannot face the Tories on a resignation over that issue. If that is the case then I go, & I go on an issue that suits me.'[29] Although the Prime Minister also received a reassuring note from Philip Sassoon that:

> Personally I have not been able in the House to discover (except of course in the smouldering Die Hard bosoms) any intense feeling on the subject of Recognition. I expect you will find more difficulty in the Cabinet than in the House of Commons. I don't think FE knows where he is at all. It is becoming increasingly difficult to find any sequence in his acts or words, on the other hand his movements are easy to follow. He and Freddie Guest, along with Mona Dunn,[30] and Scatters[31] were supping and dancing on the roof garden of the Criterion restaurant till past 1 o'clock this morning. Will you let me know if I can look forward to your dining with me on Monday. If so who would you like to have. I have got Trent ready for you if you find that Danehurst[32] is too far off.'[33]

Lloyd George stayed at Danehurst with Frances at the beginning of April where Sir Louis Mallet, also a guest of Sassoon's at Lympne, observed:

> She is afraid of letting him out of her sight and watches him like a lynx, being sincerely in love with him, as he is attached to her. It is

curious that the world at large knows nothing of this liaison which has lasted for some years now and been more or less public.[34]

On Monday 3 April, Lloyd George returned to London to open a debate in the House of Commons, which was in effect a confidence motion in the government linked to the Genoa Conference. The motion was easily carried, and Winston Churchill didn't leave the government over recognition of the Soviet Union. He wisely took the advice of Lord Birkenhead that his resignation would have made him 'the hero of the *Morning Post* and the leader of some thirty Tories in the House of Commons who would disagree with you on 90% of all the subjects about which you feel really deeply. Moreover you would cut yourself adrift, perhaps permanently, certainly for a very long time.'[35] King George V also disliked the idea of the conference and asked Lloyd George, 'I suppose you will be meeting Lenin[36] and Trotsky[37]?' To this the Prime Minister replied:

> Unfortunately, sir, I am not able to choose between the people I am forced to meet in your service. A little while ago I had to shake hands with Sami Bey,[38] a ruffian who was missing the whole day, and finally traced to a sodomy house in the East End. He was the representative of Mustafa Kemal,[39] a man who I understand has grown tired of affairs with women . . . I must confess I do not think there is very much to choose between these persons whom I am forced to meet from time to time in Your Majesty's service.

At this the King roared with laughter.[40] The Soviets, though, had been impressed with Lloyd George and his support for opening diplomatic relations with their government. The British Communist and future MP, William Gallacher,[41] remembered being told by Lenin in 1920 that he should 'study David Lloyd George. He held the opinion that David Lloyd George was the greatest political leader this country had known.'[42]

The Genoa Conference was held in the Palazzo San Giorgio, and the arrival of Lloyd George and the British delegation impressed the *Toronto Star*'s young foreign correspondent, Ernest Hemingway.[43] He observed that 'The hall is nearly full when the British delegation enters. They have come in motorcars through the troop-lined streets and enter with élan. They are the best-dressed delegation.'[44] Hemingway also thought that there was only one statesman who had 'brought any magic with him – and that was Lloyd George':

> Yet the photographers that took his picture did not capture any of that magic because Lloyd George does not look like his pictures. It is a second-rate face that photographs best. If you want to prove this, get a close-up in-the-flesh view of say one of fifty movie stars, or recall how often you have been disappointed in a photograph of your best girl. Lloyd George has no movie face. His charm, his fresh coloring – almost girlish – the complexion of a boy subaltern just out of Sandhurst, his tremendous assurance that makes him seem a tall man until you see him standing beside someone of average height; his kindly, twinkling eyes; none of these show in the photographs.[45]

In his opening remarks at the conference, Lloyd George 'makes the speech which is the star attraction of this spectacle,' noted the German diplomat Count Harry Kessler.[46] 'The effect produced by this very momentous political performance, executed in light conversational tone, was outstanding. The whole conference, including onlookers and journalists, applauded wildly for minutes on end. Lloyd George had once more evinced his magical touch and bewitched everyone.'[47] Yet to what effect? Like a theatre audience anticipating the performance of a great actor, the conference savoured the experience of seeing Lloyd George in person and then continued with their business. Raymond Poincaré had already ensured the failure of the Genoa Conference, by refusing to attend. It had attracted the representatives of 34 nations, to discuss how they could get the European economy moving again, settle the issue of German reparations, and open trade with Russia. Thomas Jones believed that for Lloyd George, it was 'the most ambitious, most heroic enterprise of his life'.[48] 'Its results,' Jones added, 'were inconclusive, and a confessed failure was avoided by the expedient of adjourning to a gathering of experts at The Hague, where no satisfactory agreement was reached.'[49] As a consequence, each nation was free to follow its own path, but without any international consensus. No such conference, on this scale and with participants from so many nations, would be attempted again until after the Second World War.

Since the signing of the Irish Treaty in December, Lloyd George had largely delegated the ratification and enforcement of the agreement to

Winston Churchill. In Dublin the Dáil Éireann had voted to endorse the settlement by 64 votes to 57, which caused De Valera and his Republican supporters to walk out of the chamber. On 16 January, in a ceremony at Dublin Castle, the official transfer of power was made by the British to the Irish Free State, with Michael Collins becoming Chairman of the Provisional Government. Yet the question of partition and the border with Northern Ireland would become an immediate problem. The Boundary Commission was an example of an often-deployed Lloyd George negotiating tactic, in that it allowed an agreement to be reached in principle while still deferring one of the most difficult decisions. It had been presented to the Unionists as a mechanism that would preserve their freedom and to Michael Collins as the means, by stealth, of reuniting Ireland. At his meeting with the Prime Minister on the morning before the treaty was signed, Collins had been encouraged to believe that 'the North would be forced economically to come in'.[50] As Lord Riddell observed of Lloyd George in conference, 'You cannot rely on what L.G. says . . . He may not actually tell a lie, but he will lead you to believe what he considers will induce you to do what he wants.'[51]

By early February violence was breaking out along the Northern Ireland border and on 8 February the Monaghan IRA kidnapped 43 Unionists in a series of cross-border raids into Fermanagh and Tyrone. In response Sir Henry Wilson, who would retire that month as Chief of the Imperial General Staff and become the Unionist MP for North Down, was advocating sending the army into the Free State territory to combat the threat from the IRA. In Belfast, brutal sectarian violence against Catholics, regardless of their involvement in the nationalist cause, was on the increase. In Dublin, on 16 April, 200 members of the anti-treaty IRA occupied the Four Courts building, which would eventually be retaken by force by the Free State army in late June, an action that led to the outbreak of civil war. A war on the border of Northern Ireland was also only narrowly averted in early June after the IRA menaced the Pettigo-Belleek triangle in County Fermanagh, a small area cut off from the rest of Northern Ireland by Lough Erne and the River Erne. On 7 June, Winston Churchill sent in 7,000 armed men to liberate this space, and although they were fired on heavily, only one soldier was wounded and there were no casualties on the Free State side of the boundary. Lloyd George, who was at Chequers at the time receiving updates, was 'furious' at what he considered to be a reckless action. Thomas Jones noted that 'the P.M. compared Winston to a chauffeur who apparently is perfectly sane and drives with great skill for months, then suddenly he takes you over a precipice. He thought that there was a strain of lunacy.'[52] Nevertheless, when news of the successful 'Battle of Belleek' was received that evening, the mood lightened. Jones recalled that 'After dinner we began innocently enough with Welsh hymns but the P.M.'s desire to celebrate the victory of Belleek led him to sing "Scots wha hae" putting in Winston's name wherever he could.'[53] Presumably, 'Wha for Ireland's king and law Winston's sword will strongly draw.'[54]

Violence resulting from dissent at the Irish agreement would also be seen on the British mainland that summer, leading to an incident that caused great shock and outrage, particularly amongst the Unionist community. On the afternoon of 22 June, wearing full uniform having just returned from unveiling the war memorial at Liverpool Street Station, Sir Henry Wilson was assassinated on the steps of his London home at 36 Eaton Place. His murderers were two London-based members of the IRA who were previously unknown to the authorities. As well as the horror at his death there was criticism of the government for withdrawing Wilson's security protection in January that year. When Austen Chamberlain called to visit Lady Wilson[55] that evening, she refused to see him, and shouted 'Murderer' at him as he left the house.[56] She also let it be known through the *Morning Post* that it would be 'distasteful'[57] to her if Lloyd George and other members of the Cabinet attended Wilson's funeral at St Paul's Cathedral, and only consented after the intervention of the King. Frances Stevenson wrote in her diary that Lloyd George was 'very upset' by the news of Wilson's death, but also that 'D. had been warned by Shortt that there were dangerous Irishmen in London, & S. advised him not to go to Chequers, but we had been rather inclined to discount the warning at this juncture. However Shortt was right.'[58] Leo Amery noted on the day of Wilson's murder, 'I have lost one of my best friends and his death raises in my mind again all the doubts I have felt about the whole hateful Irish business. I cannot help feeling that it is to these very men we have handed over Ireland.'[59]

The leadership of the Irish Free State was also dealt a terrible blow on 12 August when Arthur Griffith collapsed and died in Dublin aged just 51, his health undermined by the relentless pressure and hard work he had endured. Lloyd George wrote to Michael Collins that 'my admiration for his single-minded patriotism, his ability, his sincerity and his courage have grown steadily since I first met him . . . His loss is heavy for Ireland, but I trust that his work will go on.'[60] Tragedy would strike again in Ireland just ten days later when Michael Collins was assassinated at Béal na Bláth in west Cork, in an ambush conducted by anti-treaty forces. Lloyd George received the news at home in Criccieth and issued a statement expressing his deep regret for the loss of 'one of Ireland's brilliant sons at a moment when Ireland most needed his special qualities of courage and resolution'.[61] The prediction Collins had made to Lord Birkenhead in the Cabinet Room at 10 Downing Street had been fulfilled in just over eight months.

Closer to home another crisis would explode that summer which would rock Lloyd George and his government. On Saturday 3 June the King's birthday honours list was published and that weekend Lord Riddell was staying with Lloyd George at Criccieth. He recalled that J.T. Davies told him that 'Waring[62] has got a peerage. J.T. says that his peerage and baronetcy have cost him, "one way or another" £100,000 . . . J.T. says they have done well this time with honours. Everyone has had to pay up – whatever his qualifications. Archibald Williamson[63] who has strong political claims, £50,000, Moynihan,[64] the surgeon £10,000 etc, etc.'[65] Yet the initial public concern came from the awarding of a peerage to the 82-year-old South African mining magnate, Sir Joseph Robinson.[66] On 6 June, *The Cape Times* reported criticism of Robinson's honour and that questions had been asked in the South African parliament requiring General Smuts to confirm that their government hadn't recommended he should receive it. This was then picked up by Reuters and reported in the British press. Robinson had been convicted in South Africa for defrauding the shareholders of his mining companies and when he had appealed to the Privy Council in London his case was dismissed without being heard. Such was the outrage when this was understood that Freddie Guest asked Robinson, who had paid £30,000 for his title, if he would ask the King to withdraw it.

However, the wider significance of the Robinson case was that it burst the dam on the honours scandal. On 13 June the 'Die-Hard' Conservative-supporting *Morning Post* ran the headline, 'An appeal to the national honour. The restoration of clean government.' Beneath it was stated, 'The sale of honours has become so notorious that names and prices are openly quoted, and the profits amount to a handsome fortune. The existence of that secret hoard, available for every device of the unscrupulous politician, is a public danger.'[67] In the House of Commons the MPs Godfrey Locker-Lampson[68] and Samuel Hoare launched a campaign for a debate on the honours system, eventually gaining the support of 279 members, 134 of whom were Coalition Conservatives. Hoare was also in contact with the King's assistant private secretary Clive Wigram, who told him that he hoped the 'scandal' of selling honours would now be 'quashed for all time'.[69]

On 3 July the King wrote to Lloyd George expressing his frustration that 'For some time there have been evident signs of growing public dissatisfaction on account of the excessive number of honours conferred, the personality of some of the recipients, and the questionable circumstances under which the honours in certain instances have been granted.' He also stated that the Robinson case 'must be regarded as little less than an insult to the Crown and to the House of Lords'.[70] Five days later during golf with Riddell at St George's Hill, an indignant Lloyd George complained:

> I shall make it quite plain that if there is to be an enquiry it will have to begin with Lord Salisbury's administration, or at any rate with Arthur Balfour's. Sir George Younger tells me that Lord Northcliffe, for example gave £200,000 for his peerage, £100,000 of which went to Mrs Keppel[71] and £100,000 to King Edward.[72] And there are several other cases such as those relating to Michelham and Wandsworth[73] . . . I am going to make it clear that if I'm going down, I am going to bring the temple down with me. I am not going to be sacrificed by people and the descendants of people who have been engaged in carrying on precisely the same system.[74]

In mid-July 1922, Philip Sassoon hosted a summer party at 25 Park Lane with a number of leading politicians amongst the guests. Churchill, who stayed until 2 a.m., noted one particular incident in a letter to Clementine: 'The old boy [Asquith] turned up at Philip's party heavily loaded. The PM accompanied him up the stairs and was chivalrous enough to cede him the banister. It was a wounding sight. He kissed a great many people affectionately. I presume they were all relations. Really this letter consists in telling "sad stories of the death of Kings".'[75] Yet chivalry was the last word to be used when the cash for honours scandal exploded in Parliament on 17 July. In the House of Lords, the 'Die-Hard' Duke of Northumberland[76] cited how the coffers of the 'Prime Minister's Party' had collected 'anything from £1 million to £2 million' to fund future campaigns at a time when 'there has been a more wholesale distribution of honours than ever before'. He also highlighted that 'whole groups of newspapers have been deprived of any real independence by the sale of honours, and constitute a mere echo of Downing Street, from whence they are controlled . . . can we really call it a coincidence when we find three persons concerned with the principal newspaper in south Wales, the *Western Mail*, Cardiff, are all honoured with titles – the proprietor, one of the largest shareholders, and the editor?'[77] Then addressing the King's birthday honours list directly, the duke stated that 'three gentlemen have been honoured, either with a baronetcy or a knighthood, all three of whom have quite recently been convicted by a court of law of the most serious offences. One was sued by his divorced wife . . . Another . . . engaged in a public swindle. A third was convicted of food hoarding during the war.'[78] Northumberland also read a letter he had received from a gentleman who'd been approached by an honours tout, relaying a message that 'the Government would not last very long, and that when Lloyd George went to the country he wanted funds to contest certain seats'.[79] In a parallel debate in the House of Commons, the Conservative MP Ronald McNeill[80] called out the peerage given to the former bankrupt, Lord Waring, questioning why 'his shareholders losing large sums of money, through misfortune possibly, or bad management, while he makes a fortune for himself in the War in another direction – is singled out at this time for this very high honour?' At this point, Waring who was sitting in the Distinguished Strangers' Gallery, shouted down into the chamber, 'That is a false statement!'[81] Lloyd George responded to these charges with a poor and rambling speech, the worst performance Winston Churchill considered that he'd ever seen the Prime Minister make in the House of Commons. However, Lloyd George offered a Royal Commission to investigate the awarding of honours, which satisfied Parliament, and kicked the issue discreetly down the road until the end of the year. But the public taint of the reputation of Lloyd George remained, not least being immortalized in the music hall song, 'Lloyd George knew my father'.[82] That summer Lloyd George's son Richard also confronted his father in the wake of the honours scandal, as he was 'distressed to feel that he was slipping away from everything important to him. He had hurt mother repeatedly and needlessly; and she gave him the stability that was vital to him.'[83] Richard told his father to 'straighten things out. Clear the decks. You're surrounded by false friends who are using you and building you up to a God-almighty fall.'[84] Richard later reflected that 'I had watched him turn to sycophants, fools, flatterers, scheming women, so that important affairs began to get out of focus.'[85]

The honours scandal also galvanized Conservative opposition to Lloyd George's government, which had already been strengthened by the Anti-Waste League, opposition to the Irish Treaty, the Genoa Conference and the recognition of Soviet Russia. Two days after the parliamentary debate on the honours scandal, Austen Chamberlain and Lord Birkenhead held a very bad-tempered meeting with the Conservative junior ministers, who insisted that if they formed the largest party after the election, the Prime Minister should not be Lloyd George but a Conservative. Chamberlain recalled that in response 'F.E. scolded and browbeat them with an intellectual arrogance which nearly produced a row there and then and did infinite harm . . . Balfour spoke persuasively but it is astonishing how little weight he now carries with the Party.'[86]

On 29 July, Riddell visited Lloyd George at his new house at Churt near Hindhead in Surrey, called *Bron-y-De*, meaning 'facing south'.[87] The property, which had been designed and built for him by Philip Tilden, conformed to Lloyd George's preferences, being a new house with an excellent distant view from the downland, across Frensham Pond to the Devil's Jumps hills. Tilden also recalled that it was to be 'a modest house, but it had to have one large room approximately of the same size as the Cabinet Room at Downing Street, so that the pacing up and down could be the same in either'.[88] Riddell noted that 'We talked of his political future. It is clear that he had not made up his mind what he wants to do. Indeed, he said plainly that he "shall be guided" by events. He is feeling the constant strain, but does not wish to relinquish the position. He is preparing for a retreat (building the house at Churt and arranging to write books) but is also arranging to carry on the fight.'[89] Lloyd George and Riddell also discussed the rapidly declining physical and mental health of Lord Northcliffe, which despite their differences the Prime Minister thought 'was a tragic business, and that he felt sorry to see him end in this way'.[90] Northcliffe had become increasingly paranoid and delusional. In June he had told Wickham Steed that at Boulogne an agent of Lloyd George's had tried to murder him with a Perrier bottle.[91] On 19 June the distinguished doctor Sir Thomas Horder[92] took charge of Northcliffe's treatment and when the press baron was told who was attending to him, he took a revolver from under his pillow shouting, 'One of [Lloyd] George's bloody knights', and had to be restrained by a nurse.[93] It was claimed by some that Northcliffe was suffering from a form of clinical megalomania, no doubt encouraged by Lloyd George's remark about his 'diseased vanity'. However, his actual cause of death on 14 August, aged just 57, would be endocarditis, a serious infection of the inner lining of the heart.

In September the final act in the life of the Lloyd George coalition would come as a consequence of the distant war rumbling in the east between Greece and Turkey. The Prime Minister's support for Greece, Lord Curzon would later complain, was a policy 'carried on, sometimes in cabinet, more frequently outside it and behind the back of the Foreign Office'.[94] On 9 September the Turks launched an offensive that drove the Greeks out of the territories it administered in Asia Minor under the terms of the peace treaties. Thomas Jones remembered that 'For a moment it seemed that Mustafa Kemal might follow them and set the Balkans ablaze.'[95] Lloyd George asked for support from Italy, France and the Dominions, but there was no enthusiasm for a new war. British troops stood alone in defence of the neutral zones along the straits in Asia Minor, and at Chanak, just across the water from Gallipoli, they faced attack from Turkish forces. On 16 September the Cabinet issued a statement threatening war with Turkey if it attacked Chanak. The Turks backed down, but this was not seen as a victory for Lloyd George. As Jones recalled, 'The outcry in war-weary Britain was immediate and widespread.'[96] The Cabinet met at Chequers the following day and secretly agreed that as soon as the crisis in Turkey allowed, they would fight the next general election on a united, national platform. On 25 September, Austen Chamberlain briefed all the Conservative ministers on this plan and believed them to be in agreement, with the exception of Stanley Baldwin, President of the Board of Trade.

Two days later, Leo Amery dined with George Younger and William Bridgeman,[97] where he heard 'all about the schemes which have been on foot for an election before the National Union Conference'.[98] The following day Philip Sassoon also let slip to Sam Hoare, Lloyd George's plan to call a general election for 28 October as 'there was no particular point in giving the Prime Minister an unnecessary kick', which is what he would get from the party conference. Hoare replied that he didn't think it would make much difference 'as the majority of Conservatives were anyhow going to stand and be returned as independents at the election'.[99] Increasingly, Conservative MPs saw little value in their alliance with Lloyd George and the Coalition Liberals, a cohort dismissed by J. C. C. Davidson as a 'stage army – the same faces at every show – a façade of gilded or gold bricks with no fabric behind it'.[100] The incident at Chanak had merely added to their concerns.

On 7 October, Bonar Law took a significant step in returning to front-line politics with a carefully worded letter about Chanak that was published in *The Times*. In this, while not directly criticizing the government, he implied that matters could have been handled better. In particular, he observed that 'We cannot alone act as the policeman of the world. The financial and social condition of this country makes that impossible.'[101] On the same day, an article in *The Spectator* proclaimed, 'What is needed above all things, is a Government which will insist upon "safety first" as the rule. We suggest the idea of a remaking of the Government . . . It is out of the question just now to plunge the country into a General Election. What we suggest is that there should be a reconstruction of the Cabinet; that Mr. Lloyd George should disappear and should be replaced by Mr. Bonar Law.'[102] Two days later a backbench Conservative MP, William Ormsby-Gore,[103] wrote to *The Times* in response to Bonar Law's letter and the Chanak crisis, 'Are not half our difficulties due to the widespread distrust in France and Italy of Mr. Lloyd George's personal methods of diplomacy . . . Undoubtedly we want a change of method and probably men if we are to preserve Allied cooperation, and I am confident that the constituencies are looking anxiously for a change both of method and *personnel* in the conduct of our external affairs. Many are looking to Mr. Bonar Law, who is not identified with the more recent developments of the present Coalition on the one hand or with the "Die-Hards" on the other, to reunite the Unionist Party, if not the nation.'[104] The significance here was not just the public nature of the statement, but that Ormsby-Gore was a former parliamentary private secretary to Lord Milner who had also served as an assistant secretary to the War Cabinet.

There was growing division as well between the Conservative leadership and the members of the party. Leo Amery recalled a conversation with Austen Chamberlain on 10 October who in contrast told him that:

> ... in order to defeat Labour it is necessary to have a Coalition, that the only possible Coalition is the existing one and that neither he [Chamberlain] nor any of his colleagues are prepared to suggest to the PM that he should go, or that the Coalition should be modified to make room for a Unionist Prime Minister. He thought that the only thing was for all Unionists in a responsible position to stand together and urge this upon the Party in the hope that they would at any rate in the great majority of cases fall into line. If his advice were not accepted, he would not continue to lead. His view is to have the election as quickly as possible. I might add that this was after a meeting of the Cabinet in the afternoon at which he expressed the same views and seems to have been more or less supported by most of them. The only one who took a definite line against him being Baldwin.

However, Amery noted, ' I do not think Austen yet realises the position in the Party or the fact that in the present temper of the country the half is a great deal more than the whole, i.e. that the Unionist Party is likely to get more seats standing on its own than the whole Coalition are likely to get standing together.'[105] Three days later on 13 October, Amery also had breakfast with Bonar Law, and noted that 'He favoured my compromise of election as two Parties leaving the question of Coalition and of its terms open until after the election. He did not think that the Unionist malcontents would accept it. I said that on the contrary I thought that the Party as a whole would readily accept it ... he feared that [Lloyd George's] pugnacity would lead him to ignore the fact that there is at this moment a real tide running which no leader could stem and which it would be useless for Austen to try and stem.'[106]

Over dinner on 15 October, Lloyd George and Austen Chamberlain met with Winston and Birkenhead, at Churchill's house in Sussex Square, to devise a plan to bring the Coalition rebels back into line. It was here that Chamberlain decided to organize a meeting of Conservative MPs at the Carlton Club for the morning of 19 October in order to secure their binding agreement that they would stand on a united platform with Lloyd George's Liberals. The date was chosen to coincide with the announcement of the result of a by-election at Newport in Monmouthshire, where it was expected that the Labour candidate would come through the middle to defeat both the Coalition Liberal and the independent Conservative, thus demonstrating the need for an electoral pact. Over the next four days, Lord Beaverbrook later observed, 'the struggle became less like a battle than a series of single duels. Every man's political soul was required of him. Promises and promotions and honours were sprinkled from Downing Street on the green benches with a hose.'[107]

However, on 16 October, Sam Hoare had a letter published in *The Times* with the private support of Stanley Baldwin, calling for the return of the party system, rather than the creation of a new Centre Party to oppose Labour. He claimed that it was 'useless' for the Conservative leadership to 'attempt to impose from above the continuance of an arrangement which nine out of ten of the party desire to see ended'. Hoare added, 'When Mr Chamberlain says that the Conservative Party cannot hope for a clear majority after the general election, he may be right or he may be wrong. No one has ever been able to foretell correctly the result of any general election, least of all a general election with an electorate that has been hugely increased. But Conservatives who, like myself, believe that the vital need is not so much to form a Government as to keep the party united are not convinced by this argument.'[108]

On the day before the Carlton Club meeting, nearly 60 Conservative MPs met at Hoare's house, and the mood was very anti-coalition. Later that evening Hoare reported back to a meeting with Bonar Law at his home in Onslow Gardens, where after intense lobbying from Beaverbrook, Bonar Law told Hoare that he had 'decided to go to the [Carlton Club] meeting and I intend to make a speech at it'.[109] Sam Hoare also wrote the motion that was put to the Carlton Club meeting in the name of the MP Ernest Pretyman,[110] 'that this meeting of Conservative Members of the House of Commons declares its opinion that the Conservative Party whilst willing to co-operate with the Coalition Liberals should fight the election as an independent party with its own leader and its own programme'.[111]

On the morning of 19 October as the MPs arrived at the Carlton Club, the result of the Newport by-election was known. Disastrously for Austen Chamberlain's calculations, it had been won by the independent Conservative, Reginald Clarry,[112] who easily defeated the Labour and

Coalition Liberal candidates in a constituency that had been won by a Coalition Liberal at the 1918 general election. The meeting was held in the Smoking Room and Library of the club just after 11 a.m. and was led by Chamberlain and Lord Birkenhead. One member had asked the club steward to place two large tumblers of brandy and soda in front of them, implying they might have been ordered by the statesmen to steady their nerves. Austen looked embarrassed, whereas Birkenhead drank his. Chamberlain gave the longest speech of the meeting, restating the case for the Coalition, which was politely received. Stanley Baldwin's remarks to his fellow MPs that morning are the best remembered of the meeting, warning them that Lloyd George was a 'dynamic force and it is from that very fact that our troubles, in our opinion arise. A dynamic force is a terrible thing; it may crush you but it is not necessarily right. It is owing to that dynamic force, and that remarkable personality, that the Liberal Party, to which he formerly belonged, has been smashed to pieces; and it is my firm conviction that, in time, the same thing will happen to our party.'[113]

The great moment, though, belonged to Bonar Law, who had arrived at the meeting flanked by Lord Derby and J. C. C. Davidson. Lord Crawford[114] thought 'He looked ill . . . His voice was so weak that people quite close to him had to strain their ears – but his matter was clear and distinctly put.'[115] Bonar Law put to the meeting that the real question was not whether or not they were to fight the next election in coalition with Lloyd George, but whether or not the Conservative Party should split, something that he warned them against, stating, 'I will tell you what I think will be the result. It will be a repetition of what happened after Peel[116] passed the Corn Bills. The body that is cast off will slowly become the Conservative Party, but it will take a generation before it gets back to the influence which the Party ought to have.'[117] By this he meant that if they voted to stay with Lloyd George, the 'Die-Hards' would break away and effectively become the Conservative Party. Also, Bonar Law told them that even if as Members of Parliament they decided to support the Coalition and form a new Centre Party, 'the great bulk of our supporters would say that they refuse to leave their organisation, and would continue as members of the Unionist Party. That is the position . . . I shall vote – and for the reason that it is the best chance of keeping our Party as an integral Party – in favour of our going into the election as a Party fighting to win.'[118]

When Bonar Law sat down, Crawford thought that 'the issue was unmistakable'.[119] William Bridgeman also remembered that 'His speech made a great deal of difference in the result. If he had not come I think we should have won [anyway]. If he had spoken for Coalition I am pretty sure we should not.'[120] The motion was carried by 185 votes to 88, leading to Austin Chamberlain's resignation as leader of the party.[121] Philip Sassoon telephoned the result through to Downing Street, speaking to J. T. Davies. On receiving the news, Lloyd George simply stated, 'That's the end.'[122] The Cabinet Secretary, Maurice Hankey, wrote in his diary:

> I heard the result at 1.15 pm and went straight to 10 Downing Street . . . I met the PM in the lavatory. 'Hankey,' he said, you have written your last minutes for me. I have asked the King to come to town and this afternoon I shall resign and you will have another Prime Minister.'[123]

The King wrote in his diary after Lloyd George's resignation, 'I am sorry he is going, but some day he will be Prime Minister again.'[124]

Leo Amery had voted against the Coalition and that evening recalled going 'round to the Athenaeum after dinner to have a talk with Lord Milner who is very pleased at the turn things have taken and thinks it a unique chance for the country to have something of leadership from younger men'.[125] Their conversation marked a complete reversal of the combination of political rivals who had helped to make Lloyd George Prime Minister nearly six years before. Of those Monday Night Cabal evenings Amery and Milner were now against the Welshman, as Carson had been for several years, while Sir Henry Wilson was dead. The great axis of Lloyd George and Bonar Law that held the Coalition together had also been broken. The Carlton Club meeting may have been the final blow, but it was the culmination of a process that had been in train since the failure to achieve the fusion of the Coalition parties in the spring of 1920. Lloyd George had also greatly weakened his position by neglecting the House of Commons and relying on Austen Chamberlain and Lord Birkenhead to keep the Conservative Party on board. Bonar Law's intervention may have been important to securing the vote to end the Coalition, but the rebellion had been orchestrated by men like Baldwin and Sam Hoare, who along with Neville Chamberlain and Edward Wood,[126] would be the leading figures in the Conservative Party from 1923 until Winston Churchill formed his wartime government in 1940. These were men who Lloyd George barely knew and for whom he certainly had no regard. Frances Stevenson recalled of Stanley Baldwin that 'L.G. said he did not recollect him ever opening his mouth at a Cabinet meeting.'[127]

Bonar Law called a general election for 15 November and Frances Stevenson wrote of the campaign, 'LG. knew he was fighting a hopeless battle, but he fought well, addressing huge meetings all over the country in the dreary November weather. Enormous crowds came to see and hear him, and then, as was the fate of Churchill in 1945, voted against him.'[128] Philip Sassoon hosted an election-night party for Lloyd George at 25 Park Lane, which the artist William Orpen recorded in an unpublished verse:

> Gee it was late – that raw black night
> And we were almost all quite tight
> 'Mid beauty' and the flowing wine
> With clouds of nicotine divine
> We sat
> And watched
> And waited
> Till lo! The small machine began
> To 'tic, tic'. Then the little band
> Ran smoothly out in Philip's hand
> Curling, curling like a snake
> Till Philip's hand began to shake
> Impossible!
> 'Twas like the writing on the wall
> That told of old King Nib's sad fall
> When in the dawn we learnt it all
> Old England's choice, we clearly saw
> Was Max!
> I beg pardon! Mister B Law
>
>   Sir William Orpen, November 1922[129]

The result was an overall majority for the Conservatives with 344 seats in the new House of Commons, and Labour established as the leading opposition party with 142. The Asquith Liberals had 62 MPs and Lloyd George commanded just 53. On 17 November the leading members of the old Lloyd George coalition gathered for dinner, again at Sassoon's house on Park Lane to 'consider the results'.[130] The key question was whether they should still try to form a new Centre Party or return to their traditional Liberal and Conservative groups. Austen Chamberlain told the dinner that although he 'would not now join the Government . . . [he] was going to remain a Unionist and would not join a Centre Party and did not intend to attack or criticize the Govt unless obliged to do so . . . L.G. said that was his idea also. He did not mean to act like an ordinary chief of Opposition and to seek grounds of criticism.'[131]

Nevertheless, thanks to Freddie Guest's efforts, Lloyd George had a political fund of over £3 million. Moreover, when Lord Riddell visited him at Churt in Surrey that November, he found that Lloyd George had far from given up on the idea of creating a new political grouping. 'The change in the atmosphere since he had been out of office is amazing,' Riddell wrote. 'Now he is working like a little dynamo to break up the Conservative Party by bringing the more advanced section to his flag, to join up with the "Wee Frees" [independent Liberals] and to detach the more moderate members of the Labour Party – this with the object of forming a Centre Party of which he will be the leader.'[132] Yet out of office such dreams were harder to fulfil than when he had been Prime Minister, and while no one would have predicted so at that time, Lloyd George would never hold a government position again.

Lloyd George still commanded immense public prestige at home and overseas. In October 1923 he made his only visit to the United States where he was given a 'stupendous'[133] reception on his arrival in New York and rode in a cavalcade of more than 30 open-top motorcars for a mile-long parade along Broadway to City Hall. Every window along the route, even from 50-storey skyscrapers, was filled with people cheering and throwing down ticker-tape. To the Americans, Lloyd George was not just the man who had won the war, but someone who embodied their national dream. Like his hero Abraham Lincoln, Lloyd George had risen from the simple origins of a remote cottage home, and without a university education, to lead his nation at its time of maximum peril. The editorial column in the *New York Times* exclaimed on 5 October, 'Was there ever a more romantic rise from the humblest beginning than this? Has any statesman of our time combined in himself so many diverse and fascinating qualities as those which have made Mr Lloyd George known to the whole world? His versatility, his eloquence, his uncanny ability to read the public mind almost before it has formed itself.'[134]

When he returned to Southampton on 9 November, onboard the White Star liner, RMS *Majestic*, he received a hero's welcome and was also awarded the Freedom of the City. Lloyd George marvelled at his experiences in America, including making his first speech on the radio, which was heard by five million people. He told the crowds in Southampton that he had:

> ... delivered a speech at Chicago, and I got a telegram the following morning from Texas saying 'Listened to your speech last night.' ... This adds a new terror to existence and it will probably revolutionise public speaking ...'[135] In the future, instead of going to a hall to address a meeting, you will just sit in your own library. You will deliver your speech and take a puff at your cigar at the time when you think applause should come. There are really very great developments in front of us.'[136]

Yet such innovations would more suit new politicians like Stanley Baldwin, who had succeeded Bonar Law as Prime Minister in May that year. While he could never rival Lloyd George as a platform speaker, Baldwin's reassuring tones could instead reach his audience at their fireside. Yet whilst Lloyd George was in America, Stanley Baldwin, fearing that the former Prime Minister was going to join forces again with Birkenhead and Austen Chamberlain, and come out for greater protection of industries in order to combat rising unemployment, pre-empted him at a speech in Plymouth on 25 October. Later, Baldwin confided to Thomas Jones, 'The Goat was in America. He was on the water when I made the speech and the Liberals did not know what to say. I had information that he was going protectionist and I had to get in quick ... Dished the Goat, as otherwise he would have got the Party with Austen and F.E. [Birkenhead] and there would have been an end to the Tory Party as we know it.'[137] In a snap general election, called by Baldwin for 6 December 1923 on the single issue of protection, the Conservatives made substantial losses, leading to the formation of the first minority Labour government under Ramsay

MacDonald. However, Lloyd George and the Liberals, who remained strongly for free trade, came third but with it the spirit of the postwar coalition government was finally laid to rest.

In Parliament, Lloyd George remained a star turn. The future Prime Minister, Harold Macmillan,[138] who was first elected to the House of Commons in 1924, remembered that:

> He was still by far the most romantic figure in the House. He was the best parliamentary debater of his, or perhaps any, day. Churchill's speeches were powerful but prepared in his own style, where every word was written out beforehand. Impressive as they might be, they lacked flexibility . . . Lloyd George who spoke with few notes commanded batteries as powerful as Churchill's but much more mobile. Not being tied to a text he could adapt and change with a remarkable rapidity and pick up a point from an interruption like lightning.'[139]

Lloyd George's last significant speech in the House of Commons came during the Second World War, in the famous Norway debate on 8 May 1940, which led to Neville Chamberlain's resignation as Prime Minister. There Lloyd George, summoning up the experience of his own wartime premiership, stated that:

> The nation is prepared for every sacrifice so long as it has leadership, as long as the Government show clearly what they are aiming at and so long as the nation is confident that those who are leading it are doing their best. I say solemnly that the Prime Minister should give an example of sacrifice, because there is nothing which can contribute more to victory in this war than that he should sacrifice the seals of office.[140]

Watching from the officials' box in the House of Commons, one of Chamberlain's private secretaries, Jock Colville,[141] thought Lloyd George 'made probably the most forceful speech he has made for years: I could see that he held the House spellbound as he flung his arms about and denounced the incapacity of the P.M. and Government.'[142]

On 13 May, three days after Winston Churchill succeeded Chamberlain as Prime Minister, he appealed to the House of Commons to support his new all-party government, and famously told the members, 'I have nothing to offer but blood, toil, tears and sweat.'[143] Later in that debate, Lloyd George spoke with words that brought forth those tears from Britain's new leader when he said:

> May I, as one of the oldest friends of the Prime Minister in this House – I think on the whole that we have the longest friendship in politics in spite of a great many differences of opinion – congratulate him personally upon his succession to the Premiership. But that is a small matter. I congratulate the country upon his elevation to the Premiership at this very, very critical and terrible moment. If I may venture to say so, I think the Sovereign exercised a wise choice.[144]

Lloyd George was afterwards invited to the Prime Minister's room behind the Speaker's Chair, where Churchill asked if he would take over the Ministry for Agriculture within the War Cabinet, which he nevertheless declined. He later wrote to Winston to explain that he was 'genuinely anxious to help to extricate my country from the most terrible disaster into which it has ever been plunged by the ineptitude of its rulers. Several architects of this catastrophe are still leading members of your Government and two of them are in the Cabinet that directs the war.'[145] This was a reference to Chamberlain and Lord Halifax the Foreign Secretary. However, in a letter to Frances Stevenson's daughter Jennifer[146] he also gave his reason for declining Churchill's offer as 'I do not believe in the way we entered the war – nor the methods by which it has been conducted . . . I do not believe in the way or in the persons with which the War Cabinet is constituted.'[147] In December 1940, Lloyd George was also sounded out by Churchill about the idea of becoming the British ambassador to Washington, again with a place in the War Cabinet. This time he declined on the grounds of health and old age. However, A. J. Sylvester had a different theory about Lloyd George's reason for refusing these invitations, that 'His amazing gifts of genius were denied the nation in her hour of dire need, not because he was too old to serve, but because he would not enter the Cabinet in a subordinate position . . . he acted like the spoiled child he was.'[148]

On 20 January 1941, his wife Margaret died at home in Criccieth and in October 1943 Lloyd George married Frances, despite the disapproval of his children. Margaret's home, Brynawelon, had been left to their daughter Megan, and Lloyd George purchased Tŷ Newydd, a fine house on the edge of Llanystumdwy. There from the large bay window in the library, Lloyd George could gaze out at the distant view to the sea and the Merionethshire Hills beyond. On 21 September 1944, along with Frances, he left Churt for the last time and spent the rest of his life at Tŷ Newydd. It was there on 26 March 1945 that David Lloyd George died from cancer, missing by a few weeks the final triumph of Britain and her Allies over Nazi Germany. As Winston Churchill stated of him in his eulogy in the House of Commons, 'He faced undismayed the storms of criticism and hostility. In spite of all obstacles, including those he raised himself, he achieved his main purposes. As a man of action, resource and creative energy he stood, when at his zenith, without a rival.'[149]

In the final months of his life, every day he would walk by the banks of the River Dwyfor to the bridge in Llanystumdwy he had crossed daily as a child on the way to school. In the woods close to the shoemaker's cottage that had once been his home, and where after a storm he went out to gather kindling for the fire, Lloyd George chose the place he wanted to be buried. Instead of the pomp and circumstance of Westminster Abbey, he would take his final rest back where his journey had started – on the high bank above the Dwyfor, forever accompanied by the sound of that rushing river, whose crystal waters were drawn from the valleys he'd climbed as a boy. Back then he'd sought inspiration from those hilltops and the sight of the great mountain peaks that lay beyond them. His energy had been like a force of nature, and driven by self-belief, he had changed and saved his country. Gifted with the power of oratory to paint pictures with words, he had shown his followers the way. Lloyd George's mercurial talents found solutions when no one else could see them, but he also created suspicion and mistrust amongst his rivals. When he believed right was on his side, he was totally committed to his cause; never afraid to challenge authority and face the storm. However, he also acted with expediency when he thought he could get away with it, even when it offended those who loved him most. Now that his life had run its course, and he had taken his place once more in that sheltered valley, it would be for others to seek out as he had done, that path 'which no fowl knoweth, and which the vulture's eye hath not seen'. Lloyd George could no longer provide the direction, but for those who sought inspiration from his life's work, he had shown that nothing was impossible.

Notes

Prologue

1 The Queen's Hall in Langham Place, near Oxford Circus, opened in 1893 and was destroyed by fire on 10 May 1941 during the London Blitz – the same evening that the House of Commons chamber also suffered a direct hit.
2 London *Evening Standard*, 21 September 1914
3 Hubert Du Parcq, *The Life of David Lloyd George*, vol. 1, Caxton (1912), p. 97
4 David Lloyd George, *War Memoirs*, vol. 1, Odhams Press (1938), p. 621
5 A. J. Sylvester, *The Real Lloyd George*, Cassell (1947), p. 5
6 Richard Lloyd (1834–1917), shoemaker and pastor of the Church of the Disciples of Christ. Lloyd George's father William George had married Richard Lloyd's sister Elizabeth, and when he died in 1864, she moved with her children to live with her brother in Llanystumdwy.
7 Martin Pugh, *Lloyd George*, Taylor and Francis (2014), p. 11
8 David Lloyd George, Budget Statement, *Hansard*, 29 April 1909
9 Sir Henry Wood (1869–1944), Conductor of the Promenade Concerts from their commencement at The Queen's Hall in 1895. After the Hall was destroyed in the Blitz in 1914, the Proms concerts transferred to the Royal Albert Hall.
10 Edward Morgan Forster (1879–1970), novelist and member of the Bloomsbury Group
11 E. M. Forster, *Howard's End*, Edward Arnold (1910), p. 46
12 Frances Lloyd George, *The Years That Are Past*, Hutchinson (1967), p. 75
13 George Riddell (1865–1934), newspaper proprietor and managing director of the *News of the World*. He was ennobled at the recommendation of Lloyd George in 1918 to become 1st Baron Riddell.
14 Lord Riddell, *Lord Riddell's War Diary 1914–1918*, Nicholson & Watson (1933), p. 32
15 Ibid
16 Archduke Franz Ferdinand (1863–1914), heir to the Emperor of the Austro-Hungarian Empire
17 Sir Edward Grey (1862–1933), from 1916 1st Viscount Grey of Fallodon, Foreign Secretary 1905–16
18 Niall Ferguson, *The Pity of War*, Penguin (1998), p. 177
19 Herbert Henry Asquith, 1st Earl of Oxford and Asquith (1852–1928), Prime Minister 1908–16, raised to the peerage in 1925

20 Andrew Bonar Law (1858–1923), Prime Minister 1922–3, leader of the Conservative Party 1911–21 and 1922–3
21 Sir Rufus Isaacs QC, 1st Marquess of Reading (1860–1935), Attorney General for England and Wales 1910–13, Lord Chief Justice of England 1913–21, Viceroy of India 1921–6. Born into a Jewish family of Spitalfields fruit sellers, in 1926, he became the first commoner to rise to the rank of Marquess since the Duke of Wellington.
22 Alexander Murray, 1st Baron Murray of Elibank (1870–1920), Government Chief Whip 1910–12
23 The Marconi Wireless Telegraph and Signals Company had been formed in Britain in 1897 by the Italian inventor Guglielmo Marconi.
24 Herbert Samuel MP (1870–1963), Postmaster-General, 1910–14 and 1915–16. Home Secretary 1916 and 1931–2, and Leader of the Liberal Party 1931–5. Created 1st Viscount Samuel in 1937.
25 *Hansard official record*, 18 June 1913, vol. 54, cc391–514
26 Rudyard Kipling (1865–1936), British poet, novelist and short story writer whose works included *The Jungle Book*, *Kim* and *Just So Stories*.
27 It's hard to ignore the antisemitic undertones of this poem. Reading was being compared to Gehazi, a corrupt servant found in the Bible (2 Kings 5:20–27, King James Bible).
28 Rudyard Kipling, *The Years Between*, Methuen and Co (1919), p. 109
29 Thomas Jones, *Lloyd George*, Oxford University Press (1951), p. 45
30 When Lloyd George spoke at the Oxford Union in November 1913 his car was pelted with vegetables as he arrived. At the start of the meeting, an announcement of new books purchased by the Society included a volume supposedly entitled 'A Welshman's Reputation', and one student asked him during questions whether he had any more shares to sell.
31 John McEwen, ed., *The Riddell Diaries 1908–1923*, Athlone Press (1986), p. 90
32 The Second Boer War 1899–1902 was fought between the British Empire and the Boer Republics of South Africa.
33 Marvin Rintala, *Made in Birmingham: Lloyd George, Chamberlain and the Boer War*, Biography, vol. 11, no. 2, Spring 1988, University of Hawaii Press, p. 125
34 Ibid
35 *The Times*, 20 June 1901
36 Rintala, *Made in Birmingham*, p. 125
37 C. P. Scott (1846–1932), owner and editor of the *Manchester Guardian*, and former Liberal MP
38 Riddell, *Lord Riddell's War Diary 1914–1918*, p. 5
39 Sir John Simon (1873–1954), Attorney General 1913–15, Home Secretary 1915–16
40 Viscount Simon, *Retrospect*, Hutchinson (1952), p. 95
41 Margaret Lloyd George née Owen (1864–1941). She was married to Lloyd George in 1888 until her death in 1941 and they had five children.
42 Kenneth O. Morgan, ed., *David Lloyd George: Family Letters 1885–1936*, Oxford University Press (1973), p. 167
43 Frances Stevenson (1888–1972) became Lloyd George's personal secretary and mistress in 1913. They married in 1943 after the death of his first wife Margaret.

44 Frances Lloyd George, *The Years That Are Past*, p. 75
45 Albert James (A.J.) Sylvester (1889–1989) served as private secretary to the Committee for Imperial Defence 1914–21, private secretary to Lloyd George as Prime Minister 1921–2, and then ran Lloyd George's private office out of government 1923–45.
46 Sylvester, *The Real Lloyd George*, p. 11
47 The house at Walton Heath, now called Pinfold Manor, had been built for Lloyd George in 1913 with funds provided by George Riddell.
48 Riddell, *Lord Riddell's War Diary 1914–1918*, p. 32
49 Job 28:7, King James Bible
50 Robert Windsor-Clive, 1st Earl of Plymouth (1857–1923). A former Conservative politician and Mayor of Cardiff, he was Lord Lieutenant of Glamorganshire from 1890 until his death.
51 Hon. Archer Windsor-Clive (1890–1914) was educated at Eton College and Trinity College, Cambridge, where he was a cricket Blue, also going on to play for Glamorgan. He was the first, first-class cricketer to be killed in the war.
52 *The Times*, 20 September 1914
53 Lord Plymouth was quoting the last lines of Kipling's poem 'For All We Have and Are', first published in *The Times* on 2 September 1914.
54 *The Times*, 20 September 1914
55 Sylvester, *The Real Lloyd George*, p. 293
56 Frank Dilnot (1875–1946), journalist and at the time editor of the Labour Party-supporting *Daily Citizen*
57 Frank Dilnot, *Lloyd George: The Man and His Story*, Harper and Brothers (1917)
58 David Lloyd George, *Honour and Dishonour, a speech by the Rt Hon D Lloyd George MP Chancellor of the Exchequer at the Queen's Hall London Sept 19 1914*, Methuen & Co (1914), p. 2
59 London *Evening Standard*, 21 September 1914
60 The 1839 Treaty of London had committed Great Britain and the other powers to respecting the neutrality of Belgium.
61 Theobald von Bethmann Hollweg (1856–1921), Chancellor of Germany 1909–17
62 This was a joke at his own expense, as after the declaration of war on 4 August, Lloyd George had introduced paper £1 notes issued by the Treasury rather than the Bank of England. Given the speed of production there had been criticism of the quality of paper and design of these new notes.
63 London *Evening Standard*, 21 September 1914
64 Lloyd George is referring to Belgium and Serbia.
65 London *Evening Standard*, 21 September 1914
66 Viscount Simon, *Retrospect*, Hutchinson (1952), p. 98
67 Lloyd George, *Honour and Dishonour*, pp. 9–10
68 Ibid, p. 10
69 Ibid, p. 11
70 Theodore Roosevelt (1858–1919), 26th President of the United States of America, 1901–9. Lloyd George and Roosevelt first met in London in May 1910 after the funeral of King Edward VII. Roosevelt's 'New Nationalism' speech was delivered in Kansas on 31 August 1910.

71 https://obamawhitehouse.archives.gov/blog/2011/12/06/archives-president-teddy-roosevelts-new-nationalism-speech
72 Beverley Nichols, *Are they the same at home? Being a series of bouquets diffidently distributed*, George H Doran, New York (1927) p.165
73 David McCormick, *The Mask of Merlin: A Critical Biography of David Lloyd George*, MacDonald (1963), p. 19
74 Thomas Jones (1870–1955), Deputy Secretary to the Cabinet 1916–35
75 Thomas Jones, *Lloyd George*, Oxford University Press (1951), p. 265
76 Isaiah 2:3 (King James Bible), 'Come ye, and let us go up to the mountain of the Lord, to the house of the God of Jacob; and he will teach us of his ways, and we will walk in his paths.'
77 Most likely a reference to Cwn Pennant, the valley made by the River Dwyfor near to Lloyd George's childhood home
78 Lloyd George, *Honour and Dishonour*, p. 11
79 John F. Kennedy (1917–63), 35th President of the United States of America. Lloyd George's Queen's Hall Speech was cited by JFK in an article for *Life* magazine during the 1960 Presidential election.
80 John F. Kennedy, 'We Must Climb to the Hilltop', *Life* magazine, 22 August 1960
81 Isaac Marcosson (1876–1961), Kentucky-born journalist who wrote for the leading American weekly magazine *The Saturday Evening Post*
82 Isaac Marcosson, *Adventures in Interviewing*, Dodd Mead & Co (1931), pp. 98–9
83 McEwen, ed., *The Riddell Diaries 1908–1923*, p. 90
84 Frances Lloyd George, *The Years That Are Past*, p. 75
85 Venetia Stanley (1887–1948) was the youngest daughter of Lord Stanley of Alderley and a friend of Asquith's daughter Violet. Between 1910 and her marriage to Edwin Montagu in 1915, Asquith wrote to Venetia up to three times a day.
86 Letter dated 20 September 1914. Michael and Eleanor Brock, ed., *H. H. Asquith letters to Venetia Stanley*, Oxford (1985), p. 250
87 Pericles (c.495–429 BC), Greek politician and general during the golden age of Athens
88 William Pitt the Younger (1759–1806), Prime Minister 1783–1801, 1801, 1804–6. His father, William Pitt the Elder, 1st Earl of Chatham, had been Prime Minister 1766–8.
89 Viscount Simon, *Retrospect*, Hutchinson (1952), pp. 97–9
90 *The Times*, 21 September 1914
91 Criccieth is a small coastal town less than two miles from Llanystumdwy. The family had moved here after Lloyd George started his legal practice.
92 Letter dated 21 September 1914, Lloyd George papers
93 A. J. Sylvester, *The Real Lloyd George*, Cassell (1947), p. 1
94 Gustave Le Bon (1841–1931) is best known for his 1895 work, *The Crowd: A Study of the Popular Mind*, which was highly influential in political circles in the early twentieth century. The leading Nazi, Albert Speer, wrote after the Second World War in his memoir, *Inside the Third Reich*, 'Le Bon's study has not been surpassed to this day. I believe he did not need to observe the great demagogues

from Lloyd George to Lenin, Mussolini, and Hitler in order to fathom the mechanics of the mass psyche.'

95   Gustave Le Bon, The Psychology of the Great War, T. Fisher Unwin (1916), p. 205
96   Arthur Bourchier (1863–1927), a celebrated actor known for his performances of Shakespeare as well as Gilbert and Sullivan. He was later a successful West End Theatre manager of venues including the Garrick, His Majesty's and The Strand (now the Novello). As a student Bourchier founded the Oxford University Dramatic Society.
97   London Evening Standard, 21 September 1914

1: THE BREWING STORM

1   David Lloyd George, War Memoirs, vol. 1, p. 133
2   Reginald Brett, 2nd Viscount Esher (1852–1930), former Liberal MP who influenced many pre-First World War army reforms, also a confidant and advisor to King Edward VII
3   Herbert Kitchener, 1st Earl Kitchener (1850–1916), Secretary of State for War 1914–16, Commander-in-Chief, India 1902–9, South Africa 1900–2, Egyptian Army 1882–9
4   James Lees-Milne, The Enigmatic Edwardian: The Life of Reginald 2nd Viscount Esher, Sidgwick & Jackson (1986), p. 256
5   Sir John French, later 1st Earl of Ypres (1852–1925), Field Marshal and Commander-in-Chief, British force in France 1914–15
6   Lees-Milne, The Enigmatic Edwardian, p. 257
7   Alexandre Millerand (1859–1943), Minister for War 1914–15, and later Prime Minister 1920, and then President 1920–4
8   David Lloyd George, War Memoirs, vol. 1, p. 472
9   A. J. P. Taylor, ed., My Darling Pussy: The Letters of Lloyd George and Frances Stevenson 1913–41, Weidenfeld & Nicolson (1975), p. 8
10   Sylvester, The Real Lloyd George, p. 3
11   Sir Charles Hobhouse, 4th Baronet (1862–1941), Postmaster General 1914–15, Chancellor of the Duchy of Lancaster 1911–14
12   Edward David, ed., Inside Asquith's Cabinet, from the Diaries of Charles Hobhouse, John Murray (1977), p. 230
13   John T. ('J.T.') Davies (1881–1938), Lloyd George's principal private secretary 1912–22
14   Edward, Prince of Wales (1894–1972), the future Edward VIII and later Duke of Windsor
15   Henry Ford (1863–1907) founded the Ford Motor Company in 1903. He was the chief developer of the assembly-line production process that made automobiles affordable to the mass market.
16   Western Mail, 26 February 1935
17   Mair Lloyd George (1890–1907) died after an operation following a late diagnosis of a burst appendix. She was buried at the family plot in Criccieth and her life is commemorated in a stained-glass window commissioned by the family for the Welsh Presbyterian Chapel in Beauchamp Road, Clapham.

18 Frances Lloyd George, *The Years That Are Past*, pp. 55–6
19 David Davies (1880–1944), Liberal MP for Montgomeryshire 1906–29. His grandfather, also David Davies (1818–90), was the greatest Welsh industrialist of the nineteenth century, who founded Barry Docks and also made a fortune from coal mining and railways in south Wales.
20 Frances Lloyd George, *The Years That Are Past*, pp. 58–9
21 Ibid, pp. 68–9
22 Lloyd George, *War Memoirs*, vol. 1, p. 64
23 Nathan Rothschild, 1st Baron Rothschild (1840–1915), was head of the London branch of the N. M. Rothschild bank. Rothschild had spoken out against the new taxes for social reform in Lloyd George's 1909 Budget.
24 Austen Chamberlain (1863–1937), son of the statesman Joseph Chamberlain and first elected to the House of Commons in 1892. Chancellor of the Exchequer 1903–5.
25 Michael Hicks Beach, then Viscount St Aldwyn (1837–1916), Chancellor of the Exchequer 1885–6 and 1895–1902. At that time there were only three living former chancellors; the Prime Minister Herbert Asquith, Austen Chamberlain and Michael Hicks Beach. Lloyd George consulted with them all.
26 John Maynard Keynes (1883–1946) was called in by Treasury officials in August 1914 and joined the department as a civil servant in 1915. After the war he published his first book, *The Economic Consequences of the Peace* (1919).
27 Niall Ferguson, *The World's Banker: The History of the House of Rothschild*, Weidenfeld & Nicolson (1998), p. 966
28 Lloyd George, *War Memoirs*, vol. 1, p. 65
29 Ibid
30 Richard Davenport-Hines, *Universal Man: The Seven Lives of John Maynard Keynes*, William Collins (2015), p. 76
31 Cameron Hazlehurst, *Politicians at War, July 1914 to May 1915, a Prologue to the Triumph of Lloyd George*, Jonathan Cape (1971), p. 172
32 Herbert Du Parcq, *Life of David Lloyd George*, vol. IV: *Speeches*, Caxton (c.1913), p. 679
33 Ibid, p. 724
34 Thomas Jones, *Lloyd George*, Oxford University Press (1951), p. 54
35 Reginald, Viscount Esher, *The Tragedy of Lord Kitchener*, John Murray (1921), p. 50
36 Ibid, pp. 51–2
37 Lloyd George, *War Memoirs*, vol. 1, p. 85
38 Ibid, p. 87
39 Sir William Robertson (1860–1933), Field Marshal, Chief of Staff, British Expeditionary Force 1914–15, Chief of the Imperial General Staff 1915–18
40 Field-Marshal Sir William Robertson, *Soldiers and Statesmen 1914–1918*, Cassell (1926), pp. 58–9
41 Lloyd George, *War Memoirs*, vol. 1, p. 77
42 Ibid, p. 79
43 Société des Automobiles Renault was at that time the largest motorcar manufacturer in France.
44 Lloyd George, *War Memoirs*, vol. 1, pp. 87–8

45 The posters were created by the graphic artist Alfred Leete of the Caxton Advertising Agency, owned by Hedley Le Bas, a friend of the news publisher George Riddell. The advert first appeared on the cover of the London Opinion magazine, 5 September 1914.
46 Margot Asquith (1864–1945), from 1925 Countess of Oxford and Asquith, author and wife of Prime Minister Herbert Asquith
47 Lucinda Gosling, Brushes and Bayonets: Cartoons, Sketches and Paintings of World War I, Osprey (2008), p. 28
48 Arthur Balfour (1848–1930), Prime Minister 1902–5, Leader of the Conservative Party 1902–11
49 William Ewart Gladstone (1809–98), Prime Minister 1868–74, 1880–5, 1886, 1892–4, Leader of the Liberal Party 1868–75 and 1880–94
50 Riddell, Lord Riddell's War Diary 1914–1918, p. 5
51 The Oxford Union Society, founded in 1823, was a debating society and private members club. Its former officers include Prime Ministers William Gladstone, Lord Salisbury, Harold Macmillan, Edward Heath and Boris Johnson, as well as other leading statesmen like Lord Birkenhead and Lord Curzon.
52 Winston Churchill (1874–1965), first elected to the House of Commons in 1901 as a Conservative, then joined the Liberals in 1904. He served in Asquith's first Cabinet as President of the Board of Trade 1908–11 and First Lord of the Admiralty 1911–15. He rejoined the Conservative Party in 1924.
53 Winston Churchill, Great Contemporaries, Odhams (1937), p. 106
54 Viscount Simon, Retrospect, Hutchinson (1952), p. 141
55 Letter from Churchill to Asquith dated 29 December 1914, in Andrew Roberts, Churchill, Walking with Destiny, Allen Lane (2018), p. 196
56 The Earl of Oxford and Asquith, Memories and Reflections 1852–1927, Cassell (1928), p. 54
57 Hansard, 28 March 1945
58 Clementine Churchill, née Hozier (1885–1977), later Baroness Spencer-Churchill 1965–77
59 Winston and Clementine Churchill married at St Margaret's Church, Westminster, on 12 September 1908. The other witnesses at the wedding were the groom's mother Jennie and the bride's brother, Bill Hozier.
60 John Spencer-Churchill, 7th Duke of Marlborough (1822–1883), Lord Lieutenant of Ireland 1876–80, Lord President of the Council 1867–8
61 Lord Randolph Churchill (1849–1895) Chancellor of the Exchequer 1886, Leader of the House of Commons 1886–7
62 Benjamin Disraeli, 1st Earl Beaconsfield (1804–1881), Prime Minister 1868, 1874–80, Leader of the Conservative Party 1868–81
63 Churchill, Great Contemporaries, p. 106
64 Marvin Rintala, Lloyd George and Churchill: How Friendship Changed Politics, Madison Books (1995), p. 70
65 Lloyd George, War Memoirs, vol. 1, pp. 100–1
66 Ibid, p. 101
67 Ibid, p. 107
68 Ibid, p. 135

69 Ibid, pp. 102–3
70 Ibid, p. 105
71 Ibid, p. 103
72 John Redmond (1856–1918), leader of the Irish Parliamentary Party 1900–18
73 31 December 1914, cited in Frank Owen, *Tempestuous Journey: Lloyd George his Life and Times*, McGraw-Hill (1955), p. 280
74 Riddell, *Lord Riddell's War Diary 1914–1918*, p. 65
75 General Sir Douglas Haig (1861–1928), from 1919 1st Earl Haig. From 10 December 1915, Haig became Commander-in-Chief of the British forces on the Western Front.
76 Battle of Neuve Chapelle, 10–13 March 1915. The village is in the Artois region of northern France, 17 miles west of Lille.
77 Lieutenant Malcolm Kennedy (1895–1984), 2nd Cameronian (Scottish Rifles)
78 Imperial War Museum P392: papers of Captain Malcolm Kennedy/University of Sheffield Library
79 Report by Sir John French to Lord Kitchener, cited in Owen, *Tempestuous Journey*, p. 283
80 *The Times*, 27 March 1915
81 House of Lords, Hansard report, 15 March 1915
82 Arthur Lee (1868–1947), MP for Fareham 1900–18. From July 1919, 1st Viscount Lee of Fareham. In 1912 Lee acquired the country estate of Chequers in Buckinghamshire, which in 1917 he gifted to the nation as a residence and retreat for the exclusive use of the serving prime ministers.
83 Alan Clark, ed., *'A Good Innings': The Private Papers of Viscount Lee of Fareham*, John Murray (1974), p. 140
84 The Earl of Oxford and Asquith, *Memories and Reflections 1852–1927*, vol. II, p. 66
85 Ibid
86 Ibid, p. 69
87 *Daily Chronicle*, 29 March 1915
88 Riddell, *Lord Riddell's War Diary 1914–1918*, p. 70
89 Sir Robert Donald (1860–1933), editor of the *Daily Chronicle* from 1904, and also from 1906 *Lloyd's Weekly Newspaper*. In 1917 he was appointed by Lloyd George to conduct a review of the government's wartime propaganda.
90 Asquith letter to Venetia Stanley 29 March 1915, cited in Hazlehurst, *Politicians at War, July 1914 to May 1915*, p. 228
91 Robert Rhodes James, ed., *Memoirs of a Conservative, J. C. C. Davidson's Memoirs and Papers 1910–37*, Weidenfeld & Nicolson (1969), p. 57
92 Riddell, *Lord Riddell's War Diary 1914–1918*, p. 70
93 Reginald McKenna (1863–1943), Home Secretary 1911–15, First Lord of the Admiralty 1908–11, MP for North Monmouthshire 1895–1918
94 Margot Asquith, diary entry for 15 May 1915, Margot Asquith papers
95 The Earl of Oxford and Asquith, *Memories and Reflections 1852–1927*, vol. II, p. 71
96 Ibid, pp. 70–1
97 Ibid
98 McEwen, ed., *The Riddell Diaries 1908–1923*, p. 103
99 The Earl of Oxford and Asquith, *Memories and Reflections 1852–1927*, vol. II, p. 71

100 Taylor, ed., *My Darling Pussy*, p. 7
101 The Earl of Oxford and Asquith, *Memories and Reflections 1852–1927*, vol. II, p. 72
102 Ibid, p. 73
103 Robert Crewe-Milnes, 1st Marquess of Crewe (1858–1945), Leader of the House of Lords 1908–16
104 Edward David, ed., *Inside Asquith's Cabinet, from the Diaries of Charles Hobhouse*, John Murray (1977), p. 236
105 The Earl of Oxford and Asquith, *Memories and Reflections 1852–1927*, vol. II, p. 73
106 Alfred Harmsworth, 1st Viscount Northcliffe (1865–1922), owner of titles including *The Times* and the *Daily Mail*. In 1914 he controlled 40% of the morning newspaper circulation and 45% of the evening circulation.
107 Sir Maxwell Aitken (1879–1964), from 1917, 1st Baron Beaverbrook. Like Bonar Law, his childhood had been spent in New Brunswick, Canada. He was Conservative MP for Ashton-Under-Lyne 1910–16.
108 A. J. P. Taylor, *English History 1914–1945*, Clarendon Press (1976), p. 27
109 Lord Beaverbrook, *Men and Power 1917–18*, Hutchinson (1956), p.xxii
110 Samuel Storey (1841–1925), Liberal MP for Sunderland 1881–95, co-founder of the *Sunderland Echo*
111 Andrew Roberts, *The Chief: The Life of Lord Northcliffe, Britain's Greatest Press Baron*, Simon & Schuster (2022), p. 228
112 McEwen, ed., *The Riddell Diaries 1908–1923*, p. 108
113 George Cassar, *Asquith as War Leader*, Bloomsbury (1994), p. 87
114 *The Times*, 22 April 1915
115 Riddell, *Lord Riddell's War Diary 1914–1918*, p. 81
116 Australia and New Zealand Army Corps: 25 April is commemorated as ANZAC day in memory of those who gave their lives in the Gallipoli campaign and conflicts since.
117 Field-Marshal Viscount French of Ypres, *1914*, Constable (1919), pp. 356–7
118 Ibid, p. 357
119 Lieutenant-Colonel Brinsley Fitzgerald (1859–1931) was an Anglo-Irish stockbroker who had fought with his Yeomanry regiment in the Second Boer War, where he'd first served with Sir John French.
120 Frederick Guest (1875–1937), Liberal MP since 1910 and cousin of Winston Churchill. He would later serve as Chief Whip in Lloyd George's government from 1917 to 1921.
121 Field-Marshal Viscount French of Ypres, *1914*, p. 357
122 Lieutenant Lucas King (1894–1915), King's Royal Rifle Corps. He was the son of Northcliffe's sister Geraldine.
123 John Pollock, *Kitchener*, Constable (1998), p. 442
124 Lloyd George, *War Memoirs*, vol. 1, pp. 119–20
125 Ibid, p. 121
126 Ibid, p. 122
127 John (Jacky) Fisher, 1st Baron Fisher (1841–1920), First Sea Lord 1904–10 and 1914–15. As First Sea Lord before the war he had modernized the fleet and commissioned the construction of the world-leading Dreadnought class of all big-gun battleships.

128 Lloyd George, *War Memoirs*, vol. 1, p. 134
129 Ibid, p. 133
130 George Curzon, Earl Curzon of Kedleston (1859–1925). From 1921, 1st Marquess Curzon of Kedleston. Viceroy of India 1899–1905.
131 R. J. Q. Adams, *Bonar Law*, Stanford University Press (1999), p. 177
132 One of 40 anonymously written comic verses published in 1880 as part of a collection known as *The Balliol Masque*
133 Austen Chamberlain papers, AC 2/2/25
134 Lord Beaverbrook, *Politicians and the War 1914–1916*, Oldbourne (1960), pp. 113–14
135 Lloyd George, *War Memoirs*, vol. 1, p. 136
136 Austen Chamberlain papers, AC 2/2/25
137 17 May 1915, Winston Churchill papers, 21/38
138 Margot often referred to her husband using his middle name of Henry.
139 Henry Petty-Fitzmaurice, 5th Marquess of Lansdowne (1845–1927), Leader of the House of Lords 1903–5, Foreign Secretary 1900–5
140 Margot Asquith letter to Lloyd George, 17 May 1915, Lloyd George papers
141 Reginald, Viscount Esher, *The Tragedy of Lord Kitchener*, John Murray (1921), pp. 121–2
142 Riddell, *Lord Riddell's War Diary 1914–1918*, p. 87
143 J. L. Hammond, *C. P. Scott*, Bell (1934), p. 187
144 Tom Clarke (1884–1957), news editor, *Daily Mail*, later editor of the *News Chronicle* 1930–3
145 Tom Clarke, *My Northcliffe Diary*, Gollancz (1931), p. 75
146 Ibid, p. 78
147 Ibid, p. 79
148 Taylor, ed., *Lloyd George: A Diary by Frances Stevenson*, pp. 53–4
149 McEwen, ed., *The Riddell Diaries 1908–1923*, p. 119
150 Sir Edward Carson (1854–1935), leader of the Irish Unionist Alliance 1910–21 and campaigner against Irish Home Rule.
151 The 1912 Ulster Covenant pledged opposition to Home Rule for Ireland from a parliament and government in Dublin. It received over 470,000 signatures of support.
152 Taylor, ed., *Lloyd George: A Diary by Frances Stevenson*, pp. 50–1
153 Lloyd George, *War Memoirs*, vol. 1, p. 139
154 Marvin Rintala, *Lloyd George and Churchill: How Friendship Changed Politics*, Madison Books (1995), p. 78
155 Taylor, ed., *Lloyd George: A Diary by Frances Stevenson*, pp. 50–1

2: Man of Push and Go

1 Sir Robert Walpole (1676–1745), the first Prime Minister of Great Britain 1721–42
2 The Carlton Club, Conservative private members club, then located at 94 Pall Mall. The clubhouse was destroyed during the Blitz in 1940 and then moved to its current location at 69 St James's Street.
3 *Aberdeen Daily Journal*, 27 May 1915

4   John Colin Campbell Davidson (1889–1970), civil servant and Conservative politician. Private secretary to Bonar Law 1915–20, then parliamentary private secretary 1920–1, following his election to the House of Commons.
5   Rhodes James, ed., *Memoirs of a Conservative*, p. 42
6   Joseph Chamberlain (1836–1914), Secretary of State for the Colonies 1895–1903
7   Austen Chamberlain, *Down the Years*, Cassell (1935), pp. 109–10
8   Letter to the editor of *The Times*, 31 July 1909
9   H. Montgomery Hyde, *Carson*, Constable (1974), p. 389
10 Riddell, *Lord Riddell's War Diary 1914–1918*, p. 103
11 Lloyd George, *War Memoirs*, vol. 1, p. 445
12 6 Whitehall Gardens was built in 1825 as part of a cul-de-sac off Whitehall, which was then demolished in 1938 to make way for a new government building that is currently home to the Ministry of Defence. A road sign for the entrance to Whitehall Gardens can still be seen on the corner of Gwydyr House on Whitehall. Whitehall Gardens occupied the site of the Privy Garden of the former Tudor Palace of Whitehall, which was largely destroyed by fire in 1698.
13 William Lockett Agnew (1858–1918) was head of the Thomas Agnew and Sons gallery, currently Agnews Gallery, in St James's Place, London. He was a notable dealer in the paintings of Diego Velázquez, including the *Rokeby Venus*, currently in the National Gallery. His clients also included the American banker, J. Pierpont Morgan.
14 Paul Stevenson (1895–1915), 2nd Lieutenant, 23rd Battalion, London Regiment. Before the war he had represented Oxford University at both rugby and cricket. He died on 25 May 1915.
15 Sir Hubert Llewellyn Smith (1864–1945), appointed General Secretary of the Ministry of Munitions in 1915, Permanent Secretary of the Board of Trade 1907–19
16 Lloyd George, *War Memoirs*, vol. 1, p. 150
17 William Beveridge (1879–1963), civil servant, economist and later a Liberal politician. The 1942 Beveridge Report would lead to the creation of the National Health Service after the Second World War.
18 *The Times*, 25 September 1945
19 Christopher Addison (1869–1951), medical doctor and Liberal MP for Hoxton since 1910. Before joining the Ministry of Munitions he had been Parliamentary Secretary at the Board of Education.
20 Lloyd George, *War Memoirs*, vol. 1, p. 151
21 Under the National Insurance Act 1911, workers who earned less than £160 per year paid 4 pence per week into the scheme, their employer paid 3 pence, and 2 pence was paid by the government. Hence Lloyd George told the workers that they were getting 'ninepence for fourpence'. During periods of sickness a worker would be paid from the scheme 10 shillings per week for the first 13 weeks and 5 shillings a week for the next 13 weeks if required. The National Insurance Act also provided free medical care for tuberculosis and the right for workers to receive treatment for sickness from a panel doctor.
22 Isaac Marcosson, *Adventures in Interviewing*, Dodd Mead & Company (1931), p. 98

23 Ibid
24 Lloyd George, *War Memoirs*, vol. 1, p. 147
25 Ibid
26 Eric Geddes (1875–1937), appointed in 1915 Deputy Director General for munitions supply
27 Lloyd George, *War Memoirs*, vol. 1, p. 151
28 Clark, ed., 'A Good Innings', p. 144
29 Lloyd George, *War Memoirs*, vol. 1, pp. 359–60
30 Richard Lloyd George (1889–1968), a graduate of Christ's College, Cambridge, was commissioned into the Royal Engineers, rising to the rank of major.
31 Richard Lloyd George, *Lloyd George*, Frederick Muller (1960), p. 150
32 Lloyd George, *War Memoirs*, vol. 1, p. 149
33 Walter Hines Page (1855–1918), United States Ambassador to the United Kingdom 1913–18
34 Burton Hendrick, *The Life and Letters of Walter H. Page*, Part II, Heinemann (1923), p. 259
35 Lieutenant Colonel Edward House (1858–1938), Texas businessman, political strategist and advocate of progressive politics. He'd been a close friend and advisor to Wilson since 1911.
36 Woodrow Wilson (1856–1924), 28th President of the United States 1913–21
37 Lloyd George, *War Memoirs*, vol. 1, p. 394
38 Ibid, p. 147
39 Ibid, p. 145
40 Brooks's Club at 60 St James's Street, gentlemen's dining club originally founded in 1764
41 Richard Haldane, 1st Viscount Haldane (1856–1928), Secretary of State for War 1905–12, Lord Chancellor 1912–15
42 J. Lee Thompson, *Theodore Roosevelt Abroad: Nature, Empire and the Journey of an American President*, Palgrave Macmillan (2010), p. 153
43 *A King's Funeral*, letter from Theodore Roosevelt to David Gray, 5 October 1911, Harvard Library, Cambridge, MA
44 David Lloyd George, *The Truth About the Peace Treaties*, Gollancz (1938), p. 227
45 William Jennings Bryan (1860–1925), US Secretary of State 1913–15. Democratic Party presidential candidate in the 1896, 1900 and 1908 elections. A renowned orator, his 1896 'Cross of Gold' speech at the 1896 Democratic National Convention transformed him from relative obscurity into a national figure, as well as securing him the party's presidential nomination.
46 Isaac Marcosson, *Adventures in Interviewing*, Dodd Mead & Company (1931), pp. 107–8
47 Christabel Pankhurst (1880–1958), co-founder of the Women's Social and Political Union
48 Elizabeth Crawford, *We Wanted to Wake Him Up: Lloyd George and Suffragette Militancy* (2013), history.blog.gov.uk
49 Emmeline Pankhurst (1858–1928), organizer of the UK suffragette movement and co-founder of the Women's Social and Political Union
50 *Daily Citizen*, 27 February 1913

51 Advert for the march published in the *Daily Mail*, 14 July 1915. Imperial War Museum collection ref Q107082.
52 *Derby Daily Telegraph*, 19 July 1915
53 Houldsworth Hall, 90 Deansgate, Manchester, had opened in 1911 and was the administrative centre for the Church of England Diocese of Manchester.
54 Lloyd George, *War Memoirs*, vol. 1, pp. 155–6
55 Abraham Lincoln (1809–1865), 16th President of the United States of America, 1861–5
56 Gwilym Lloyd George (1894–1967), a graduate of Jesus College, Cambridge, was commissioned into the Royal Welsh Fusiliers in 1914. In 1915 he was ADC to Major-General Ivor Philipps, commander of the 38th (Welsh) Division, and in 1916 joined the anti-aircraft branch of the Royal Garrison Artillery, where he rose to the rank of major.
57 Olwen Elizabeth Lloyd George (1892–1990). In 1917 she married Captain Thomas Carey Evans (1884–1947), a surgeon in the Indian Medical Service. She is the maternal grandmother of the historian Margaret MacMillan, and the maternal great-grandmother of the historian and broadcaster Dan Snow.
58 John Gulland (1864–1920), Government Chief Whip 1915–16, Liberal Chief Whip 1916–18
59 The Earl of Oxford and Asquith, *Memories and Reflections 1852–1927*, vol. 2, pp. 109–10
60 *Daily Mail*, 7 September 1915
61 Taylor, ed., *Lloyd George: A Diary by Frances Stevenson*, p. 58
62 Frederick Edwin Smith KC (1872–1930), from 1919 1st Earl of Birkenhead. He was appointed Solicitor General in June 1915.
63 Morgan, ed., *David Lloyd George: Family Letters 1885 to 1936*, p. 180
64 Geoffrey Dawson (1874–1944) changed his surname to Dawson from Robinson in 1917, but for ease of reference in this book I have referred to him as Dawson throughout. Assistant private secretary to Lord Milner as Colonial administrator in Southern Africa 1901–5, editor of the *Johannesburg Star* 1905–11, editor of *The Times* of London 1912–19.
65 John Evelyn Wrench, *Geoffrey Dawson and Our Times*, Hutchinson (1955), p. 122
66 John Sholto Douglas, 9th Marquess of Queensbury (1844–1900). He also gave his name to the rule book for modern boxing.
67 Oscar Wilde (1854–1900), Irish poet and playwright. The Marquess of Queensbury was the father of Wilde's lover Lord Alfred Douglas. Evidence prepared for the trial caused Wilde to drop his case and led to charges being brought against him for acts of 'gross indecency'. Homosexual activity between consenting adults remained a criminal offence in the UK until 1967.
68 George Archer-Shee (1895–1914), Lieutenant 1st Battalion, South Staffordshire Regiment
69 Edith Vane-Tempest-Stewart (1878–1959), Marchioness of Londonderry
70 Hyde, *Carson*, p. 275
71 Ibid
72 Sir Terence Rattigan (1911–1977), playwright and screenwriter. The 1948 screen film of *The Winslow Boy* was directed by Anthony Asquith, son of the former

      Prime Minister. The *Winslow Boy* play is also dedicated to the future Conservative Cabinet minister Paul Channon (1935–2007), son of Rattigan's friend the MP, Sir Henry 'Chips' Channon (1897–1958).
73 Francis Robinson (1895–1914), Lieutenant 3rd Battalion, South Staffordshire Regiment
74 Walter Long (1854–1924), President of the Local Government Board 1915–16, Leader of the Ulster Unionist Party 1906–10, and great rival of Sir Edward Carson
75 William Palmer, 2nd Earl of Selborne (1859–1942), President of the Board of Agriculture and Fisheries 1915–16, First Lord of the Admiralty 1900–5
76 Taylor, ed., *Lloyd George: A Diary by Frances Stevenson*, p. 60
77 Alfred Milner, 1st Viscount Milner (1854–1925), 1st Governor of the Transvaal Colony and Orange River Colony 1902–5, Administrator of the Transvaal Colony and Orange River Colony 1901–2, Governor of the Cape Colony and High Commissioner for Southern Africa 1897–1901
78 *Hansard*, 17 June 1901
79 Ibid, 24 March 1904
80 *Daily News*, 2 March 1905
81 The Battle of Loos was fought just north of Lens in Northern France, and was also the first time that the British used poison-gas shells against the Germans.
82 Robert Graves (1895–1985). His autobiographical war memoir, *Goodbye to All That*, was published in 1929.
83 Robert Graves, *Goodbye to All That*, Jonathan Cape (1929), p. 144
84 Wrench, *Geoffrey Dawson and Our Times*, p. 123
85 John Kipling (1897–1915), Second Lieutenant Irish Guards. His grave was not identified until 1992, and he is recorded as having been killed in action on 27 September 1915.
86 Rudyard Kipling, 'My Boy Jack', first published in *The Times*, 19 October 1916
87 Lloyd George, *War Memoirs*, vol. 1, p. 289
88 Riddell, *Lord Riddell's War Diary 1914–1918*, pp. 123–4
89 Keith Murdoch (1885–1952) at that time worked for the Australian United Cable Service, based in London, which supplied news to the *Melbourne Herald* and *Sydney Sun* newspapers. He is the father of Rupert Murdoch.
90 Andrew Fisher (1862–1928), Prime Minister of Australia 1908–9, 1910–13 and 1914–15, Australian High Commissioner to the United Kingdom 1916–21
91 Australian *Daily Telegraph*, 15 September 2015
92 Sir Maurice Hankey (1877–1963), Secretary to the War Council
93 The alternative name then used for the War Council of the Cabinet
94 Lloyd George letter to Carson and Bonar Law, dated 25 September 1915, Lloyd George papers
95 Sir Ian Hamilton (1853–1947), Commander-in-Chief of the Mediterranean Expeditionary Force, had previously served as Chief of Staff to Lord Kitchener during the Second Boer War.
96 *Hansard*, 25 September 1915
97 Lloyd George, *War Memoirs*, vol. 1, p. 311
98 Hyde, *Carson*, p. 393

99   Lloyd George, *War Memoirs*, vol. 1, p. 306
100 Reginald, Viscount Esher, *The Tragedy of Lord Kitchener*, p. 168
101 Letter dated 18 September 1915, Asquith papers
102 Riddell, *Lord Riddell's War Diary 1914–1918*, p. 129
103 Lloyd George, *War Memoirs*, vol. 1, p. 309
104 Lloyd George papers
105 The Committee members were Asquith, Lloyd George, McKenna, Bonar Law, Balfour and Kitchener.
106 *Hansard*, 20 December 1915
107 Lloyd George, *War Memoirs*, vol. 1, p. 433
108 Edward Stanley, 17th Earl of Derby (1865–1948), Conservative politician and former soldier
109 Figures from David Lloyd George, *War Memoirs*, vol. 1, Odhams Press (1938), p. 436
110 Morgan, ed., *David Lloyd George: Family Letters 1885 to 1936*, p. 180
111 Ibid, p. 181. Walter Runciman (1870–1949), President of the Board of Trade 1914–16, Liberal MP for Oldham from 1899 to 1900, and MP for Dewsbury from 1902 to 1918.
112 Letter from Asquith to Pamela McKenna, 1 January 1916, McKenna papers
113 Lloyd George, *War Memoirs*, vol. 1, pp. 445–6
114 Clark, ed., *'A Good Innings'*, p. 144
115 Ibid
116 The Hotel Metropole was created by the hotelier Frederick Gordon and opened in 1885. The building is currently the Corinthia Hotel.
117 *Illustrated London News*, 26 January 1916
118 Viscount Grey of Fallodon, *Twenty-Five Years 1892–1916*, vol. 2, Hodder & Stoughton (1925), pp. 242–3
119 Clark, ed., *'A Good Innings'*, p. 142

3: THE CABAL

1   Known as 'Plug Street' by the British forces, Ploegsteert was located close to the France/Belgium border between Ypres to the north and Armentières to the south.
2   Martin Gilbert, *Winston S. Churchill, Companion vol. 3: Part 2 Documents, 1915–1916*, Heinemann (1972), letter dated 25 January 1916, p. 1,395
3   Leo Amery (1873–1955), Liberal Unionist, and then Conservative MP from 1911. War Correspondent for *The Times* during the Boer War, he had also turned down the opportunity to become editor of *The Times* in 1912. Amery had also been a year above Churchill at Harrow School.
4   Memo written by Lord Milner on 12 March 1916. See P. A. Lockwood, 'Milner's Entry into the War Cabinet, December 1916', *The Historical Journal*, vol. 7, no. 1 (1964), pp. 124–5.
5   Leo Amery, *My Political Life: War and Peace, 1914–1929*, Hutchinson (1953), pp. 81–2
6   John Barnes and David Nicholson, eds, *The Leo Amery Diaries*, vol. 1: 1896–1929, Hutchinson (1980), letter from Amery to his wife Florence, dated 21 July 1915, pp. 123–4

7   Frederick Scott Oliver (1864–1934), Scottish political writer and Unionist. His 1906 biography, *Alexander Hamilton: An Essay on American Union*, had been much admired by Lord Milner and his followers.
8   Milner's Kindergarten were mostly Oxford-educated young men, handpicked from the civil service to support Milner's colonial administration of Southern Africa. They all favoured the unification of South Africa and greater co-ordination between Great Britain and the Empire Dominions.
9   Geoffrey Dawson letter to Philip Sassoon dated 20 October 1916, Sir Philip Sassoon papers, Houghton Hall archives
10 Niall Ferguson, *The Square and the Tower, Networks, Hierarchies and the Struggle for Global Power*, Penguin (2017) pp.184–5
11 Sir Henry Wilson (1864–1922), Commander IV army corps on the Western Front, previously sub-chief of staff to the British Expeditionary Force
12 Waldorf Astor (1879–1952), owner of *The Observer*. MP for Plymouth from 1910 until succeeding his father as 2nd Viscount Astor in 1919. In 1906 he had married Nancy Langhorne.
13 Barnes and Nicholson, eds, *The Leo Amery Diaries*, vol. 1: 1896–1929, letter from Milner to Amery dated 9 January 1916, p. 127
14 Leo Amery, *My Political Life: War and peace, 1914–1929*, Hutchinson (1953), p. 81
15 Gilbert, *Winston S. Churchill*, Companion vol. 3: Part 2 Documents, 1915–1916, letter dated 1 February 1916, p. 1,409
16 Amery papers, 'Notes for Monday's Meeting', 19 February 1916
17 William Hughes (1862–1952), Prime Minister of Australia 1915–23 and leader of the Australian Labor Party
18 Howell Arthur Gwynne (1865–1950), editor of the London *Morning Post* 1911–37
19 Llandudno is about 50 miles from Lloyd George's childhood village of Llanystumdwy.
20 Riddell, *Lord Riddell's War Diary 1914–1918*, p. 162
21 Ibid, pp. 161–2
22 Ibid
23 McEwen, ed., *The Riddell Diaries 1908–1923*, p. 148
24 W. M. Hughes, *'The Day' and After* (1916). The book was edited by Keith Murdoch and contained a foreword from Lloyd George.
25 Christopher Addison, *Politics from Within 1911–1918*, vol. I, Herbert Jenkins (1924), p. 246
26 Riddell, *Lord Riddell's War Diary 1914–1918*, pp. 161–2
27 Addison, *Politics from Within 1911–1918*, vol. I, pp. 246–7
28 Ibid, p. 247
29 Frederick Kellaway (1870–1933), Liberal MP for Bedford, December 1910–22
30 William Glyn-Jones (1869–1927), Liberal MP for Stepney, January 1910–18
31 Addison, *Politics from Within 1911–1918*, vol. I, p. 260
32 Ibid, p. 252
33 Ibid, p. 248
34 Clark, ed., *'A Good Innings'*, p. 158
35 Lieutenant-Colonel Arthur John Bigge, 1st Baron Stamfordham (1849–1931), Private Secretary to the sovereign, 1895–1901 and 1910–31

36 Riddell, *Lord Riddell's War Diary 1914–1918*, p. 175
37 Gilbert, *Winston S. Churchill, Companion vol. 3: Part 2 Documents, 1915–1916*, Heinemann (1972), letter dated 16 April 1916, p. 1.491
38 Taylor, ed., *Lloyd George: A Diary by Frances Stevenson*, pp. 105–6
39 Clark, ed., *'A Good Innings'*, p. 149
40 Alfred George Gardiner (1865–1946), editor of the *Daily News* 1902–19. Gardiner resigned due to disagreement with the proprietor George Cadbury over his opposition to Lloyd George.
41 John Julius Norwich, ed., *The Duff Cooper Diaries 1915–1951*, Weidenfeld & Nicolson (2005), entry for 28 April 1916, p. 28
42 Sir Henry Dalziel (1868–1935), Liberal MP and journalist, owner of *Reynolds's News*
43 Reverend Dr Sir William Robertson Nicoll (1851–1923), former Minister of the Free Church of Scotland, and founder of the non-conformist newspaper, the *British Weekly*
44 *Daily News*, 22 April 1916
45 Patrick Pearse (1879–1916), teacher, barrister and writer. He had been the person most responsible for drafting the 'Proclamation of the Irish Republic'. He was proclaimed President of the Republic after reading the declaration, and it was he who would issue the order to surrender after six days of fighting.
46 Morgan, ed., *David Lloyd George: Family Letters 1885 to 1936*, p. 182
47 An 8,000-strong British army garrison besieged by the forces of the Ottoman Empire at Kut Al Amara, about 100 miles south-east of Baghdad, surrendered on 29 April 1916.
48 Tom Clarke, *My Northcliffe Diary*, Gollancz (1931), p. 99
49 A. M. Gollin, *Proconsul in Politics: A Study of Lord Milner in Opposition and in Power*, Anthony Blond (1964), p. 345
50 Addison, *Politics from Within 1911–1918*, vol. I, p. 252
51 Letter dated 2 May 1916, Lloyd George papers
52 *The Times*, 5 May 1916
53 Riddell, *Lord Riddell's War Diary 1914–1918*, p. 183
54 McEwen, ed., *The Riddell Diaries 1908–1923*, p. 156
55 Jean, Lady Hamilton (1861–1941). She was the daughter of the millionaire Scottish businessman, Sir John Muir, partner of Finlay Muir & Co. Jean was a close friend of Winston and Clementine Churchill, and the first person to buy one of his paintings.
56 John Alfred Spender (1862–1942), editor of the *Westminster Gazette* 1896–1922
57 Celia Lee, *Jean, Lady Hamilton 1861–194: A Soldier's Wife*, Celia Lee (2001), diary entry for 24 May 1916, p. 165
58 Lloyd George, *War Memoirs*, vol. 1, p. 420
59 Ibid, p. 418
60 Of the nine counties of Ulster, it was proposed that Donegal, Cavan and Monaghan, where no Unionist MPs had been returned to the UK Parliament since 1885, should be included as part of southern Ireland for the purpose of the Home Rule settlement. The border dispute concerned the exclusion from Home Rule of the counties of Fermanagh and Tyrone, and the boroughs of Newry and Derry/Londonderry where there were also nationalist majorities.

61 Notes from meeting of the Unionist Party, 7 July 1916, Bonar Law papers
62 Stephen Gwynn, ed., *The Anvil of War: Letters between F. S. Oliver and his Brother 1914–1918*, Macmillan (1936), p. 151
63 Lloyd George, *War Memoirs*, vol. 1, p. 422
64 Beaverbrook, *Politicians and the War 1914–1916*, vol. 2, p. 272
65 Gwynn, ed., *The Anvil of War*, pp. 151–3
66 Barnes and Nicolson, eds, *The Leo Amery Diaries*, vol. 1, letter from Wilson to Amery, dated 19 August 1915, p. 124
67 Major-General Sir Charles Callwell, ed., *Field-Marshall Sir Henry Wilson: His Life and Diaries*, vol. I, Cassell (1927), p. 285
68 Maurice Bonham-Carter (1880–1960), principal private secretary to the Prime Minister 1910–16. In 1915 he had married Herbert Asquith's daughter Violet.
69 Lloyd George, *War Memoirs*, vol. 1, p. 456
70 Robert Blake, *The Unknown Prime Minister: The Life and Times of Andrew Bonar Law 1858–1923*, Eyre & Spottiswoode (1955), p. 289
71 Edwin Montagu (1879–1924), Chancellor of the Duchy of Lancaster in 1915, and again in 1916. Liberal MP for Chesterton 1906–18.
72 Runciman papers
73 Owen, *Tempestuous Journey*, p. 319
74 Hugh Powell Williams (1883–1916), Captain 14th Battalion Royal Welsh Fusiliers. He was killed in action close to Hellfire Corner, near Ypres. He died on 5 June, the same day as Kitchener, but was initially reported as missing in action.
75 Griffith Powell Williams (1845–1917) ran the Eifion Stores on the High Street in Criccieth. He was also an elder of the Berea chapel in the town.
76 Lloyd George, *War Memoirs*, vol. 1, pp. 458–9
77 Roy Jenkins, *Asquith*, Collins (1986), p. 410

4: The Powers That Be

1 The building, now known as the Old War Office, was designed by William Young (1843–1900) and opened in 1906. It is now home to the Raffles OWO hotel and residences.
2 Clark, ed., '*A Good Innings*', p. 153
3 Siegfried Sassoon MC (1886–1967), Second Lieutenant 3rd Battalion, Royal Welch Fusiliers
4 *Sassoon Journals*, 1 July 1916, University of Cambridge Library
5 Lloyd George, *War Memoirs*, vol. 1, p. 321
6 *The Battle of the Somme* was a 74-minute silent film made by the cinematographers Geoffrey Malins and John McDowell between 26 June and 9 July 1916. It was distributed by the British Topical Committee for War Films.
7 Taylor, ed., *Lloyd George: A Diary by Frances Stevenson*, p. 112
8 Stephen Badsey, *The Battle of the Somme: British War Propaganda*, Historical Journal of Film, Radio and Television (1983), p. 99
9 Christopher Williams (1873–1934). His 1916 painting, *The Charge of the Welsh Division at Mametz Wood*, was purchased in 1920 by the investment banker Sir

Archibald Mitchelson (1878–1945), another friend of Lloyd George, as a gift for the National Museum of Wales.
10 David Jones (1895–1974), painter and modernist poet. He fought with the Royal Welch Fusiliers at Mametz Wood and in 1917 at Pilckem Ridge during the Battle of Passchendaele. His long poem In Parenthesis, published in 1937, was inspired by his experiences during the war.
11 John Mathias, ed., Selected Works of David Jones, University of Maine (1992), p. 90
12 Hywel Williams (1894–1916), Captain 17th Battalion Royal Welch Fusiliers. He was killed in action sometime between 10 and 12 July during the attack on Mametz Wood. Hywel has no known grave and is commemorated on the Thiepval Memorial.
13 W. R. P. George, 88 Not Out, Gwasg Dwyfor (2001)
14 William George, My Brother and I, Eyre & Spottiswoode (1958), p. 255
15 David Robert Daniel (1859–1931), political commentator and organizer, from Merionethshire in north Wales
16 Ffion Hague, The Pain and the Privilege: The Women in Lloyd George's Life, Harper Press (2008), p. 180
17 Taylor, ed., Lloyd George: A Diary by Frances Stevenson, p. 259
18 Gilbert, Winston S. Churchill, Companion vol. 3: Part 2 Documents, 1915–1916, Heinemann (1972), letter dated 16 April 1916, pp. 1,537–8
19 Harold Harmsworth, 1st Viscount Rothermere (1868–1940)
20 Taylor, ed., Lloyd George: A Diary by Frances Stevenson, p. 112
21 Gary Sheffield and John Bourne, eds, Douglas Haig: War Diaries and Letters 1914–1918, Weidenfeld and Nicolson (2005), p. 213
22 Lloyd George, War Memoirs, vol. 1, p. 468
23 Ibid, p. 466
24 Ibid, pp. 466–7
25 Aristide Briand (1862–1932), Prime Minister of France 1909–11, 1913, 1915–17. He was a member of the Republican-Socialist Party in the National Assembly, which campaigned for progressive reform. He was born in Nantes in the west of France.
26 Lloyd George, War Memoirs, vol. 1, p. 467
27 Sandringham, the private estate in Norfolk of the Royal Family, created by King Edward VII when Prince of Wales
28 Sir Philip Sassoon Bt (1888–1939), Conservative MP for Hythe since 1912. He had volunteered at the start of the war as a Second Lieutenant in the reservist East Kent Yeomanry Regiment and became a staff officer at GHQ in 1915. He had inherited great wealth as the heir of the Sassoon trading and banking family, and his mother was the daughter of Baron Gustave de Rothschild, head of the house of Rothschild in Paris. Philip was also the second cousin of the war poet, Siegfried Sassoon.
29 Sir Philip Sassoon papers, Box 12, Houghton Hall Archives
30 Roberts, The Chief, p. 280
31 Oliver, Viscount Esher, ed., Journals and Letters of Reginald Viscount Esher, vol. 4: 1916–1930, Nicholson & Watson (1938), journal entry for 6 May 1916, p. 22
32 Ibid, letter addressed to H.M. Queen Mary dated 14 August 1916, pp. 49–50

33 Lord Birkenhead, *Rudyard Kipling*, Weidenfeld and Nicolson (1978), p. 264
34 Sheffield and Bourne, eds, *Douglas Haig*, p. 220
35 Lloyd George, *War Memoirs*, vol. 1, p. 468
36 Ibid, pp. 2,014–15
37 Richard Lloyd George, *Lloyd George*, p. 148
38 Gary Mead, *The Good Soldier: The Biography of Douglas Haig*, Atlantic (2007), p. 242
39 Megan Arvon Lloyd George (1902–1966)
40 John Grigg, *Lloyd George from Peace to War 1912–16*, Methuen (1985), pp. 416–17
41 *The Times*, 18 August 1916
42 Ibid, 19 August 1916
43 Ibid
44 Ibid
45 Evan Roberts (1878–1951), leader of the 1904–5 Welsh revivalist Christian movement. Born in Loughor in south Wales, his ministry began while preaching and studying at Newcastle Emlyn, and his congregations soon numbered in the thousands.
46 *Liverpool Daily Post*, 12 June 1905
47 Wilfred Owen (1893–1918), 2nd Lieutenant Manchester Regiment and war poet. He was killed in action crossing the Sambre-Oise canal in Northern France on 4 November 1918, just a week before the war's end.
48 Guy Cuthbertson, *Wilfred Owen*, Yale University Press (2014), pp. 201–2
49 Rupert Hart-Davis, ed., *Siegfried Sassoon: The War Poems*, Faber and Faber (1983), p. 134
50 The Honourable Society of Cymmrodorion was founded in London in 1751 to promote the language, literatures, arts and science of Wales. The dinner was held at the Trocadero restaurant in London on 19 May 1916, and the Australian Prime Minister Billy Hughes was also a guest speaker.
51 Graves, *Goodbye to All That*, p. 253
52 Ferdinand Foch (1851–1929), French military commander and strategist
53 Callwell, ed., *Field-Marshal Sir Henry Wilson*, vol. I, p. 292
54 Sheffield and Bourne, eds, *Douglas Haig*, diary entry for 17 September 1916, p. 213
55 Winston Churchill had sponsored the development of the 'landships' that became known as 'tanks' while First Lord of the Admiralty. The term 'tank' was a code name that then stuck. In order to keep the project secret, the prototype machines were referred to as water tanks for export to Russia.
56 Rudolph Lambart, 10th Earl of Cavan (1865–1946), commanding officer of the XIV infantry corps
57 Joseph Joffre (1852–1931), Commander-in-Chief of the French forces on the Western Front 1914–16
58 Raymond Asquith (1878–1916), Lieutenant 3rd Battalion, Grenadier Guards
59 The Earl of Oxford and Asquith, *Memories and Reflections 1852–1927*, vol. II, pp. 158–9
60 Roberts, *The Chief*, p. 286
61 Lord Northcliffe letter to Philip Sassoon, 6 October 1916, Northcliffe papers, British Library
62 Roberts, *The Chief*, p. 287
63 Winston S. Churchill, *The World Crisis*, vol. 3: 1916–1918, part 1, Thornton Butterworth (1927), p. 244

64 Lord Northcliffe letter to Philip Sassoon dated 18 October 1916, Northcliffe papers, British Library
65 Sir Louis du Pan Mallet notes from a conversation with Philip Sassoon, 11 March 1917, Sir Louis du Pan Mallet papers, Balliol College, Oxford University
66 Oliver, Viscount Esher, ed., *Journals and Letters of Reginald Viscount Esher*, vol. 4: 1916–1930, letter to Lord Murray of Elibank, 28 November 1916, p. 68
67 Battle of Jutland, 31 May–1 June 1916. The British and German fleets engaged off the North Sea coast of Denmark. The Royal Navy lost more ships but forced the German fleet back to port.
68 Roy Howard (1883–1964), President of the United Press news agency
69 *The Weekly Dispatch*, 15 October 1915
70 *The Weekly Freeman*, 30 September 1916
71 Harry Levy-Lawson, 2nd Baron Burnham (1862–1933), former Liberal MP, inherited the family control of the *Daily Telegraph* following the death of his father in January 1916.
72 Lord Burnham papers, Imperial War Museum, London, 1 November 1916
73 St James's Court at 54 Buckingham Gate, Westminster, was also a short walking distance from these other properties, as well as Downing Street. The flat may have been a haven for Lloyd George in case he was required to resign from the government. If he did, he would now have somewhere to live after giving up 11 Downing Street.
74 Trevor Wilson, ed., *The Political Diaries of C. P. Scott 1911–1928*, Collins (1970), diary entry for 20–22 November 1916, p. 236
75 Donald Hankey (1884–1916), 2nd Lieutenant Royal Warwickshire Regiment, was killed in action during the Battle of the Somme on 12 October 1916 near Le Transloy. He has no known grave and is commemorated on the memorial at Thiepval.
76 Stephen Roskill, *Hankey: Man of Secrets*, vol. I, Collins (1970), p. 312
77 Leslie Scott KC (1869–1950), barrister and Conservative MP for Liverpool Exchange 1910–29. In 1910, Scott had also assisted Edward Carson in the successful defence of the 15-year-old former Royal Navy cadet, George Archer-Shee. In Parliament, Scott was a member of Carson's backbench Unionist War Committee. F. E. Smith's pupilage as a barrister had also been at Scott's chambers in Cook Street, Liverpool.
78 *Hansard*, 8 November 1916, debate on 'Sale of Enemy Property'
79 Bonar Law, private interview with Robert Donald, 29 December 1916, published in H. A. Taylor, *Robert Donald*, Stanley Paul and Co (1931), p. 128
80 Sir Alfred Mond (1868–1930), Liberal MP since 1906
81 Sir Hamar Greenwood Bt (1870–1948). Born in Canada, Greenwood had been a Liberal MP since 1906.
82 Royal Archives, Windsor Castle, RA/PS/PSO/GV/C/K/1048A
83 Beaverbrook, *Politicians and the War 1914–1916*, vol. 2, p. 301
84 Robert Self, ed., *The Austen Chamberlain Diary Letters, the Correspondence of Sir Austen Chamberlain with his Sisters Hilda and Ida, 1916–1937*, Cambridge University Press (1995), pp. 36–7
85 Taylor, ed., *Lloyd George: A Diary by Frances Stevenson*, p. 122
86 Beaverbrook, *Politicians and the War 1914–1916*, vol. 2, p. 131
87 Chamberlain, *Down the Years*, p. 113

88 Lloyd George, *War Memoirs*, vol. 1, p. 572
89 Ibid, p. 574
90 Ibid
91 Napoleon Bonaparte (1769–1821), First Consul of France 1799–1804, Emperor of France 1804–14 and 1815. The Vendôme Column had been built to commemorate the victory of Napoleon over the Austrian Empire at the Battle of Austerlitz in 1805.
92 Lloyd George, *War Memoirs*, vol. 1, pp. 574–5

5: Submit or Resign

1   This is the present-day Mandarin Oriental Hyde Park Hotel in Knightsbridge.
2   Hyde, *Carson*, p. 407n
3   Beaverbrook, *Politicians and the War 1914–1916*, vol. 2, p. 140
4   Bonar Law, private interview with Robert Donald, 29 December 1916, published in H. A. Taylor, *Robert Donald*, Stanley Paul & Co (1931), pp. 129–30
5   Beaverbrook, *Politicians and the War 1914–1916*, vol. 2, p. 155
6   First World War nickname for the Germans
7   Callwell, ed., *Field-Marshal Sir Henry Wilson*, vol. I, p. 299
8   Wrench, *Geoffrey Dawson and Our Times*, p. 139
9   Ibid
10 Ibid, p. 140
11 Chamberlain, *Down the Years*, p. 117
12 Beaverbrook, *Politicians and the War 1914–1916*, vol. 2, p. 161
13 Ibid, p. 164
14 Ibid, p. 169
15 Chamberlain, *Down the Years*, p. 117
16 Riddell, *Lord Riddell's War Diary 1914–1918*, pp. 225–6
17 Lord Burnham papers, Imperial War Museum, London, record dictated by Burnham on 1 December 1916
18 Clark, ed., *'A Good Innings'*, p. 160
19 *The Times*, 2 December 1916
20 Lloyd George, *War Memoirs*, vol. 1, p. 588
21 The Berkeley Hotel was then on the corner of Berkeley Street and Piccadilly opposite The Ritz. The hotel moved to its current location in Wilton Place, Knightsbridge, in 1972.
22 Walter Cunliffe, 1st Baron Cunliffe (1855–1920), Governor of the Bank of England 1913–18
23 Lloyd George, *War Memoirs*, vol. 1, p. 589
24 Ibid, pp. 588–9
25 J. M. McEwen, 'Northcliffe and Lloyd George at War, 1914–1918', *The Historical Journal*, 24, 3 (1981), p. 663
26 Walmer Castle in Kent is the grace and favour home of the Lord Warden of the Cinque Ports, then William Lygon, 7th Earl Beauchamp. He had offered the use of the castle to Asquith as a weekend retreat for the duration of the war.
27 Notes from Robert Donald interview with Edwin Montagu in H. A. Taylor, *Robert Donald*, Stanley Paul & Co (1931), p. 137

28 Denis Judd, *Lord Reading*, Weidenfeld & Nicolson (1982), p. 132
29 S. D. Waley, *Edwin Montagu, a Memoir and an Account of His Visits to India*, Asia Publishing House (1964), p. 104
30 Grigg, *Lloyd George from Peace to War 1912–16*, p. 453
31 Lord Newton, *Lord Lansdowne*, Macmillan (1929), pp. 452–3
32 Hammond, *C. P. Scott*, Bell (1934), p. 203
33 H. A. Taylor, *Robert Donald*, Stanley Paul and Co (1931), p. 131
34 Lloyd George, *War Memoirs*, vol. 1, p. 589
35 Arthur Henderson (1863–1935), MP for Barnard Castle since 1903, Leader of the Labour Party 1908–10, 1914–17, Paymaster General since August 1916. Former iron worker and trades unionist.
36 Taylor, *Robert Donald*, p. 125
37 Grigg, *Lloyd George from Peace to War 1912–16*, p. 457
38 Lloyd George, *War Memoirs*, vol. 1, p. 590
39 King George V, diary entry for 4 December 1916, Royal Archives, Windsor Castle
40 Roskill, *Hankey*, vol. I, p. 327
41 Michael and Eleanor Brock, eds, *Margot Asquith's Great War Diary 1914–1916: The View from Downing Street*, Oxford (2014), p. 297
42 This dispute occurred in 1933 between Lloyd George and Wilson Harris, editor of *The Spectator*. In 1916 Harris had been a political reporter on the Asquith-supporting *Daily News*. In his 1954 autobiography, *Life So Far*, Harris attributed knowledge of the meeting between Northcliffe and Lloyd George on the evening of 3 December 1916 to his editor at that time, A. G. Gardiner.
43 McEwen, 'Northcliffe and Lloyd George at War, 1914–1918', *The Historical Journal*, 24, 3 (1981), p. 664
44 Clark, ed., *'A Good Innings'*, p. 161
45 Clarke, *My Northcliffe Diary*, p. 106
46 Lloyd George, *War Memoirs*, vol. 1, p. 590
47 Hammond, *C. P. Scott*, p. 205
48 Cecil Harmsworth (1869–1948), Liberal MP for Droitwich 1906–10 and Luton 1911–22, Home Office Minister 1915.
49 J. Lee Thompson, *Politicians, the Press and Propaganda: Lord Northcliffe and the Great War, 1914–1919*, Kent State University Press (1999), p. 114
50 The Earl of Oxford and Asquith, *Memories and Reflections 1852–1927*, vol. II, p. 132
51 *Daily News*, 4 December 1916
52 *The Times*, 4 December 1916
53 Ibid
54 *Daily Mirror*, 4 December 1916
55 *Daily Telegraph*, 4 December 1916
56 Wrench, *Geoffrey Dawson and Our Times*, p. 140
57 Ibid, p. 141
58 Lloyd George, *War Memoirs*, vol. 1, p. 590
59 Trevor Wilson, ed., *The Political Diaries of C. P. Scott 1911–1928*, Collins (1970), p. 245
60 Viscount Samuel, *Memoirs*, Cresset Press (1945), pp. 120–5
61 Léon Gambetta (1838–1882), lawyer and politician who proclaimed the French Third Republic in 1870

62 The Earl of Oxford and Asquith, *Memories and Reflections 1852–1927*, vol. II, p. 138
63 Wrench, *Geoffrey Dawson and Our Times*, p. 142
64 Hyde, *Carson*, p. 410
65 Lloyd George, *War Memoirs*, vol. 1, p. 594
66 Blake, *The Unknown Prime Minister*, pp. 331–2
67 Addison, *Politics from Within 1911–1918*, vol. I, p. 269
68 Waley, *Edwin Montagu*, pp. 108–9
69 King George V, diary entry for 5 December 1916, Royal Archives, Windsor Castle, RA/GV/PRIV/GVD/1914–1927
70 As discussed in Clark, ed., 'A Good Innings', p. 163
71 Roy Jenkins, *Churchill*, Macmillan (2001), pp. 318–19
72 Addison, *Politics from Within 1911–1918*, vol. I, p. 270
73 Clarke, *My Northcliffe Diary*, p. 107
74 Lord Burnham papers, Imperial War Museum, London. Record dictated by Burnham on 7 December 1916.
75 Named after the room used to receive Tsar Nicholas I of Russia during his state visit in 1844. The room is still used today for meetings of the Privy Council and for the private audiences given by the King for the Prime Minister and other dignitaries.
76 King George V, diary entry for 6 December 1916
77 Viscount Samuel, *Memoirs*, Cresset Press (1945), pp. 120–5
78 Grigg, *Lloyd George from Peace to War 1912–16*, p. 470
79 Lord Burnham papers, Imperial War Museum London. Record dictated on 7 December 1916.
80 Ibid
81 McEwen, ed., *The Riddell Diaries 1908–1923*, p. 177
82 Ibid
83 The Athenaeum Club, private members club at 107 Pall Mall. The Carlton Club, Conservative leaning private members club, then located at 94 Pall Mall. John Evelyn Wrench, *Geoffrey Dawson and Our Times*, Hutchinson (1955) p.142
84 The Reform Club, private members club at 104 Pall Mall
85 Addison, *Politics from Within 1911–1918*, vol. I, pp. 270–1
86 Lord Edmund Talbot (1855-1947) Conservative MP for Chichester from 1894 to 1921. Conservative Chief Whip 1915-21. Lord Lieutenant of Ireland 1921-2, when he became 1st Viscount FitzAlan of Derwent.
87 Beaverbrook, *Politicians and the War 1914–1916*, vol. 2, p. 300
88 Churchill, *Great Contemporaries*, p. 204
89 Captain David Henderson (1889–1916), Middlesex regiment, killed in action at High Wood (Bois des Fourcaux), near Longueval on 15 September 1916 during the Battle of the Somme
90 Mary Agnes Hamilton, *Arthur Henderson: A Biography*, William Heinemann (1938), p. 113
91 Ramsay MacDonald (1866–1937), MP for Leicester since 1906, Leader of the Labour Party 1911–14
92 Philip Snowden (1864–1937), MP for Blackburn since 1906
93 Ernest Bevin (1881–1951), national organizer for the Dock, Wharf, Riverside and General Labourers' Union

94 These were the figures given in Snowden's memoirs. Lloyd George claimed that there was just one vote in it, in favour of joining the government.
95 McEwen, ed., *The Riddell Diaries 1908–1923*, p. 177
96 H. A. Taylor, *Robert Donald*, Stanley Paul and Co (1931), p. 135
97 Hyde, *Carson*, p. 411
98 Harold Nicholson, *King George V: His Life and Reign*, Constable (1952), p. 292
99 William George (1865–1967) was born in the cottage at Llanystumdwy just over seven months after the death of his father. He was a solicitor and partner in the firm he established in Criccieth with his brother.
100 William George, *Richard Lloyd, Criccieth*, Western Mail A'r Echo (1934), p. 161
101 Oliver Cromwell (1599–1658), Lord Protector of the Commonwealth of England, Scotland and Ireland 1653–8
102 *Hansard*, 28 March 1945
103 The full quotation Churchill was referring to was, 'To decide about ambition, whether it is bad or not, you have two things to take into view. Not the coveting of the place alone, but the fitness for the man of the place withal: that is the question. Perhaps the place was his, perhaps he had a natural right, and even obligation to seek the place!' From Thomas Carlyle's lecture on Oliver Cromwell published in *Heroes and Hero-Worship* (1840).
104 George Hamilton-Gordon, 4th Earl of Aberdeen (1784–1860), Prime Minister 1852–5. His government lasted two years and 42 days. Lord Aberdeen at that time led the breakaway Peelite faction of the Conservative Party and formed a coalition government with the Whigs. Lord Stamfordham prepared a memorandum for King George V on the precedent, a copy of which is in the Royal Archives at Windsor Castle.

6: Gentlemen and Players

1 *Hansard*, 19 December 1916
2 In his first speech to Parliament as Prime Minister, on 13 May 1940, Churchill told the House of Commons that the 'aim' of the government was 'Victory at all costs, victory in spite of all terror, victory however long and hard the road may be'.
3 Beaverbrook, *Men and Power 1917–1918*, p. 54
4 Blanche Dugdale, *Arthur James Balfour, 1st Earl of Balfour*, vol. 2: 1906–1930, Hutchinson (1936), p. 170
5 Robert Self, ed., *The Austen Chamberlain Diary Letters: The Correspondence of Sir Austen Chamberlain with his Sisters Hilda and Ida, 1916–1937*, Cambridge University Press (1995), pp. 37–8
6 Neville Chamberlain (1869–1940), Lord Mayor of Birmingham 1915–17. On 19 December 1916 he was appointed Director of National Service. Later, Prime Minister and Leader of the Conservative Party, 1937–40.
7 Robert Self, ed., *The Neville Chamberlain Diary Letters*, vol. 1: *The Making of a Politician*, Ashgate (2000), pp. 174–5
8 Referring to the Jewish council of elders in the ancient land of Israel that in the New Testament condemned Jesus Christ to death. Another example of Lloyd George's preference for biblical points of reference.

9   Robert Shepherd, *Westminster: A Biography: From Earliest Times to the Present*, Bloomsbury (2012), p. 305
10 McEwen, ed., *The Riddell Diaries 1908–1923*, p. 177
11 Lloyd George, *War Memoirs*, vol. 1, p. 643
12 William George Stewart Adams (1874–1966). In 1912 he had been appointed as Gladstone Professor of Political Theory and Institutions at the University of Oxford.
13 Thomas Jones, *Lloyd George*, Oxford University Press (1951), p. 93
14 Philip Kerr (1882–1940) from 1930, 11th Marquess of Lothian. In 1910 Kerr founded the *Round Table Journal: A Quarterly Review of the Politics of the British Empire*.
15 The Round Table movement had been founded by Lord Milner to promote stronger political ties between Great Britain and the English-speaking peoples of the Empire dominion states.
16 John Buchan (1875–1940) from 1935 1st Baron Tweedsmuir. Diplomat, politician and novelist; his most famous work being the spy thriller, *The Thirty-Nine Steps*.
17 A. M. Gollin, *Proconsul in Politics: A Study of Lord Milner in Opposition and in Power*, Anthony Blond (1964), pp. 393–4
18 Christopher, Viscount Addison, *Four and a Half Years: A Personal Diary from June 1914 to January 1919*, vol. II, Hutchinson (1934), p. 392
19 Clark, ed., 'A Good Innings', p. 164
20 Ibid, p. 166
21 Sarah Jones (1872–1960) from Criccieth worked for the Lloyd George family from 1899 until the death of Dame Margaret in 1941.
22 Thomas Jones, *Lloyd George*, Oxford University Press (1951), p. 93
23 McEwen, ed., *The Riddell Diaries 1908–1923*, diary entry for 5 April 1917, p. 188
24 Frances Lloyd George, *The Years That Are Past*, p. 73
25 Taylor, ed., *Lloyd George: A Diary by Frances Stevenson*, entry for 15 January 1917, p. 137
26 Thomas Jones often used biblical references to describe Lloyd George. 'It is of the Lord's mercies that we are not consumed, because his compassions fail not. They are new every morning' (Lamentations 3:22–23, King James Bible).
27 Jones, *Lloyd George*, pp. 89–90
28 Oliver, Viscount Esher, ed., *Journals and Letters of Reginald Viscount Esher*, vol. 4: 1916–1930, letter addressed to Sir Douglas Haig, dated 4 December 1916, pp. 71–2
29 Ibid, journal entry for 7 December 1916, p. 73
30 Philip Sassoon letter to Douglas Haig, December 1916, Haig papers, National Library of Scotland
31 Peter Stansky, *Sassoon: The Worlds of Philip and Sybil*, Yale University Press (2003), p. 67
32 Lord Northcliffe letter to Philip Sassoon, 8 December 1916, Northcliffe papers, British Library
33 Lloyd George, *War Memoirs*, vol. 1, p. 817
34 Albert Thomas (1878–1932), French Socialist politician, Minister for Artillery and Munitions 1915–16, Minister of Armaments 1916–17. First Director General of the International Labour Office 1919–32
35 Oliver, Viscount Esher, ed., *Journals and Letters of Reginald Viscount Esher*, vol. 4: 1916–1930, journal entry for 4 January 1917, p. 81
36 Ibid, journal entry for 29 December 1916, p. 79

37 Lloyd George, *War Memoirs*, vol. 1, p. 818
38 General Luigi Cadorna (1850–1928), Chief of Staff of the Italian Army 1914–17
39 Robert Nivelle (1856–1924), commander of the Second Army of France 1916, commander-in-chief 1916–17. He had replaced Joseph Joffre on 12 December 1916.
40 The route, named after two daughters of Louis XV, Marie Adélaïde and Victoire, runs for 20 miles along a ridge between the valleys of the rivers Aisne and Ailette, about 85 miles north-east of Paris.
41 Lloyd George, *War Memoirs*, vol. 1, p. 876, memo dated 21 December 1916
42 Ibid, p. 859
43 *The Times*, 8 January 1917
44 William Orpen (1878–1931), Irish artist. In January 1917 he was appointed as an official war artist by Douglas Haig. Orpen was also a friend of Haig's private secretary, Philip Sassoon.
45 William Orpen, *An Onlooker in France 1917–1919*, Williams and Norgate (1921), p. 50
46 Leon Wolff, *In Flanders Fields: Passchendaele 1917*, Penguin (1979), p. 42
47 Alfred Duff Cooper (1890–1954) worked in the Foreign Office 1913–17, and then served in the Grenadier Guards from June 1917 until the end of the war. He first entered Parliament in 1924.
48 Duff Cooper, *Haig*, vol. II, Faber & Faber (1935), p. 24
49 Taylor, ed., *Lloyd George: A Diary by Frances Stevenson*, entry for 15 January 1917, p. 138
50 Ibid, entry for 15 January 1917, p. 139
51 Lloyd George, *War Memoirs*, vol. 1, p. 860
52 The Ypres Salient was a bulge in the front line to the north-east and east of the town of Ypres in Belgium.
53 Lloyd George, *War Memoirs*, vol. 1, p. 891
54 War Cabinet minutes, 24 February 1917, CAB 23/1, National Archives
55 Memorandum from a conversation between Stamfordham and Curzon on 4 March 1917. Royal Archives, Windsor Castle, RA GV Q1079/17.
56 Notes taken by Sir Louis du Pan Mallet from a conversation with Philip Sassoon on 11 March 1917. Louis du Pan Mallet (1864–1936), private secretary to the Foreign Secretary Sir Edward Grey 1905–7, British ambassador to the Ottoman Empire 1913–14
57 Sir Louis du Pan Mallet notes from a conversation with Philip Sassoon, 11 March 1917, Sir Louis du Pan Mallet papers, Balliol College, University of Oxford
58 David R. Woodward, *Lloyd George and the Generals*, Frank Cass (2004), p. 147
59 Sir Louis du Pan Mallet notes from a conversation with Philip Sassoon, 11 March 1917
60 Roskill, *Hankey*, vol. I, pp. 362–3
61 Major-General Sir Edward Spears Bt (1886–1974), liaison officer between the British and French army commands
62 Edward Spears, *Prelude to Victory*, Cape (1939), p. 143
63 Tommy Atkins or just 'Tommy' was the common nickname for British private soldiers during the First World War.

64 Roskill, *Hankey*, vol. I, p. 363
65 Wolff, *In Flanders Field*, p. 45
66 Ibid, p. 46
67 Ibid
68 Douglas Haig letter to Lord Curzon, 2 March 1917, copy held in the Sir Philip Sassoon papers, Houghton Hall archives
69 Roskill, *Hankey*, vol. I, p. 364
70 HRH Prince Edward (1894–1972), as King Edward VIII in 1936, then Duke of Windsor 1936–72
71 Jane Marguerite Tippett, *Once a King: The Lost Memoir of Edward VIII*, Hodder & Stoughton (2023), p. 37
72 Roskill, *Hankey*, vol. I, p. 283
73 Helen Hardinge, *Loyal to Three Kings: A Memoir of Alec Hardinge, Private Secretary to the Sovereign, 1920–1943*, Kimber (1967), p. 85
74 Beaverbrook, *Men and Power 1917–18*, pp. 147–8, relating to an audience granted to Haig with the King on 11 March 1917
75 King George V, diary entries for 1 and 2 March 1917, Royal Archives, Windsor Castle, RA/GV/PRIV/GVD/1914–1927
76 Sir Henry Rawlinson (1864–1925), Commander of the British 4th Army division in France, who played a leading role in the execution of the Battle of the Somme.
77 Lieutenant Colonel Clive Wigram (1873–1960), assistant private secretary and equerry to King George V 1910–31, then private secretary to the King from 1931 until the end of his reign in 1936.
78 David R. Woodward, *Lloyd George and the Generals*, Frank Cass (2004), p. 150
79 William Sutherland (1880–1949) had worked as a civil servant for Lloyd George at the Board of Trade and the Ministry of Munitions, and was then appointed as one of his private secretaries at 10 Downing Street. Sutherland was a policy advisor, press fixer and fundraiser for Lloyd George, and would be elected to Parliament as a Coalition Liberal in 1918.
80 Rhodes James, ed., *Memoirs of a Conservative*, p. 67
81 Woodward, *Lloyd George and the Generals*, p. 152
82 Taylor, ed., *Lloyd George: A Diary by Frances Stevenson*, entry for 16 March 1917, p. 147
83 Woodward, *Lloyd George and the Generals*, p. 152
84 Colonel Neville Bulwer-Lytton (1879–1951), later 3rd Earl of Lytton. After being wounded in action with the Royal Sussex Regiment, he was appointed in 1916 as controller of press censorship and guidance at GHQ. In 1908 he won a bronze medal in real tennis at the Olympic Games held in London.
85 Gary Mead, *The Good Soldier: The Biography of Douglas Haig*, Atlantic (2007), p. 277
86 Joseph Micheler (1861–1931), commander of the Tenth Army during the Battle of the Somme. In 1917 he was commander of the Army Group Reserve, created to fight the offensive at Chemin des Dames.
87 Philippe Pétain (1856–1951), known as 'The Lion of Verdun'. On 30 April 1917 he became Chief of Staff to the French Army. In July 1940 he would become the head of state of France after its surrender to Nazi Germany.

88   Noël Édouard, vicomte de Curières de Castelnau (1851–1944), commander of the French Eastern Army Group
89   Oliver, Viscount Esher, ed., *Journals and Letters of Reginald Viscount Esher*, vol. 4: 1916–1930, letter dated 8 March 1917, p. 92

7: THE VALLEY OF THE SHADOW OF DEATH

1   The *Irish Mail* ran early in the morning and late at night from London Euston to the port of Holyhead on the Isle of Anglesey where it connected with the ferry services to Dublin.
2   Sir Thomas Edwards Roberts (1851–1926), businessman and High Sheriff of Caernarvonshire in 1911. He had been included on the approved list of proposed new Liberal members of the House of Lords, should they have been required to force through Lloyd George's 1909 'People's Budget'.
3   Taylor, ed., *Lloyd George: A Diary by Frances Stevenson*, entry for 24 February 1917, p. 145
4   Ibid
5   William George, *My Brother and I*, Eyre & Spottiswoode (1958), p. 27
6   'Dai' being the family nickname for Lloyd George, the short form of David often used in Wales
7   Taylor, ed., *Lloyd George: A Diary by Frances Stevenson*, entry for 24 February 1917, p. 145
8   Owen, *Tempestuous Journey*, p. 368
9   Elizabeth George née Lloyd (1828–1896), born in Llanystumdwy, she died in Criccieth, after many years of poor health.
10 *Evening Mail*, 5 March 1917
11 William George (1820–1864), born in Trefwrdan in Pembrokeshire, south-west Wales. Whilst teaching at Pwllheli near Llanystumdwy, he met and married Elizabeth Lloyd. They moved to Manchester where he had secured a teaching position, and it was there that Lloyd George was born in 1863. William George suffered from poor health and the family moved back to Pembrokeshire in 1864, where he died of pneumonia. Elizabeth then returned to Llanystumdwy to live with her brother.
12 Harriet Beecher Stowe, *Uncle Tom's Cabin*, first published in instalments in the abolitionist journal, *The National Era*, in 1851, and then as a book in 1852. In the United States of America, it was the second best-selling book of the nineteenth century, after the Bible.
13 Lincoln Day is a legal public holiday observed by several states in the USA, marking the anniversary of Abraham Lincoln's birth.
14 Theodore Roosevelt, *Fear God and Take Your Own Part*, Hodder & Stoughton (1916), p. 353
15 Lincoln's response to the bombardment of Fort Sumter in South Carolina in April 1861 was the start of the American Civil War.
16 Peter Appleseed, *Franklin Delano Roosevelt's Life and Times*, Lulu (2014), p. 182
17 Lloyd George, *War Memoirs*, vol. 1, p. 446
18 Charles Evans Hughes (1862–1948), Republican Party candidate for the Presidency of the United States of America in 1916. Governor of New York

1907–10, member of the Supreme Court of the United States 1910–16. Hughes's father David Charles Hughes, a Methodist preacher, had emigrated to America from south Wales in 1855.
19 Lord Burnham papers, Imperial War Museum, London, notes of a conversation on 1 November 1916
20 David Lloyd George, *New York Times*, 12 February 1917
21 *Hansard*, 19 December 1916
22 The interview was syndicated by the Press Association and Reuters in Great Britain and appeared in most newspapers, for example, the *Birmingham Mail*, 26 January 1917.
23 Lloyd George, *War Memoirs*, vol. 1, pp. 1,050–7
24 General Jan Christian Smuts (1870–1950). Born to Afrikaner parents in the British Cape Colony, he read law at Christ's College, Cambridge. He fought for the Boers in the Second Boer War and played a leading role in negotiating the treaty that ended it. In 1917 he was Minister for Finance and Defence in the government of the Union of South Africa.
25 J. C. Smuts, *Jan Christian Smuts by his Son*, Cassell (1952), p. 187
26 Ibid
27 Ibid, p. 225
28 Tsar Nicholas II (1868–1918), Emperor of Russia from 1894 until 1917 when the monarchy was abolished
29 Lloyd George, *War Memoirs*, vol. 1, p. 1,050
30 Prince Georgy Lvov (1861–1925), Head of the Provisional Government of the Russian Republic, as created by the Russian Duma, 15 March–20 July 1917, when he resigned in favour of the Minister for War, Alexander Kerensky
31 Kenneth Rose, *King George V*, Weidenfeld & Nicolson (1983), pp. 209–10
32 *The Times*, 19 March 1917
33 Hammond, *C. P. Scott*, p. 212
34 Tsar Nicholas II was a first cousin of King George V.
35 Harold Nicolson, *King George V: His Life and His Reign*, Constable (1952), p. 301
36 Alexandra, Empress of Russia (1872–1918), born Princess Alix of Hesse and by Rhine, granddaughter of Queen Victoria
37 *The Globe*, 5 April 1917
38 Sir George Buchanan (1854–1924), British ambassador to Russia, 1910–17
39 Pavel Milyukov (1859–1943), Liberal politician and member of the Russian Duma. Russian Minister for Foreign Affairs, 2 March–20 May 1917.
40 Stamfordham letters to Balfour dated 6 April 1917, Lloyd George papers, Parliamentary Archive
41 There was press speculation that the Imperial family would stay at Claremont House near Esher, then a Royal residence, which had previously been used by the exiled King Louis-Philippe of France.
42 Speech made on 2 April 1917, in Lloyd George, *War Memoirs*, vol. 1, p. 991
43 1 Samuel 30:17. David attacked them from dawn until the evening of the next day. Not one of them escaped, except for 400 young men who jumped on camels and got away.
44 *Companionship in Arms: Speeches Delivered in London on April 12, 1917, by the Prime Minister of Great Britain, the United States Ambassador, Viscount Bryce, and Lord Robert Cecil, and in the House*

of Commons on April 18 by Mr. Bonar Law, Mr. Asquith, Mr. Dillon, and Mr. Wardle, to celebrate America's Adhesion to the Allies' Cause, Hodder & Stoughton (1917)

45 Daily News, 13 April 1917
46 The term 'special relationship' was first used in this context by Winston Churchill during his famous 'Iron Curtain' speech at Fulton, Missouri, on 5 March 1946
47 On the same day communist revolutionary Vladimir Lenin disembarked from his train at the Finland Station in Petrograd intent on replacing the liberal Russian Provisional Government with a Marxist Bolshevik one.
48 The Hindenburg Line was a fortification of concrete, steel and barbed wire, which ran for seventy miles from Arras in the north to Laffaux near Soissons on the River Aisne.
49 Louis-Hubert Lyautey (1854–1934), Minister of War 12 December 1916–15 March 1917. Soldier and colonial administrator.
50 Spears, Prelude to Victory, p. 202
51 Alexandre Ribot (1842–1923), Prime Minister of France on four separate occasions and never for more than one year: in 1892–3, 1895, 1914 and 1917.
52 Paul Painlevé (1863–1933), Minister of War, 20 March–13 November 1917. An acclaimed mathematician who had applied his work to the theory of flight, in 1909 he had created the first university course in France in aeronautics.
53 David Lloyd George, War Memoirs, vol. II, Odhams Press (1938), p. 1,602
54 Raymond Poincaré (1860–1934), President of France 1913–1920, Prime Minister of France 1912–1913. A centre-right politician, he had been one of the founders of the Democratic Republican Alliance of followers of Léon Gambetta.
55 Callwell, ed., Field-Marshal Sir Henry Wilson, vol. I, p. 336
56 Winston Churchill, The World Crisis 1911–1918, Penguin (2007), p. 713
57 Callwell, ed., Field-Marshal Sir Henry Wilson, vol. I, p. 338
58 Ibid, p. 339
59 Oliver, Viscount Esher, ed., Journals and Letters of Reginald Viscount Esher, vol. 4: 1916–1930, journal entry dated 17 April 1917, p. 104
60 Lloyd George, War Memoirs, vol. 2, p. 1,258
61 Roskill, Hankey, vol. I, p. 385
62 Ibid, diary entry for 4 May 1917, p. 386
63 Paul Mantoux (1877–1956), Professor of French History and Institutions at the University of London. He acted as interpreter at the Inter-Allied conferences 1915–18 and was the official interpreter for the leaders at the Paris Peace Conference at Versailles in 1919.
64 Roskill, Hankey, vol. I, diary entry for 4 May 1917, p. 386
65 Oliver, Viscount Esher, ed., Journals and Letters of Reginald Viscount Esher, vol. 4: 1916–1930, journal entry for 25 April 1917, p. 109
66 Woodward, Lloyd George and the Generals, p. 164
67 Lloyd George, War Memoirs, vol. 2, p. 1,258
68 Richard M. Watt, Dare Call It Treason, Chatto & Windus (1963), p. 182
69 Lloyd George, War Memoirs, vol. 1, p. 873
70 Ibid, p. 891
71 Ibid, p. 831

72 'The General' was written in April 1917 while Sassoon was convalescing at Denmark Hill hospital, now King's College Hospital in Camberwell, South London.
73 Siegfried Sassoon, The War Poems, Faber & Faber (1983), p. 67
74 Erich Ludendorff (1865–1937), First Quartermaster General of the Great General Staff of the German Army (1916–18)
75 Erich Ludendorff, My War Memoirs, Naval & Military Press (2005), pp. 421–2
76 Beaverbrook, Men and Power 1917–18, p. 115
77 Taylor, ed., Lloyd George: A Diary by Frances Stevenson, entry for 12 May 1917, p. 157
78 Sir Archibald Murray (1860–1945), Commander-in-Chief of the Egyptian Expeditionary Force, January 1916–June 1917. During 1915 he had been Deputy Chief of the Imperial General Staff.
79 2 Samuel 5:7, King James Bible
80 William George, My Brother and I, letter dated 30 March 1917, p. 258
81 General Sir Edmund Allenby (1861–1936), previously commander of the Third Army on the Western Front. In the Middle East, Allenby increased support for irregular warfare, in particular Lawrence of Arabia's revolt in the desert.
82 Lieutenant Charles John Law (1897–1917), 3rd Battalion King's Own Scottish Borderers
83 Lloyd George, War Memoirs, vol. 1, pp. 447–8
84 Churchill, The World Crisis 1911–1918, p. 713
85 Beaverbrook, Men and Power 1917–18, p. 153
86 Lloyd George, War Memoirs, vol. 1, p. 650
87 John Jellicoe, 1st Earl Jellicoe (1859–1935), First Sea Lord 1916–18. Jellicoe commanded the Grand Fleet in the Battle of Jutland in May 1916.
88 Lloyd George, War Memoirs, vol. 1, p. 673
89 Taylor, English History 1914–1945, p. 122
90 Lloyd George, War Memoirs, vol. 1, p. 609
91 The Aldwych Club, founded in 1906, was a club for leading London advertisers and media owners, rather like its contemporary rival The Thirty Club, which still exists today.
92 The Connaught Rooms, 61–65 Great Queen Street, Covent Garden, London
93 Beaverbrook, Men and Power 1917–18, p. 151
94 Clarke, My Northcliffe Diary, p. 111
95 Joseph Kenworthy, 10th Baron Strabolgi (1886–1953). In 1919, Kenworthy became a Liberal MP, later joining the Labour Party.
96 Sir Frederick Whitley-Thomson (1851–1925), Liberal MP for Skipton 1900–6, Mayor of Halifax 1908–11
97 Jim Ring, How the Navy Won the War: The Real Instrument of Victory 1914–1918, Pen & Sword (2018)
98 Joseph Kenworthy, Sailors, Statesmen and Others: An Autobiography, Rich & Cowan (1933), p. 70
99 Reginald Henderson (1881–1939), later Third Sea Lord and Controller of the Navy 1934–9
100 Churchill, The World Crisis 1911–1918, p. 745
101 Beaverbrook, Men and Power 1917–18, p. 153

102 Ibid, p. 115
103 Ibid, pp. 120–1
104 Martin Gilbert, *Winston S. Churchill, vol. IV: 1917–1922*, Heinemann (1975), p. 17
105 Martin Gilbert, *Winston S. Churchill, Companion vol. IV: Part 1, January 1917 to June 1919*, Heinemann (1977), p. 60
106 Beaverbrook, *Men and Power 1917–18*, p. 122
107 Ibid, p. 123
108 The Other Club is a dining club founded by Winston Churchill and F. E. Smith in 1911. It met fortnightly in the Pinafore Room at The Savoy Hotel when parliament was in session.
109 McEwen, ed., *The Riddell Diaries 1908–1923*, p. 189
110 Taylor, ed., *Lloyd George: A Diary by Frances Stevenson*, entry for 19 May 1917, p. 158
111 Letter from Esher to Haig dated 30 May 1917, Sir Philip Sassoon papers, Houghton Hall, Norfolk
112 Denis Judd, *Lord Reading*, Weidenfeld & Nicolson (1982), pp. 134–5
113 William Randolph Hearst (1863–1951), businessman, news publisher and founder of the Hearst Corporation. His titles included the *San Francisco Examiner*, *New York Journal*, *Chicago Herald and Examiner* and *Washington DC Times*. Hearst was the inspiration for the character of Charles Foster Kane in Orson Welles's 1941 film, *Citizen Kane*. Hearst tried to prevent the release of the film and banned any mention of it in his publications.
114 *New York Tribune*, 30 June 1918
115 Karl von Wiegand (1874–1961), born in Hesse in Germany, was the only American correspondent allowed to stay in Berlin during the First World War.
116 William Dodd (1869–1940), advisor to President Woodrow Wilson and later, American ambassador to Germany 1933–7
117 Letter from William Dodd, American ambassador to Germany, to President Franklin D. Roosevelt, 20 March 1935, Franklin D. Roosevelt Presidential Library archive
118 Eric Rauchway, 'How "America First" Got its Nationalistic Edge', *The Atlantic*, 6 May 2016
119 Pomeroy Burton (1869–1947). Born in Pennsylvania and having previously edited Joseph Pulitzer's *New York World*, in 1906 he was hired by Northcliffe and went on to become General Manager of Associated Newspapers. In 1927 he commissioned the construction of the Château de la Croë, a large, detached villa on the Cap d'Antibes in the south of France, which in 1938 he leased to the Duke and Duchess of Windsor.
120 Thompson, *Lord Northcliffe and the Great War, 1914–1919*, p. 127
121 Isaac Marcosson, *Adventures in Interviewing*, Dodd Mead & Company (1931), p. 103
122 Sir Cecil Spring-Rice (1859–1918), British ambassador to the United States of America 1912–18. He was a contemporary and friend of Lord Curzon from their time as undergraduates at Balliol College, Oxford. Spring-Rice was also a close friend of President Theodore Roosevelt and had been best man at his wedding to his second wife, Edith Carow. He also wrote the words to the hymn 'I Vow to Thee My Country'.

123   Beaverbrook, *Men and Power 1917–18*, pp. 71–2
124   The St Regis Hotel at Fifth Avenue and 55th Street in Manhattan, New York City, had been founded by John Jacob Astor IV, who had also partnered with his cousin, William Waldorf Astor, in the creation of New York's Waldorf Astoria hotel. John Jacob Astor IV died when the *Titanic* sank in 1912. William Waldorf Astor moved to England in 1891 and became 1st Viscount Astor in 1917. He was the father of the politician Waldorf Astor, and gave his son the Cliveden estate in Berkshire in 1906.
125   Beaverbrook, *Men and Power 1917–18*, p. 75
126   Barnes and Nicolson, eds, *The Leo Amery Diaries*, vol. 1, p. 159
127   Roskill, *Hankey*, vol. I, p. 391
128   McEwen, ed., *The Riddell Diaries 1908–1923*, p. 190
129   Gilbert, *Winston S. Churchill, Companion vol. IV: Part 1, January 1917 to June 1919*, Heinemann (1977), p. 75
130   Beaverbrook, *Men and Power 1917–18*, p. 134
131   Ibid, p. 125
132   Ibid, letter dated 18 June 1917, p. 129
133   McEwen, ed., *The Riddell Diaries 1908–1923*, p. 191
134   Beaverbrook, *Men and Power 1917–18*, p. 170
135   Ibid, p. 173
136   Hyde, *Carson*, p. 423
137   The Mesopotamian campaign had been planned and run by the India Office and the British Indian Army. There had been particular criticism following the surrender of British forces following the siege of Kut in April 1916.
138   Self, ed., *The Austen Chamberlain Diary Letters*, dated 25 July 1917, p. 49
139   Andrew Roberts, *Churchill, Walking with Destiny*, Allen Lane (2018), p. 249
140   Beaverbrook, *Men and Power 1917–18*, p. 137
141   Ibid
142   Richard Lloyd George, *Lloyd George*, p. 185

8: Mud Sticks

1   *Dundee Courier*, 8 June 1917
2   It has been disputed whether the sound of the explosions could have carried over such a long distance. However, Maurice Hankey who was also staying in Surrey that night, claimed to have heard the explosion. Reports of residents in Kent hearing the guns from the front, particularly on days of wet weather, were not uncommon. In the early hours of 7 June, the weather conditions in Kent and Surrey were still, with a very gentle breeze from the south-east. The thunderstorms that took place earlier that night may have also created atmospheric conditions helping the sound to travel.
3   Sir Herbert Plumer KCMG (1857–1932), commander of the Second Army on the Western Front
4   Callwell, ed., *Field-Marshal Sir Henry Wilson*, vol. I, p. 342
5   Jones, *Lloyd George*, p. 117
6   John Grigg, *Lloyd George: War Leader 1916–18* Allen Lane (2002), p. 159

NOTES

7 Woodward, *Lloyd George and the Generals*, p. 178
8 Ibid, p. 168
9 Callwell, ed., *Field-Marshal Sir Henry Wilson*, vol. I, diary entry for 20 May 1917, p. 355
10 Woodward, *Lloyd George and the Generals*, Frank Cass (2004), p. 168
11 Callwell, ed., *Field-Marshal Sir Henry Wilson*, vol. I, diary entry for 2 June 1917, p. 359
12 Brigadier-General John Charteris (1877–1946), Chief of Intelligence at the British Expeditionary Force general headquarters 1915–18. A professional soldier who had worked as one of Haig's trusted officers since before the war.
13 Brigadier-General John Charteris, *Field Marshal Earl Haig*, Cassell (1929), p. 272
14 Lloyd George, *War Memoirs*, vol. 1, p. 1,297
15 Wolff, *In Flanders Fields*, p. 113
16 Woodward, *Lloyd George and the Generals*, Frank Cass (2004), letter from Robertson to Haig, 13 June 1917, p. 176
17 *The Woman's Dreadnought*, 28 July 1917
18 Sylvia Pankhurst (1882–1960), socialist campaigner in the East End of London. Sister of the suffragette Christabel Pankhurst and daughter of Emmeline Pankhurst.
19 The Brotherhood Church on the corner of Southgate Road and Balmes Road in Hackney closed in 1934 and no longer stands. It was often used for Socialist meetings, including in 1907 for a congress organized by the Russian Social-Democratic Labour Party, which was attended by Lenin, Stalin, Trotsky, Zinoviev and Rosa Luxembourg.
20 The Workers' and Soldiers' Council had been inspired by the revolution in Russia and was supported by Sylvia Pankhurst, and some leading Labour MPs, including Ramsay MacDonald and Philip Snowden.
21 Bertrand Russell (1872–1970), mathematician, philosopher and public intellectual. His pacifism during the First World War meant he was sentenced to six months in Brixton Prison. In 1931 he succeeded his brother to become 3rd Earl Russell.
22 *Hansard*, 28 November 1916
23 Lady Ottoline Morrell (1873–1938), aristocrat and society hostess, a friend of Bertrand Russell and Siegfried Sassoon. She was also a member of the Bloomsbury Group and married to the Asquith-supporting Liberal MP, Philip Morrell.
24 Nicholas Griffin, *The Selected Letters of Bertrand Russell*, vol. 2: *The Public Years 1914–1970*, Taylor and Francis (2013), p. 116
25 George Lansbury (1859–1940), Labour MP for Tower Hamlets, Bow and Bromley 1910–12. Editor of the *Daily Herald* 1913–22. He returned to Parliament in 1922 as Labour MP for Poplar, Bow and Bromley, becoming leader of the Labour Party 1932–5.
26 *Daily Herald*, 4 August 1917
27 Henry Chancellor (1863–1945), MP for Haggerston in East London 1910–18. In 1918 he was defeated for the new constituency of Shoreditch by Christopher Addison.

28   *Birmingham Mail*, 31 July 1917
29   Ethel Snowden (1881–1951), Socialist and human-rights activist. Before the First World War she was one of the leading campaigners for women's suffrage, and during the war founded the Women's Peace Crusade.
30   Peter Brock, *The Pacifist Impulse in Historical Perspective*, University of Toronto (1996), p. 356
31   Hastings Lees-Smith (1878–1941), MP for Northampton 1910–18. In 1919 he joined the Labour Party.
32   *The Woman's Dreadnought*, 28 July 1917
33   The Craiglockhart war hospital opened in 1916 as a psychiatric hospital for the recovery of shell-shocked officers. It was here that Siegfried Sassoon and Wilfred Owen met.
34   Alexander Kerensky (1881–1970), Minister-Chairman of the Russian Provisional Government, July–November 1917
35   *L'humanité*, 29 July 1917
36   The delegation comprised four Social Democrats, I. P. Goldenberg, Henryk Ehrlich, A. N. Smirnov, V. N Rozanov, and a Socialist revolutionary, N. S. Rusanov. All were from the Menshevik faction of the Russian Soviet.
37   Lloyd George, *War Memoirs*, vol. 1, p. 1,127
38   Ibid, vol. 2, p. 1,129
39   Barnes and Nicholson, eds, *The Leo Amery Diaries*, vol. 1, diary entry for 11 August 1917, describing Lord Milner's recollection of the proceedings, p. 166
40   George Barnes (1859–1940), MP for Glasgow Blackfriars and Hutchesontown 1906–18 and then Glasgow Gorbals 1918–22, Leader of the Labour Party 1910–11. Minister for Pensions, December 1916–August 1917. Minister without Portfolio August 1917–January 1920.
41   Chris Wrigley, *Arthur Henderson*, GPC Books (1990), p. 118
42   Sidney Webb (1859–1947), co-founder of the London School of Economics and early member of the Fabian Society. He was married to the social reformer and writer Beatrice Webb née Potter. He became a Labour MP in 1922 and member of the House of Lords in 1929.
43   Wrigley, *Arthur Henderson*, p. 120
44   Members of the Women's Land Army, founded in 1917, were known as Land Girls. They helped to provide farmers with the workers they needed to replace men called to serve at the front.
45   *Mid Sussex Times*, 28 August 1917
46   Ibid
47   Grigg, *Lloyd George: War Leader 1916–18*, p. 22, from Riddell diary entry for 13 August 1917
48   Barnes and Nicholson, eds, *The Leo Amery Diaries*, vol. 1, letter from Amery to his wife dated 25 September 1917, describing a dinner conversation with Smuts, p. 172
49   George Cassar, *Lloyd George at War 1916–1918*, Anthem Press (2011), p. 129
50   Ernest Dunlop Swinton, *Twenty Years After: The Battlefields of 1914–1918: Then and Now*, G. Newnes Ltd (1936), p. 1,083
51   Lloyd George, *War Memoirs*, vol. 2, p. 1,248

NOTES

52 Sir Hubert de la Poer Gough (1870–1963), commanding officer of the Fifth Army 1916–18. Like Haig, Gough had been a cavalry officer, and had fought in the colonial wars in South Africa.
53 General Hubert Gough, *The Fifth Army*, Hodder & Stoughton (1931), p. 205
54 Lloyd George, *War Memoirs*, vol. 2, p. 1,310
55 Woodward, *Lloyd George and the Generals*, p. 195
56 Simon Heffer, *Staring at God: Britain in the Great War*, Penguin (2019), p. 559
57 Callwell, ed., *Field-Marshal Sir Henry Wilson*, vol. II, p. 10
58 Lloyd George, *War Memoirs*, vol. 2, pp. 1,415–17
59 Wrench, *Geoffrey Dawson and Our Times*, p. 153
60 Woodward, *Lloyd George and the Generals*, p. 198
61 Heffer, *Staring at God*, p. 561
62 Frances Lloyd George, *The Years That Are Past*, p. 92
63 Woodward, *Lloyd George and the Generals*, letter dated 15 September 1917, p. 201
64 Roskill, *Hankey*, vol. I, pp. 434–5
65 William Lever, 1st Viscount Leverhulme (1851–1925), British industrialist and philanthropist. In 1886 he established along with his brother James the soap manufacturing business, Lever Brothers, now part of the global firm, Unilever. Lever had also been Liberal MP for The Wirral 1906–09.
66 Brigadier-General Sir Owen Thomas (1858–1923), formerly commanding officer of the North Wales Brigade. He had stood unsuccessfully in 1895 as a Liberal to become Member of Parliament for Oswestry. In 1918 he would be elected MP for Anglesey, standing as an independent Labour candidate.
67 *Illustrated London News*, 15 September 1917
68 Frances Lloyd George, *The Years That Are Past*, p. 92
69 *The Times*, 7 September 1917
70 *Liverpool Daily Post*, 7 September 1917
71 The Bardic Chair was made by the master craftsman Eugeen Vanfleteren (1880–1950), a refugee from Mechelen in Belgium, who was then living in Birkenhead. Since 1917 it has been known as the 'Black Chair' and the Birkenhead Eisteddfod as the 'Black Eisteddfod'.
72 Evan Rees (1850–1923), a Calvinist Minister, was known by his bardic name of Dyfed, as the Archdruid of Wales 1905–23. The Archdruid is the presiding officer of the Gorsedd, a society of Welsh-language poets, writers and musicians.
73 Ellis Humphrey Evans (1887–1917), Private, 15th Battalion, Royal Welch Fusiliers. He is buried at Artillery Wood Cemetery near Ypres. His home in Trawsfynydd was less than 20 miles from Lloyd George's in Criccieth. His winning awdl, entitled *Yr Arwr (The Hero)*, was inspired by Percy Bysshe Shelley's poem *Prometheus Unbound*.
74 *The Guardian*, 30 July 2014, interview with Gerald Williams, nephew of Hedd Wyn
75 Silyn Roberts (1871–1930), a Calvinist Minister and poet, had won the National Eisteddfod in 1902.
76 McKinley Terry, 'The Bard and the Black Chair: Ellis Evans and Memorializing the Great War in Wales', *Aletheia, The Alpha Chi Journal of Undergraduate Scholarship*, vol. 3, issue 1 (2018)

77 Y Brython, 20 September 1917
78 Gloucestershire Echo, 7 September 1917
79 Liverpool Daily Post, 7 September 1917
80 Glyn Welden Banks, 'Hedd Wyn: Poet as Hero', in Anders Ahlqvist, Harri Nyberg, Glyn Welden Banks and Tom Sjöblom (eds), Celtica Helsingiensia: Proceedings from a Symposium on Celtic Studies, Helsinki: Societas Scientiarum Fennica (1996), p. 8 (from the translation by Professor Alan Llwyd)
81 Chamberlain, Down the years, p.242
82 Taylor, ed., My Darling Pussy, p. 21
83 Roskill, Hankey, vol. I, p. 435
84 Lord Riddell, Lord Riddell's War Diary 1914–1918, Nicholson & Watson (1933), entry for 13 September 1917, p. 272
85 Wolff, In Flanders Fields, p. 175
86 Captain James Kidston Law (1893–1917). His body was never identified and he was commemorated on the memorial to missing airmen at Arras.
87 Rhodes James, ed., Memoirs of a Conservative, p. 57
88 McEwen, ed., The Riddell Diaries 1908–1923, diary entry for 21 September 1917, pp. 199–200
89 Lord Robert Cecil (1864–1958), Parliamentary Under-Secretary of State for Foreign Affairs 1915–19, MP for Marylebone East 1906–10, MP for Hitchin, 1911–23. He was the sixth child and third son of the former Prime Minister, the 3rd Marquess of Salisbury.
90 Woodward, Lloyd George and the Generals, letter dated 12 September 1917, p. 215
91 Pope Benedict XV (1854–1922), Archbishop of Bologne 1907–14, elected Pope 3 September 1914
92 Baron Richard von Kühlmann (1873–1948), German Foreign Minister, 6 August 1917–9 July 1918
93 Lloyd George, War Memoirs, vol. 2, p. 1,238
94 Roskill, Hankey, vol. I, diary entry for 24 September 1917, p. 438
95 Lloyd George, War Memoirs, vol. 2, p. 1,242
96 This meeting was discussed by Painlevé in his memoir, Comment j'ai nommé Foch et Pétain la politique de guerre de 1917 le commandement unique interallié, F. Alcan (1923).
97 'G.S.O.' [Sir Frank Fox], G.H.Q. (Montreuil-sur-Mer), Philip Allan (1920), p. 51
98 Ibid, p. 53
99 In the novel Montreuil is the town where Jean Valjean rebuilds his life and becomes mayor. Victor Hugo visited the town in 1837 and the famous scene of the runaway cart in the novel is based on an incident he witnessed in Montreuil on the steep cobbled street of Cavée Saint-Firmin.
100 Jones, Lloyd George, p. 34
101 Taylor, ed., Lloyd George: A Diary by Frances Stevenson, p. 269
102 Victor Hugo, Les Misérables, Simon & Schuster (2005), p. 52
103 Woodward, Lloyd George and the Generals, p. 203
104 Gary Sheffield, Douglas Haig from the Somme to Victory, Aurum Press (2011), p. 245
105 The Battle of Caporetto (24 October–19 November 1917) took place near the town of Kobarid, now in north-west Slovenia. Caporetto was the Italian name for the town. The Austrian and German forces advanced 150 kilometres and the Italian army lost over 250,000 men taken prisoner, along with vast

       numbers of guns, stores and equipment. The battle was also documented by
       Ernest Hemingway in his novel, *A Farewell to Arms*.
106   Vittorio Orlando (1860–1952), Prime Minister of Italy 1917–19. A Sicilian
       Liberal, Orlando had previously been a professor of law at the University of
       Palermo, and first entered the Italian National Assembly in 1897.
107   Paolo Boselli (1838–1932), Prime Minister of Italy 1916–17. Before entering
       politics he had been the first professor of science at the University of Rome.
108   Lloyd George, *War Memoirs*, vol. 2, pp. 1,435–7
109   Oliver, Viscount Esher, ed., *Journals and Letters of Reginald Viscount Esher*, vol. 4: 1916–
       1930, journal entry dated 3 November 1917, p. 151
110   Sheffield and Bourne, eds, *Douglas Haig*, diary entry for 4 November 1917, p. 338
111   Ibid
112   Oliver, Viscount Esher, ed., *Journals and Letters of Reginald Viscount Esher*, vol. 4: 1916–
       1930, letter to Lord Stamfordham dated 9 November 1917, pp. 155–6
113   Lloyd George, *War Memoirs*, vol. 2, p. 1,441
114   A. J. P. Taylor, *The First World War, an Illustrated History*, Perigee Trade (1972), pp.
       181–2
115   Wolff, *In Flanders Fields*, p. 262
116   Ibid, p. 227
117   Brigadier-General John Charteris, *At GHQ*, Cassell (1931), notes from 10
       October 1917, p. 259
118   Lloyd George, *War Memoirs*, vol. 2, p. 1,368
119   Lieutenant-General Sir Launcelot Kiggell (1862–1954), Chief of the General
       Staff for the British Expeditionary Force in France 1915–18
120   Lloyd George, *War Memoirs*, vol. 2, p. 1,242

9: THE MAN WHO WON THE WAR

1   Letizia Bonaparte (1750–1836). After Napoleon's defeat at Waterloo in 1815,
    she moved to Rome where she lived for the rest of her life. The Hôtel de Brienne,
    at 14 Rue Saint Dominique in the 7th arrondissement of Paris, was sold to the
    French government in 1817, when it became the home of the Ministry of War.
2   *The Scotsman*, 13 November 1917
3   Ibid
4   Ibid
5   *The Times*, 14 November 1917
6   Quoted in *The Times*, 14 November 1917
7   McEwen, ed., *The Riddell Diaries 1908–1923*, p. 205
8   Jones, *Lloyd George*, p. 120
9   *The Scotsman*, 13 November 1917
10 Ibid
11 Barnes and Nicholson, eds, *The Leo Amery Diaries*, vol. 1, p. 179
12 McEwen, ed., *The Riddell Diaries 1908–1923*, diary entry for 27 November 1917,
    p. 207
13 Lord Hankey, *The Supreme Command 1914–1918*, vol. II, Allen & Unwin (1961),
    p. 728
14 *The Times*, 16 November 1917

15 Beaverbrook, *Men and Power 1917–18*, p. 87
16 Ibid, p. 84
17 McEwen, ed., *The Riddell Diaries 1908–1923*, p. 205
18 Weetman Pearson, 1st Viscount Cowdray (1856–1927), engineer and oil industrialist. He was the Liberal MP for Colchester 1895–1910, when he was elevated to the House of Lords as Baron Cowdray. He had been raised to the rank of Viscount after Lloyd George became Prime Minister, when he was also appointed as President of the Air Board.
19 Beaverbrook, *Men and Power 1917–18*, p. 87
20 Stanley Morison, *Personality and Diplomacy in Anglo-American Relations, 1917*, R&R Clark (1956), pp. 39–40
21 Self, ed., *The Austen Chamberlain Diary Letters*, p. 63
22 *Vorwärts*, meaning 'Forward', was founded in 1876, and is published by the Social Democratic Party of Germany.
23 *Vorwärts*, 15 November 1917
24 Self, ed., *The Austen Chamberlain Diary Letters*, p. 64
25 McEwen, ed., *The Riddell Diaries 1908–1923*, diary entry for 24 November 1917, p. 206
26 Self, ed., *The Austen Chamberlain Diary Letters*, p. 65
27 *Hansard*, 19 November 1917
28 Ibid
29 Lloyd George, *War Memoirs*, vol. 2, p. 1,602
30 Ibid, p. 1,603
31 Georges Clemenceau (1841–1929), Prime Minister of France 1906–9 and 1917–20
32 Paul Déroulède (1846–1914), nationalist politician and author, and member of the French National Assembly. He was a co-founder of the right-wing League of Patriots.
33 Émile Zola (1840–1902), journalist, author and playwright
34 Alfred Dreyfus (1859–1935). In 1895 Dreyfus, an artillery officer of Jewish ancestry, was falsely convicted in a secret court martial of spying for Germany and sentenced to life imprisonment on Devil's Island in French Guiana. Dreyfus was pardoned by the President of France, Émile Loubet, in 1899, following a public campaign protesting his innocence. He was formally exonerated by a military commission in 1906 and promoted to the rank of major. He returned to the army as a reservist artillery officer at the outbreak of the First World War and served throughout.
35 Churchill, *Great Contemporaries*, pp. 310–11
36 Lloyd George, *War Memoirs*, vol. 2, p. 1,602
37 Ibid, pp. 1,603–4
38 The nickname was acquired by Clemenceau during his political career for the way he would pursue and devour French government ministers.
39 Lloyd George, *War Memoirs*, vol. 2, p. 1,609
40 Ibid, p. 1,674
41 Georges Clemenceau, *Grandeur and Misery of Victory*, George G. Harrap & Co (1930), p. 92

42 General Sir Julian Byng (1862–1935), later 1st Viscount Byng of Vimy, commander of the Third Army. He served as Governor-General of Canada 1921–6.
43 Lord Esher, 'War Journals', 1 December 1917, Esher papers, University of Cambridge
44 Ibid
45 Roberts, *The Chief*, p. 341
46 *The Times*, 12 December 1917
47 Lord Northcliffe letter to Philip Sassoon, 13 December 1917, Northcliffe papers, British Library
48 Vyvyan Harmsworth MC (1894–1918), Captain 2nd Battalion Irish Guards. His younger brother Vere Harmsworth (1895–1916), a Lieutenant in the Royal Naval Division, had been killed in action at the Battle of Ancre on the Somme on 13 November 1916. They were the elder of three sons of Northcliffe's brother, Lord Rothermere.
49 The Balfour Declaration was issued by the Foreign Secretary, Arthur Balfour, on 2 November 1917.
50 *Aberdeen Evening Express*, 13 December 1917
51 Peter Frankopan, *The Silk Roads: A new history of the world*, Bloomsbury (2015) p.343
52 Major-General Sir Ronald Maxwell, Quartermaster General 1852–1924
53 Barnes and Nicholson, eds, *The Leo Amery Diaries*, vol. 1, p. 187
54 McEwen, ed., *The Riddell Diaries 1908–1923*, diary entry for 23 December 1917, p. 211
55 Ibid
56 Barnes and Nicholson, eds, *The Leo Amery Diaries*, vol. 1, p. 196
57 Ibid, p. 198
58 Ibid, p. 199
59 Lord Beaverbrook, *Men and Power 1917–18*, Hutchinson (1956), pp. 181–2
60 Letter from Lord Northcliffe to Philip Sassoon, 17 January 1918, Northcliffe papers, British Library
61 Trevor Wilson, ed., *The Political Diaries of C. P. Scott 1911–1928*, Collins (1970), p. 336
62 Woodward, *Lloyd George and the Generals*, p. 255
63 Captain Peter E. Wright, *At the Supreme War Council*, G.P. Putnam's Sons (1921), p. 62
64 Letter from Robertson to Lord Derby, dated 2 February 1918, Derby papers, Liverpool Records Office
65 Letter from Robertson to Lord Stamfordham, dated 2 February 1917, Royal Archives, Windsor Castle
66 *Morning Post*, 11 February 1918
67 *Western Times*, 25 January 1918
68 Lloyd George, *War Memoirs*, vol. 2, p. 1,671
69 Ibid, p. 1,678
70 *Daily Mail*, 21 February 1918
71 Lilias, Countess Bathurst (1871–1965), proprietor of *The Morning Post* since the death of her father, Lord Glenesk, in 1908. At that time she was the only female owner of a major newspaper in the world, and she eventually sold the newspaper in 1924.

72 Clarisse Berthezene and Julie Gottlieb (eds), *Considering Conservative Women in the Gendering of Modern British Politics*, Routledge (2021), p. 1,921
73 *Hansard*, 12 February 1918
74 Ibid
75 *Dundee Courier*, 13 February 1918
76 *Hansard*, 12 February 1918
77 Beaverbrook, *Men and Power 1917–18*, Lord Stamfordham memorandum dated 13 February 1918, p. 409
78 King George V, diary entry for 13 February 1918, Royal Archives, Windsor Castle, RA/GV/PRIV/GVD/1914-1927
79 Woodward, *Lloyd George and the Generals*, p. 269
80 Lloyd George, *War Memoirs*, vol. 2, p. 1,672, Lord Milner letter to Lloyd George dated 8 February 1918
81 Callwell, ed., *Field-Marshal Sir Henry Wilson*, vol. II, p. 61
82 Beaverbrook, *Men and Power 1917–18*, Lord Stamfordham memorandum dated 13 February 1917, p. 412
83 King George V, diary entry for 16 February 1918, Royal Archives, Windsor Castle, RA/GV/PRIV/GVD/1914–1927
84 McEwen, ed., *The Riddell Diaries 1908–1923*, diary entry for 17 February 1918, p. 218
85 *The Times*, 20 February 1918
86 Ibid
87 Woodward, *Lloyd George and the Generals*, p. 275
88 *Hansard*, 19 February 1918
89 *The Times*, 20 February 1918
90 *Hansard*, 19 February 1918
91 Charles Repington, *The First World War, 1914–1914: Personal Experiences of Lieutenant-Colonel Charles Repington*, vol. 2, Constable (1920), letter from Robertson to Repington dated 25 February 1918, p. 236
92 Roberts, *The Chief*, p. 349
93 Callwell, ed., *Field-Marshal Sir Henry Wilson*, vol. II, p. 73
94 Major-General Sir Frederick Maurice (1871–1951) had seen action during the Battle of Mons in 1914, and then been posted to London as Director of Military Operations in 1915. In 1916 he had been promoted to the rank of major-general.
95 Lloyd George, *War Memoirs*, vol. 2, p. 1,725
96 John Toland, *No Man's Land: 1918, the Last Year of the Great War*, University of Nebraska Press (2002), p. 8
97 Lloyd George, *War Memoirs*, vol. 2, p. 1,726
98 Callwell, ed., *Field-Marshal Sir Henry Wilson*, vol. II, pp. 73-4
99 Lloyd George, *War Memoirs*, vol. 2, p. 1,727
100 Callwell, ed., *Field-Marshal Sir Henry Wilson*, vol. II, p. 74
101 Philip Sassoon letter to Lord Esher, 23 March 1918, Esher papers
102 Jones, *Lloyd George*, p. 145
103 Riddell, *Lord Riddell's War Diary 1914–1918*, p. 320
104 Callwell, ed., *Field-Marshal Sir Henry Wilson*, vol. II, p. 76

105 Clemenceau, *Grandeur and Misery of Victory*, p. 35
106 Lloyd George, *War Memoirs*, vol. 2, p. 1,740
107 Callwell, ed., *Field-Marshal Sir Henry Wilson*, vol. II, p. 78. The room at the town hall, now known as the 'Hall of the Unified Command' has been preserved as it was in 1918 but now displays murals and a stained glass window depicting scenes from the conference.
108 *Die Ursachen des Deutschen Zusammenbruchs im Jahre 1918*, vol. III, Deutsche Verlagsgesellschaft für Politik (1928), p. 138
109 Haig's Order of the Day, 11 April 1918, Sir Philip Sassoon papers, Houghton Hall archive
110 Lloyd George, *War Memoirs*, vol. 2, p. 1,835
111 *Hansard*, 9 April 1918
112 Lloyd George, *War Memoirs*, vol. 2, p. 1,778
113 Ibid, p. 1,675
114 *The Times*, 7 May 1918
115 Barnes and Nicholson, eds, *The Leo Amery Diaries*, vol. 1, entry for 7 May 1918, p. 219
116 *Morning Post*, 24 January 1918
117 Letter from Colonel Repington to Philip Sassoon dated 2 April 1918, Sir Philip Sassoon papers, Houghton Hall archive
118 Stanley Baldwin (1867–1947), Conservative MP for Bewdley from 1908. Financial Secretary to the Treasury 1917–21. Former parliamentary private secretary to Bonar Law.
119 Keith Middlemas and John Barnes, *Baldwin: A Biography*, Weidenfeld & Nicolson (1969), p. 68
120 *Hansard*, 9 May 1918
121 Times change, as Boris Johnson, Lloyd George's successor 100 years later, could testify.
122 *Hansard*, 9 May 1918
123 Heffer, *Staring at God*, p. 715
124 Rhodes James, ed., *Memoirs of a Conservative*, pp. 73–4
125 Ibid, p. 73
126 Frances Lloyd George, *The Years That Are Past*, p. 127
127 Oliver, Viscount Esher, ed., *Journals and Letters of Reginald Viscount Esher*, vol. 4: 1916–1930, letter from Esher to Maurice Hankey dated 9 May 1918, p. 199
128 *Hansard*, 9 May 1918
129 *The Times*, 10 May 1918
130 Barnes and Nicholson, eds, *The Leo Amery Diaries*, vol. 1, diary entry for 9 May 1918, p. 220
131 *Hansard*, 9 May 1918
132 Rhodes James, ed., *Memoirs of a Conservative*, p. 73
133 McEwen, ed., *The Riddell Diaries 1908–1923*, diary entry for 11 May 1918, p. 226
134 Jones, *Lloyd George*, p. 152
135 Roberts, *The Chief*, p. 352
136 Michael Neiberg, *The Second Battle of the Marne*, Indiana University Press (2008), p. 130

137 *Edinburgh Evening News*, 9 August 1918
138 *The Times*, 10 August 1918
139 *Western Mail*, 10 August 1918
140 Maurice Elvey (1887–1967) was one of the most prolific early British film directors, making nearly 200 films 1913–57.
141 *The Life Story of David Lloyd George* (1918) was widely advertised but not in the end released. Long believed to have been destroyed, it was discovered in the archive of the Wales Film and Television Archive in 1994. Fully restored, it finally received its world premiere in Cardiff in 1996.
142 John Thomas Job (1867–1938) from Llandybie in Carmarthenshire was the winner of the Bardic Chair on three occasions: 1897, 1903 and 1918.
143 In order to vote, women aged 30 or over, or their husband, were required to own property or land with a rateable value of more than £5, in the constituency where they were registered to vote. As a result of the new legislation, the male electorate increased from 5.2 million to 12.9 million. Some 8.5 million women were also included in the electorate for the first time. It would not be until 1928 that men and women would be able to vote on an equal basis in the UK.
144 Danny House is a large Elizabethan red-brick mansion near Hurstpierpoint, and at the foot of Wolstonbury Hill.
145 Sir Henry Norman (1858–1939), Liberal Member of Parliament for Wolverhampton South 1900–10 and for Blackburn 1910–23. In 1909–10 he organized the Budget League, to rally support in the country for Lloyd George's People's Budget.
146 McEwen, ed., *The Riddell Diaries 1908–1923*, p. 233
147 Admiral Lord Charles de la Poer Beresford (1846–1919), former naval commander and Member of Parliament
148 According to the Bank of England, that amount would have been worth over £4.5 million in 2023.
149 Sir Howard Spicer (1872–1926), businessman, wholesale stationer and printer. He was also a technical advisor at the War Office during the First World War.
150 McEwen, ed., *The Riddell Diaries 1908–1923*, p. 233
151 Roskill, *Hankey*, vol. I, pp. 502–3
152 William Dudley Ward (1877–1946), MP for Southampton 1906–22. He won a bronze medal for Great Britain in rowing at the 1908 Olympic games, having three times previously rowed for Cambridge against Oxford in the University Boat Race. In 1913 he married Freda, 17 years his junior, who after the war would have a long-standing affair with the Prince of Wales.
153 Letter from Guest to Lloyd George dated 3 August 1918, Lloyd George papers, Parliamentary Archives, Westminster
154 Barry McGill, 'Lloyd George's Timing of the 1918 Election', *The British Journal of Politics*, Cambridge (1974), notes made by Norman following a telephone conversation with Lloyd George on 19 September 1918, p. 118
155 Imperial preference had been one of the great causes of both Bonar Law and Lord Beaverbrook. This was that free trade should exist within the Empire to protect industries, but that there should be trade tariffs imposed on other imported

goods. Lloyd George and the Liberals had always previously believed in complete free trade. This had also been one of the main issues that had caused Winston Churchill to leave the Conservatives and join the Liberals in 1904.

156 McGill, 'Lloyd George's Timing of the 1918 Election', *The British Journal of Politics*, p. 117
157 McEwen, ed., *The Riddell Diaries 1908–1923*, p. 234
158 Sir Alexander Porter (1853–1926), Liberal politician and Lord Mayor of Manchester 1917–18
159 The Manchester Hippodrome at 44–50 Oxford Street was designed by the well-known theatre architects, Frank Matcham and Co, who had also built the London Hippodrome and Coliseum. It opened in 1904 but was demolished in 1935 to make way for the Gaumont Cinema. The site today is a multi-storey car park.
160 *Manchester Evening News*, 12 September 1918
161 Ibid
162 *Pall Mall Gazette*, 13 September 1918
163 Lloyd George was born in a small, terraced house at 5, New York Place, in Chorlton-on-Medlock, Manchester. The house was painted by L. S. Lowry before it was demolished in 1958.
164 *Manchester Evening News*, 12 September 1918
165 Ibid
166 Ibid
167 Ibid
168 Ibid
169 Ibid
170 The Midland, on St Peter Street, serves today as the main hotel when the annual political party conferences are held in Manchester. This grand Edwardian baroque building was opened in 1903 by the Midland railway in connection with Manchester Central station, the northern terminus for its services to London's St Pancras station. At that time the hotel included a 1,000-seat theatre.
171 Albert Hall, 27 Peter Street, Manchester, was built in 1908 as the Methodist Central Hall in the city, on land that was a short distance from the site of the 1819 Peterloo Massacre. It is now a music venue.
172 The Reform Club was a private members club located in Spring Gardens in the city centre, for the leading members of the Liberal Party in Manchester. The building is now home to the Grand Pacific bar and restaurant.
173 Sir William Milligan M.D. (1864–1929) was a consultant aurist and laryngologist at the Manchester Royal Infirmary. A committed Liberal, he stood unsuccessfully for Parliament in Salford in 1922.
174 Lloyd George had succumbed during the peak period of infection of the H1N1 flu pandemic, known as the Spanish Flu. In the UK the virus killed an estimated 250,000 people and is believed to have caused the deaths of at least 50 million people around the world. When Prime Minister Boris Johnson was admitted to hospital for COVID-19 during the pandemic in 2020, he was the same age as Lloyd George had been in 1918.

175 *The Scotsman*, 14 September 1918
176 George Newnham (1865–1954) was resident office keeper and personal attendant to the Prime Minister at 10 Downing Street.
177 Roskill, *Hankey*, vol. I, diary entry for 24 September 1917, p. 604
178 *Manchester Evening News*, 23 September 1918
179 Frances Lloyd George, *The Years That Are Past*, p. 136
180 McEwen, ed., *The Riddell Diaries 1908–1923*, p. 236
181 Ibid, p. 237
182 Since the surrender of the Serbian state in 1915, the remnants of the government and armed forces had established themselves on the Greek island of Corfu, before re-engaging with the Allied cause on the Salonika front. With the assistance of the Royal Navy, by the end of February 1916, 135,000 Serbians had been evacuated to Corfu.
183 Prince Max von Baden (1867–1929), Chancellor of Germany, 3 October–8 November 1918
184 Wilson had set out his 'Fourteen Points' in a speech to the United States Congress on 8 January 1918, proposing criteria upon which the post-war world could be reconstructed. These included the restoration of Belgium, the return of Alsace-Lorraine to France, the freedom of the seas, disarmament, the creation of the League of Nations, the creation of independent states for Poland and Serbia with access to the sea, and the autonomous development for the peoples of the Austro-Hungarian Empire.
185 McEwen, ed., *The Riddell Diaries 1908–1923*, diary entry for 27 October 1918, p. 244
186 Woodrow Wilson Presidential Library, reference WWP25239
187 McEwen, ed., *The Riddell Diaries 1908–1923*, diary entry for 27 October 1918, p. 244
188 Ibid, p. 242
189 Ibid
190 Sir Rosslyn Wemyss (1864–1933), from 1919 1st Baron Wester Wemyss. He was raised at his ancestral home Wemyss Castle on the coast of Fife in Scotland and joined the Royal Navy as a cadet in 1877.
191 Cabinet Office Papers, National Archives, Kew. Minutes of War Cabinet 485, 14 October 1918.
192 Ibid
193 Kaiser Wilhelm II (1859–1941), Emperor of Germany 1888–1918
194 King George V, diary entry for 14 October 1918. Royal Archives, Windsor Castle, RA/GV/PRIV/GVD/1914–1927
195 Friedrich Ebert (1871–1925), Head of the German government 9 November 1918–13 February 1919. President of Germany 11 February 1919–28 February 1925.
196 Horace Marshall (1865–1936), Lord Mayor of London 1918–19, later 1st Baron Marshall of Chipstead. Marshall was a wholesale newspaper publisher and distributor. His elder daughter Nellie married the British film producer and distributor J. Arthur Rank.
197 Ibid
198 *The Times*, 11 November 1918
199 Frances Lloyd George, *The Years That Are Past*, p. 136

200 Horatio Nelson had lost his life commanding the British victory against the navies of France and Spain off Cape Trafalgar on 21 October 1805. The news first reached London on 6 November 1805.
201 R. Coupland, ed., *The War Speeches of William Pitt, the Younger*, Oxford (1915), p. 351
202 *The Times*, 11 November 1918
203 Frances Lloyd George, *The Years That Are Past*, p. 136
204 Ibid
205 *The Times*, 11 November 1918
206 Ibid
207 McEwen, ed., *The Riddell Diaries 1908–1923*, p. 246
208 Richard Rhys O'Brien, *The Campaigns of Margaret Lloyd George, the Wife of the Prime Minister 1916–1922*, Y Lolfa (2022), p. 25

10: PRIME MINISTER FOR LIFE

1 Barnes and Nicolson, eds, *The Leo Amery Diaries*, vol. 1, p. 243
2 *Evening News*, 13 November 1918
3 Churchill, *The World Crisis 1911–1918*, pp. 839–40
4 *Evening News*, 13 November 1918
5 Ibid
6 *The Times*, 12 November 1918
7 James Lowther (1855–1949), later 1st Viscount Ullswater. Speaker of the House of Commons 1905–21, MP for Penrith 1886–1921
8 *The Times*, 12 November 1918
9 Callwell, ed., *Field-Marshal Sir Henry Wilson*, vol. II, p. 149
10 Jones, *Lloyd George*, p. 158
11 Robert Boothby (1900–1986), Conservative Member of Parliament for Aberdeen and Kincardine East 1924–50, and then for East Aberdeenshire 1950–8.
12 Robert Blake and William Roger Louis (eds), *Churchill*, Clarendon Press (1996), p. 106
13 *Hansard*, 28 March 1945
14 Jones, *Lloyd George*, p. 160
15 It was an unfortunate turn of phrase, given the permanent link today between 'National Socialism' and the ideology of Adolf Hitler's Nazi Party (Nationalsozialistische Deutsche Arbeiterpartei/National Socialist German Workers Party), which was founded in 1920. However, it may also in part explain the slowness of Lloyd George in the 1930s to recognize the danger presented by Hitler's regime.
16 Riddell, *Lord Riddell's War Diary 1914–1918*, entry for 'April' 1918, p. 324
17 Ibid, pp. 309–12
18 Rhodes James, ed., *Memoirs of a Conservative*, p. 56
19 Ibid, pp. 58–9
20 Chamberlain was a member of the Liberal Unionist group in Parliament, which in 1886 had broken with Gladstone's Liberal Party over the question of Home Rule for Ireland. The Liberal Unionists supported the Conservative Party in government and Chamberlain served as Colonial Secretary in the governments

of Lord Salisbury and Arthur Balfour. In 1912 the Liberal Unionists formally merged with the Conservatives to create the Conservatives and Unionist Party.
21. Wrench, *Geoffrey Dawson and Our Times*, p. 153
22. *Sheffield Daily Telegraph*, 18 November 1918
23. Ibid
24. Ibid
25. McEwen, ed., *The Riddell Diaries 1908–1923*, letter from Northcliffe to Riddell dated 3 October 1918, p. 419
26. H. A. L. Fisher (1865–1940), President of the Board of Education 1916–22. From 1926 until his death he was Warden of New College, Oxford.
27. H. A. L. Fisher, diary entry for 6 November 1918, H. A. L. Fisher papers, Bodleian Library, Oxford
28. The Earl of Oxford and Asquith, *Memories and Reflections 1852–1927*, vol. II, p. 171
29. Jones, *Lloyd George*, p. 160
30. George Bernard Shaw (1856–1950), Irish playwright, writer and political activist
31. Kenneth O. Morgan, *Revolution to Devolution: Reflections on Welsh Democracy*, University of Wales Press (2014), p. 112
32. *St Helen's Examiner*, 30 November 1918
33. *Liverpool Daily Post*, 25 November 1918
34. Roberts, *The Chief*, p. 369
35. Wrench, *Geoffrey Dawson and Our Times*, pp. 169–70
36. Clarke, *My Northcliffe Diary*, p. 117
37. Riddell, *Lord Riddell's Intimate Diary of the Peace Conference and After*, p. 3
38. McEwen, ed., *The Riddell Diaries 1908–1923*, letter from Northcliffe to Riddell dated 3 October 1918, p. 250
39. Moreton Frewen (1853–1924), writer and adventurer. He had also been MP for North East Cork 1910–11. Frewen married the American heiress Clara Jerome, who was the sister of Winston Churchill's mother Jennie.
40. John St Loe Strachey (1860–1927), editor of *The Spectator* 1887–1925. He was a contemporary of both Lord Curzon and Cecil Spring-Rice at Eton College and Balliol College, Oxford.
41. Sir Gilbert Parker Bt (1862–1932), Conservative MP for Gravesend 1900–18. A Canadian-born novelist, during the war he had also worked to disseminate pro-British propaganda in the United States of America.
42. G. R. Steele, *Corruption in British Politics, 1895–1930*, Oxford (1987), p. 314
43. Letter from Walter Long to Lloyd George, 23 January 1919, Lloyd George papers, Parliamentary Archives, Westminster
44. McEwen, ed., *The Riddell Diaries 1908–1923*, letter from Northcliffe to Riddell dated 3 October 1918, p. 419
45. *The Times*, 4 December 1918
46. *The Times*, 3 December 1918
47. Viscount Simon, *Retrospect*, Hutchinson (1952), p. 120
48. The Earl of Oxford and Asquith, *Memories and Reflections 1852–1927*, vol. II, pp. 171–2
49. Roberts, *The Chief*, p. 374
50. Ibid

51 The Drill Hall was built in 1914 in East Road, Cambridge. It was demolished in 1993 and the Cambridgeshire County Court now stands on its site.
52 Roberts, *The Chief*, p. 374
53 Jones, *Lloyd George*, p. 162
54 King George V diary, entry for 28 December 1918. Royal Archives, Windsor Castle, RA/GV/PRIV/GVD/1914-1927
55 Among the Sinn Féin members elected was the first woman MP, Constance Markievicz, although the first woman to take her seat in the House of Commons would be Nancy Astor in November 1919.
56 Sinn Féin, meaning 'Ourselves' in Gaelic, was founded by Arthur Griffith in 1905 as a political party committed to establishing an independent Republic of Ireland.
57 McEwen, ed., *The Riddell Diaries 1908–1923*, diary entry for 16 February 1919, p. 257
58 Wrench, *Geoffrey Dawson and Our Times*, p. 180
59 Self, ed., *The Austen Chamberlain Diary Letters*, letter dated 19 January 1919, p. 108
60 Elmwood was Northcliffe's country estate near Broadstairs on the east Kent coast.
61 Roberts, *The Chief*, p. 377
62 Winston S. Churchill, *The World Crisis*, vol. IV: *The Aftermath 1918–1922*, Bloomsbury (2015), p. 85
63 The Hotel Majestic, today called the Peninsula Paris, was a large luxury hotel that had opened in 1908. During the war it had served as a field hospital for wounded officers. The Hotel Astoria has also been a hospital for wounded officers during the war. The hotel no longer exists, and its address is the headquarters of the global media company, Publicis Groupe.
64 Harold Nicolson (1886–1968), British diplomat, writer and politician
65 Harold Nicolson, *Peacemaking 1919*, Methuen (1964), p. 44
66 Sir Clement Wakefield Jones (1880–1963), Assistant Secretary to the War Cabinet 1916–18, Secretary to the British Empire Delegation, 1919
67 Clement Wakefield Jones papers, Bodleian Library, Oxford. Letter dated 22 January 1919.
68 Leila Megáne (1891–1960), Welsh mezzo-soprano opera singer. She was born Margaret Jones in Bethesda, north Wales. She had won first prize in the singing contest at the National Eisteddfod in Colwyn Bay in 1910. Lloyd George had helped her to move to France to advance her career. During the war she had sung to entertain injured soldiers in France.
69 Clement Wakefield Jones papers, Bodleian Library, Oxford. Letter dated 24 January 1919.
70 Jones, *Lloyd George*, p. 167
71 This address is now 23 Rue de l'Amiral d'Estaing. The apartment building today is a co-working office space called Morning, Iéna.
72 Herbert Stern, 1st Baron Michelham (1851–1919), was a member of the Stern banking family. He was also a renowned art collector, philanthropist and horse breeder. The Michelhams' London home, Strawberry Hill house in Twickenham, was one of the social centres of Edwardian high society.

73 Sir Joseph Duveen (1843–1908), Henry Duveen (1854–1919). From 1908 the business was run by Joseph's son, Joseph Duveen, 1st Baron Duveen (1869–1939), considered one of the most influential art dealers of all time. Duveen clients included Henry Clay Frick, William Randolph Hearst, Andrew Mellon and John D. Rockefeller.
74 James Shotwell, *At the Paris Peace Conference*, Macmillan (1937), p. 170
75 Frances Lloyd George, *The Years That Are Past*, p. 165
76 Kaiser Wilhelm I (1797–1888), King of Prussia 1861–88, Emperor of Germany 1871–88. Grandfather of Kaiser Wilhelm II.
77 The Franco-Prussian War of 1870–1 led to the defeat of Napoleon III, the collapse of the government of the Second Empire, and the proclamation of the French Third Republic.
78 The Paris Commune was a revolutionary government that seized power in the city 18 March–22 May 1871, following the Franco-Prussian War.
79 David Lloyd George, *The Truth about the Peace Treaties*, vol. I, Gollancz (1938), p. 133
80 Their representatives included Robert Borden for Canada, Billy Hughes for Australia, Smuts for South Africa, the Maharaja Sir Ganga Singh for India, and Prime Minister William Massey from New Zealand.
81 Sir Robert Borden (1854–1937), Conservative politician and Prime Minister of Canada 1911–20.
82 Tim Cook, *Warlords, Borden, Mackenzie King, and Canada's World Wars*, Penguin (2013), p. 141
83 *Hansard*, 16 April 1919
84 *Sheffield Independent*, 2 December 1918
85 The British interest in Mosul was to secure the oil they believed existed in northern Iraq.
86 James Barr, *A Line in the Sand: Britain, France and the Struggle that Shaped the Middle East*, Simon & Schuster (2011), p. 72
87 Ibid, p. 387
88 Clemenceau, *Grandeur and Misery of Victory*, p. 113
89 Ibid
90 Riddell, *Lord Riddell's Intimate Diary of the Peace Conference and After*, p. 42
91 Sean Dennis Cashman, *America in the Age of the Titans: The Progressive Era and World War I*, NYU Press (1988), p. 526
92 Margaret MacMillan, *Peacemakers: Six Months that Changed the World*, John Murray (2001), p. 48
93 James Lees-Milne, *Harold Nicolson: 1886-1929*, Chatto and Windus (1980), p. 113
94 Clemenceau, *Grandeur and Misery of Victory*, p. 138
95 Stephen Bonsal, *Unfinished Business*, Doubleday Doran (1944), p. 72
96 Clemenceau lived at 8 Avenue Benjamin Franklin in the 16th *arrondissement* of Paris from 1895 until his death in 1929. The Musée Clemenceau preserves the apartment as it was when he lived there.
97 Émile Cottin (1896–1936) was a cabinet maker from Creil in northern France. He was initially sentenced to death but this was reduced to ten years' imprisonment. In 1936 he joined the anarchist Durruti Column that fought against General Franco in the Spanish Civil War and was killed in action at the Battle of Farlete in Aragon.

NOTES

98 Taylor, ed., *Lloyd George: A Diary by Frances Stevenson*, p. 174
99 Robert Smillie (1857–1940), President of the Scottish Miners Federation 1894–1918 and 1922–8.
100 Self, ed., *The Austen Chamberlain Diary Letters*, letter dated 9 February 1919, p. 108
101 Jones, *Lloyd George*, p. 171
102 The Spartacist Uprising in Berlin, 5–12 January 1919, was led by the Communists Karl Liebknecht and Rosa Luxemburg. They founded the Marxist Spartacus League and had wanted to establish a Bolshevik-style republic. Both were killed in the suppression of the uprising.
103 Churchill, *The World Crisis*, vol. IV: *The Aftermath 1918–1922*, pp. 126–7
104 Clemenceau, *Grandeur and Misery of Victory*, p. 220
105 Jones, *Lloyd George*, p. 171
106 Paul Mantoux, *The Deliberations of the Council of Four (March 24–June 29, 1919)*, vol. 1, Princeton University Press (1992), p. 51
107 John Maynard Keynes, *Essays in Biography*, Macmillan (1933), p. 36
108 MacMillan, *Peacemakers*, p. 192
109 Peter Clarke, *Keynes in Action: Truth and Expediency in Public Policy*, Cambridge University Press (2022), p. 34
110 John Maynard Keynes, *Essays in Biography*, Macmillan (1933), p. 10
111 MacMillan, *Peacemakers*, p. 48
112 Keynes, *Essays in Biography*, p. 12
113 Self, ed., *The Austen Chamberlain Diary Letters*, letter dated 21 December 1919, p. 122
114 Wickham Steed (1871–1956), editor of *The Times* 1919–22
115 McEwen, ed., *The Riddell Diaries 1908–1923*, diary entry for 28 March 1919, p. 262
116 Ibid
117 Ibid
118 Ibid, diary entry for 5 April 1919, p. 265
119 Ibid, diary entry for 9 April 1919, p. 266
120 Beaverbrook, *Men and Power 1917–1918*, pp. 329–34
121 *Hansard*, 16 April 1919
122 Ibid
123 A reference to a German warship firing at Lord Northcliffe's country house at Broadstairs in February 1917
124 Self, ed., *The Neville Chamberlain Diary Letters*, p. 322
125 Ibid, letter dated 18 April 1919, p. 112
126 Bernard Baruch (1870–1965), American financier and advisor to President Wilson. Baruch was also a great friend of Winston Churchill and would save him from financial ruin following the Wall Street Crash of 1929.
127 Patrick Weil, *The Madman in the White House: Sigmund Freud, Ambassador Bullitt, and the Lost Psychobiography of Woodrow Wilson*, Harvard University Press (2023), p. 113
128 Ibid
129 Louis XIV (1638–1715), King of France 1643–1715. The 'Sun King' and creator of the Palace of Versailles.
130 Taylor, ed., *Lloyd George: A Diary by Frances Stevenson*, p. 187
131 Callwell, ed., *Field-Marshal Sir Henry Wilson*, vol. II, p. 201

132 Ibid
133 Clemenceau, *Grandeur and Misery of Victory*, pp. 373–4
134 *Citizenships: France, Poland and Germany since 1789*, German History Museum, Berlin, exhibition catalogue published by Piper Munich (2022).
135 Riddell, *Lord Riddell's Intimate Diary of the Peace Conference and After*, pp. 101–2
136 Alderman Sir Stephen Penfold (1842–1925), Mayor of Folkestone 1913–19
137 *The Scotsman*, 30 June 1919
138 Clement Wakefield Jones papers, Bodleian Library, Oxford. From the unpublished work *The Dominions and the Peace Conference* by Clement Wakefield Jones.
139 The Prince of Wales, later Edward VIII; his last Christian name was David.
140 King George V, diary entry for 29 June 1919, Royal Archives, Windsor Castle, RA/GV/PRIV/GVD/1914–1927
141 That laurel wreath has been preserved and is on display at the Lloyd George Museum in Llanystumdwy.
142 Taylor, ed., *Lloyd George: A Diary by Frances Stevenson*, p. 187
143 The Order of Merit was created in 1902 by Edward VII, is restricted to a maximum of 24 members, and is regarded as the highest civil honour the Monarch can bestow. The only British Prime Ministers to have received it are, in order, Arthur Balfour, Lloyd George, Winston Churchill, Clement Attlee, Harold Macmillan and Margaret Thatcher.
144 King George V, diary entry for 12 August 1919, Royal Archives, Windsor Castle, RA/GV/PRIV/GVD/1914–1927
145 Beaverbrook, *Men and Power 1917–1918*, p. 324
146 Ibid, p. 325

11: THE RULES OF THE ROAD

1 Arthur John Maundy Gregory (1877–1941). In 1933 he was convicted under the 1925 Honours (Prevention of Abuses) Act, and is still the only person to have been successfully prosecuted for that offence.
2 These buildings are now known as the Norman Shaw Buildings (after the architect who designed them) on Victoria Embankment and are part of the Parliamentary estate: 38 Parliament Street also now contains offices for Members of Parliament.
3 Prince Albert, Duke of York (1895–1952), second son of King George V, later King George VI 1936–52
4 Arthur Askew was Head of the Metropolitan Police's Criminal Investigation Department from 1934 to 1938.
5 *The Spectator* (1974), vol. 232, p. 612
6 Andrew Cook, *Cash for Honours: The True Life of Maundy Gregory*, History Press (2008), p. 81
7 Tom Cullen, *Maundy Gregory, Purveyor of Honours*, Bodley Head (1974), p. 93
8 Ibid, p. 107
9 H. J. Hanham, *The Sale of Honours in Late Victorian England*, Victorian Studies, vol. 3, no. 3 (1960), p. 277
10 Queen Victoria (1819–1901), Queen of the United Kingdom 1837–1901. Empress of India 1876–1901.

11 Coincidentally, this was also Lord Stamfordham, then Arthur Bigge, who served as private secretary to Queen Victoria from 1895 until her death in 1901. He then returned to serve King George V in the same position from 1910.
12 Hanham, *The Sale of Honours in Late Victorian England*, p. 281
13 Rhodes James, ed., *Memoirs of a Conservative*, p. 279
14 At 2023 prices, according to the Bank of England, that would be more than £2 million.
15 Cullen, *Maundy Gregory, Purveyor of Honours*, p. 95
16 Sir Colin Reith Coote (1893–1979), Member of Parliament for Wisbech 1917–18, then the Isle of Ely 1918–22. Later editor of *The Daily Telegraph* 1950–64.
17 Cullen, *Maundy Gregory, Purveyor of Honours*, p. 95
18 Letter from Freddie Guest to Lloyd George dated 16 May 1919, Lloyd George papers, Parliamentary Archive
19 The by-election was held on 1 March but the result not declared until 14 March to allow time for the ballots of servicemen overseas to be counted.
20 Beaverbrook, *Men and Power 1917–1918*, p. 395, letter from Lloyd George to Birkenhead dated 15 March 1919.
21 Sir Mark Sykes (1879–1919). In 1916 he had drafted the secret Sykes-Picot agreement between the British and French governments concerning the partition of the Ottoman Empire after the war. He died in Paris of Spanish Flu during the Peace Conference.
22 Viscount Birkenhead, *Points of View*, vol. II, Hodder & Stoughton (1922), pp. 198–9
23 McEwen, ed., *The Riddell Diaries 1908–1923*, diary entry for 12–15 July 1919, p. 285
24 Sir George Younger Bt (1851–1929), MP for Ayr Burghs 1906–22, created Viscount Younger of Leckie in 1923. From 1916 to 1923 he was Chairman of the Conservative and Unionist Party Organisation.
25 *The New York Times*, 25 July 1919
26 Ibid
27 The Royal Commission chaired by Sir John Sankey, established in February 1919, produced its report in June that year.
28 *Sunday Mirror*, 7 December 1919
29 *Reynolds's Newspaper*, 7 December 1919
30 Lady Aline Sassoon (1867–1909), wife of Sir Edward Sassoon Bt MP (1856–1912)
31 Baron Gustave de Rothschild (1829–1911), financier and head of the Rothschild family business in France
32 The address for this property, which no longer stands, is today 45 Park Lane. The site is currently occupied by the hotel 45 Park Lane.
33 Taylor, ed., *Lloyd George: A Diary by Frances Stevenson*, entry dated 11 December 1919, p. 190
34 Ibid, p. 192
35 The Spen Valley by-election was held on 20 December 1919 but the result not declared until 3 January 1920.
36 H. A. L. Fisher, diary entry 28 January 1920, Bodleian Library, Oxford
37 Ibid, 4 February 1920
38 Riddell, *Lord Riddell's Intimate Diary of the Peace Conference and After*, pp. 159–60

39 Sir Robert Horne (1871–1940), MP for Glasgow Hillhead 1918–37. Minister for Labour January 1919–20, President of the Board of Trade 1920–1, and Chancellor of the Exchequer 1921–2.
40 Sir Laming Worthington-Evans (1868–1931), MP for Colchester 1910–29, junior Minister at the Ministry of Munitions 1916–18, Minister of Blockade 1918–19, Pensions Minister 1919–20, Minister without Portfolio 1920–1, Secretary of State for War 1921–2
41 Riddell, *Lord Riddell's Intimate Diary of the Peace Conference and After*, diary entry for 1 February 1920, p. 166
42 Philip Lloyd-Greame (1884–1972) after 1924 was known as Philip Cunliffe-Lister and from 1935 as The Viscount Swinton. In 1955 he was created 1st Earl of Swinton. Conservative Member of Parliament for Hendon 1918–35.
43 Philip Cunliffe-Lister, *I Remember*, Hutchinson (1948), p. 156
44 The election was held on 12 February but the result not declared until 25 February 1920.
45 Sir Samuel Hoare (1880–1959), Conservative MP for Chelsea 1910–44
46 McEwen, ed., diary entry for 28 March 1919, p. 307
47 Fiume in the northern Adriatic, known today as Rijeka, is the main seaport in Croatia. Between 1920 and 1924 it became an independent state before being incorporated into Italy. After the Second World War it became part of Yugoslavia.
48 Taylor, ed., *Lloyd George: A Diary by Frances Stevenson*, entry dated 14 February 1920, p. 198
49 Sir David Low (1891–1963), New Zealand born cartoonist who worked in Australia before moving to England in 1919. He is particularly known for his character Colonel Blimp, and for his satirical portrayals of Hitler, Stalin and Mussolini in the 1930s.
50 David Low, *Lloyd George and Co*, Allen & Unwin (1921)
51 David Low, *Low's Autobiography*, Simon & Schuster (1957) p.144
52 Riddell, *Lord Riddell's Intimate Diary of the Peace Conference and After*, diary entry for 1 February 1920, pp. 168–9
53 Taylor, ed., *Lloyd George: A Diary by Frances Stevenson*, entry dated 14 February 1920, p. 201
54 Trent Park is located on the ancient Enfield Chase, on the northern edge of London.
55 Lord Curzon switched positions in the Cabinet with Balfour, who took his place as Lord President of the Council. Francesco Nitti (1868–1953), a member of the centre left Radical Party, was Prime Minister of Italy from 23 June 1919 until 15 June 1920.
56 Maurice Hankey diaries, 8 May 1920, Hankey papers, Churchill Archives Centre, University of Cambridge
57 Lloyd George's health had failed at the end of 1910 following his gruelling schedule during the general election of December that year. Sir Arthur Markham, 1st Baronet Markham of Beachborough Park (1866-1916), MP for Mansfield from 1900 to 1916.
58 Henry 'Chips' Channon (1897–1958), future Conservative MP for Southend West 1935–58. Channon himself was bisexual.

59 Simon Heffer, ed., *Henry 'Chips' Channon: The Diaries:1938–43*, Hutchinson (2021), pp. 134–5
60 Josep Maria Sert (1874–1945), Catalan artist based in Barcelona and friend of Salvador Dalí
61 The Ballets Russes company was regarded as one of the most influential in the twentieth century. It performed between 1909 and 1929, giving performances across Europe and the Americas.
62 Glyn Philpot (1884–1937), British painter and sculptor who painted the portraits of both Siegfried Sassoon and his cousin Philip
63 This frieze is still at Port Lympne, although now located in a different room.
64 Hansard, 22 December 1919.
65 General Sir Nevil Macready (1862–1946), General Officer Commanding-in-Chief in Ireland
66 David Lloyd George to Winston Churchill, letter dated 10 May 1920, Lloyd George papers, Parliamentary Archives. Éamon de Valera (1882-1975) President of Sinn Féin and President of the Dáil Éireann
67 Lloyd George letter to Andrew Bonar Law, 10 May 1920, Lloyd George papers, Parliamentary Archives
68 Andrew Bonar Law letter to Lloyd George, 11 May 1920, Lloyd George papers, Parliamentary Archives
69 Hankey diaries, 14 May 1920, Hankey papers, Churchill Archive Centre, University of Cambridge
70 Ibid
71 Thomas Jones, *Whitehall Diary*, vol. 1: 1916–1925, Oxford University Press (1969), p. 113
72 Hankey diaries, 14 May 1920, Hankey papers, Churchill Archive Centre, University of Cambridge
73 *Daily Mail*, 15 May 1920
74 Riddell, *Lord Riddell's Intimate Diary of the Peace Conference and After*, p. 194
75 Philip Tilden (1887–1956), English society architect whose notable patrons included Philip Sassoon, Winston Churchill, Beaverbrook and Lloyd George.
76 Philip Tilden, *True Remembrances: The Memoirs of an Architect*, Country Life (1954), p. 74
77 Maurice Hankey, note from 'The Conversations at Hythe', The National Archives, Kew (TNA), CAB 24/105/97, 17 May 1920
78 Clemenceau, *Grandeur and Misery of Victory*, p. 288
79 Philip Sassoon letter to Lloyd George relating to his meeting with Lord Derby on 2 June 1920, Lloyd George papers, Parliamentary Archives
80 Paul Deschanel (1855–1922), President of France 18 February–21 September 1920
81 Philip Sassoon letter to Lloyd George relating to his meeting with Lord Derby on 2 June 1920, Lloyd George papers, Parliamentary Archives
82 CAB 24/109/1 11 July 1920, Cabinet memorandum on the presentation by the German delegation at the Spa conference, National Archives, Kew
83 The proportions were 52 per cent to France, 22 to Britain, 10 to Italy, 8 to Belgium, and the rest to the other Allies. Belgium, in view of its sufferings during the German occupation, was to have priority up to the amount of £100 million.

84 Constantin Fehrenbach (1852–1926), leader of the Centre Party, Chancellor of Germany 25 June 1920–10 May 1921
85 Otto Gessler (1875–1955), liberal politician, Defence Minister 1920–8, Mayor of Nuremberg 1913–19
86 Philip Sassoon letter to Lady Desborough, 6 July 1920, Desborough papers, Hertfordshire County Archive
87 Reginald Dyer (1864–1927), a career soldier and officer of the British Indian Army who had commanded the Seistan Force during the First World War
88 William, Lord Hunter (1865–1957), former Liberal MP for Govan and Solicitor General for Scotland, 1910–11. In 1911 he was appointed as a Senator of the College of Justice in Scotland.
89 *Reports on the Punjab Disturbances April 1919*, H. M. Stationery Office (1920), p.30
90 'Frocks' referred to the frock coats worn by civilian government ministers.
91 Callwell, ed., *Field-Marshall Sir Henry Wilson*, vol.II, p. 238
92 Hansard 8th July 1920
93 Ibid
94 Sir William Sutherland to David Lloyd George, 9 July 1920, in Martin Gilbert, *The Churchill Documents, vol. 9, Disruption and Chaos*, July 1919–March 1921 (Hillsdale College Press, 2008), pp.1140–41.
95 *Aberdeen Press and Journal*, 13 July 1920
96 Mohandas K. Gandhi (1869–1948) later known as Mahatma Gandhi, was a lawyer and anti-colonial Indian nationalist. Gandhi was the leader of the movement of nonviolent resistance against British rule in India.
97 The Montagu–Chelmsford reforms were introduced through the Government of India Act 1919. These increased the role of representative institutions in India but reserved the ultimate executive authority with the Viceroy, who could overrule them.
98 Frederic Thesiger, 1st Viscount Chelmsford, Viceroy of India 1916 to 1921.
99 V. Geetha (ed), Mohandas K. Gandhi, *Soul Force: Gandhi's writings on peace*, Tara (2004) p.160
100 The term 'lynch-pin' was used by Winston Churchill in his history of the First World War, *The World Crisis, vol. IV, The Aftermath 1918–1922* (1929).
101 Lev Kamenev (1883–1936), Bolshevik politician and close associate of Lenin. He was later executed during one of Stalin's purges.
102 Leonid Krasin (1870–1926), Soviet diplomat who became his country's first ambassador to France in 1924 and then ambassador to the United Kingdom from 1925 until his death, of natural causes, the following year
103 Churchill, *The World Crisis*, vol. 4: *The Aftermath, 1918–1922*, p. 179
104 Riddell, *Lord Riddell's Intimate Diary of the Peace Conference and After*, p. 230
105 Ibid
106 Albert I (1875–1934), King of Belgium 1909–34
107 Giovanni Giolitti (1842–1928), Prime Minister of Italy 15 June 1920–4 July 1921. A politician from the liberal left, he had been Prime Minister on four previous occasions before the First World War.
108 Riddell, *Lord Riddell's Intimate Diary of the Peace Conference and After*, p. 232
109 Ibid

110 Stella Rudman, *Lloyd George and the Appeasement of Germany 1919–1945*, Cambridge Scholars Publishing (2011), p. 70
111 McEwen, ed., *The Riddell Diaries 1908–1923*, diary entry for 28 March 1919, p. 322
112 Ibid, pp. 322–3

12: Solver of the Insoluble

1 From the poem 'Casement' by Terence MacSwiney
2 Terence MacSwiney, *Battle-Cries*, The Bank and File (1918), p. 53
3 Terence MacSwiney (1879–1920), Sinn Féin MP for Mid Cork 1918–20, Lord Mayor of Cork March–October 1920
4 Sir Roger Casement (1864–1916), Irish diplomat and nationalist executed for treason for colluding with the German state to smuggle arms to Ireland for use by the IRA
5 Irish Republican Army, the nationalist paramilitary organization
6 James Vernon, *Hunger: A Modern History*, Harvard University Press (2009), p. 68
7 Edward Shortt (1862–1935), Home Secretary 1919–22, Coalition Liberal MP for Newcastle upon Tyne West
8 Seán McConville, *Irish Political Prisoners 1848–1922: Theatres of War*, Taylor & Francis (2005), p. 745
9 Riddell, *Lord Riddell's Intimate Diary of the Peace Conference and After*, p. 234
10 *Liverpool Daily Post*, 26 August 1920
11 McConville, *Irish Political Prisoners 1848–1922*, p. 745
12 Morgan, ed., *David Lloyd George: Family Letters 1885–1936*, p. 192
13 Ibid
14 Michael Collins (1890–1922), President of the Irish Republican Brotherhood 1920–2, Minister for Finance in the Ministry of Dáil Éireann 1919–22 (the self-declared government and parliament of the Irish Republic), and Sinn Féin MP for Cork South 1918–22
15 Frank Thornton (1891–1965) was at that time the third-ranking member of the intelligence staff of the IRA. He had also taken part in the 1916 Dublin Easter Rising.
16 Seán Flood (1898–1920) had also taken part in the Easter Rising.
17 The Squad was a special unit created by Michael Collins, also known as the Twelve Apostles.
18 McGreevy, *Great Hatred*, p. 203
19 The Act received Royal Ascent on 23 December 1920 and would come into force on 21 May 1921. It maintained the control of the UK Parliament on international matters like foreign, defence and trade policy. Northern Ireland was defined as the six of the nine counties of Ulster, with a similar border to that which exists today, and would have an opt-in to an all-Ireland Parliament, but could not be coerced.
20 *Freeman's Journal*, 11 October 1920
21 Ibid
22 *Hamilton Daily Times*, 11 October 1920
23 William George, *My Brother and I*, p. 266
24 Sir John Lavery (1856–1941), Belfast-born painter known best for his portrait and conversation-piece works. He established his studio in London in 1888 and was also an official war artist during the First World War.

25 *Western Gazette* 12 November 1920
26 Ibid
27 The Cairo Gang were British intelligence officers of the Dublin District Special Branch. It's believed that the officers had previously served in the Middle East, based in Cairo. Others claim that the gang's name came about because they all frequented the Cairo Café, then in Grafton Street in Dublin.
28 The game was a charity match between Dublin and Tipperary to raise funds for the dependants of Republican prisoners.
29 Tipperary player Michael Hogan (1896–1920). The Hogan Stand at Croke Park is named in his memory.
30 *Hansard*, 22 November 1920
31 *The Observer*, 8 May 2011
32 *New York Times*, 27 November 1920
33 Callwell, ed., *Field-Marshal Sir Henry Wilson*, vol. II, p. 270
34 *The Times*, 22 November 1920
35 Ibid, 27 November 1920
36 Callwell, ed., *Field-Marshal Sir Henry Wilson*, vol. II, p. 270
37 Ibid, p. 275
38 The popular Irish song about the Dubliner Molly Malone.
39 Riddell, *Lord Riddell's Intimate Diary of the Peace Conference and After*, p. 259
40 Grigg, *Lloyd George*, p. 265
41 This seems to be a bit harsh. It is correct to say that Chequers doesn't have a long-range view from an elevated position, but it nevertheless overlooks a lovely garden and extensive parkland.
42 Frances Lloyd George, *The Years That Are Past*, p. 182
43 Lord Derby letter to Philip Sassoon, 23 December 1920, papers of 17th Earl of Derby, Liverpool Record Office
44 Riddell, *Lord Riddell's Intimate Diary of the Peace Conference and After*, diary entry for 21 January 1921, p. 266
45 *Blackwood's Magazine*, vol. 209 (1921), p. 263
46 Self, ed., *The Austen Chamberlain Diary Letters*, p. 14
47 Ibid, letter dated 20 March 1921, pp. 154–5
48 James Denman and Paul McDonald, *Unemployment Statistics from 1881 to the Present Day*, Labour Market Trends, Office of National Statistics (January 1996), p. 6
49 Taylor, *English History 1914–1945*, p. 195
50 *Weekly Dispatch*, 13 February 1921
51 Taylor, *English History 1914–1945*, p. 197
52 Sir Alfred Mond (1868–1930) First Commissioner of Works from 1916 to 1921. Minister for Heath 1921–2. In 1928 he was created 1st Baron Melchett. His father had made a fortune through his chemicals business Brunner Mond & Company, which is today Tata Chemicals Europe. Alfred Mond was also a Zionist who backed the campaign for a Jewish national state in the British Mandate of Palestine.
53 William Peel, 1st Earl Peel (1867–1937), Viscount Peel from 1912 to 1929 when his Earldom was created. He was a grandson of the former Prime Minister Sir Robert Peel.
54 William Butler Yeats (1865–1939), Irish poet, dramatist, writer and politician. Winner of the 1923 Nobel Prize for Literature.

55 *Freeman's Journal*, 19 February 1921
56 St John Brodrick, 1st Earl of Midleton (1856–1942), Conservative and Unionist politician, Secretary of State for War 1900–3 and Secretary of State for India 1903–5
57 Jones, *Whitehall Diary*, vol. III: Ireland 1918–1925, pp. 54–5
58 Callwell, ed., *Field-Marshal Sir Henry Wilson*, vol. II, p. 283
59 Riddell, *Lord Riddell's Intimate Diary of the Peace Conference and After*, pp. 288–9
60 *The Times*, 25 April 1921
61 They met at the house of the businessman and MP James O'Mara (1873–1948), 43 Fitzwilliam Place
62 Randolph Churchill, *Lord Derby, 'King of Lancashire'*, Heinemann (1959), p. 410
63 Ibid
64 Sir James Craig (1871–1940), first Prime Minister of Northern Ireland 1921–40, created Viscount Craigavon in 1927
65 Lord Beaverbrook, *The Decline and Fall of Lloyd George*, Collins (1963), p. 56
66 Taylor, ed., *Lloyd George: A Diary by Frances Stevenson*, entry dated 1 June 1921, p. 219
67 Churchill, *The World Crisis*, vol. 4: *The Aftermath, 1918–1922*, p. 195
68 Jones, *Whitehall Diary*, vol. III: Ireland 1918–1925, p. 75
69 H.M. Queen Mary (1867–1953)
70 Mabell Ogilvy, Countess of Airlie (1866–1956). She had been a childhood friend of Queen Mary and served as a lady-in-waiting from 1901 until the Queen's death in 1953.
71 Jane Ridley, *George V: Never a Dull Moment*, Penguin (2021), p. 286
72 Lord Stamfordham papers, Royal Archives, Windsor Castle, GEO V K 1702
73 King George V, diary entry for 18 June 1921, Royal Archives, Windsor Castle, RA/GV/PRIV/GVD/1914–1927
74 *Belfast News Letter*, 21 June 1921
75 Letter dated 23 June 1921, Royal Archives, Windsor Castle, GEO V K 1702
76 Ronan Fanning, *Fatal Path: British Government and Irish Revolution 1910–1922*, Faber & Faber (2013), pp. 262–3
77 Beaverbrook, *The Decline and Fall of Lloyd George*, p. 86
78 Fanning, *Fatal Path*, p. 264
79 Tim Pat Coogan, *De Valera: Long Fellow, Long Shadow*, Penguin (2015), p. 234
80 Beaverbrook, *The Decline and Fall of Lloyd George*, p. 89
81 Coogan, *De Valera*, p. 234
82 *East Galway Democrat*, 30 July 1921
83 *New York Times*, 30 July 1921
84 *Birmingham Daily Gazette*, 30 July 1921
85 *New York Times*, 30 July 1921
86 *Western Mail*, 5 August 1921
87 Arthur Griffith (1871–1922), founder of Sinn Féin and leader 1911–17, deputy leader 1917–22
88 Robert Barton (1881–1975). He was born into a Protestant landowning family and became an officer in the Royal Dublin Fusiliers at the outbreak of the First World War. He had joined the Irish nationalist movement as a consequence of the British actions in suppressing the 1916 Easter Rising.

89 Eamonn Duggan (1878–1936). He fought in the Easter Rising and was elected to Parliament for Meath South for Sinn Féin at the 1918 general election.
90 George Gavan Duffy (1882–1951), an Irish lawyer who had unsuccessfully defended Roger Casement in his trial for treason. He was elected to Parliament for Dublin South for Sinn Féin at the 1918 general election.
91 Tim Pat Coogan, *Michael Collins*, Penguin (2015), p. 256
92 Peter Hart, *Mick: The Real Michael Collins*, Macmillan (2006), p. 307
93 Taylor, ed., *Lloyd George: A Diary by Frances Stevenson*, entry dated 14 November 1921, p. 237
94 The National Union of Conservative and Unionist Associations represented the grassroots Conservative Party members and local organizations. The National Union organized the annual conference, which was the forerunner to the modern party conferences.
95 Self, ed., *The Austen Chamberlain Diary Letters*, pp. 170–1
96 John Gretton (1867–1947), Colonel in the North Staffordshire Regiment of the territorial army. MP for Derbyshire South 1895–1906, Rutland 1907–18 and Burton 1918–43. He won two gold medals for sailing at the 1900 Paris Olympic Games.
97 Sir Robert Bruce (1871–1955), journalist and editor of the *Glasgow Herald* 1917–36
98 Sir Robert Bruce, *The House of Memories*, Glasgow: Royal Philosophical Society (1946–7), p. 13
99 *Hansard*, 15 December 1921
100 Taylor, ed., *Lloyd George: A Diary by Frances Stevenson*, entry dated 14 November 1921, p. 237
101 Fanning, *Éamon De Valera*, p. 118
102 Ibid
103 Ibid, p. 121
104 Chamberlain, *Down the Years*, p. 149
105 Ibid
106 Churchill, *The World Crisis*, vol. 4: *The Aftermath, 1918–1922*, p. 205
107 Coogan, *Michael Collins*, p. 276
108 Jones, *Whitehall Diary*, vol. III: *Ireland 1918–1925*, entry for 6 December 1921, p. 184
109 King George V, diary entry for 6 December 1921, Royal Archives, Windsor Castle, RA/GV/PRIV/GVD/1914–1927
110 Beaverbrook, *The Decline and Fall of Lloyd George*, p. 123

13: THINGS FALL APART

1 W. B. Yeats, *Selected Poems and Four Plays*, Scribner (2011), p. 89
2 Royal Historical Society, *Transactions of the Royal Historical Society*, vol. 11, Cambridge University Press (2003), p. 144
3 Elizabeth Cullingford, *Yeats, Ireland and Fascism*, Macmillan (1981), p. 110
4 Villa Valetta was located at 71 Boulevard Métropole in Cannes, with commanding views of the Côte d'Azur. It was demolished in 1958.

5   Sir Albert Stern (1878–1966) was a member of the Stern banking family, and a cousin of Lord Michelham, in whose apartment at Rue Nitot in Paris, Lloyd George had stayed during the 1919 Peace Conference. Stern had also worked for Lloyd George at the Ministry of Munitions during the war.
6   Walter Rathenau (1867–1922), German Minister for Reconstruction 1921–2, and Foreign Minister 1 February–22 June 1922.
7   David Lloyd George, *The Truth about Reparations and War-Debts*, Heinemann (1932), p. 66
8   Ibid
9   Sylvester, *The Real Lloyd George*, p. 71
10 The deflationary spiral that saw the peak of the Great Depression
11 Lloyd George, *The Truth about Reparations and War-Debts*, p. 68
12 Viscount Farquhar (1844–1923). He was created 1st Earl Farquhar on 30 November 1922. He served as the first Treasurer of the Conservative Party 1911–23.
13 Sylvester, *The Real Lloyd George*, p. 69
14 Beaverbrook, *The Decline and Fall of Lloyd George*, p. 127
15 Ibid
16 Beaverbrook, *The Decline and Fall of Lloyd George*, p. 129
17 Self, ed., *The Austen Chamberlain Diary Letters*, letter dated 1 January 1922, p. 177
18 Beaverbrook, *The Decline and Fall of Lloyd George*, p. 289
19 Ibid, pp. 290–1
20 McEwen, ed., *The Riddell Diaries 1908–1923*, diary entry for 25 February 1922, pp. 364–5
21 Sylvester, *The Real Lloyd George*, pp. 78–9
22 Ibid, p. 79
23 Self, ed., *The Austen Chamberlain Diary Letters*, letter dated 26 February 1922, p. 181
24 Ibid, letter dated 4 March 1922, p. 182
25 Philip Sassoon letter to Lord Esher, 6 March 1922, Esher papers, Churchill Archive Centre, Churchill College, University of Cambridge
26 *Weekly Dispatch*, 12 March 1922
27 Philp Sassoon letter to David Lloyd George, 13 March 1922, Lloyd George papers, Parliamentary Archive
28 Taylor, ed., *My Darling Pussy*, letter dated 21 March 1922, p. 39
29 Ibid, letter dated 22 March 1922, p. 40
30 Mona Dunn (1902–28), beautiful socialite and mistress of Lord Birkenhead. She was the daughter of the Canadian industrialist Sir James Hamet Dunn (1874–1956). In 1925 Mona married the war hero Edmund Tattersall (1897–1968). She died in 1928 of peritonitis.
31 Sir Mathew Wilson Bt (1875–1958), Conservative MP for Bethnal Green 1914–22.
32 Danehurst was a house on the edge of the Port Lympne estate that Lloyd George often used.
33 Philip Sassoon letter to David Lloyd George, 24 March 1922, Lloyd George papers, Parliamentary Archives
34 Sir Louis du Pan Mallet diary notes for April 1922, Sir Louis du Pan Mallet papers, Balliol College, University of Oxford

35 Alan Clark, *The Tories: Conservatives and the Nation State 1922–1997*, Weidenfeld & Nicolson (1998), p. 10
36 Vladimir Lenin (1870–1924), Marxist revolutionary and leader of the Soviet Union from 1917 until his death.
37 Leon Trotsky (1879–1940), a leader of the Bolshevik revolution and founder of the Soviet Red Army. From 1918 to 1925 he was People's Commissar for Military and Naval Affairs of the Soviet Union.
38 Bekir Sami Bey (1867–1933), also known as Bekir Sami Kunduh. Turkish politician and Minister for Foreign Affairs 1920–1.
39 Mustafa Kemal Pasha, later known as Atatürk (1881–1938), was the leader of the Turkish National Movement in the Turkish War of Independence (1919–22). A former army officer, who had been a front-line commander at Gallipoli during the First World War, he would become the first President of Turkey from 1923 until his death in November 1938.
40 Beaverbrook, *The Decline and Fall of Lloyd George*, p. 135
41 William Gallacher (1881–1965) was a founding member of the Communist Party of Great Britain and MP for West Fife 1935–50.
42 *Hansard*, 28 March 1945
43 Ernest Hemingway (1899–1961), American writer and novelist. At the time he was foreign correspondent for the *Toronto Star* based in Paris. His first novel, *The Sun Also Rises*, would be published in 1926.
44 *Toronto Star*, 24 April 1922, reprinted in Ernest Hemingway, *By-Line*, Collins (1968)
45 Ernest Hemingway, *Dateline Toronto*, Scribner (2002), p. 216
46 Harry Graf Kessler (1868–1937), Anglo-German diplomat, writer and patron of the arts. He was the son of the Hamburg banker Adolf Wilhelm Graf von Kessler (1838–95) and his British mother Alice Blosse-Lynch (1844–1919).
47 Count Harry Kessler, *The Diaries of a Cosmopolitan 1918–1937*, Weidenfeld & Nicolson (1999), pp. 162–3
48 Jones, *Lloyd George*, p. 184
49 Ibid
50 Documents on Irish Foreign Policy, No. 212NAI DE 2/304/1, National Archive of Ireland, Dublin
51 Fanning, *Fatal Path*, p. 317
52 Jones, *Whitehall Diary*, vol. III: Ireland 1918–1925, entry for 8 June 1922, p. 212
53 Ibid
54 'Scots Wha Hae' is a patriotic song that had previously served as a national anthem for Scotland. The lyrics were written by Robert Burns (1759–96) and were based on the speech given by Robert the Bruce before the Battle of Bannockburn in 1314.
55 Lady Cecil Mary Wilson (1861–1930) was from an Irish family and was born in Monasterevin, County Kildare.
56 McGreevy, *Great Hatred*, p. 219
57 Ibid, p. 221
58 Taylor, ed., *Lloyd George: A Diary by Frances Stevenson*, entry dated 22 June 1922, p. 242
59 Barnes and Nicolson, eds, *The Leo Amery Diaries*, vol. 1, diary entry dated 22 June 1922, p. 287

60 *Sunday Illustrated*, 13 August 1922
61 *Daily News*, 24 August 1922
62 Samuel Waring, 1st Baron Waring (1860–1940), Liverpool-born industrialist
63 Archibald Williamson, 1st Baron Forres (1860–1931), Liberal MP 1906–18 for Elginshire and Nairnshire, and then 1918–22 for Moray and Nairn. He also had business interests in oil and the railways.
64 Sir Berkeley Moynihan Bt (1865–1936) from 1929 1st Baron Moynihan. He was awarded a baronetcy in the 1922 honours list. Moynihan was a noted abdominal surgeon.
65 McEwen, ed., *The Riddell Diaries 1908–1923*, pp. 368–9
66 Sir Joseph Robinson Bt (1840–1929), Chairman of the Robinson South African Banking Corporation and the owner of numerous gold mines in Transvaal.
67 *Morning Post*, 13 June 1922
68 Godfrey Locker-Lampson (1875–1946), Conservative MP for Salisbury 1910–18 and then for Wood Green 1918–35. In 1918 he had been parliamentary private secretary to the assistant Foreign Secretary Lord Salisbury.
69 Letter from Clive Wigram to Samuel Hoare dated 4 July 1922, Templewood papers, University of Cambridge library
70 G. R. Seale, *Corruption in British Politics, 1885–1930*, Clarendon Press (1987), pp. 363–4
71 Alice Keppel (1868–1947), Society hostess and mistress and confidante of King Edward VII
72 Edward VII (1841–1910), King Emperor of the British Empire 1901–10
73 Sydney Stern, 1st Baron Wandsworth (1844–1912), Liberal MP for Stowmarket 1891–5. He was elevated to the peerage as Lord Wandsworth in 1895. Like his cousin Lord Michelham, he was a member of the Stern banking family.
74 McEwen, ed., *The Riddell Diaries 1908–1923*, p. 371
75 Stansky, *Sassoon*, p. 106
76 Alan Percy (1880–1930), 8th Duke of Northumberland 1918–30, and a 'Die-Hard' Conservative
77 *Hansard*, 17 July 1922, House of Lords
78 Ibid
79 Ibid
80 Ronald McNeill (1861–1934), MP for St Augustine's in Kent 1911–18, and then for Canterbury 1918–27. In 1927 he was elevated to the peerage as Lord Cushendun.
81 *Hansard*, 17 July 1922, House of Commons
82 Taylor, *English History 1914–1945*, p. 110
83 Richard Lloyd George, *Lloyd George*, p. 209
84 Ibid
85 Ibid, p. 210
86 Self, ed., *The Austen Chamberlain Diary Letters*, letter dated 20 November 1922, referring to the meeting that took place on 19 July 1922, p. 203
87 The house was actually on the north-facing slope of the Downs in that part of Surrey.
88 Tilden, *True Remembrances*, p. 77
89 McEwen, ed., *The Riddell Diaries 1908–1923*, p. 372

90 Ibid, entry for 17 June 1922, p. 369
91 Roberts, The Chief, p. 448
92 Sir Thomas Horder (1871–1955) was the physician to the King and had received his knighthood in 1918. He was made a Baronet in 1923 and elevated to the peerage as 1st Baron Horder in 1933.
93 Roberts, The Chief, p. 452
94 A. E. Montgomery, 'Lloyd George and the Greek Question, 1918–22', in A. J. P. Taylor, ed., Lloyd George: Twelve Essays, Hamish Hamilton (1971), p. 257
95 Jones, Lloyd George, p. 199
96 Ibid
97 William Bridgeman (1864–1935), Conservative MP for Oswestry 1906–29, Secretary for Mines 1920–2, Home Secretary 1922–4. In 1929 he was created 1st Viscount Bridgeman.
98 Barnes and Nicolson, eds, The Leo Amery Diaries, vol. 1, diary entry dated 27 September 1922, p. 292
99 John Cross, Sir Samuel Hoare: A Political Biography, Jonathan Cape (1977), p. 71
100 Letter from J. C. C. Davidson to Bonar Law dated 13 January 1922, Bonar Law papers, Parliamentary Archive
101 The Times, 7 October 1922
102 Article reprinted in The Times, 7 October 1922
103 William Ormsby-Gore (1885–1964), Conservative MP for Denbigh 1910–18, and for Stafford 1918–38. In 1938 he succeeded to his father's peerage as 4th Baron Harlech. In 1917 he served as parliamentary private secretary to Lord Milner and as assistant secretary to the War Cabinet.
104 The Times, 9 October 1922
105 Barnes and Nicolson, eds, The Leo Amery Diaries, vol. 1, pp. 293–4
106 Ibid, p. 294
107 Beaverbrook, The Decline and Fall of Lloyd George, p. 190
108 The Times, 16 October 1922
109 Cross, Sir Samuel Hoare, p. 77
110 Ernest Pretyman (1859–1931), Conservative MP for Woodbridge in Suffolk 1895–1906 and for Chelmsford 1908–23.
111 M. S. R. Kinnear, The Fall of Lloyd George: The Political Crisis of 1922, Macmillan (1973), p. 128
112 Reginald Clarry (1882–1945), Conservative MP for Newport, Monmouthshire, 1922–9 and 1931–45
113 R. J. Q. Adams, Bonar Law, Stanford University Press (1999), p. 327
114 David Lindsay, 27th Earl of Crawford (1871–1940), First Commissioner of Works 1921–2. Conservative MP for Chorley 1895–1913, when he succeeded his father as Earl of Crawford and took his seat in the House of Lords.
115 Adams, Bonar Law, p. 327
116 Sir Robert Peel Bt (1788–1850), a founder of the modern Conservative Party. Prime Minister 1834–5 and 1841–6.
117 Adams, Bonar Law, p. 328
118 Ibid
119 Ibid, p. 327
120 Ibid, p. 328

121 A full breakdown of how members voted can be found in Rhodes James, ed., *Memoirs of a Conservative*.
122 Sylvester, *The Real Lloyd George*, p. 99
123 Roskill, *Hankey*, vol. I, p. 296
124 King George V, diary entry for 23 October 1922, Royal Archives, Windsor Castle, RA/GV/PRIV/GVD/1914–1927
125 Barnes and Nicolson, eds, *The Leo Amery Diaries*, vol. 1, p. 300
126 Edward Wood (1881–1959), Conservative MP for Ripon 1910–25. In 1925 he was elevated to the House of Lords as Lord Irwin ahead of becoming Viceroy of India. In 1934 he became Viscount Halifax and then 1st Earl Halifax in 1944. Foreign Secretary 1938–40.
127 Frances Lloyd George, *The Years That Are Past*, p. 206
128 Ibid, p. 207
129 'November 1922' is the title of the poem, an undated copy of which can be found in the Lloyd George papers in the Parliamentary Archives.
130 Self, ed., *The Austen Chamberlain Diary Letters*, letter dated 21 November 1922, p. 203
131 Ibid
132 McEwen, ed., *The Riddell Diaries 1908–1923*, p. 382
133 *New York Times*, 7 October 1923
134 *New York Times*, 5 October 1923
135 The BBC had made its first radio broadcast in November 1922, just after the fall of Lloyd George's government. The first general election to feature radio addresses by the party leaders was in October 1924.
136 *The Times*, 10 November 1923
137 Roy Jenkins, *Baldwin*, William Collins (1987), p.73
138 Harold Macmillan (1894–1986), Conservative MP for Stockton-on-Tees 1924–9 and 1931–45. From 1945 until his retirement in 1964 he was the MP for Bromley. In 1984 he was created 1st Earl Stockton. Prime Minister 1957–63.
139 Harold Macmillan, *The Past Master: Politics and Politicians 1906–1939*, Macmillan (1975), p. 56
140 David Lloyd George, *Hansard*, 8 May 1940
141 Sir John Colville (1915–87), civil servant who served as assistant private secretary to Neville Chamberlain 1939–40, Winston Churchill 1940–1 and 1943–5, and Clement Attlee in 1945
142 John Colville, *The Fringes of Power: Downing Street Diaries 1939–1955*, Hodder & Stoughton (1985), p. 119
143 *Hansard*, 13 May 1940
144 Ibid
145 Colville, *The Fringes of Power*, p. 143
146 Jennifer Longford née Stevenson (1929–2012) was also believed to be Lloyd George's daughter.
147 Jennifer Stevenson private collection, referenced in Roy Hattersley, *David Lloyd George: The Great Outsider*, Little Brown (2010), p. 6
148 Sylvester, *The Real Lloyd George*, p. 12
149 Winston Churchill, *Hansard*, 28 March 1945

Acknowledgements

In April 2017 I was invited by the American historian Peter Stansky to give a talk at Stanford University about my biography of Philip Sassoon, a subject we had both written about. Then aged 85, Peter assured me that he was looking to gift books from his personal library and sent me on my way home with a copy of Lord Beaverbrook's *The Decline and Fall of Lloyd George*, A. J. P. Taylor's biography, *Beaverbrook*, and R. J. Q. Adams's *Bonar Law*. Whilst I had not then decided to write my own biography of Lloyd George, these books certainly pointed me in that direction. In late 2019, just before the outbreak of the COVID-19 pandemic, the British broadcaster and political writer Iain Dale asked me if I would write an essay on a former British Prime Minister, for a collection to be published the following year in a book called *The Prime Ministers*. I suggested Lloyd George, which he readily agreed to, and the reception of that work led one way or another to this book. I would like to thank my literary agent Diane Banks for encouraging me along that path, together with her former colleague at Northbank Talent Management, Martin Redfern.

The background to writing this book was also a difficult time for my father Fearghal and our whole family, with the death of my mother Diane on 1 October 2023, after a long illness. The progress of the manuscript was a subject she often asked me about in her final months and I'm sorry that she was not able to see the completion of the project. Needless to say that my wife Sarah has been a tower of strength throughout the whole period, whilst also managing her own busy career and the reconstruction of our home in Kent! None of this would have been possible without her love and support, and she also made several critical interventions to improve the dramatic quality of some key passages in the book.

Thanks are due as well to our children Claudia and Hugo, who have once again supported my writing of this book and the inevitable distraction that it brings. At the same time Claudia has been working hard at her public examinations and preparation for university applications next year, as well as acting and performing, and campaigning on the harms that social media can cause young people. Hugo even journeyed with me, with reasonably good grace, on that cold wet November day when we visited Lloyd George's cottage in Llanystumdwy. Thankfully the Imperial War Museum in London is equipped with five-a-side football pitches outside in Geraldine Mary Harmsworth Park, which are a greater source of inspiration for Hugo than the First World War galleries, although he has engaged with both.

His Majesty King Charles III has granted permission for the use of documents in this book, sourced from the Royal Archive at Windsor Castle. I would like to thank Julie Crocker and the team at the archive for their assistance with my research.

I am grateful to Megan Cynan Corcoran and the volunteers at the Lloyd George Museum in Llanystumdwy, for allowing me to experience both the museum and Lloyd George's childhood home outside of the normal visiting period, and also for their subsequent help in sourcing images for use in this book.

I would like to thank David Cholmondeley, the Marquess of Cholmondeley, for allowing me to access his family archive at Houghton Hall in Norfolk, for papers relating to Sir Philip Sassoon's work both for David Lloyd George and Sir Douglas Haig. Also, to Charles Cholmondeley for giving his permission for the use of images from the Port Lympne visitors' books, and my friend Anthony Tynan-Kelly who photographed the pages.

Catherine Ross, the Library and Archive Manager at the Met Office, provided invaluable assistance in understanding the weather conditions in Flanders and south-east England on the night of 6 June 1917, in response to my enquiry as to whether or not it was likely that Lloyd George could have heard the explosions from the Western Front, whilst at home in Walton Heath. On balance, I concluded that he probably did.

My parliamentary colleague Lord Tim Clement-Jones very kindly gave me a copy of a privately published volume of his grandfather's letters from the Paris Peace Conference, the original documents being held at the Bodleian Library in Oxford. Pierre Andrews was also a great help with research into the French politicians of the era.

The team at the House of Commons Library have once again provided me with invaluable assistance, and I would also like to thank my parliamentary colleagues who are fellow regulars of Room C in the members' library for their encouraging enquiries about the progress of the book, in particular Siobhan Baillie, Danny Kruger and Robert Jenrick.

Finally I would like to thank my editor Tomasz Hoskins and all of the team at Bloomsbury, including Sarah Jones and Richard Mason, who have been a joy to work with.

Damian Collins,
Elham, Kent,
May 2024

Picture credits

1. Lloyd George with his uncle Richard Lloyd © Hulton Archive/Getty Images
2. Lloyd George family © Pictorial Press / Alamy Stock Photo
3. Frances Stevenson © History and Art Collection / Alamy Stock Photo
4. LG walking by the sea in Llanystumdwy with Lord Milner and Philip Kerr © Parliamentary Archives
5. Golf at Walton Heath by permission of Llyfrgell Genedlaethol Cymru/The National Library of Wales
6. Golf at Cannes © Photo 12/ Universal Images Group via Getty Images
7. LG conferring with Joffre and Haig © Chronicle / Alamy Stock Photo
8. LG accompanied by Lord Reading on the western front in France, 1916 © Ernest Brooks, Public domain, via Wikimedia Commons
9. LG conferring with Sir Henry Wilson and Ferdinand Foch © Charles Cholmondeley, photographed by Anthony Tynan-Kelly
10. Queen's Hall in London © Topical Press Agency/Getty Images
11. LG speaking at the 1916 Eisteddfod © PA / Alamy Stock Photo
12. LG with Bonar Law © Hulton Archive/Getty Images
13. LG and Austen Chamberlain © Charles Cholmondeley, photographed by Anthony Tynan-Kelly
14. LG and Churchill by permission of Llyfrgell Genedlaethol Cymru/The National Library of Wales
15. LG and Asquith by permission of Llyfrgell Genedlaethol Cymru/The National Library of Wales
16. Hall of Mirrors © Parliamentary Archives
17. Paris peace conference © Bettmann/Getty Images
18. Anglo-French conference at Port Lympne © Charles Cholmondeley, photographed by Anthony Tynan-Kelly
19. LG sketch by William Orpen © Charles Cholmondeley, photographed by Anthony Tynan-Kelly
20. David Low cartoon © dmg media licensing
21. David Low cartoon © dmg media licensing

Index

Aberdeen, Lord 85
Adams, George 88
Addison, Christopher 28, 46–7, 79–83, 88–9, 122, 171, 191, 214, 229–30
Admiralty 21, 24, 33, 115–16, 122, 153
Agnew, William Lockett 27
Air Ministry 145–6
Airlie, Countess of 233
Aisne Valley 93–4
Aitken, Max, *see* Beaverbrook, Lord
Albert I, King of Belgium 220
Albert, Prince, Duke of York 205, 212
Aldwych Club 115
Alexandra, Empress 107–8
Allenby, General Edmund 113, 151, 175
Allied Joint Council 132
Alsace-Lorraine 137–8, 193, 198
American Civil War 32, 193–4
American Luncheon Club 108
Amery, Leo 43–4, 47, 88, 130, 145, 152–3, 165, 167, 180, 252
    and end of coalition 257–9, 262
Amiens, Battle of 168
ammunition shortages 6–7, 13–14, 18–20, 22–3, 35
Amritsar massacre 217–19
Anglo-French conferences (Port Lympne) 215–16, 219–20
antisemitism 218, 228
Anti-Waste League 229, 256
ANZACs 19
Archer-Shee, George 33
Armistice 180–3, 201
Army Council 48, 143, 218
Arras, Battle of 109, 112–13
Asquith, Herbert xi, xiii, xix, 7–25, 37–9, 43, 45–6, 48–54, 58, 86, 117, 119, 136, 210, 224, 244, 254
    challenges Lloyd George 145–7, 153–6, 159, 165, 167–8
    and general election (1918) 170–2, 185–6, 188–90
    and Lloyd George coup 68, 70–83
    son killed in action 63–4, 83, 143
Asquith, Margot 8, 16, 22, 54, 76
Asquith, Raymond 63–4, 83
Asquith Liberals 128, 188, 207, 209, 263
Associated Newspapers 120
Astor, Waldorf 44, 50, 78, 88
Athenaeum Club 82
Aubers Ridge 13, 19, 35
Australian United Cable Service 105
Austria 126, 128, 132, 154, 177–9
Austro-Hungarian Empire x, 37, 194

Baden, Max von 175
Baldwin, Stanley 165, 190, 257, 259–63, 265
Balfour, Arthur 8, 12, 19, 24, 26, 38, 53, 87, 107, 120, 176, 212, 254, 256
    and general election (1918) 186, 191
    and Lloyd George coup 81, 83, 85
    and Paris Peace Conference 192, 200
    secret memorandum 137
Balfour Declaration 151
Bank of England 5, 73
Barnes, George 129, 155
Barton, Robert 237, 240
Baruch, Bernard 202
Bathurst, Lady 155
Battle of the Somme (film) 56–7
Beauquesne 59–60, 63
Beaverbrook, Lord (Max Aitken) 18, 21, 52–3, 86, 88, 107, 154, 171, 187, 204, 232, 241, 244, 260
    and Churchill's return 118, 121–2
    and Lloyd George coup 68–70, 72–3, 80
    and Northcliffe letter 146
    and secret session debate 116–7

INDEX

Belgium x, xiii, xv, 124, 137–8, 213, 216, 231
'Belleek, Battle of', 251–2
Benedict XV, Pope 137
Beresford, Lord Charles 170
Beveridge, William 27
Bevin, Ernest 84
Bible, the xvii, 113
Birkenhead, Lord (F. E. Smith) 32, 48, 58, 80, 168, 182, 191, 200, 205, 232, 249, 265
 and Centre Party plan 207–8, 210
 and end of coalition 256, 259, 261–2
 and Ireland 236, 238, 240, 253
Black and Tans 215, 225, 227
Blackwood's Edinburgh Magazine 228
Blenheim Palace 10, 21
Bloody Sunday 225–6
Board of Agriculture 90
Boer War xii–xiii, xvi, 12–13, 26, 34, 127, 224, 232
Bonar Law, Andrew xi, 11–12, 19–22, 36, 38–9, 45–6, 48, 53, 87, 147, 155, 265
 and Armistice 176, 179, 181
 and Centre Party plan 206, 208, 210, 244–6
 and Churchill's return 121–3
 and coalition 24–6
 and conscription 32, 34
 and end of coalition 258–63
 and general election (1918) 171–2, 175, 184–6, 191
 and German offensive 164–6
 and Ireland 51–2, 214–15, 234, 236–9
 and Lloyd George coup 68–83, 85
 and Lloyd George 'dictator' 98–100
 and Paris Peace Conference 192, 200, 203–4
 and Passchendaele offensive 126, 136–7
 resignation 228–9
 sons killed in action 113, 136, 143
Bonar Law, Charles 113
Bonar Law, James 136
Bonham-Carter, Maurice 53, 74–5
Book of Job xiv
Book of Samuel 109
Boothby, Bob 182
Borden, Robert 194
Boselli, Paolo 139–40
Bourchier, Arthur xx
Bow Street Magistrates' Court 155
Briand, Aristide 59–60, 92–3, 97, 110, 243–4

Bridgeman, William 257, 262
British Empire xii, 7, 61, 66, 99, 106, 109, 113, 134, 173, 178–9, 214, 218, 231, 233–4, 239
British Expeditionary Force 1, 7–8, 19, 36
British Medical Association 28
Brooks's Club 30
Brotherhood Church, Hackney, riot 127–8
Bruce, Sir Robert 238
Bryan, William Jennings 30
Brynawelon 3, 213, 267
Buchan, John 89, 120
Buchanan, Sir George 108
Bulgaria 37, 175, 178
Burnham, Lord Harry 66, 72, 81–3, 104, 136, 231
Burton, Pomeroy 120
by-elections
 Hull Central 207
 Leyton West 207
 Newport 260–1
 Paisley 210
 Spen Valley 209
 Wrekin 210
Byng, General Sir Julian 150

Cadorna, General Luigi 93, 139
'Cairo Gang', 225
Cambrai, Battle of 150–1
Cannes conference 243–4
Cape Times 253
Caporetto, Battle of 139–40, 143, 167
Carlsbad 148
Carlton Club 25, 82, 170, 259–60
Carlyle, Thomas 85
Carson, Sir Edward 26, 36–7, 39, 44, 46–8, 54, 67, 88, 123, 163, 168, 191
 and conscription 32–4, 43, 50
 and Ireland 24, 51–2, 238–9
 and Lloyd George coup 68, 72, 75–6, 78–84
 and the navy 114–15, 121–2, 153
Casement, Roger 222
Castelnau, General Vicomte de 101
Cavan, General the Earl of 63
Cecil, Lord Robert 137, 210
Chamberlain, Austen 5, 21–2, 24, 26, 34, 68, 72, 87, 92, 121–2, 135, 163, 191, 200, 202, 245–6, 248, 264–5
 and end of coalition 256–7, 259–62
 and Ireland 236, 238, 240, 252
 leads Conservative Party 228–30
 and Paris speech 146–7
Chamberlain, Hilda 87, 228, 238, 245–6

Chamberlain, Ida 87, 122, 191, 202, 246
Chamberlain, Joseph 184
Chamberlain, Neville 87, 202, 210, 262, 266–7
Chanak incident 257–8
Channon, Henry 'Chips' 213
Charteris, Brigadier-General John 125, 130, 142, 150–2
Chelmsford, Lord 219
Chemin des Dames 93–4, 110, 112
Chequers 227, 231–2, 251–2, 257
Cherkley Court 53
Churchill, Clementine 10, 44, 161, 254
Churchill, Lord Randolph 10
Churchill, Winston 9–10, 17, 20, 24, 47, 86, 88, 106, 111, 148, 161–2, 208, 214–15, 219, 228, 243, 247–9, 254–5
  and Amritsar massacre 218
  and Armistice 176, 179, 181–3
  and Battle of the Somme 58–9, 64
  and conscription 32, 34, 38
  and end of coalition 259
  eulogy for Lloyd George 268
  and general election (1918) 191–2
  and Ireland 226, 232, 237, 251–2
  and Lloyd George coup 67–8, 80, 83, 85
  and Marconi affair 24, 123
  and the navy 115–16
  return to active service 37, 43
  return to government 117–19, 121–3
  wartime government 263, 266–7
  The World Crisis 64, 111, 162, 182
Clarke, Tom 23, 76, 81, 115, 187
Clarry, Reginald 260
Clemenceau, Georges 148–9, 154, 162–3, 175, 193–8, 203, 211, 216
Cliveden 78, 90
Collins, Michael 223, 225, 231, 237, 240, 251, 253
Colville, Jock 266
Committee for Imperial Defence 12
Committee on Munitions 14, 17, 20
Congress of Vienna 194
conscription 31–5, 38–40, 43, 46–50, 161, 182–3
Conservative Party
  and Bonar Law resignation 228–9
  and Centre Party plan 206–10, 245, 260–1, 264
  and Churchill's return 117, 122
  and coalition government 25–6
  and conscription 32

  and general election (1918) 170–2, 184–8
  and general election (1922) 244–6
  and general election (1923) 265
  and end of coalition 260–4
  and Ireland 26, 51–2, 234, 237–8
  and Lloyd George coup 68, 72, 79
  mistrust of Lloyd George's statistics 166
  and Nigeria debate 67
convoy system 115–16, 121, 125, 152, 182
Cooper, Duff 94
Coote, Colin 207
Corn Bills 261
Cottin, Émile 196–7
Cowdray, Lord 146
Craig, Sir James 232, 240
Craiglockhart 128
Crawford, Lord 261–2
Crewe, Lord 17, 75–6, 78
Criccieth xix, 3, 54, 90, 102–3, 133, 136–7, 143, 170–1, 174, 193, 208, 213, 247–8, 253, 267
  Chapel of the Disciples of Christ xvii, 102
Crimean War 85
Cromwell, Oliver 85
Cunliffe, Walter 73
Curzon, Lord 21–2, 24, 32, 34, 44, 74, 87, 92, 98, 100, 121, 176, 191–2, 200, 212, 243, 247, 257
Czechoslovakia 194

Dáil Éireann 251
Daily Chronicle 15–16
Daily Express 18, 123
Daily Herald 127
Daily Mail 18, 23, 32, 50, 81–2, 92, 115, 129, 155, 215, 235
  and Northcliffe's attack 200–1
Daily Mirror 18, 77
Daily News 33–4, 48, 77, 109, 129
Daily Telegraph 77, 81
Dalziel, Sir Henry 48, 67, 74
Damascus 175
Daniel, D. R. 57
Danny House 170–1, 175–6, 213
Dardanelles 9, 14, 17, 19–20, 24, 36–8, 64
Dardanelles Commission 122
David, King 109, 113
Davidson, J. C. C. 26, 99, 166, 168, 184, 206, 229, 258, 261
Davies, David 4, 47, 66, 88, 112, 120
Davies, J. T. 2, 4, 27, 88, 99, 192, 220, 253, 262

Dawson, Geoffrey 33–4, 44, 64, 132, 153, 191–2
   and general election (1918) 184, 191
   and Lloyd George coup 71–2, 77–8, 82
Dawson, Robin 120
De Valera, Éamon 214, 231–7, 239–40, 251
Defence of the Realm Act 155
democracy ix, 31, 103, 106, 108
Derby, Lord 39, 88, 92, 99, 111, 145, 152, 154, 157–8, 163, 213, 215–16, 228, 261
   and Ireland 231–2, 238
Derby Scheme 39–40
Déroulède, Paul 148
Deschanel, Paul 216–17
Dilnot, Frank xv
Disraeli, Benjamin 8, 10, 12
Donald, Robert 15–16, 45, 84, 121
Doullens conference 162–3
Dreyfus, Alfred 148
Dublin Custom House 232
Duffy, George Gavan 237
Duggan, Eamonn 237, 239
Dunn, Mona 248
Duveen brothers 193
Dyer, Brigadier-General 217–19
Dyfed the Archdruid 134–5

Ebert, Friedrich 177
Écho de Paris 144
Economist, The 229
Education Act (1918) 230
Edward VII, King 254
Edward, Prince of Wales (later King Edward VIII) 2, 98–9, 204, 211–12
Egyptian Expeditionary Force 113
Elvey, Maurice 169
Erzberger, Matthias 180
Esher, Lord 1–2, 6, 14, 22, 38, 65, 91, 112, 150, 161, 167, 247
   and Battle of the Some 58–60
   and Nivelle offensive 93, 101, 111–12
   and Rapallo conference 140–1
Estonia 194
Evans, Ellis Humphrey (Hedd Wyn) 134–5, 143, 222
Evans, Lance-Corporal Samuel 133
Evening Mail 181
Evening News 73

Farquhar, Horace 244
Fehrenbach, Constantin 217
Festubert 27
Finance Act (1910) 102

financial crisis (1914) 5
Finland 194
Fisher, Andrew 36
Fisher, H. A. L. 185, 209, 229–30
Fisher, Lord Jacky 20–2, 24, 114
Fitzgerald, Colonel Brinsley 19–20
Fiume 211
Flood, Seán 223–4
Foch, Marshal Ferdinand 62–3, 125, 132, 138, 154–5, 162–3, 173, 180, 194, 219–20
Ford, Henry 2–3
Forster, E. M. x
Fort Douaumont 93
Franco-Prussian War 193
Franz Ferdinand, Archduke x, 202
Free Church of Scotland 11
free trade 11, 26, 185, 210, 266
Freeman's Journal 231
French, General Sir John 1, 6–7, 13, 19, 36, 43, 132, 214
French army mutiny 112, 117
French National Assembly 110, 143, 148–9, 193, 243
Frewen, Moreton 188
Frohman, Charles 104

Gallacher, William 249
Gallipoli 9, 19, 36–7, 43, 257
Gambetta, Léon 78
Gandhi, Mohandas K. 219
Gardiner, A. G. 48–9, 129
Gare du Nord 94
Gaza 113, 151
Geddes, Eric 29, 60, 96, 116, 121, 152, 189, 191, 209, 229–30
Geddes Axe 230
general elections
   1918 186–92
   1922 263–4
   1923 265–6
Genoa conference 243, 248–50, 256
George V, King 59, 75, 81, 84, 92, 155, 157, 176, 190, 204, 223
   and Asquith resignation 80
   dislike of Lloyd George 98–100
   and end of coalition 262
   and Genoa conference 249
   and Ireland 233–5, 239, 241
   and Russian revolution 107–8
   and sale of honours 254–5
George, William 103
German colonies 67, 118, 194, 196
German Mark, falls in value 80

German navy   177, 195
German offensive   160–8, 173
German peace offer   137–8
German reparations   189, 198, 201–2, 213, 216–17, 243, 250
Gessler, Otto   217
Ginchy   64
Giolitti, Giovanni   220
Gladstone, William Ewart   8
Glasgow Herald   238
Glasgow strike   197
Globe, The   107
Glyn-Jones, William   47, 83
gold standard   5
Gough, General Sir Hubert de la Poer   131, 142
Government of Ireland Act (1920)   224
Graves, Robert   35, 62
Great Walstead   129
Greece   9, 37, 221, 247, 257
Greenwood, Sir Hamar   67, 225–6
Gregory, Maundy   205, 206, 207
Gretton, John   238
Grey, Sir Edward   x, 17, 37, 41, 53, 78
Griffith, Arthur   237–40, 252
Guest, Freddie   19–20, 83, 117–18, 121, 171, 174, 248
    and sale of honours   205–7, 253, 264
Gulland, John   32
Gwynne, H. A.   45, 132, 155

Haig, Field Marshal Douglas   13, 36, 55–6, 58–60, 63, 133, 209
    and Churchill's return   118
    and German offensive   160, 163–5, 167
    and Lloyd George government   91–2
    and Nivelle offensive   94–100, 112–13
    and Passchendaele offensive   124–6, 130–3, 136, 138–44, 150
    and Rapallo conference   140–1
    and Robertson's dismissal   151–4, 157–8
Haldane, Lord   30
Halifax, Lord   267
Hamilton, Sir Ian   37
Hamilton, Jean   50
Hankey, Donald   66–7
Hankey, Sir Maurice   37, 53, 66, 69, 74, 88, 97–8, 112, 115, 121, 125, 130–1, 133, 136–9, 141, 145, 154, 157, 162, 166, 171, 174, 176, 192, 213, 215, 220, 262
    brother killed in action   66–7, 143
Harcourt, Lord   78
Harmsworth, Cecil   76, 88

Harmsworth, Vyvyan   151
Hearst, William Randolph   119–20
Hemingway, Ernest   249
Henderson, Arthur   75–8, 81, 83–4, 87, 184
    doormat incident   128–9
    son killed in action   143
Henderson, David   83
Henderson, Reginald   115
Hindenburg Line   110, 150
HMS *Hampshire*   53
Hoare, Samuel   210, 254, 257–8, 260, 262
Hobhouse, Charles   2, 17
Honourable Society of Cymmrodorion   62
Horder, Sir Thomas   257
Horne, Sir Robert   210, 228, 243–4
Hôtel de Crillon, Paris   1, 69, 93, 140, 150, 196
Houldsworth Hall   31
House, Colonel   29, 145–6, 159, 182, 196
House of Lords   xi, 6, 13, 65, 102, 191, 254–5
    reform   8, 26
    and sale of honours   206–7
house-building   229
Howard, Roy   66
Hughes, Billy   45–6, 89
Hughes, Charles Evans   104
Hugo, Victor   138–9, 193
Hungary   194
Hunter, Lord   218

Illustrated London News   41
Imperial Committee   189
Imperial War Conference   107
Imperial War Council   105–7, 111, 113
India   217–19, 247
Indian Corps   13
industrial unrest   197, 208
Inter-Allied conferences   68–9, 93–4, 99
Inter-Allied Supreme War Council   140–1, 145, 149, 153–5
International News Service   119
IRA   222–5, 232, 251–2
Iraq   213
Ireland   214–15, 218, 222–7, 230–41, 251–3
    Bloody Sunday   225–6
    Boundary Commission   237, 239, 251
    conscription   161
    Easter Rising   49–51
    Home Rule   11, 24, 26, 51–2, 117, 161, 185, 210
    martial law   226
    War of Independence   223
Irish Citizen Army   49

INDEX

Irish Executive 226
Irish Free State 239, 242, 251–2
Irish nationalists 51–2, 161, 214, 251
Irish Parliamentary Party 12, 214
Irish Treaty 239–42, 246, 250, 256
Irish Volunteers 49
Isaacs, Rufus, see Reading, Lord
Isonzo, Battle of the 132
Italian Front 93, 139–40, 150
Italy 68, 96, 141, 144, 151, 167, 201, 211, 220–1, 243, 257–8

Jellicoe, Admiral John 114, 116, 125, 152–4, 168
Jerusalem 113, 151–2, 195
Job, J. T. 169
Joffre, General Joseph 63, 112
Jones, Clement 192–3, 204
Jones, David 57
Jones, Rev. Richard 6
Jones, Sarah 90
Jones, Thomas xvii, 6, 88, 90–1, 125, 138, 144, 168, 183, 250, 265
 and Ireland 234, 236, 241, 252
Jordan 213
Jutland, Battle of 66

Kamenev, Lev 219
Kellaway, Frederick 47, 83
Kemal, Mustafa 249, 257
Kennedy, John F. xviii
Kennedy, Lieutenant Malcolm 13
Kenworthy, Commander Joseph 115
Keppel, Mrs 254
Kerensky, Alexander 128, 141
Kerr, Philip 88, 153, 171
Kessler, Count Harry 250
Keynes, John Maynard 5, 198–9
Kiggell, Lieutenant-General Sir Launcelot 142, 152
King, Lucas 20
Kipling, Jack 35
Kipling, Rudyard xii, xiv, 35, 60
Kitchener, Lord 1, 7–9, 13–14, 17–24, 28–9, 35, 37–9, 43, 51, 53
Krasin, Leonid 219
Kühlmann, Baron Richard von 137
Kut 50

La Crèche de Bailleul 43
L'Aurore 148
Labour Party 12, 83–4, 117, 209, 259, 264
 break with Liberals 129
 and conscription 45–6
 and general election (1918) 184, 186

 minority government 265–6
 and Stockholm conference 128–9
labour shortages 31
Land Girls 129
Lansbury, George 127
Lansdowne, Lord 22, 34, 52, 72, 74
Latvia 194
Lavery, John 225
Le Bon, Gustave xix
League of Nations 195–6, 202, 211
Lebanon 194, 213
Lee, Arthur 14, 28–9, 40–2, 47–8, 54–5, 66–8, 72, 89–90, 217, 228
 gifts Chequers to nation 227
Lee, Ruth 72, 76, 89, 227
Lees-Smith, Hastings 128
Lenin, V. I. 141, 249
Leverhulme, Lord 133, 135
Liberal Party
 break with Labour 129
 and Brotherhood Church riot 127–8
 and Centre Party plan 206–10, 245, 264
 and conscription 32–4, 183
 and general election (1918) 170–2, 183–90
 and general election (1923) 266
 and Lloyd George coup 80, 83
 and Maurice affair 168
 radicals break with Lloyd George 35–6, 43
Liddell Hart, Basil 167
Lincoln, Abraham 31, 103–4, 264
Lithuania 194
Llanystumdwy ix, xiv, 84, 103, 268
Llewellyn Smith, Sir Hubert 27
Lloyd, Elizabeth 103
Lloyd, Richard ix, xix, 57, 84, 102–3, 109
Lloyd George, David
 appointed Secretary of State for War 52–4, 198
 and Armistice 180–3
 assassination attempt 223–4
 attitude to authority 5–6
 awarded Order of Merit 204
 becomes Prime Minister 70–85
 break with radical Liberals 35–6, 43
 and Brotherhood Church riot 127–8
 capacity for work 129–30
 and conscription 31–5, 38–40, 46–7, 50
 and daughter's death 57
 domestic arrangements 90–1
 draft letter to Asquith 54, 58
 election campaign (1918) 170–5, 183–92

first speech as Prime Minister 105
forms government 86–90
forms Ministry of Munitions 23–4,
    26–30, 40–2
and German offensive 160–8, 173
ill health 174–5, 213, 215, 217
increasingly autocratic 200
and Irish negotiations 236–41
last significant speech 266
Lincoln Day message 103–6, 108
low points of war 133, 136, 141,
    159–60, 162
Manchester speech 172–4, 185
and Marconi affair xi–xii, 24, 51, 65,
    123, 188
marriage with Frances Stevenson 267–8
as 'Nationalist-Socialist' 183–4
and Nivelle offensive 93–101, 109–12
and Northcliffe's attack 200–1
pacifism xiii
and Paris Peace Conference 192–204
Paris speech 143–7
and Passchendaele offensive 124–6,
    130–2, 136–42, 144
and peace negotiations 187–9
philandering 3
Queen's Hall speech ix–xx, 38, 128,
    230
relations with king 98–100
relationship with Frances Stevenson
    3–4, 90–1
and rhetoric of democracy 106–9
and sale of honours 206–7, 244,
    253–6
and secret session debate 116–18
sings 'cockles and mussels' 227
and uncle's death 102–3
and unity of command 154–5, 173
visits United States 264–5
War Memoirs 1, 27, 38, 54, 56, 76,
    92–3, 95, 110–11, 113, 125, 131,
    142, 144, 148, 164
working style 2–3
Lloyd George, Gwilym 32, 57, 220
Lloyd George, Mair 3, 57
Lloyd George, Margaret xiii, 3, 32, 61, 67,
    90–1, 133, 168, 172, 174, 179, 204,
    223, 236, 267
Lloyd George, Megan 61, 133, 168, 174,
    192, 220, 223, 236, 268
Lloyd George, Olwen 32
Lloyd George, Richard 29, 32, 57, 60,
    103, 255–6
Lloyd George, William 224

Lloyd-Greame, Philip 210
Locker-Lampson, Godfrey 254
London Stock Exchange 23
Londonderry, Lady 37
Long, Walter 34, 52, 188, 191, 228
Loos, Battle of 35–6, 55–6
Louis XIV, King 202
Low, David 211
Ludendorff, General Erich 113, 168, 175
Lvov, Prince 107
Lyautey, General Hubert 110
Lytton, Neville 100

MacDonald, Ramsay 84, 128, 183, 265–6
McKenna, Pamela 40, 75
McKenna, Reginald 16–17, 24, 34, 40, 48,
    53, 78–9, 172, 190
Macmillan, Harold 266
McNeill, Ronald 255
Macready, General Nevil 214–15
MacSwiney, Terence (Lord Mayor of
    Cork) 222–6
Mallet, Sir Louis 248
Mametz Wood 57, 127, 133
Manchester Evening News 172, 174
Manchester Guardian xiii, 22, 75, 107, 223
Manchester Hippodrome 172–4
Manchester Reform Club 174
Mantoux, Paul 112
Marconi affair xi–xii, 24, 51, 65, 123, 188
Marcosson, Isaac xviii, 28, 30, 120
Markham, Sir Arthur 213
Marlborough, Duke of 10
Marne, Battle of the xiv
Mary, Queen 233
Maurice, Major-General Sir Frederick 160,
    164–8, 171
Maxwell, Major-General Sir Ronald 152
Mayfair Society Journal 205
Méaulte 63
Megáne, Leila 192
Megiddo, Battle of 175
Menin Gate 33
merchant shipping 114
Mesopotamia 118, 122, 194–5
Messines Ridge 124
Metropolitan Police 205
Micheler, General Joseph 101
Michelham, Lord 193, 254
Midleton, Lord 231
Military Service Act (1916) 40, 46
Millerand, Alexandre 1, 212, 215–16,
    219–20
Milligan, Dr William 174–5

INDEX

Milner, Lord   34–5, 43–4, 48–50, 52, 67–8, 78, 87–9, 121, 136, 162–3, 176, 184, 191, 200, 214, 228, 258, 262
   and Robertson dismissal   153–4, 157–8
'Milner's Kindergarten' (Round Table)   44, 88–9
Milyukov, Prince   108
mining industry   208
Ministry of Munitions   23–4, 26–30, 40–2, 51–2, 55, 57, 88, 170, 181
Ministry of Reconstruction   122, 191
Mond, Sir Alfred   67, 230
Monday Night Cabal   43–5, 47–53, 71, 78–9, 85, 87–8, 117, 120, 145, 153, 214, 262
Mons, retreat from   xiv
Montagu, Edwin   53–4, 122, 192, 218–19, 247
   and Lloyd George coup   73–5, 77, 79
Montagu, Venetia   73
Montreuil-sur-Mer   59, 138–9
Morning Post   15, 22, 45, 155, 165, 249, 252–3
Morrell, Lady Ottoline   127
Moynihan, Sir Berkeley   253
Murdoch, Keith   36–7, 105
Murray, Sir Archibald   113
Murray of Elibank, Lord   xi–xii, 65, 185, 205–6

Napoleon Bonaparte   69, 101, 143, 196
Napoleonic Wars   194
'national factories'   41–2
National Insurance Act (1911)   28, 213
National Liberal Club   41
National Service League   35
National Union Conference   257
Navy Board   115, 121
Nelson, Admiral Horatio   177
Neuve Chapelle, Battle of   13–14, 35, 55, 64
New York Times   103–4, 208, 226, 235, 264
Newnham George   174
Nicholas II, Tsar   106, 108
Nicoll, Rev. Dr Sir William Robertson   48
Nicolson, Harold   192
Nigeria debate   67
Nitti, Francesco   212
Nivelle, General Robert   93–8, 100–1, 109–13, 124, 142, 153
Norman, Sir Henry   170–1
North Eastern Railway   29
Northcliffe, Lord   18, 20, 22–3, 32, 39, 47–51, 58–9, 64–6, 92–3, 100, 115, 151, 153, 155, 159, 168
   attacks Lloyd George   200–1
   and conscription   32, 47
   and general election (1918)   185, 191–2
   illness and death   256–7
   and Ireland   235–6
   and Lloyd George coup   72–3, 76–8, 81–2
   and Marconi affair   51, 65, 188
   open letter to Lloyd George   145–6
   and peace negotiations   187–9
   and sale of honours   254
   and war propaganda   119–21, 123, 154
Northern Ireland   233, 237, 239, 251
Northumberland, Duke of   255
Norway debate   266

Oberndorff, Count Alfred von   180
Observer   15
Oliver, F. S.   44, 52, 71, 88, 153
Orlando, Vittorio   139–40, 211
Ormsby-Gore, William   258
Orpen, Sir William   94, 263
Ostend   125, 150
Other Club   118
Ottoman Empire   38, 65, 113, 118, 126, 151, 175, 194, 213
Owen, Wilfred   62
Oxford Union Society   9, 230

Page, Walter Hines   29, 108
Painlevé, Paul   110–11, 138, 140, 144, 148
Palestine   113, 118, 151, 194–5, 213
Pankhurst, Christabel   30–1, 170
Pankhurst, Emmeline   30–1
Pankhurst, Sylvia   127
Paris Commune   193
Paris Opera House   192
Paris Peace Conference   135, 187, 192–204, 211–12, 216
   British Empire Delegation   192, 194, 203–4
Parker, Gilbert   188
Passchendaele, Battle of   124–6, 130–3, 135–42, 150–1, 222
Pearse, Patrick   49
Peel, Robert   261
Peel, Viscount   230
Penfold, Sir Stephen   204
'People's Budget'   ix, 6, 102
Pericles   xix
Pétain, General Philippe   101, 110–12, 117, 124–6, 163
Philpot, Glyn   214

Pilckem Ridge 135
Pitt, William, the Elder, Earl of
  Chatham xix
Pitt, William, the Younger xix, 177, 206
Plumer, General Sir Hubert 124
Plymouth, Lord xiv–xv, 143
Poincaré, Raymond 110, 148, 162, 216,
  243–5, 250
Poland 219–20
Polygon Wood, Battle of 139
Pontius Pilate 104
Port Lympne 212–15, 227, 236, 245–6,
  248
Press Association 124
Pretyman, Ernest 260
Psalm 23 102–3

Queen's Own Oxfordshire Hussars 37
Queensbury, Marquess of 33
queues, as British institution 133

railways 208, 230
Rapallo conference 140–1, 144
Rathenau, Walter 243
Rattigan, Terence 33
Rawlinson, George 99
Reading, Lord (Rufus Isaacs) xi–xii, 5, 33,
  53, 63, 73–4, 77, 88, 119, 132, 146,
  159, 168, 214, 228
Red Cross 32
Redmond, John 12, 51
Reform Club 82–3, 208
Renault motor works 7
Repington, Colonel 19, 155, 159, 165
Restoration of Order in Ireland Act 222
Reynolds's News 74
Rhineland 197–8, 202
Ribot, Alexandre 110–11, 138
Riddell, George (Lord) x, xii–xiv, xviii, 4,
  8, 12, 15–16, 18–19, 22–3, 26, 36,
  38, 45–6, 50, 66, 88, 90, 118, 121,
  129, 131, 136, 146, 162, 168, 176,
  179, 187, 212, 214–15, 219–22,
  227–8, 231, 251, 256
  and Centre Party plan 208, 210,
    245–6, 264
  and general election (1918) 170–1,
    175, 183–5, 190
  and Lloyd George coup 72, 81–3
  and Paris Peace Conference 195, 197,
    200, 204
  and Paris speech 144–5
  and Robertson dismissal 152, 158
  and sale of honours 253–4
RMS *Lusitania* 19, 103–4, 202

RMS *Majestic* 265
Roberts, Evan 62
Roberts, Sir Thomas 102
Roberts, non-conformist family 6
Robertson, Sir William 7, 47, 50, 57–9,
  65–6, 141, 164, 168
  dismissal 151–5, 157–9
  and Nivelle offensive 94, 96–8
  and Passchendaele offensive 126,
    131–3, 136, 138, 141–4
Robinson, Francis 33
Robinson, Sir Joseph 253–4
Romania 141
Roosevelt, Theodore xvii, xix, 14, 30, 40,
  104
Rothermere, Lord 58, 185, 187, 229
Rothschild, Baron Gustave de 209
Rothschild, Lord Nathan 5
'Rough Riders' 14
Round Table, *see* 'Milner's Kindergarten'
Royal Courts of Justice 6
Royal Engineers 57
Royal Flying Corps 136
Royal Military Academy, Sandhurst 59
Royal Naval College 33
Royal Navy 66, 104, 115
Royal Scots Fusiliers 43
Royal Welsh Fusiliers 133
Ruhr occupation 217
Runciman, Walter 53, 78, 172, 190
Russell, Bertrand 127
Russia 51, 53, 65
  'Argonauts of Peace' 128
  Bolshevik revolution 141, 151, 194,
    198, 201, 208
  collapse of regime 106–9, 113, 117
  exit from war 156
  see *also* Soviet Union

Saarland 197, 202
St Aldwyn, Lord 5
St Paul's Cathedral 150, 252
St Petersburg 107, 141
Salisbury, Lord 206, 254
Salonika 9, 37, 69, 93, 175
Sami Bey 249
Samuel, Herbert xi, 78, 81, 190
San Remo conference 217
Sandringham 59, 99, 241
Sankey Commission 208
Sassoon, Aline 209
Sassoon, Sir Philip 59, 64–5, 92, 96–7,
  150–1, 154, 161, 165, 209, 211–17,
  223, 227–8, 232, 236–7, 245–8,
  254, 257, 262–3

INDEX

Sassoon, Siegfried 56, 62, 113, 127–8, 131
Scott, C. P. xiii, 22, 47, 66, 75–6, 107, 152, 154
Scott, Leslie 67
Selborne, Lord 34, 52
Serbia x, 9, 37–8, 43, 141
Sert, Josep Maria 213
Shaw, George Bernard 186
Shortt, Edward 222, 252
Simon, Sir John xiii, xix, 9, 40, 189–90, 209
Sinn Féin 190, 214, 222, 224–5, 231–2, 238–40
Smith, F. E. *see* Birkenhead, Lord
Smuts, Jan Christian 106, 130, 141, 152, 179, 198, 232–3, 253
Snowden, Ethel 128
Snowden, Philip 84, 127–8
social reform ix, xvii, 6, 8, 10, 26, 28, 188
Somme, Battle of the 55–67, 83, 94, 124–5, 130, 133
Soviet Union 219–20, 243, 249, 256
  see also Russia
Spa conference 216–17, 221
Spanish flu pandemic 174
Spanish–American War 14
Spartacists 201
Spears, Edward 97, 110
Spectator, The 188, 258
Spender, J. A. 50
Spender, Mary 50
Spicer, Sir Howard 170
Spring-Rice, Sir Cecil 120
Stamfordham, Lord 47, 68, 85, 96, 99, 101, 107, 141, 157, 222
  and Ireland 233, 235–6
Stanley, Venetia xix, 15
Star, The 211
Steed, Wickham 200, 235–6, 257
Stern, Sir Albert 243–4
Stevenson, Frances xiii, xviii, 2, 17, 23, 32, 48, 57, 68, 73, 84, 118, 133, 175, 220, 248
  brother killed in action 27, 56, 143
  and Chequers 227
  and coalition government 88, 90–1
  and disagreement with king 100
  and end of war 177–8
  and general election (1922) 263
  and Irish negotiations 235, 238–9
  marriage 267–8
  and Nivelle offensive 94–5, 113
  and Paris Peace Conference 192–3, 196–7, 203–4
  and Philip Sassoon 209, 212, 214, 232
  relationship with Lloyd George 3–4, 90–1
  and Stanley Baldwin 263
  and Uncle Lloyd's death 102
  and Victor Hugo 138–9
  and Wilson assassination 252
Stevenson, Jennifer 267
Stevenson, Paul 27, 56
Stockholm conference 128–9
Strachey, John 188
submarine warfare, unrestricted 104, 113–16
Sutherland, William 'Bronco Bill' 99, 170, 174, 205, 218
Suvla Bay 36
Sykes, Sir Mark 207
Sylvester, A. J. xiii, xix, 2, 243–4, 246, 267
Syria 194

Talbot, Edmund 83
tanks, first deployment of 63
tariff reform 11, 185, 234, 237
taxation ix, 6, 26, 185
Thomas, Albert 92–3, 111
Thomas, Brigadier-General Sir Owen 133
Thornton, Frank 223–4
Tilden, Philip 215, 256
Times, The 13, 15, 18–19, 22, 50, 61, 107, 115, 144, 151, 154–5, 158–9, 167, 177
  and end of coalition 258, 260
  and general election (1918) 188, 191–2
  and Ireland 226, 231, 235–6
  and Lloyd George coup 73, 76–8
  Northcliffe letter 145–6
  and Northcliffe's attack 200–1
Trade Union Congress 190
trades unions 83, 133, 208, 227
Trafalgar, Battle of 177
Treaty of Versailles 198, 203–4, 208, 211, 219–20, 243–4
Trent Park 212, 223, 238
Trotsky, Leon 249
Turkey 132, 178, 247, 257

U-boats 19, 66, 115–17, 125, 164, 182
Ukraine 194, 219
Ulster Covenant 24
Ulster Hall 233
Ulster Unionists 33, 165, 231–2, 239
Uncle Tom's Cabin 103
unemployment 229

United States
  Congress 175–6, 211
  entry into war 103–6, 108–9, 113, 117
  war propaganda 119–20
Upper Silesia 197, 202

Vanderbilt, Alfred Gwynne 104
Vanselow, Captain Ernst 180
Verdun 55, 65, 93, 95, 124, 163
Versailles 149, 154–6, 158, 178
  Hall of Mirrors 193, 202–3
  see also Treaty of Versailles
Victoria, Queen 206
Vimy Ridge, Battle of 108–9
Vorwärts 147

Walmer Castle 74
Walpole, Sir Robert 25
Walton Heath xiv, xviii, 4, 15, 23, 30, 38, 66, 71, 75–6, 91, 118, 124, 146, 152–3, 157–9, 162, 179, 187
Wandsworth, Lord 254
War Cabinet 84, 87–9, 93, 95–6, 98, 100, 106, 111, 116, 119, 121–2, 125–6, 128, 130–2, 137, 140, 145, 150, 153, 159–60, 163, 165–7, 176, 191, 233, 258, 267
War Committee 39, 69, 73–8, 80, 98, 125
War Council 9, 12, 38, 53, 68, 70–1, 76–7, 85, 105–6, 111, 113, 154
War Intelligence Department 120
War Office 6–7, 14, 17, 22–3, 32, 37–9, 44, 53–8, 60–1, 66, 68, 73, 76, 78, 80, 83–4, 92, 151, 160–1, 165–6, 168, 179, 218, 228
  building 55
  and Ministry of Munitions 28–9, 42
  recruitment figures 47
War Policy Committee 126
Ward, William Dudley 171
Waring, Lord 253, 255
Warsaw, Battle of 220
Webb, Sidney 129
Weekly Dispatch 229
Welsh National Eisteddfods 61–2, 133–5, 168–9, 219, 236
Welsh Regiment 169
Wemyss, Sir Rosslyn 176, 180
Western Mail 169, 255
Westminster Gazette 51, 146
Whitehall Gazette 205

Whitley-Thomson, Sir Frederick 115
Wiegand, Karl von 119
Wigram, Clive 99, 254
Wilde, Oscar 33
Wilhelm I, Kaiser 193, 202
Wilhelm II, Kaiser 177–8, 182, 189, 192, 217
Wilhelmshaven 177
Williams, Christopher 57
Williams, G. P. 54, 57
Williams, Hugh Powell 54, 143
Williams, Hywel 57, 143
Williamson, Archibald 253
Wilson, General Sir Henry 44, 52, 62–3, 71, 98, 100, 110–11, 124–5, 131–2, 141, 176, 262
  and Amritsar massacre 218
  and Armistice 182
  assassination 252
  and German offensive 160–4
  and Ireland 226, 231, 239, 251–2
  and Paris Peace Conference 203
  and Robertson dismissal 153–4, 157–9
Wilson, Lady 252
Wilson, Woodrow 29, 104, 108–9, 119, 132, 161, 182, 211–12
  early life 193–4
  Fourteen Points 175–6
  and Paris Peace Conference 192–200, 202–3
Winterfeldt, Major-General Detlof von 180
Woman's Dreadnought, The 127
women's suffrage 26, 30–1, 170
Women's War Pageant 30
Wood, Edward 262
Wood, Sir Henry x
Woolwich Arsenal 7
Workers' and Soldiers' Council 127
Worthington-Evans, Sir Laming 210, 228, 243–4

Yeats, W. B. 230–1, 242
Younger, Sir George 208, 229, 245, 254, 257
Ypres, First Battle of 33, 163
Ypres, Third Battle of, *see* Passchendaele, Battle of
Ypres Salient 95–6, 124–5
Yugoslavia 194

Zeebrugge 125, 150
Zeppelins 49
Zola, Émile 148